This lucid, scholarly, accessible, and reverent commentary will be invaluable for preachers, Bible study leaders, and any thoughtful Christian wanting to study the books of Chronicles. It is detailed enough to address the puzzles, for example when putting Chronicles side by side with Samuel and Kings, and yet without being dauntingly dense. The Application sections are pure gold, informed by a robust confidence that the whole Bible finds its fulfilment in Christ. It is likely to be my 'go to' commentary on these books.

Christopher Ash
Writer in Residence, Tyndale House, Cambridge

These two volumes display excellent linguistic knowledge, fine theological discernment, and most useful practical application of passages. This is what makes them so significant, and they will be welcomed as an outstanding contribution to the books of Chronicles. That Philip Eveson has taken years over this work means that we have the mature mind of the author, and so he presents us with an enlightening discussion that will be of assistance to many.

Allan Harman
Research Professor,
Presbyterian Theological College,
Melbourne, Australia

One's head hurts to think of all the labour Philip Eveson poured into this study of Chronicles – he does the indispensable 'dirty work' and beavers us through the details we need to understand the text. And yet all along his applications keep the kingship of Jesus in clear view. Makes me want to go back and study through 1–2 Chronicles all over again.

Dale Ralph Davis
Author, *My Exceeding Joy: Psalms 38-51*

T0270364

1 & 2 CHRONICLES

Volume 2

Solomon to Cyrus

Philip H. Eveson

CHRISTIAN
FOCUS

Philip Eveson is the author of a number of Old Testament commentaries that have been well received. After ministering for over twenty-five years at Kensit Evangelical Church and serving as Resident Tutor in Biblical Exegesis and Theology at the London Theological Seminary, he became the Seminary's second principal. In retirement, he has continued to teach the Old Testament and to preach in many parts of the world. He and his wife, Jennifer, now attend Borras Park Church, Wrexham, where his family also worships.

Copyright © 2024 Philip H. Eveson

ISBN 978-1-5271-1104-2
Ebook ISBN 978-1-5271-1152-3

10 9 8 7 6 5 4 3 2 1

Printed in 2024
by
Christian Focus Publications Ltd.,
Geanies House, Fearn, Ross-shire,
IV20 1TW, Scotland, U.K.

www.christianfocus.com

Cover design by Daniel van Straaten

Printed and bound by
Bell & Bain, Glasgow

Contents

Abbreviations

AD	Anno Domini (In the year of our Lord)
AV/KJV	Authorised/King James Version
BC	Before Christ
BDB	Brown, Driver and Briggs *A Hebrew and English Lexicon of the Old Testament* (Oxford: Clarendon Press, 1962)
ESV	English Standard Version
LXX	The Septuagint (The Hebrew Old Testament in Greek)
MSS	Manuscripts
MT	Masoretic Text
NIV	New International Version
NKJV	New King James Version

Preface

I count it a privilege to have had some of the best teachers in their fields of scholarship. They have included three Welshmen. The Reverend Dafydd Rhys ap Thomas introduced me to Biblical Hebrew and the Reverend Professor Dr Bleddyn Roberts first aroused my interest in the various Old Testament ancient texts and versions including the Qumran material that had, at that time, only recently been discovered.[1] Both these men belonged to the faculty of Hebrew and Biblical Studies at the University College of North Wales Bangor. The third Welshman to whom I owe much was Dr David Winton Thomas, Regius Professor of Hebrew at Cambridge University. Additional encouragement in Hebrew at Bangor came from the Reverend Brian Mastin, while the Reverend John St John Hart of Queens' College, Cambridge, encouraged a deeper appreciation of biblical Hebrew in his students through his regular Tuesday evening readings from the Hebrew Bible followed by Lapsang Souchong tea and Madeira cake.

More importantly, I thank God for the blessing of being brought up from birth in a home where the Bible was appreciated as God's inerrant and authoritative word and for opening my eyes to its truths and leading me to know God's Son, Jesus Christ, as my own personal Saviour and Lord. It was in the environment of my home church that I grew up from my earliest years to teenage life listening to challenging messages from the Bible through the ministries of the Reverends D. O. Calvin Thomas and J. Glyn Owen in Trinity Presbyterian Church of Wales, Wrexham. I was also

---

1. The Qumran or Dead Sea Scrolls were found on the northwest shores of the Dead Sea between 1947 and 1956.

privileged in those formative years of my life to be gripped by the powerful preaching of Dr D. Martyn Lloyd-Jones when he visited our town from time to time. In addition, it is important to put on record that I owe it to the Lord for keeping me trusting in the veracity of God's Word and enabling me, however imperfectly, to preach that Word and to teach and write on biblical books and themes.

When I first began studying the Bible as an academic discipline, it was at a period when the negativism of liberal Old Testament scholarship had reached its full flowering in British university circles. One of my Old Testament lecturers, Dr Charles Whitley, recommended as a text-book R. H. Pfeiffer's *Introduction to the Old Testament* (London: A & C Black, 1952), a work that Professor G. R. Driver of Oxford considered to be an 'admirable book … beyond all praise'. On Chronicles, this is what I read: 'The Chronicler made no important contributions to theological thought but presented the notions about God found in the Pentateuch and later in the Psalms' (p. 789). Further on I was informed, 'It is an error to consider the Chronicler as a writer of history. It is futile to inquire seriously into the reality of any story or incident not taken bodily from Samuel or Kings. His own contributions would be classed … as historical fiction … the Chronicler is utterly devoid of historical sense and even of a genuine curiosity about the actual events …' (p. 806).

Thankfully, that incredibly pessimistic estimate of Chronicles has long been superseded by a much more positive appreciation of the work, although its infallibility is still denied by many. I had the advantage of engaging in post-graduate studies when this change of thinking in academic circles was in its earliest stages. Dr Peter Ackroyd, the Samuel Davidson Professor of Old Testament at the University of London, was at the forefront of the new outlook and I profited from the personal tuition I received from him in the theological department of King's College London.

The translation of the Masoretic Text of Chronicles is my own and is purposefully as word for word as possible, in order for readers to appreciate the difficulties of translating some sentences and to observe more easily how the compiler used key words throughout his work. Words or phrases placed in *italics* indicate the additions needed in an English translation to help convey the sense of Hebrew sentences. In transliterating the original languages, I have generally followed the Society of Biblical Literature's academic system. When versification between the printed editions of the Hebrew and English Bibles differs, the Hebrew verse number (and chapter if necessary) is placed in square brackets after the English; for example, 1 Chronicles 6:1 [5:27]. As this is a Christian commentary, I continue to use B.C. and A.D. when referring to historical dates.

I have valued the encouragement of Graham Hind and others who have urged me to complete this daunting assignment which was first given me by John Currid. During a sabbatical in 2005, my wife and I spent over a month at the Reformed Theological Seminary in Jackson, Mississippi, and I place on record my immense gratitude to the Seminary board for allowing me free accommodation and access to all their resources. We first met Dr Currid and his wife while at Jackson and very much appreciated their kindness to us.

An important word of appreciation must go to Malcolm Maclean and all at Christian Focus for their helpful support.

It is only in more recent years since my retirement from the principalship of the London Seminary that I have been able to speed up and finish what I began so long ago. I am grateful that a number of former students have also spurred me on to keep going and not give up. The study and writing of this commentary has been a pleasurable project and it has been exciting to appreciate how the whole of Chronicles leads to Jesus Christ.

Finally, I am indebted to my wife, Jenny, for her love, patience and willingness to read through the whole script, checking my references and correcting flaws in my English. It has been a blessing in retirement to have our family close by and I dedicate this commentary to Ruth and Andrew, my daughter and son-in-law, and to Joshua, Nia, Hannah and Joseph, my grandchildren.

PHILIP H. EVESON
Wrexham, North Wales
May, 2023

PART TWO (Contd.):
The David–Solomon Kingdom
(I Chron. 9:35–2 Chron. 9:28)

6

The reign of Solomon
(2 Chron. 1:1–9:31)

Having already emphasised the joint nature of the David–Solomon rule as a picture of the ideal kingship to which the post-exilic community can look forward (see especially 1 Chron. 29), the Chronicler now presents the chief events of Solomon's reign. The material is divided into two main parts: part one is concerned with Solomon's task of building the temple (1:1–7:22) while the second part considers his position as an international monarch (8:1–9:31). It is structured in such a way that the building and dedication of the temple are seen as the central concern (3:1–7:22) with Solomon's wisdom, wealth and worldwide renown forming a frame around his whole reign (1:1–2:18; 8:17–9:28).

The introduction to Solomon's reign (1:1-17)
After a brief introduction to his reign (v. 1), the chapter recounts Solomon's sacrifices at Gibeon and God's revelation to him (vv. 2-13) and closes by describing his wealth and commercial enterprises (vv. 14-17). Further words concerning Solomon's wisdom and wealth occur at 9:22-28.

Solomon worships at Gibeon (1:1-6)

> 1:1. Now Solomon the son of David strengthened himself over his kingdom, and Yahweh his God was with him and made him exceedingly great. 2. And Solomon spoke to all Israel, to the commanders of the thousands and of the hundreds

and to the judges and to every chief of all Israel, the heads of the fathers. 3. Then Solomon and all the assembly with him, went to the high place which was at Gibeon; for God's tent of meeting was there, which Moses the servant of Yahweh had made in the wilderness. 4. However, David had brought up the ark of God from Kiriath-jearim to the place David had prepared for it; for he had pitched a tent for it in Jerusalem. 5. Furthermore, the bronze altar, which Bezalel the son of Uri, the son of Hur, had made, was there before the tabernacle of Yahweh, and Solomon and the assembly sought it. 6. And Solomon went up there to the bronze altar before Yahweh which was at the tent of meeting, and offered one thousand burnt offerings on it.

David had urged his son to 'be strong' (1 Chron. 28:10, 20), and the Chronicler uses the same verb but in an intensive reflexive form to indicate that Solomon was firmly in charge of his kingdom ('strengthened himself,' v. 1). It becomes one of the Chronicler's favourite verbal forms especially when indicating how a king gains authority after a difficult period (2 Chron. 12:13; 13:21; 15:8; etc.). Its use here is perhaps a veiled recognition of the troubles that surrounded the succession (1 Kings 1–2). Yahweh, who is as much Solomon's God as David's, is with him, as his father had assured him, and had made him 'exceedingly great' (see 1 Chron. 14:2; 22:11-12, 16; 28:20; 29:2-3, 25).

As 'all Israel' rallied to David, so Solomon is able to summon 'all Israel' as represented by the army commanders, judges and family heads (see 1 Chron. 11:1, 4, 10; 27:1; 28:1). For the term 'chief' or 'leader' (nāśî', v. 2), see 1 Chron. 2:10; 4:38; 2 Chron. 5:2. Meeting with God was as centrally important for Solomon as for David. While Kings makes no mention of the whole assembly accompanying him to Gibeon, the Chronicler indicates that this was no private affair, but an important event witnessed by 'all the assembly' (1 Kings 3:4-15; see 1 Chron. 13:2, 4; 29:1, 20). It is emphasised that Gibeon, unlike other 'high places', was to be seen as a legitimate site for the worship of Yahweh, as the original Mosaic tabernacle was there as well as the bronze altar. In addition, Zadok the priest had been appointed to officiate at the altar (1 Chron. 16:39-40; 21:29). Moses' special status as 'the servant of Yahweh', the reference to Bezalel the skilled craftsman who made the altar

(v. 5; Exod. 31:2; 38:1-2; 1 Chron. 2:19-20), and especially the additional unique expression 'God's tent of meeting' (which could also be translated 'the tent for meeting God,' v. 3), all add further weight to the legitimacy of the location. Though a semi-permanent building seems to have been erected at Shiloh, which was later destroyed, this did not mean that the original tabernacle had been replaced or ruined (1 Sam. 1:9; 3:3; Jer. 7:12, 14; 26:9).

It was 'there' at Gibeon, in Yahweh's presence, 'at the tent of meeting', 'on the bronze altar' that Solomon sacrificed his thousand animals as burnt offerings – the build-up of phrases again indicates that this was an acceptable high place (v. 6; see 1 Chron. 16:1-2 where David offered sacrifices before the ark in Jerusalem). The addition of one of the Chronicler's favourite verbs, 'seek' (*dāraš*), in reference to inquiring of Yahweh, indicates that Solomon follows David's example and not that of Saul (1 Chron. 10:14; 13:3; 14:10, 14). There is also a reminder, however, that David had pitched a tent in Jerusalem to house the ark he had brought from Kiriath-jearim (v. 4; 1 Chron. 13:1–17:1). This anomalous, unsatisfactory situation would be rectified by Solomon, so that meeting with God and the offering of sacrifices would take place in association with the ark. Solomon would complete what had begun under David. All would be brought together with the construction of the temple in Jerusalem.

God's revelation to Solomon (1:7-13)

1:7. In that night God appeared to Solomon and said to him, 'Ask what I shall give you'. 8. Then Solomon said to God, 'You have shown great steadfast love to my father David and have made me king in his place. 9. Now, Yahweh God, let your word to my father David be confirmed; for you have made me king over a people as numerous as the dust of the earth. 10. Give me now wisdom and knowledge, that I may go out and come in before this people; for who can judge this great people of yours?' 11. And God said to Solomon, 'Because this was in your heart and you did not ask for riches, wealth and honour, or the life of those who hate you, nor have you even asked for long life, but you have asked for yourself wisdom and knowledge, that you may judge my people, over whom I have made you king, 12. wisdom and knowledge have been granted to you. And I will give you riches and wealth and honour, which was not so to the kings who were before you, and after you it will not be so. 13. Then Solomon went from the high place which was at Gibeon, from the tent of meeting, to Jerusalem and he reigned over Israel.

Chronicles abbreviates the account in 1 Kings 3:5-15 of God's appearance to Solomon and the promises made in response to his prayer (vv. 7-12). The phrase 'in that night' (v. 7) implies that the revelation was by means of a dream, as Kings makes clear. In Solomon's reply to God's generous offer, the king begins by acknowledging God's great faithfulness or 'enduring love' toward his father (v. 8). God had kept His promise by enabling Solomon to reign in his father's place. In the light of the enormity of the task, he asks for wisdom and knowledge to govern – the old word 'judge' (*šāpaṭ*) being used in this sense here (v. 10). The phrase 'go out and come in' has military overtones (1 Chron. 11:2), but can be used more generally for those in a leadership position (Deut. 31:2). The David–Solomon era had brought about the fulfilment of the promises to the patriarchs, with God's people as numerous as the 'dust of the earth' (v. 9; see Gen. 13:16; 28:14).

Because Solomon had got his priorities right, God not only granted him his request but promised him the things he did not ask for! The king's main task was to judge or govern God's people (vv. 10-11) and to that end wisdom and knowledge were essential, while the trappings of status in the form of riches, wealth and honour unsurpassed by any other king before or after, would set Solomon apart as the ideal monarch reigning over God's people on God's behalf (see Ps. 72).

Solomon's wealth (1:14-17)

1:14. And Solomon amassed chariots and horsemen. He had one thousand four hundred chariots, and twelve thousand horsemen, and he situated them in the chariot cities and with the king at Jerusalem. 15. And the king made silver and gold in Jerusalem as plentiful as stones, and he made cedars as plentiful as the sycamore in the Shephelah. 16. And Solomon's horses were imported from Egypt; and from Kue, the king's traders procured them from Kue at a price. 17. And they went up and brought out a chariot from Egypt for six hundred *shekels* of silver and a horse for one hundred and fifty, and thus by their hand they brought out to all the kings of the Hittites and the kings of Aram.

The details concerning Solomon's wealth and commercial ventures are also found in 1 Kings 10:26-29 but whereas in Kings they appear toward the end of the account of his reign and immediately before the compiler's critical remarks, in Chronicles they are placed at the beginning to indicate that God was true to his promise and that Solomon had ample means to build the temple. As was customary in powerful states like Assyria, Solomon had the chariots and horses placed in strategic locations throughout the country as well as in Jerusalem (v. 14). Wealth poured into the capital (v. 15), no doubt through tribute money and the commercial activities that are described in the final verses (vv. 16-17). The sycamore-fig trees were common along the coastal plain ('Shephelah' verse 15) and produced fruit that only the poor ate, but the wood was useful as was that from the more expensive and impressive cedars that grew in abundance in Lebanon. The king's traders imported and exported horses from Egypt and as far away as Kue, probably the ancient name for Cilicia, one of the small neo-Hittite states which lay in what is now an area of northern Syria and southern Turkey.

Application

The Chronicler's account would have certainly encouraged those in the post-exilic community to be united ('all Israel') in the service of God, to be wholehearted ('of one heart and mind') in worship as they offered their sacrifices at the temple, to give themselves to prayer on the basis of God's promises to David and to look expectantly to the fulfilment of those promises. As it has been emphasised in 1 Chronicles, God uses the prayers of His people to fulfil His purposes, even when the odds seem stacked against any realisation of them. We are to pray for wisdom in testing circumstances, without doubting God's ability to answer our requests (James 1:1-8). Solomon is but a shadowy picture of David's greater Son. Psalms 68 and 72 speak of the future Messiah in terms of prosperity and international acclaim. Through Jesus, the promise of an innumerable company of people from all nations and people groups truly fulfils the promises to the patriarchs (Rev. 7:9).

Solomon's temple (2:1[1:18]–7:22)

This section begins with Solomon's preparations to build (ch. 2), followed by an account of the actual building of the temple (ch. 3), the production of the temple furnishings (ch. 4), the bringing of the ark to the temple (ch. 5), Solomon's address to the people and prayer of dedication (ch. 6) and finally God's reply (ch. 7). There are many parallels with the Kings account (1 Kings 5–8) but Chronicles uses all the material at his disposal to present his own distinctive message. This meant that he also leaves out what he did not deem necessary or significant, knowing that people had the Kings account on which to fall back for further details.

Preparations for building (2:1-18[1:18–2:17])

There is a chiastic arrangement of the material. At the core is the correspondence between Solomon and Huram in which Solomon writes to Huram (2:3-10[2-9]) and Huram replies to Solomon (2:11-16[10-15]). This is encompassed by references to the conscription of labour (v. 2[1] and vv. 17-18[16-17]). Balancing this chapter concerning Solomon's relations with Tyre is the passage toward the end of the Chronicler's account of Solomon's reign that deals further with international recognition (8:17–9:21). The English text makes the final verse of chapter one in the Hebrew Bible (1:18) the first verse of chapter two which has the advantage of providing a suitable introduction to the new chapter. It does mean, however, that the Hebrew verse numbers for chapter 2 are one less than the English.

> 2:1.[1:18] Now Solomon intended to build a house for the name of Yahweh and a house for his kingdom. 2.[2:1] So Solomon counted seventy thousand men to bear burdens and eighty thousand men to quarry in the mountain and three thousand six hundred supervisors over them.
>
> 3.[2] Then Solomon sent to Huram the king of Tyre, saying: 'As you have dealt with David my father and sent him cedars to build him a house to dwell in, 4.[3] – here I am building a house for the name of Yahweh my God to dedicate it to him and to burn fragrant incense before him, and for the row of continuity, and for the burnt offerings morning and evening for the sabbaths and for the new moons and for the appointed

festivals of Yahweh our God; this *being a requirement* on Israel for ever. 5.[4] And the house which I am going to build is great, for our God is greater than all the gods. 6.[5] But who is able to build a house for him, for the heavens and the highest heavens cannot contain him, and who am I that I should build a house for him except to burn sacrifices before him? – 7.[6] now then send me a skilled man to work in gold and in silver and in bronze and in iron and in purple, and crimson and violet, and who knows how to engrave with the skilful men who are with me in Judah and in Jerusalem, whom David my father provided. 8.[7] Also send to me cedar, cypress and algum wood from Lebanon, for I know that your servants know how to cut the timber of Lebanon; and in fact my servants *will work* with your servants, 9.[8] even to prepare for me timber in abundance, for the house which I am building will be great and wonderful. 10.[9] And indeed I will give to your servants, to the woodmen who cut the timber, twenty thousand kors of ground wheat and twenty thousand kors of barley, and twenty thousand baths of wine, and twenty thousand baths of oil.'

11.[10] Then Huram king of Tyre replied in writing, which he sent to Solomon: 'Because Yahweh loves his people, he has made you king over them.' 12.[11] And Huram also said, 'Blessed be Yahweh, the God of Israel, who has made heaven and earth, who has given king David a wise son, endowed with discretion and understanding, who will build a house for Yahweh and a house for his kingdom. 13.[12] And now I send Huram-abi, a skilled man endowed with understanding, 14.[13] the son of a woman from the daughters of Dan, and his father a Tyrian man, who knows how to work in gold and in silver, in bronze, in iron, in stone and in wood, in purple, in violet, and in linen and in crimson, and to make any engraving and to devise any design which may be assigned to him, together with your skilful men and the skilful of my lord David your father. 15.[14] Now then, let my lord send to his servants the wheat and the barley, the oil and the wine, of which he has spoken, 16.[15] and we will cut timber from Lebanon, as much as you need and bring them to you on rafts by sea to Joppa, and you will carry them up to Jerusalem.'

17.[16] Then Solomon numbered all the aliens who were in the land of Israel, following the numbering which his father David had counted them, and there were found one hundred and fifty-three thousand six hundred. 18.[17] And he made seventy thousand of them bearers of burdens, eighty thousand as quarriers in the mountain and three thousand six hundred as supervisors to make the people work.

The introductory verse mentions in passing that Solomon intended or purposed[1] to build a royal residence for himself, something of which the king of Tyre was aware (vv. 1, 12) and referred to later (2 Chron. 7:11; 8:1; 9:3, 11); but, unlike 1 Kings 7:1-12, the Chronicler gives no details of its construction. All the attention is focused on the temple, where Yahweh's 'name' is to dwell. The 'name of Yahweh' is another way of referring to God Himself with particular focus on His revealed character in His dealings with people. It denotes not only His reputation (1 Chron. 17:21, 24) but His gracious presence in the place associated with Him (see Deut. 12:3b-5, 11). By referring to the 'name', the biblical writer is distancing himself from any thought that one could house the infinite God. The ark of the covenant represented God's presence and the temple was to house this ark. God confirmed His association with the ark when it was placed in the inner sanctuary of the newly-built temple, for the divine glory cloud filled the house. If Yahweh's name or presence dwelt there, that was the place to go to meet and worship Him (see 1 Chron. 13:6; 22:7-8, 10, 19; 28:2-3; 29:16; 2 Chron. 5:2-14; 6:5-10, 20, 24; 7:16, 20, etc.). The king's royal house or 'house of his kingdom' is closely associated with Yahweh's house for the kingdom is Yahweh's (see 1 Chron. 28:5).

In verse 2 and more fully in verses 17-18 reference is made to the labourers who were conscripted. The census or 'count' that is mentioned here, unlike David's census of his own people (1 Chron. 21), is made up of resident aliens, those descendants of the Canaanites who remained after the Israelite conquest, the ones that David had begun to gather in preparation for temple building (see 1 Chron. 22:2, 15-16; 2 Chron. 8:7-10). The parallel text in 1 Kings 5:16 mentions three thousand three hundred overseers instead of three thousand six hundred. Various Greek versions give different figures which may suggest problems in the transmission of the text or that the number fluctuated over the period. On the other hand, the figure in Kings may be referring to a separate group of Israelite officials from the ones mentioned in Chronicles.

---

1. See 1 Kings 5:5[19] for this use of the verb generally translated 'said' (*'āmar*).

Huram (v. 3[2]) is the Chronicler's consistent way of spelling Hiram. This Tyrian king was on friendly terms with David and had provided him with timber for his own palace as well as cedar in preparations for the temple (see 1 Chron. 14:1; 22:4). He had also made an initial contact with Solomon (1 Kings 5:1[15]), but then Solomon wrote to Hiram, wisely indicating the precedent already set, then breaking off to explain the need (vv. 4-6[3-5]),[2] before returning to make his request for men and materials (vv. 7-10[6-9]). The point that Solomon forcefully makes is that as Hiram had helped David to build a palace for himself, how much greater should be his help when David's son is building a palace for Yahweh. Solomon spells out the purpose of the temple in terms of that holy place where the various features of Israel's worship would take place and that were first introduced for the tabernacle in the time of Moses (v. 4).

The incense is associated with the most holy place where God met with His people (Exod. 30:6-7). Also standing in the holy place and associated with God's presence in the inner sanctuary was the regular 'showbread', often described in Hebrew as 'the bread of the face' but here called literally 'continual rows' (*ma'areket tāmîd*), which referred to the bread being placed in rows and always present on the table (see Exod. 25:23-30; Lev. 24:5-9; Num. 4:7). The burnt offerings took place on the bronze altar that was outside in the tabernacle courtyard (Lev. 1; 6:8-13). The burning of incense was closely associated with the twice daily burnt offerings and spoke of propitiation, atonement and wholehearted commitment. As for the weekly renewal of the twelve loaves before each Sabbath (1 Chron. 9:32), this symbolised Israel and the need for renewal in the presence of God. These regular rituals whether daily, weekly, monthly or at the annual festivals (see Num. 28:1–29:39) represented the whole ceremonial law that was to be observed without fail and, for the Chronicler, they provided a way of measuring how true the kings of Judah were to the Mosaic religion (see 2 Chron. 13:10-11). Like the Unleavened Bread festival, these rituals were perpetual ordinances for Israel to keep (Exod. 12:17).

---

2. The sentence breaks off, with verses 4-6 in parenthesis and the main point continues in verse 7.

In addition to the purpose of the temple, Solomon explains why it was to be the very best in terms of materials and magnificence (vv. 5-6, 9). This was to be, as David had emphasised, an impressive structure for other countries to admire (1 Chron. 22:5). It was a house for Yahweh who is described as greater than all the gods that other nations worship (see Exod. 18:11; Pss. 77:13[14]); 95:3; 135:5; 1 Chron. 29:1). David's absolute monotheism (1 Chron. 17:20) is not denied by this statement. Solomon is merely acknowledging that Israel was surrounded by people groups who believed in multiple gods. Lest it should be simplistically thought that the temple was to be built large enough to house this great God, Solomon explains that God cannot be confined to any house built by humans. Not even the temple-like spacious sky above could contain Yahweh. Like Moses and David (Exod. 3:11; 1 Chron. 17:16; 29:14), Solomon expresses his unworthiness as he contemplates the task of building a house that would be appropriate for this transcendent God as a house of prayer and sacrifice (see 2 Chron. 7:12, 15).

After this important theological aside (vv. 4-6), Solomon makes his requests in the form of commands so that he becomes almost like an overlord with Hiram as a vassal king (vv. 7-10; see also 1 Kings 5:6[20]). Later, Hiram also gives that impression by referring to David and then to Solomon as 'my lord' (vv. 14-15). Only the offer to pay wages to Hiram's workers indicates that Hiram is not in subjection to the king of Israel (v. 10). Solomon's first request is for a highly skilled, versatile craftsman, able to work with all types of metal and fabrics as well as to engrave. This expert is to assist those in Israel that David had already provided (v. 7; 1 Chron. 22:15-16; 28:21; 29:5). The verse calls to mind the materials and craftsmen associated with the construction of the tabernacle. Bezalel and Oholiab were experts in the same materials and worked with other skilled workers among the people (Exod. 35:30-36:2; see 2 Chron. 1:5 for Bezalel). Secondly, Solomon asks for the famous Lebanon timber that included cedar, cypress and the unidentified almug wood, a wood that is also mentioned in Akkadian and Ugaritic texts. Famous too are the Tyrian workers skilled in felling and cutting the trees. Solomon's servants are pledged to work alongside Hiram's lumberjacks. After repeating the importance of the building project (v. 9), Solomon mentions the amount he is prepared to pay the workers. This is probably one of Solomon's negotiating positions,[3] which, as Kings describes, was subsequently changed (1 Kings 5:6, 11[20, 25]). It is impossible to be sure, as all the details are not available, but these initial amounts are not excessive compared with the Kings account, especially as thirty kors of flour and sixty kors of cereal were needed daily to support Solomon's court (1 Kings 4:22).

Hiram's written reply begins diplomatically (vv. 11-12). He recognises that Solomon's kingship is due to Yahweh's love for His people, a conclusion that the Queen of Sheba also acknowledged, and both Hiram and the Queen worship Yahweh for putting Solomon on the throne (2 Chron. 9:8). In this way the Chronicler emphasises at the beginning and end of his account of Solomon's reign how Gentile monarchs witness to Israel's God and His love for His people (Deut. 7:7-8; Mal. 1:2; Ps. 47:4[5]). Hiram also confesses that Yahweh is the creator God (see Gen. 14:19; 2 Chron. 36:23) and that Solomon is a wise son of David, who has been given the kind of discretion and understanding that David had desired for his son (1 Chron. 22:12). Such theological declarations by pagan rulers are found elsewhere (Dan. 4:34-35; 6:26-27) and do not necessarily imply conversion to Israel's God. Compared with the Kings account, Chronicles contains more information that draws particular attention to the divine wisdom given to Solomon in relation to the building of Yahweh's house as well as his own royal residence. The temple is seen as the crowning achievement of the David–Solomon era and thus magnifies Yahweh's greatness.

Hiram grants Solomon's requests by sending his namesake as a skilled worker to Jerusalem (vv. 13-14) and arranging for the required timber to be cut and transported by sea in rafts to the port of Joppa (v. 16; see Jonah 1:3; Ezra 3:7), as well as accepting payment in kind to Hiram's lumberjacks who are actually referred to as working for Solomon ('his servants,' v. 15). It may be that Huram-abi, called simply 'Hiram' in 1 Kings 7:13-14, 40, 45 and 'Huram' in 2 Chronicles 4:11, is his

---

3. See Selman, *2 Chronicles*, p.301.

full name to distinguish him from the Tyrian king. At the same time, the Chronicler may well have wanted to make a link between this skilled craftsman and Bezalel's assistant, Oholiab, who had engaged in similar work for the tabernacle, especially as Huram-abi's mother, like Oholiab's father, was from Dan (Exod. 31:6; 35:34-35; 38:23). The parallel text in Kings states that this Hiram was the son of a widow from the tribe of Naphtali. Until the Danites migrated north from their allotted coastal plain region, that included Joppa, to seize Laish or Leshem and rename it Dan, Naphtali was the northernmost inland tribe. While this city called Dan lay just outside the Israelite territory near to the sources of the Jordan, it is more than likely that some Danite inhabitants occupied the border regions of Naphtali (Josh. 19:40-48; Judg. 18:1, 7, 27-29). It is interesting that both Dan and Naphtali were the two sons of Jacob's concubine Bilhah, Rachel's maid (Gen. 30:6, 8) and Dan is the one tribe not mentioned in the genealogies of 1 Chronicles 2–8. Huram-abi's father, on the other hand, was from Tyre, a not unusual relationship, because the nearest access of the Danites to the sea was the Phoenician coastline, with the closest port being Tyre. The wisdom or skill of Huram-abi gave him the kind of 'understanding' Solomon possessed so that he had the combined abilities of both Bezalel and Oholiab (see Exod. 31:1-4; 35:31-35).

Application

The Chronicler has shown that everything associated with the temple and its location involved people of other races, from Jerusalem which was itself won from the Hittites to the Moriah site obtained from a Jebusite and including the help obtained from the Phoenicians. Writing in the same era, Malachi also emphasised that Yahweh's name is great among the Gentile nations and one to be feared (Mal. 1:11, 14). It is as if the Chronicler is pressing home the prophet's message and encouraging his people to understand that there is continuity between the original temple and the one they have recently built, even mentioning that it was the same port, Joppa, to which the Sidonians and Tyrians brought the logs for the construction of the second temple (Ezra 3:7). That continuity is shown to extend further back in history as witnessed by the references to the tabernacle materials, sacrifices and festivals, as well as the parallels between Huram-abi's skills and those of Bezalel and Oholiab. That continuity continues through to the new covenant where Jesus brings to realisation all that the old tabernacle and temple pictured.

God's spiritual temple is one for all the nations of the world, and the Tyrian king's worship of God is an example of the praise encouraged by the Psalter and the post-exilic prophets (Ps. 117; Hag. 2:7; Zech. 8:18-23; 14:16-21). With Jesus and the Church that He is building, we have a greater than Solomon. Jesus has been made head over all things to the Church. Jew and Gentile are brought together and likened to a building that 'grows into a holy temple in the Lord ... for a habitation of God in the Spirit' (Eph. 1:22; 2:19-22; see 1 Pet. 2:4-10). And Jesus does involve His servants in this building project with Paul describing himself as a master builder and others like Apollos seen as co-workers (1 Cor. 3:5-17).

The temple building and its furnishings (3:1–5:1)
The building of the various rooms of the temple is given in chapter three while the furnishings are recorded in chapter four with a concluding note at 5:1a.

1. Building the temple (3:1-17)
Compared to 1 Kings 6:1-7:51, Chronicles gives a much briefer account and does not mention the building of Solomon's own royal palace (but see 2 Chron. 8:1). Only what the Chronicler considered important to his message relating to the temple is presented with a few details not recorded elsewhere. After the introduction (vv. 1-2), the chapter deals with the construction of the temple itself and its rooms (vv. 3-9), the formation of the cherubim and the veil (vv. 10-14) and the creation of the two named pillars (vv. 15-17).

> 3:1. Now Solomon began to build the house of Yahweh in Jerusalem on Mount Moriah, where he had appeared to David his father, which he had prepared on David's site,[4] on the

---

4. The ancient versions support a readjustment of the Hebrew to give 'at the place that David had prepared,' which most English versions follow, including the AV text.

threshing-floor of Ornan the Jebusite. 2. And he began to build on the second in the second month, in the fourth year of his reign. 3. Now these Solomon established to build the house of God. The length in cubits according to the former standard *was* sixty cubits and the width twenty cubits. 4. And the porch that was in front: the length corresponded to the breadth of the house, twenty cubits, and the height was one hundred and twenty. He overlaid the inside with pure gold.

5. And the great house he panelled with cypress wood and overlaid it with fine gold, and he put palms and chains on it. 6. And he overlaid the house with precious stones for beauty, and the gold was gold from Parvaim. 7. He also overlaid the house – the beams, the thresholds and its walls and its doors – with gold; and he carved cherubim on the walls. 8. And he made the most holy house. Its length corresponded to the width of the house, twenty cubits, and its width twenty cubits. He overlaid it with six hundred talents of fine gold. 9. The weight of the nails was fifty shekels of gold; and he overlaid the upper *part* with gold. 10. And in the most holy house he made two cherubim of sculptured work, and overlaid them with gold. 11. The wings of the cherubim were twenty cubits long: the wing of one *was* five cubits, touching the wall of the house, and the other wing *was* five cubits, touching the wing of the other cherub; 12. and the wing of one cherub *was* five cubits, touching the wall of the house, and the other wing *was* five cubits, joining the wing of the other cherub. 13. The wings of these cherubim extended twenty cubits and they stood on their feet, and they were facing the house. 14. And he made the veil of blue and purple and crimson and fine linen, and he worked cherubim on it.

15. Also he made in front of the house two pillars thirty-five cubits long, and the capital that was on the top of it was five cubits. 16. And he made chains, *as* in the inner sanctuary, and set them on top of the pillars; and he made one hundred pomegranates and put *them* on the chains. 17. Then he set up the pillars in front of the temple, one on the right and the other on the left; and he called the name of the one on the right Jachin, and the name of the one on the left Boaz.

The introduction (vv. 1-2) provides important information not found elsewhere. Particularly significant is the actual place in Jerusalem where the temple was to be built. The reference to Mount Moriah associates the temple site with Abraham and with the binding of his son Isaac and God's provision of a lamb in place of his son (Gen. 22). Moriah is also called the 'mountain of Yahweh' (Gen. 22:14) which prophets and psalmists associate with Zion and its temple (Isa. 2:2-3//Micah 4:1; 30:29; Ps. 24:3; Zech. 8:3; 2 Chron. 33:15; see Exod. 15:17). The temple site is also connected with David and the altar he built after purchasing Ornan's threshing floor, with the propitiatory sacrifices he offered to appease Yahweh's wrath and the fire from heaven that gave approval to David's action. While the post-exilic temple structure was no match for the one built by Solomon, the Chronicler encouraged his people by showing how the site had a long history associated with such illustrious figures as Abraham and David who had met God there.

Like Kings, Chronicles gives the starting date of the whole project as the fourth year of the second month but unlike Kings makes no reference to the years since the exodus from Egypt. There are other parallel passages where the exodus is omitted (1 Chron. 17:5//2 Sam. 7:6; 2 Chron. 6:11, 39-40//1 Kings 8:21, 50-53) but we ought not to read too much into this as the Chronicler assumes familiarity with the text of Kings. The 'second' refers to the day,[5] while the second month (between April and May) relates to the religious calendar that began with the festival of Passover and Unleavened Bread in the first month – a good time to start building. The repetition of 'began to build' in verses 1 and 2 indicates that the Chronicler is more concerned to link the date with David's choice of the site and the preparations he had already made for its construction (see 1 Chron. 22). Further building projects are mentioned later with a time reference that matches the one found here in verse 2 (8:1-16).

The account first gives the dimensions of the main building and the porch (vv. 3-4) and, interestingly, it informs us of measurement variations in ancient Israel, one cubit being longer than the other (see Ezek. 40:5; 43:13). Scholars are not sure which is to be considered the 'former standard', but overall Solomon's main temple structure that included the holy and most holy rooms was not large, measuring

---

5. The word for 'second' is missing in a few Hebrew MSS and the ancient versions, and scholars often omit it as being due to dittography, especially as it has no accompanying word for 'day'.

somewhere in the region of either a hundred and five feet by thirty-five feet (32x10.6 metres) according to the larger cubit or for the short cubit, eighty-eight feet by thirty feet (27x9 metres). Separate measurements are given for the porch or vestibule which was in front at the entrance to the temple. To give it an impressive appearance, the inside was overlaid with pure gold.[6]

Moving on to describe the holy place (vv. 5-7; see Exod. 26:33; Lev. 16:2; 2 Chron. 5:11), which is sometimes referred to as the 'nave' or 'palace' (2 Chron. 4:7-8, 22) but here called 'the great house' (v. 5), the Chronicler mentions the cypress panelling which was decorated with palm trees, chains, precious stones and cherubim. The whole area was gilded, and the gold was described as 'good' or 'fine', a high-quality 'Parvaim' gold. No such place with this name has yet been identified with any certainty. What David had in mind and planned for is executed (see 1 Chron. 22:5). It was an exquisite, glorious room that befitted the God to whom it was dedicated (1 Chron. 29:11, 13). In addition, there are, like the tabernacle, reminders of the original lost temple-like garden in Eden with the references to the gold, the precious stones, the trees and the cherubim (Gen. 2:9, 11-12; 3:24).

The Chronicler then proceeds to describe the holy of holies or 'most holy house' (vv. 7-9; see Exod. 26:33) and termed 'the inner sanctuary' in verse 16. A vast amount of gold was used to line the room, but this was only a fraction of what David had obtained for the work (1 Chron. 22:14). The nails were made of iron (see 1 Chron. 22:3) and then overlaid with gold. As for 'the upper *part*', which was probably the ten-cubit space between the ceiling and the roof (see 1 Kings 6:2, 20 where the height of the building is thirty cubits and the height of the most holy place twenty cubits),[7] this too was covered with gold. Despite the scepticism of many scholars

---

6. The text of verse 4 is difficult and the meaning uncertain. 120 cubits cannot be its height as this would be far too high. There is no word for 'cubit' with the numeral as in the case of the previous measurements, so it may refer to a measure that is much smaller than a cubit. See Raymond B. Dillard, *2 Chronicles*, Word Biblical Commentary, Volume 15 (Nashville: Thomas Nelson, 2000), p. 26, who suggests that a confusion has arisen between the word for hundred (*m'wt*) and cubit (*'mwt*), in which case the height would be a more acceptable twenty cubits.

7. See Dillard, *2 Chronicles*, p. 29, for more details.

who cannot understand why such areas of the temple unseen by the human eye and completely dark should have such gold, this was meant for the unseen God and appropriate for the place that was to house the ark, the symbol of the glorious presence of God.

Associated with the most holy place, the account describes how Solomon constructed the cherubim (vv. 10-13; see 1 Chron. 13:6; 28:18; Exod. 25:18-20). Their wingspan stretched from one wall to the other, with the other wing of each touching in the middle. They were self-supporting, standing on their own feet and they faced the main room of the temple. When the ark was in place they would have given it complete protection (2 Chron. 5:7-8). In the Ancient Near East such creaturely figures guarded sacred places.

The remaining item associated with the most holy place relates to the veil or curtain that separated the holy from the most holy place (v. 14). There are clear reminders of the tabernacle (Exod. 26:31-33; 36:35) where similar coloured fabrics and white linen separate the two rooms. Like the tabernacle, the coloured cloths suggest the colours seen in the sky, intimating that the temple is a miniature universe and along with the other materials speak of the lost temple garden in Eden where God dwelt with his image bearers. Although it is stressed all through this section that Solomon not only built the temple but made all the various rooms and furnishings, that must not be taken literally, any more than is done when hearing that Wren built St Paul's cathedral. In the case of the temple curtain, this was Huram-abi's direct responsibility as he was used to working with the coloured materials mentioned (2 Chron. 2:7[6]). Kings makes no allusion to the veil but does report that double olive wood doors were made to separate the rooms (1 Kings 6:31-32). Though the Chronicler makes no reference to these doors here, he does mention them later (2 Chron. 4:22). Clearly, there were wooden doors as well as a curtain in Solomon's temple.

In the porch and immediately before the entrance to the holy place, two free-standing pillars were made (vv. 15-17): one called Jachin ('he establishes') erected on the south side of the entrance and one on the north side called Boaz ('in strength'). They were made of bronze (1 Kings 7:13-14; see

1 Chron. 18:8; 2 Chron. 4:11-16). The capital on the top of each pillar was five cubits and their combined height is put at thirty-five cubits (eighteen cubits each in 1 Kings 7:15). There is no certainty over the significance of the pillars and their names, but they probably underline two important themes of the Chronicler. It is God who 'established' David as king and promised to establish his kingdom which is very closely associated with Yahweh's temple (see 1 Chron. 14:2; 17:11-12, 14, 23-24; 22:10). In addition, Yahweh's 'strength' is emphasised in David's thanksgiving (1 Chron. 16:11, 27-28) and coupled with the ark (2 Chron. 6:41). Thus at the entrance to the holy place the pillars proclaimed Yahweh's stability and strength. They are decorated on top with capitals that had chains around them with a hundred pomegranates hanging from the chains. Pomegranates were embroidered on Aaron's robe, and they are sometimes mentioned as an example of the good foods of Egypt (Exod. 28:34; Num. 20:5). The chain design is like that found in the most holy place (v. 16; 1 Kings 6:21) as well as in the holy place (v. 5). Mentioning 'the inner sanctuary' at this point (v. 16) suggests that the Chronicler was indicating that the pillars were an integral part of the main temple structure with its decoration in harmony with the most holy part (see 1 Kings 6:21).[8] The description, in fact, moves in and then out again, from the porch to the holy place and to the inner sanctuary and then retreating to the curtain at the entrance to the most holy place and finally back to the pillars in the porch at the entrance to the holy place.

Application

For the Chronicler's contemporaries, it was more important to appreciate the significance of the site on which their temple had been recently built than all the details described in Kings. There was continuity not only with Solomon and David but with Moses and Abraham. While Jesus indicated that He Himself was the true temple (John 2:21-22), Revelation shows how the old tabernacle/temple is patterned on the original

---

8. Most modern versions and commentaries emend the text to 'chains like a necklace' while some suggest it is a 'misplaced gloss'. See Japhet, *I & II Chronicles*, p. 558.

temple garden in Eden and anticipates the future new world order where Eden is surpassed. The new Jerusalem, a perfect cube, needs no temple for it is itself the holy of holies where God dwells with His people. It is to this Mount Zion associated with Mount Moriah that Christians already come (Heb. 12:22-24). The awesome beauty of Solomon's temple pales into insignificance in the light of the reality associated with Jesus's achievement through His atoning death. By the blood of Jesus, God's people enter into the real holy of holies (Heb. 9:24; 10:19-20).

2. Temple furnishings and conclusion (4:1–5:1)

The passage can be compared with the account in 1 Kings 7:23-51. From the emphasis on the structures of the temple in chapter three, the Chronicler considers the fittings and furniture along with the various temple vessels and the metals used. There are four paragraphs: the temple furnishings (vv. 1-11a, with the continuing refrain 'and he made'); the bronze items summarised (vv. 11b-18); the gold items summarised (vv. 19-22); and the work completed (5:1).

> 4:1. He also made a bronze altar, twenty cubits its length, twenty cubits its width and ten cubits its height. 2. Then he made the molten sea, ten cubits from rim to rim round its perimeter and five cubits its height and a line of thirty cubits encircled it round. 3. And the likeness of oxen was under it encircling it all around, ten to a cubit, encompassing the sea around. Two rows of oxen *were* cast when it was cast. 4. It stood upon twelve oxen, three facing northward, three facing westward, three facing southward, and three facing eastward. The sea *was set* on top of them and all their back parts *were* inward. 5. And its thickness was a handbreadth; and its rim was made like the rim of a cup, like the flower of a lily. It held three thousand baths. 6. He also made ten lavers, and he put five on the right and five on the left in which to wash. They rinsed in them the work associated with the burnt offerings and the sea *was* for the priests to wash in.
>
> 7. And he made ten golden lampstands according to the ruling given them, and set them in the temple, five on the right and five on the left. 8. He also made ten tables and placed them in the temple, five on the right and five on the left; and he made a hundred basins of gold. 9. And he made the court of

the priests, and the great enclosure and doors for the enclosure and overlaid their doors with bronze. 10. And the sea he set on the right side at the southeast. 11. Hiram also made the pots, the shovels and the basins.

So Huram finished doing the work that he did for king Solomon in the house of God: 12. the two pillars and the bowls and the capitals on top of the two pillars and the two lattice-works to cover the two bowls of the capitals that were on the top of the pillars; 13. and the four hundred pomegranates for the two lattice-works, two rows of pomegranates for each lattice-work, to cover the two bowls of the capitals that were on the pillars. 14. He also made the stands and he made the lavers on the stands, 15. the one sea and the twelve oxen under it, 16. and the pots and the shovels and the forks, and all the utensils Huram-abi made of burnished bronze for king Solomon for the house of Yahweh. 17. In the plain of the Jordan the king cast them, in the clay ground between Succoth and Zarethan. 18. And Solomon made all these utensils in great abundance that the weight of the bronze could not be ascertained.

19. So Solomon made all the utensils that *were for* the house of God, and the golden altar and the tables on which was the bread of the presence, 20. and the lampstands and their lamps of pure gold to burn in front of the inner sanctuary according to the ruling; 21. and the flowers and the lamps and the tongs of gold, that is of purest gold; 22. and the snuffers and the basins and the ladles and the firepans of pure gold. And the entrance of the house, its inner doors to the most holy place and the doors of the nave of the temple *were* of gold.

5:1. So all the work that Solomon had done for the house of Yahweh was finished. And Solomon brought in the dedicated things of David his father; and he put the silver and the gold and all the utensils in the treasuries of the house of God.

The chapter begins with the construction of the large bronze altar that stood in the courtyard immediately outside the temple (v. 1). Its purpose was for the burning of the animal and grain sacrifices (see 2 Chron. 7:7). The ascending smoke of the offerings represented their acceptance by God and the removal of His wrath. Even though the old Mosaic altar was still in existence at Gibeon, a new, bigger altar was needed for a new temple (see 2 Chron. 1:6; Exod. 27:1-8). Its dimensions in modern equivalents made it about thirty feet square and fifteen feet high (9x9x4.5 metres).

Like the pillars, the 'sea' was made of the bronze that David had dedicated from the spoils of war (vv. 2-5; 1 Chron. 18:8). It, too, was placed in the courtyard on the south side of the temple (v. 10). The cast-metal tank was about fifteen feet (4.5 metres) in diameter, 7.5 feet (2.25 metres) high, forty-five feet (13.5 metres) in circumference and a handbreadth thick and held 3,000 baths, equivalent to about 17,500 gallons (66 kilolitres) of water (v. 5). The figure of 2,000 baths in 1 Kings 7:26 is probably due to different ways of measuring. Verse 3 is difficult, but the Chronicler's text should be kept. The 'gourds' of the 1 Kings 7:24 text looked more like the heads of oxen as they peered out from under the rim of the 'sea'. The whole cistern rested on twelve oxen with three facing each of the four points of the compass and represented the twelve tribes that made up the nation of Israel, while the 'sea' probably spoke of Yahweh's universal rule and presence that would cover the waters of the sea in every direction (Isa. 11:9; Hab. 2:14; Ps. 72:19). The Chronicler briefly mentions the ten lavers or basins that stood five on the south side and five on the north side of the temple (v. 6; 1 Kings 7:38-39). While the lavers were for cleaning and preparing the sacrifices, the 'sea' was set aside for the priests to cleanse themselves. In the tabernacle, there was only the one basin for the priests to wash their hands and feet before entering the tent or preparing to sacrifice (Exod. 30:18-21; 40:31-32).

The Chronicler then describes the furnishings in the main hall of the temple: the ten golden lampstands and the ten tables (vv. 7-8) in contrast to the single lampstand and table that stood in the tabernacle (Exod. 25:23-30; 31-40; 37:10-16; 17-24). While the lampstand in the tabernacle was on the south side, opposite the table that was on the north side, in Solomon's temple five lampstands and five tables were on each side, north and south. This difference was by divine approval (kᵊmišpāṭām, 'according to their ruling,' vv. 7, 20; 1 Chron. 24:19), as were the original furnishings in the tabernacle (Exod. 25:40). David had provided the gold for the tables of 'showbread' and for the basins (1 Chron. 28:16-17). Both the lamps and the bread on the tables spoke of God's special presence with His people, bringing them salvation and life (see vv. 19-20).

In verses 9-11a the Chronicler returns to say more about the courtyard where the altar and sea stood (vv. 1-6). The structure of these verses has the advantage of acting like the courtyard itself surrounding the holy place. Whereas the tabernacle had only one court (Exod. 27:9-19), two courts are mentioned here: the court of the priests, elsewhere described as the 'inner' court next to the temple where the sea and lavers stood (1 Kings 6:36; 7:12); and a 'great enclosure' where the unusual term 'enclosure' (*ʿᵃzārāh*) is used for court (see also 2 Chron. 6:13 and used elsewhere only for the surrounding ledge of the altar in Ezek. 43:14, 17, 20; 45:19). This larger outer enclosure, called the 'great court' in 1 Kings 7:12 is probably the one referred to as the 'upper courtyard' in Jeremiah 36:10 where the people could assemble. Reference is also made later to two temple courts (2 Kings 21:5//2 Chron. 33:5; 2 Kings 23:12; see also the outer and inner courts in the visionary temple of Ezek. 40:17-19, 44). The bronze-covered doors that separated the two courts would have helped protect the priestly court from inadvertent entry by the people.

The pots, shovels and basins (v. 11a; see Exod. 27:1-3; 38:3; Num. 4:14) would each have their purpose: the pots for boiling the sacrificial meat; pots and shovels for clearing away the ash from the altar; and the basins for catching the blood of animals and for sprinkling it at the appropriate places according to the ceremonial laws. This verse together with the remaining verses of this section follows closely the parallel account in 1 Kings 7:40-50.

The final paragraphs (4:11b–5:1) provide a summary of what has already been described in detail, although some items are new. The two bronze pillars and capitals with the decorative pomegranates (vv. 12-13) were mentioned in 3:15-17. As for the lavers (v. 14), there was no mention earlier of the stands on which they stood (4:6). Interestingly, the Chronicler prefers to emphasise Hiram's action in making the lavers and their stands ('he made') whereas 1 Kings 7:43 is more interested in recording that there were 'ten' stands and basins. For the sea with the oxen beneath (v. 15), see the fuller description in 4:2-6. In verse 16, 'forks' are an additional item not mentioned before or in Kings (see Exod. 27:3; 38:3; 1 Chron. 28:17). All the utensils of polished bronze were made in the valley east of the

Jordan and to the north of the Dead Sea and the weight of the bronze was deemed to be incalculable (vv. 17-18).[9]

The casting was probably done by pressing the clay earth into moulds. As for the remaining items, it is made clear that whereas Huram-abi was responsible to Solomon for making the bronze furnishings for the temple courtyard, it is Solomon who is more directly responsible for the golden items belonging to the holy place (vv. 19-22). Also of note is that more costly metals were used in the holier areas – bronze for outside the temple but gold for the interior.

The golden altar was not described earlier, as might have been expected in verses 7-8, but its presence has been assumed (1 Chron. 28:18). It is to be identified with the similar altar that stood near the entrance to the holy of holies in the tabernacle and known as the altar of incense (Exod. 30:1-10; 40:5, 26; Lev. 16:12). The tables for the showbread, the lampstands and the bowls have been mentioned earlier (see vv. 7-8). Significantly, in this one case only in Chronicles is the showbread referred to as the 'bread of the presence' (literally 'the bread of the faces,' v. 19; see Exod. 25:30; 35:13; 39:36). It was perhaps called this because it lay near the most holy place and 'especially meaningful in a passage anticipating the reality of God's glorious presence'.[10] Because there was to be a continual supply (Exod. 25:30), it is also referred to as 'the regular … bread' (Num. 4:7). Added here are the flower-like buds, the lamps and the tongs associated with the lampstands (see Exod. 25:31, 33, 37-38). The spoon-shaped ladles and firepans were necessary for the incense altar (see Exod. 25:38; 27:3). Both the entrance to the holy place and the inner sanctuary had golden doors. This was in addition to the brightly coloured veil that separated the holy place from the holy of holies (3:14).

The concluding summary (5:1) is in two parts. First, there is a statement that the work that was begun in 3:1-2 was now finished. To emphasise that Solomon had carried out what he had been called to do, there is a word play on Solomon's

---

9. The parallel text of 1 Kings 7:46 reads Zarethan. See Dillard, 2 Chronicles, p. 33, who suggests that Zeredah may be an alternative name for the same site.

10. See Selman, 2 Chronicles, p. 314.

name. All the work of building God's house undertaken by Solomon (š^elōmôh) was completed (tišlam). Second, David's part in preparing for this conclusion is not forgotten. Solomon brought into the temple all David's dedicated treasures and placed them in the treasuries (see 1 Chron. 9:26; 26:26), just as Joshua had done in his day (Josh. 6:24). In this way, the Chronicler stresses again that the temple construction was a joint David–Solomon project.

Application

The Chronicler shows that Solomon did precisely what was expected of him and finished what his father had planned and purposed. The old altar from the time of Moses was not used. A new temple demanded a new altar. Jesus accomplished all that His Father had purposed in bringing to realisation all that the old tabernacle and temple had symbolised. Jesus is God's new temple and, as we are told, 'we have an altar from which those who serve the tabernacle have no right to eat' (Heb. 13:10). Jesus sanctified His people by His own blood when He suffered outside the camp. We are urged to go out to Him bearing His reproach, knowing we have no continuing city in the present world, but we seek one that is to come. Thus we are called to offer continually sacrifices of praise and thanksgiving to God and urged to do good and share (Heb. 13:11-16). The Chronicler presents the construction of Solomon's temple against the background of the original tabernacle and with an eye to the present concerns of his own post-exilic community. There is continuity with the past, but the people are left with a longing for something more and far better than Solomon's temple.

The ark is brought to the temple (5:2–6:2)
This section parallels closely the text of 1 Kings 8:1-11 and is a continuation of the narrative concerning Solomon's temple begun in chapter 1. Up to this point (1:1–5:1) the account has covered the necessary preparations and building process; now the focus is on God's presence in the temple. It begins with the final and most important item brought into the temple and closes with the manifestation of Yahweh's presence in the temple and Solomon's initial response.

5:2. Then Solomon assembled to Jerusalem the elders of Israel and all the heads of the tribes, the chiefs of the fathers of the sons of Israel, to bring up the ark of the covenant of Yahweh from the city of David, which is Zion. 3. And all the men of Israel assembled themselves to the king at the feast, that is *in* the seventh month. 4. Then all the elders of Israel came and the Levites took up the ark. 5. And they brought up the ark and the tent of meeting and all the holy utensils which *were* in the tent; the Levitical priests brought them up. 6. And king Solomon and all the congregation of Israel who were assembled with him before the ark were sacrificing sheep and oxen that could not be counted or numbered for being so many. 7. Then the priests brought the ark of the covenant of Yahweh to its place, into the inner sanctuary of the house, to the most holy place, under the wings of the cherubim. 8. For the cherubim spread their wings over the place of the ark, so that the cherubim made a covering over the ark and over its poles above. 9. And the poles were so long that the ends of the poles of the ark[11] could be seen in front of the inner sanctuary, but they could not be seen outside; and it is there to this day. 10. There was nothing in the ark except the two tablets that Moses put *there* at Horeb, where Yahweh made a covenant with the sons of Israel, when they came out of Egypt. 11. And it was when the priests came out from the holy place (for all the priests who were present had sanctified themselves, regardless of divisions), 12. and all the Levitical singers, Asaph, Heman, Jeduthun and their sons and brothers, clothed in fine linen, with cymbals, harps, and lyres, standing east of the altar, and with them one hundred and twenty priests blowing trumpets, 13. and it was when in unison the trumpeters and the singers were to make themselves heard with one voice to praise and to give thanks to Yahweh, and when they lifted up their voice accompanied by trumpets and cymbals and instruments of music, and when they praised Yahweh, 'For *he is* good for his steadfast love *is* for ever,' then the house was filled with a cloud, the house of Yahweh, 14. so that the priests were not able to stand to minister because of the cloud, for the glory of Yahweh filled the house of God. 6:1. Then Solomon said, 'Yahweh purposed to dwell in the thick cloud. 2. But I have built an exalted house for you and a place for you to dwell for ever.'

As Solomon involved all the various leaders of Israel in worship at Gibeon where the Mosaic tabernacle was situated

11. The LXX, a few Hebrew MSS and 1 Kings 8:8 read 'from the holy place'.

(2 Chron. 1:2-3), so he gathered them together for this important event. Every Israelite man (v. 3) – represented by the elders (1 Chron. 11:3; 15:25; 21:16), the tribal heads (Num. 30:1[2]) and family leaders (1 Chron. 7:11, 40; 8:13; etc.) – was in effect assembled to move the ark from the tent that David had provided for it to its new site in the temple. It was the final move that had begun with David's act of transferring it from Kiriath-jearim to Jerusalem (1 Chron. 15-16). The reference to Zion is a reminder of David's capture of this stronghold which became the original city of David (1 Chron. 11:5). By the time the Chronicler wrote, prophecies as in Isaiah and so many of the psalms had used the name Zion to speak of it as a mountain associated with God's presence with His people that transcended the temporal city and that was closely associated with an eschatological Davidic ruler.

Though the temple is said to have been completed in the eighth month of Solomon's eleventh year (1 Kings 6:38), it was not ready to be used until the following year for it was in the holy seventh month at the festival of Tabernacles which began on the fifteenth day of that month that the events surrounding the dedication of the temple took place. It was an appropriate time, for it marked the end of the harvest season, an occasion of great joy and a reminder of Israel's years of wandering in the wilderness with the portable sanctuary (Lev. 23:35-44; Deut. 16:13-17). When the returning exiles built an altar on the temple site, it was similarly dedicated at the time of Tabernacles (Ezra 3:4).

In view of David's initial abortive attempt to bring the ark to Jerusalem, Chronicles is careful to indicate that only those from the tribe of Levi could carry the ark of the covenant (vv. 4-5, 7; Num. 1:50; 4:15; 1 Chron. 15:14-15; see 1 Kings 8:3). It was only natural that those Levites who had been attending to the ark in Jerusalem, would be involved in carrying the ark on this occasion (1 Chron. 16:37-42). The priests, who were of course Levites[12] and had been based in Gibeon (1 Chron. 16:39; 2 Chron. 1:3), brought from there Moses' tent of meeting and all its holy utensils and presumably they were placed

---

12. Instead of the MT, 'the priests the Levites', the LXX, Vulgate and many Hebrew MSS plus 1 Kings 8:4 read 'the priests and the Levites'.

somewhere safe within the temple precincts. In this way the continuity between the original tabernacle and the temple is again indicated and at the same time the centralisation of Israel's worship is achieved. There is one place of worship centred on the temple in Jerusalem. As a symbolic number of sacrifices – seven bulls and seven rams – had been offered on the ark's journey to Jerusalem, so Solomon and the assembly made similar sacrifices (v. 6), only this time they could not be numbered (v. 6; 1 Chron. 15:26).

As only the priests were allowed to enter the holy and most holy place (see Num. 4:5-20), it was they who brought the ark to its final resting place in the inner sanctuary, beneath the wings of the cherubim (vv. 7-8; Exod. 25:10-21; 1 Chron. 28:18; 2 Chron. 3:13). The 'poles' placed in the rings on either side of the ark are specifically mentioned in the light of the Uzza incident when the ark was carried on a cart instead of on the shoulders of Levites by means of poles. These poles were to remain in position when the ark was placed in the inner sanctuary (v. 9; Exod. 25:14-15) and could be seen by the priests in the main holy nave, presumably when the doors were opened revealing a bulge in the veil. Apparently, only when the ark was being prepared for transportation in the wilderness were the poles temporarily taken out (Num. 4:6). Now that this was to be the ark's permanent home they would be there 'in perpetuity' which is probably the meaning of 'it is there until this day'.[13]

Continuity with the tabernacle is further emphasised by reference to the two tablets on which were written the Ten Commandments. They represented the Sinai covenant (v. 10; see 2 Chron. 6:11; Deut. 9:9; 10:2, 5). Far from thinking the Chronicler had little interest in the events surrounding the exodus and Sinai, he noted this important fact that is also included in the parallel account in Kings. Often the exodus event is taken as read by Chronicles, but there are enough references to indicate it was basic to the compiler's understanding of David and the temple (1 Chron. 17:5, 21; 2 Chron. 6:5; 7:22; 20:10). The strong statement that there was

---

13. The LXX, Syriac, some Hebrew MSS and 1 Kings 8:8 read the plural 'and they are'. The Vulgate retains the singular verb but adds 'the ark' as the subject. But the singular is probably meant in the sense of the sight, the phenomena.

nothing else in the ark suggests that there was a time when other items were deposited there besides the stone tablets (see Exod. 16:32-34; Num. 17:10-11[25-26]; Heb. 9:4).

As the divine glory cloud filled the tabernacle when it was erected and the ark and all the furnishings were in place, so the same occurred with the newly-constructed temple. Because of the cloud, the priests could not enter the temple to minister, just as Moses was unable to enter the tabernacle (vv. 13-14; Exod. 40:34-35). Even more clearly than at the Sinai tabernacle, the ark symbolised Yahweh's presence among His people in the temple. The Chronicler adds to the account in Kings by giving more attention to the activities of the priests and Levites (vv. 11b-13a) and in this way shows how important was the information recorded in 1 Chronicles 13–16. In the first place, regardless of the roster (see 1 Chron. 23:6; 24:1-19), a large number of priests were present for this unique occasion, having ceremonially sanctified themselves as they had done when David brought the ark to Jerusalem (1 Chron. 15:14). A second additional note is that the Levitical singers with their musical instruments were out in force in their best robes ('fine linen'; see 1 Chron. 15:27) and they stationed themselves east of the bronze altar near to the temple entrance. Whereas David had divided the Levites, with Asaph associated with the ark in Jerusalem and Heman and Jeduthun with the tabernacle at Gibeon (1 Chron. 16:37, 41), they are now united at the temple. A third additional piece of information is the large number of priests playing trumpets (see 1 Chron. 15:24, 28). Finally, with this massive choir and orchestra, nothing was out of place, but all were together (v. 13, 'in unison', 'with one voice') praising and giving thanks to Yahweh. They sang one of their favourite choruses that is also found a number of times in the Psalter (see 1 Chron. 16:34, 41; 2 Chron. 7:3; Pss. 107:1; 118:1; 136:1). God's goodness and His faithful love can never be underestimated or taken for granted.

Solomon was lost for words as he responded to God's gracious presence (6:1-2; 1 Kings 8:12-13). As he faced the temple, he first acknowledged that Yahweh is the mysterious, unseen God, but then immediately he addressed God, indicating what his own intention had been in building the temple. The thick cloud of Yahweh's presence had been seen at Sinai (Exod. 20:21; Deut. 4:11; 5:22; see also 2 Sam. 22:10; Ps. 97:2) and the windowless inner sanctuary spoke of that unseen, hidden God. On the other hand, Solomon had also built the temple according to specifications in order to convey the loftiness or magnificence of God (6:2, 'an exalted house'; see 7:21) and as a permanent place for God's special presence to dwell on earth in contrast to the mobile tabernacle.

Application

The passage teaches that God is both transcendent and immanent. As Isaiah reminds us, God dwells in eternity in the high and holy place but also with those of a contrite and humble spirit (Isa. 57:15). The Son of God, our Lord Jesus Christ who humbled Himself to become God's suffering servant, is the glorious sovereign high over all who also promises to be with those who gather in His name (Matt. 18:20; Rev. 1).

When David brought the ark to Jerusalem, he expressed lively unrestrained worship in front of the ark. Nothing is said of any similar action by Solomon on this occasion. Nevertheless, the offerings indicated that Solomon was wholehearted in his worship. This perhaps is a reminder that expressions of worship by individuals can differ not only according to personality and culture but contingent on the nature of the divine presence. The book of Acts tells of great joy on some occasions when the Spirit was powerfully at work while at other times there was great fear.

Solomon addresses Israel (6:3-11)

Again, Chronicles parallels closely what is found in 1 Kings 8:14-21. Solomon blessed the assembly, worshipped God and reminded the people of God's promises.

> 6:3. Then the king turned his face and blessed all the assembly of Israel, while all the assembly of Israel was standing. 4. And he said, 'Blessed be Yahweh, the God of Israel, who has spoken by his mouth with David my father and by his hand has fulfilled *it*, saying, 5. "From the day I brought my people out from the land of Egypt, I have not chosen a city from all the tribes of Israel to build a house that my name might be there, nor did I choose a man to be prince over my people Israel. 6. But I have chosen

Jerusalem that my name might be there and I have chosen David to be over my people Israel." 7. Now it was in the heart of David my father to build a house for the name of Yahweh, the God of Israel. 8. But Yahweh said to David my father, "Because it was in your heart to build a house for my name, you did well that it was in your heart. 9. Nevertheless, you shall not build the house, but your son who will come out of your loins, he will build the house for my name." 10. So Yahweh has fulfilled his word that he spoke, for I have risen in the place of David my father, and I have sat on the throne of Israel as Yahweh promised and I have built the house for the name of Yahweh, the God of Israel. 11. And there I have set the ark in which is the covenant of Yahweh, which he made with the sons of Israel.'

From facing the temple, Solomon turned to the people to bless them (v. 3), as David had done when the ark was brought to Jerusalem (1 Chron. 16:1-3). He then worshipped Yahweh who had kept His promise to David (v. 4; see 1 Chron. 17:1-15; 22:7-11; 28:2-10). The following verses 5-11 proceed to spell out those promises and their fulfilment. Stress is placed on God's covenant at Sinai and with David, and especially the link with God's choice of Jerusalem and David (see Pss. 2:6-7; 78:67-72). In addition, David's heartfelt desire to build a temple for God is seen as good and all part of God's plan which had come to fruition through the son that had been born to him (vv. 9-10). Interestingly, there is a play on the verb 'to arise, stand' (*qûm*) in verse 10, where it reads that Yahweh's word 'arises' or 'stands' in the sense of 'is established' or 'fulfilled' and David's son who is 'risen up' or 'established' in the place of his father. David was disqualified from building the temple, but it was not on account of any particular sin in him. It was David's part to prepare for the necessary peace and rest that would follow under his son's reign.

There is great emphasis on God's 'name' which is mentioned in each verse from 5 to 10. It stands for Yahweh Himself and particularly His special presence among His people in a place chosen by Him (see Deut. 12:5, 11; 14:23; 16:2; 26:2; 28:58). Weight is also placed on Israel as God's people and on Yahweh as Israel's God ('my people,' vv. 5-6; 'God of Israel,' vv. 7, 10), which expresses the very heart of God's covenant with His people – 'you shall be my people and I will be your God'

(Exod. 6:7; Lev. 26:12; 2 Cor. 6:16). It is this same emphasis on Israel that probably led Solomon to speak of inheriting the 'throne of Israel' (v. 10) rather than the throne of his father David. It is, however, not too far removed from David's idea of his son sitting 'on the throne of the kingdom of Yahweh over Israel' (1 Chron. 28:5). Instead of referring, as usual, to 'the ark of the covenant of Yahweh' (2 Chron. 5:2, 7), the text reads that 'the covenant' that Yahweh had made with the people was in the ark (v. 11). This is a reference to the tablets containing the Ten Commandments that were placed in the ark (2 Chron. 5:10), and which are described as 'the words of the covenant' (Exod. 34:28). Those tablets represented the whole Sinai agreement.

Solomon's prayer of dedication (6:12-42)

Solomon's prayer ranks among the great prayers of the Bible. Key theological themes running through it include an exalted view of God, an awareness of the people's depravity and waywardness, and the emphasis on the temple as a place of prayer for all peoples. The prayer follows closely the parallel passage in 1 Kings 8:12-53. It consists of an introduction (vv. 12-13), a prayer for the continuation of the dynasty (vv. 14-17), a general appeal that God would listen to the supplications of king and people (vv. 18-21), specific petitions (vv. 22-39) and a concluding appeal (vv. 40-42).

6:12. Then he stood before the altar of Yahweh in the presence of all the assembly of Israel and spread out his hands. 13. Now Solomon had made a bronze platform five cubits long, five cubits wide and three cubits high, and he had set it in the middle of the court and he stood on it; then he knelt on his knees before all the assembly of Israel, and spread out his hands toward heaven. 14. And he said, 'Yahweh, God of Israel, there is no god in heaven or on earth like you, keeping the covenant and the steadfast love to your servants who walk before you with all their heart, 15. you who have kept for your servant, David my father, what you promised him. Indeed, you promised with your mouth and by your hand you fulfilled, as *it is* this day. 16. And now, Yahweh, God of Israel, keep for your servant David my father what you promised him, saying "You shall not fail to have a man before me to sit on the throne of Israel, if only your sons guard their way to walk in my law as you have walked before me." 17. And now, Yahweh, God of Israel, let your word be confirmed which you promised to your servant David.

18. 'But will God truly dwell with humans on the earth? Even heaven and the highest heaven cannot contain you, how much less this house that I have built. 19. But have regard to the prayer of your servant and his supplication, Yahweh my God, to listen to the cry and to the prayer which your servant is praying before you, 20. that your eyes may be open day and night toward this house – to the place where you promised to put your name – to listen to the prayer that your servant prays toward this place. 21. And may you hear the supplications of your servant and of your people Israel, when they pray toward this place; may you hear from your dwelling-place, from heaven; and may you hear and forgive. 22. If a person sins against his neighbour and is made to take an oath, and he comes taking an oath before your altar in this house, 23. then may you hear from heaven, and act, and judge your servants, repaying the wicked one by putting his way on his own head, justifying the righteous by giving him according to his righteousness. 24. If your people Israel are defeated before an enemy, because they sinned against you, and they repent and confess your name, pray and make supplication before you in this house, 25. then may you hear from heaven and forgive the sin of your people Israel and bring them back to the land which you gave to them and to their fathers. 26. When the heaven is shut up and there is no rain because they have sinned against you, and when they pray toward this place, and confess your name, and repent of their sin, because you afflict them, 27. then may you hear from heaven and forgive the sin of your servants and your people Israel, that you teach them in the good way in which they should walk; and put rain on your land, which you have given to your people as an inheritance. 28. When there is famine in the land, when there is pestilence, blight or mildew, when there is locust or caterpillar, when their enemy besieges them in the land of its gates; whatever plague or sickness there is; 29. whatever prayer, whatever supplication which is from any human or from all your people Israel, each one of whom knows his own affliction and his own pain so that he stretches out his hands toward this house; 30. then may you hear from heaven, your dwelling-place, and forgive, and give to each one whose heart you know, according to all his ways, for you alone know the hearts of the sons of humanity, 31. in order that they may fear you to walk in your ways all

the days that they are alive on the face of the land that you gave to our fathers. 32. And also, concerning a foreigner who is not from your people Israel but comes from a distant land for the sake of your great name and your strong hand and your outstretched arm, when they come and pray toward this house, 33. then may you hear from heaven, from your dwelling-place, and do according to all for which the foreigner calls to you, so that all the peoples of the earth may know your name and fear you, as *do* your people Israel, and that they may know that this house which I have built is called by your name. 34. When your people go out to battle against their enemies, by the way you send them, and they pray to you toward this city that you have chosen and the house that I have built for your name, 35. then hear from heaven their prayer and their supplication, and maintain their cause. 36. When they sin against you – for there is no human who does not sin – and you are angry with them and you deliver them to an enemy, and they take them captive to a land far or near, 37. and they have a change of heart in the land where they are captive, and repent and make supplication to you in the land of their captivity, saying, "We have sinned; we have done wrong; we have acted wickedly"; 38. and they repent with all their heart and with all their soul in the land of their captivity, where they have been taken captive, and they pray toward their land that you gave to their fathers, the city that you have chosen, and the house that I have built for your name, 39. then hear from heaven, from your dwelling-place, their prayer and their supplications, maintain their cause and forgive your people who have sinned against you.

40. 'Now, my God, please let your eyes be open and your ears attentive to the prayer of this place. 41. And now arise, Yahweh God, to your resting place, you and the ark of your strength. Let your priests, Yahweh God, be clothed with salvation, and let your loyal ones rejoice in goodness. 42. Yahweh God, do not turn away the face of your anointed ones. Remember the loyal deeds of David your servant.'

The scene is depicted in some detail (vv. 12-13) with Solomon again facing the temple by the bronze altar with arms outstretched, before he proceeded to step onto a bronze platform which had the same dimensions as the bronze altar that was made for the tabernacle (Exod. 27:1-2), a detail missing from the Kings text. Here Solomon knelt and again with hands stretched out toward heaven (see Exod. 9:29;

Ezra 9:5; Ps. 44:20[21]) he began to utter this long and moving prayer on behalf of himself, others and Israel as a whole.

Solomon's prayer is full of biblical associations, particularly from Deuteronomy. He begins by praising God's incomparability (v. 14; see Exod. 15:11; Deut. 4:39) and His loving commitment to His covenant promises to those who are devoted to Him. What God says, He means; mouth and hand are one in fulfilling His words of promise (v. 15). Solomon turns into prayer what he had said to the people and echoes what he had prayed earlier (vv. 16-17; see vv. 4, 10; 2 Chron. 1:9). David had himself prayed in a similar way that the Davidic dynasty would last for ever (v. 17; 1 Chron. 17:23). It is made clear that walking before God means living in accordance with God's revealed will as found in the written law of Moses (v. 16; see 1 Kings 8:25, 'walk before me').

Having witnessed the stunning presence of God filling the temple in the form of the glory cloud, Solomon could state that he had built a place for God to dwell in for ever (v. 2). However, Solomon's rhetorical question (v. 18) indicates his amazement at the thought of the God whom even the highest heavens cannot contain condescending to live on the earth, and not only with Israel but with humanity ('ādām) in general (see 2 Chron. 2:6; Deut. 10:14; Neh. 9:6). It is rightly maintained that the transcendent God cannot be contained. But throughout his prayer, Solomon believes that the infinite God has made heaven His home. It is His 'dwelling-place' (literally 'the place of your sitting'; vv. 21, 27, 30, 33, 35, 39) and conveys the idea of the place where God sits enthroned. Isaiah 66:1 actually states that heaven is God's throne. Prayers are directed to God's heavenly throne (vv. 21, 30, 33, 39). On the other hand, the earthly temple is described as the place where God has ordained to place His 'name' (v. 20), something Solomon had repeatedly made clear to his people (vv. 7, 8, 9, 10), and the temple is called by God's name and built for his name (vv. 33, 34, 38). The presence of God in the temple, symbolised by the ark, makes it a special place through which prayer can be channelled to where God particularly reveals himself in his heavenly dwelling-place. Describing the ark as the footstool of God also indicates the close connection between the heavenly and earthly realms. In this way the passage carefully preserves God's transcendence and immanence as well as His immensity and localised presence. Solomon also saw the temple as a place to burn sacrifices that were pleasing to God (see 2 Chron. 2:6).

Humbly, Solomon asks three times that God would accept the temple as a place where prayer to God by him and God's people would be effective (vv. 19-21). From speaking of David as God's 'servant' (vv. 15, 17), Solomon applies this same self-deprecating term to himself. Three different words for prayer are used in verse 19: 'prayer' (*t˚pillāh*) is the general term that covers praise and petition (vv. 20, 29, 39, 40); 'supplication' (*t˚ḥinnāh*) has the thought of pleading for mercy and help (vv. 19, 21, 29, 35, 39); 'cry' (*rinnāh*) suggests a resounding sound of joy or sorrow. In the prayer items that follow, it is about God's forgiveness that the king is most concerned (v. 21; see vv. 25, 27, 30, 39).

Solomon provides seven examples of the kind of petitions that can be made either in or toward the temple. In most cases, Solomon has in mind the covenant curses for disobedience to God's law. While the first two cases are introduced by the hypothetical conjunction 'if,' the remainder suggest situations that can be expected and commence with 'when'. The first petition (vv. 22-23) concerns a person who has wronged a neighbour and an oath is involved. It probably involved circumstances where a human judge was unable to make just decisions. The prayer is that the guilty person will be punished by finding that the wrong conduct ('his way') has turned to the guilty person's own disadvantage ('on his own head') leading to the innocent ('righteous') being vindicated. Such cases considered in Exodus 22:7-13[6-12] and Leviticus 6:1-5 might have been in Solomon's thoughts.

The second petition (vv. 24-25) has in mind a situation where the whole nation has been defeated in battle because of some sin that has been committed (see Lev. 26:17; Deut. 28:25, 36). Prayer, confession of God's name and repentance are the marks of a contrite spirit and Solomon urges God to listen and forgive. Confessing the divine name probably means praising God by acknowledging their sin and the rightness of God in punishing them (see Josh. 7:19). The Chronicler will give the example of how wicked king Manasseh, who was taken

into exile by the enemy, was brought back when he repented
(2 Chron. 33:10-13). In the time of the judges, when there was
'no king in Israel', the nation's history had been one of sin,
punishment, repentance and deliverance. A new situation
was now in place, with the David–Solomon era paralleling
the period of Moses and Joshua.

Solomon's third petition (vv. 26-27) deals with the curse
of drought due to Israel's sin (Lev. 26:18-20; Deut. 28:23-24).
Here Solomon adds the importance of a contrite people
being taught by God the good way in which they should
conduct themselves. Moses was called to instruct the people
concerning God's law and the priests were to continue that
work (Deut. 6:1-3; Lev. 10:8-11; Mal. 2:7). The land, as stressed
often in the law, belonged to God and was his gift to his
people as an inheritance (see vv. 25, 27, 31, 38; Deut. 4:21,
38;11:17; 26:1).

The fourth petition (vv. 28-31) concerns seven situations
where natural catastrophes, epidemics or enemy action have
caused individuals or the nation as a whole much pain and
suffering. Covenant curses included famine, pestilence, blight,
mildew, locusts, caterpillar plus city gates besieged (Lev. 26:25;
Deut. 28:22, 38). No actual sin is mentioned but Solomon still
assumes that forgiveness is necessary, especially as only God
knows the very inner being of a person (see Jer. 11:20; 17:9-10).
The plea is that all who in their affliction stretch out their
hands toward the temple will find relief and that they will
humbly revere, worship and live to please God. Walking in
God's 'ways' means living as God has revealed in His written
law (Deut. 5:33; 30:16; Pss. 78:10; 119:1).

Petition five relates to any foreigner who prays toward the
temple (vv. 32-33). There were people from other lands and
nations, like Ruth the Moabite, who had joined themselves
to God's people. The Canaanite Rahab was another who
reported how her people had heard of Yahweh's action at
the Red Sea (Josh. 2:9-13; Ruth 1:16). Yahweh's 'name' or
reputation was great and was well-known, for instance,
to the Philistines (1 Sam. 4:7-8). It was at the exodus that
He revealed His 'strong hand and an outstretched arm'
(Deut. 4:34; 5:15; etc.; Ps. 136:12). That 'all the peoples of
the earth' would worship God as Israel was seeking to do,

expressed the great purpose of Israel's priestly election to be a light to the nations (Exod. 19:5-6). God promised to bless Abraham in order that all nations and families of the earth might be blessed (Gen. 12:1-3; 22:18). The prophets and psalmists looked to a day when many Gentiles would be one with Israel and worship Yahweh (Isa. 19:24-25; 56:6-8; Zech. 2:11; 8:20-23; Pss. 67:1-7; 87:1-7; 117:1-2).

The sixth petition concerns a situation where Israel is sent to war by Yahweh (vv. 34-35). This is a plea for protection and to uphold their cause. Like the previous petition, there is no mention of sin or the need for forgiveness. The Chronicler will give numerous examples where king and people humbly prayed and trusted God in the context of enemy aggression (2 Chron. 13:13-16; 14:9-15; 18:31-32; 20:1-30; 32:20-22).

Finally, the seventh petition has Israel's exile in mind (vv. 36-39) and there is a fine display of alliteration using words containing the Hebrew letters $š$ and b. This is the ultimate curse – removal from the promised land (Lev. 26:33-39; Deut. 28:63-68) – and sin is the cause. The universality of sin is acknowledged (see Eccles. 7:20; Pss. 14:2-3; 143:2), but not in order to encourage God to be more sympathetic to their waywardness. God's anger in punishing the nation with exile is not seen as unjust or excessive and even at the close of this petition Solomon still emphasises the enormity of their offence in that God's people have sinned against God (v. 39b). It is only when there is confession of sin and of their wrong and wicked ways, all such confession being indications of a change of heart and a repentant spirit, that the plea for mercy and forgiveness is made. A complete turnaround in their lives is called for which involves their innermost being. It is what is termed in the Mosaic law as a 'circumcised heart' (Deut. 30:1-6; see Jer. 24:7). Daniel was one such exile who prayed 'toward' Jerusalem with a contrite and humble spirit (Dan. 6:10-11).

The concluding appeal (vv. 40-42) differs greatly from what is found in 1 Kings 8:50b-53. It is very possible that the Chronicler and the compiler of Kings have used only those parts of Solomon's concluding words that suited their purposes. The king begins by repeating his earlier fervent plea that God would see and hear prayer associated with the temple (v. 40; 1 Kings 8:52). He then rounds off the prayer with a poetic piece that is strikingly similar to Psalm 132:8-10 (vv. 41-42). There is a concern first for the ark that had been safely placed in the inner sanctuary (5:7-10; 6:11), then for the priests and people, and finally for the king, and in all three the divine title 'Yahweh God' is used. The phrase 'Arise, Yahweh God' recalls the time when the ark led the people through the wilderness (Num. 10:35; see Ps. 68:1). This symbol of God's power (v. 41) as well as of His presence was now at rest, and the ark at rest had also become symbolic of the rest that had only now been achieved for the people of God (Deut. 12:9-11; 1 Chron. 22:9; 28:2).

For the priests, Solomon requests that they will appropriate to themselves this saving way into God's presence. Salvation includes righteousness which means being in a right relationship with God (see Ps. 132:9, 16; Isa. 61:10). As for the people, they are described as God's 'loyal ones' (A.V. 'saints'), a term that belongs to the same word family as the noun translated 'steadfast love'. The request is that those committed to Yahweh and His people will be full of joy at God's goodness associated with all that the temple represents for their spiritual and physical well-being.

Finally, Solomon prays for the Davidic kingship (42; see vv. 16-17). There are two parts to the request. First comes a plea that the 'anointed ones' will not be rejected. In Psalm 84:9 the prayer is in a positive form: 'look upon the face of your anointed'. The plural form, if accepted,[14] in contrast to the singular in Psalm 132:10, is referring to Davidic kings in general or perhaps to the David and Solomon kingship in particular (see 2 Chron. 7:6). The second part of the request is that God would be mindful of David's 'loyalties', the plural of the word for 'steadfast love'. There were occasions when requests were made for God to hear and answer prayer 'for David's sake' (see Ps. 132:1). Evidences of David's steadfast love would include his bringing of the ark out of obscurity to Jerusalem and making preparation for the building of the temple.

---

14. Most of the English translations, including the AV, follow the ancient versions and some Hebrew MSS in reading the singular, as in Psalm 132:10.

Application

Prayer is one of the major themes in Chronicles and this prayer is presented as a prime example to follow for the post-exilic community. Their temple might not match Solomon's, but it is on the site of the old building, and it was toward the city and site that faithful Israelites like Daniel had prayed (Dan. 6:10; 9; Ps. 5:7; Jon. 2:4). Furthermore, God had answered prayer and had brought the exiles back along with the vessels that belonged to the old temple, all with the support of the Persian authorities. The prayer is helpful to Christians in its use of biblical allusions and divine promises, showing how God's word is to influence the prayers we offer. Praise comes before supplication; recognising who God is encourages faith to call on God with large petitions.

Jesus reminded the Jews of His day that the temple was to be a house of prayer for all nations (Mark 11:17; Isa. 56:7) which is why He was so concerned about the court of the Gentiles being used by traders (Mark 11:15-17). Such activity detracted from its function as a picture of the true temple where people of all nations would find blessing by looking to Jesus for salvation. Jesus taught, especially in His model prayer, that God is associated with heaven, yet when Jesus was born, God actually did dwell on the earth and the apostles saw His glory (John 1:1-18). As the temple typologically portrayed, Jesus is the true channel or way to God. It is through Jesus and His sacrificial death that we are accepted and our prayers are heard by our heavenly Father. It is in the name of Jesus that prayer is to be offered to God. Previously, the disciples had not offered prayer in the name of Jesus, but they were assured that He was the only way to the Father and that their prayers would be effective (John 14:6; 16:23-24; see also Heb. 7:25).

Yahweh's reply (7:1-22)

God answers Solomon's prayer in two distinct ways: first, by means of the heavenly fire and the glory cloud (vv. 1-3); and second, by a special revelation to Solomon (vv. 12-22). Between these two divine responses, there is an account of the temple dedication celebrations (vv. 4-11). Much of the material is paralleled in 1 Kings 8:54-9:9 but there are some omissions (for example 1 Kings 8:54b-61) as well as some significant additions (see vv. 13-15).

> 7:1. Now when Solomon had finished praying, fire came down from heaven and consumed the burnt offering and the sacrifices; and the glory of Yahweh filled the house. 2. And the priests were not able to enter the house of Yahweh because the glory of Yahweh filled the house of Yahweh. 3. And all the sons of Israel were looking as the fire came down and the glory of Yahweh on the house, and they knelt down on the pavement their faces to the ground and worshipped and gave thanks to Yahweh: 'For *he is* good, for his steadfast love *is* for ever.'
> 4. Then the king and all the people offered sacrifice before Yahweh. 5. And king Solomon offered a sacrifice of twenty-two thousand oxen and one hundred and twenty thousand sheep. So the king and all the people dedicated the house of God. 6. And the priests stood at their posts; also the Levites with instruments of music for Yahweh, that David the king had made to give thanks to Yahweh – 'for his steadfast love *is* for ever' – whenever David offered praise by their hand; while the priests opposite them sounded trumpets and all Israel stood. 7. Then Solomon consecrated the middle of the court that was in front of the house of Yahweh; for there he offered the burnt offerings and the fat of the peace offerings because the bronze altar that Solomon had made was not able to contain the burnt offerings, the grain offering and the fat.
> 8. Thus Solomon held the festival at that time for seven days, and all Israel with him, a very great assembly from the entrance of Hamath to the wadi of Egypt. 9. And on the eighth day they held a solemn assembly: for they held the dedication of the altar seven days and the festival seven days. 10. Then on the twenty-third day of the seventh month, he sent the people to their tents, rejoicing and good of heart on account of the goodness that Yahweh had done for David and for Solomon and for Israel his people. 11. Thus Solomon finished the house of Yahweh and the house of the king, and all that came into the heart of Solomon to do in the house of Yahweh and in his house, he successfully completed.

The Chronicler's first important additional piece of information not found in Kings is that the glory cloud again filled the temple (v. 1; see 2 Chron. 5:13-14). Even more significant is the account of the heavenly fire that consumed the offerings. As Aaron had lifted his hands and blessed the people in the presence of Moses, and fire had kindled the first sacrifices that had been prepared in the tabernacle, so it had happened on this occasion, indicating that the temple was the true replacement of the tabernacle (Lev. 9:22-24). Fire from heaven had also ignited David's burnt and peace offerings at the threshing floor of the Jebusite (1 Chron. 21:26). As Moses was unable to enter the tabernacle because of Yahweh's glory cloud so the priests were unable to enter the temple (v. 2; see Exod. 40:35). The people too saw the fire descend and the cloud over the temple and they prostrated themselves in worship, with king and people offering sacrifice for the dedication of God's house (vv. 3-5). This is the first mention of a 'pavement' (v. 3), and it recurs in Ezekiel's temple vision (Ezek. 40:17-18; 42:3; see also Esther 1:6). The rare verb for to 'dedicate' (v. 5) is only used elsewhere for the dedication of a house (Deut. 20:5; the root letters form the word 'Hanukkah' which is the term for the Jewish festival that commemorated the rededication of the temple in 164BC). At the king's command thousands of animals were slaughtered, needing much more space and many more altars than the large bronze altar if they were to be offered within a short period. The courtyard was set apart as holy for this very purpose (see v. 7). These sacrifices were of the communal type which enabled all the people to be fed during the extended event. Whether the term 'thousand' is used hyperbolically is debatable. The 'fat' like the blood of the sacrifices was not for human consumption (Lev. 3:17).

A number of the Chronicler's concerns are evident in the account. It is stressed that the king and 'all the people' were involved (vv. 4-5; see 1 Chron. 15:28; 2 Chron. 1:3). It is also stated that 'all Israel stood' in reverence (v. 6; see v. 8). The Levites led the congregation with musical accompaniment and the priests as usual played the trumpets (see 1 Chron. 15:24; 16:6; 2 Chron. 5:12). David is mentioned to indicate how important his contribution was to the celebrations, especially concerning the music (v. 6; see 1 Chron. 23:5; Amos 6:5). It was he who had used the ministry of the Levites as he led the people in worship, especially the favourite chorus concerning Yahweh's enduring love (see 1 Chron. 16). Both David and Solomon belong together in the whole temple enterprise, including its dedication, and their reigns are thought of jointly as the David–Solomon era (see 2 Chron. 11:17).

Again, king and people acted together to celebrate (v. 8) and this time, the greatness of the assembly is stressed with citizens from every part of the kingdom, from the northernmost reaches of the empire to the borders of Egypt. Hamath is in southern Syria while the wadi or brook of Egypt is identified with the wadi that empties into the Mediterranean Sea forty miles (sixty-four kilometres) south of Gaza. These were the ideal boundaries of the promised land (Gen. 15:18; Num. 34:5, 8; Josh. 15:4, 47; see 1 Chron. 21:2; 2 Chron. 30:5 for the Chronicler's usual wording). The Chronicler provides more detail concerning the celebration period from what is found in 1 Kings 8:65. First, there was a week-long festival for the dedication of the altar which would have taken place from the eighth to the fourteenth of the month, with no mention made of the Day of Atonement, on the tenth day of the month (Lev. 23:26-32). Following this was the festival of Tabernacles from the fifteenth to the twenty-second of the month before the people disbanded the following day (vv. 9-10). An extra eighth day, 'the solemn assembly,' was added to Tabernacles as directed by the Mosaic law (Lev. 23:36, 39; Num. 29:35). Like David after the celebrations for the transfer of the ark, Solomon dismissed the people with traditional language being used: 'to their tents' (v. 10; see 1 Chron. 16:1-3, 43; Judg. 19:9; 2 Chron. 10:16). Further emphasis is given to the people's wholehearted endorsement of the festivities by recording that they returned home, rejoicing in God's goodness to them all (v. 10). That goodness is spelled out in terms of Yahweh's activity toward the united monarchy and His own people Israel. Such joyful celebrations are especially noted by the Chronicler (2 Chron. 15:8-15; 30:23; 35:17-18).

The paragraph closes with a concluding statement that both Yahweh's house and Solomon's were completed, and that Solomon had finished successfully all that he had set out to do (v. 11). The verb for 'successfully completed' (ṣlḥ) in its various forms is another of the Chronicler's favourite terms and expresses the idea of prospering or advancing effectively (1 Chron. 22:11; 2 Chron. 20:20; 26:5; 31:21; 32:30). This is only so for those who follow God's commands, while those who disobey God are warned that they will not prosper (2 Chr. 13:12; 24:20). This verse 11 together with 2 Chron. 2:1[1:18], which speaks of Solomon's plan to build a house for Yahweh as well for himself, acts as a frame around the whole temple building project.

Application

The temple is to be seen for the post-exilic community as the unifying point for God's people and the legitimate place of worship. Neither the temple that the Jews built on the island of Elephantine in Egypt during the sixth century nor the Gerizim temple of the Samaritans was to be considered a legitimate site for worship. Jesus, in pointing to Himself as the fulfilment of the Jerusalem temple worship which would make even that place redundant, was firm in His reply to the Samaritan woman that her worship associated with Gerizim was not acceptable. Not all worship is acceptable to the true and living God. There is only one God and only one way to God, through His Son, the Lord Jesus Christ (John 14:6).

The glory cloud that filled the temple and the fire that consumed the sacrifice not only became a reminder of what happened when the tabernacle was erected but it draws attention to the significance of Jesus's transfiguration. On the holy mountain, the disciples witnessed the divine cloud and glory of Jesus (Mark 9:2-8; 2 Pet. 1:16-18). The presence of Moses and Elijah recalled their experiences of God at Sinai or Horeb, the mount of God, and both were heard talking to Jesus of His 'exodus', meaning His death and resurrection (Exod. 33:18-34:8, 29-35; 1 Kings 19:8-13; Luke 9:30). Jesus, God's unique Son, is the radiance of God's glory and exact image of His being (Heb. 1:3), so that John could testify that 'we saw his glory, glory as of the only-begotten of the Father, full of grace and truth' (John 1:14).

> 7:12. Then Yahweh appeared to Solomon in the night and he said to him, 'I have heard your prayer and I have chosen this place for myself for a house of sacrifice. 13. If I shut up the heavens so that there is no rain or if I command the locust to devour the land, or if I send a pestilence among my people, 14. and my people over whom my name is called humble

themselves and pray and seek my face and turn from their evil
ways, then I will hear from heaven and I will forgive their sin
and will heal their land. 15. Now my eyes will be open and my
ears will be attentive to the prayer of this place. 16. And now I
have chosen and consecrated this house that my name may be
there for ever; and my eyes and my heart will be there always.
17. And as for you, if you walk before me as David your father
walked, even to do according to all that I have commanded
you and you keep my statutes and my rulings, 18. then I will
establish the throne of your kingdom, as I covenanted with
David your father, saying You shall not lack a man ruling in
Israel. 19. But if you turn away and forsake my statutes and
my commandments that I have set before you and you go and
serve other gods and bow down to them, 20. then I will uproot
them from my land which I gave to them and this house which
I have consecrated to my name I will cast out of my presence
and I will make it a proverb and a taunt among all peoples. 21.
And this house, which was exalted, everyone who passes by it
will be appalled and will say, Why has Yahweh done like thus
to this land and to this house? 22. And they will say, Because
they forsook Yahweh, the God of their fathers who brought
them from the land of Egypt, and they took hold of other gods
and worshipped them and served them; therefore he brought
against them all this evil.'

This second appearance of Yahweh to Solomon did not take
place immediately after the temple was dedicated, but thirteen
years later, during which time he had completed his own
house (vv. 11-12; 1 Kings 7:1; 9:1-2, 10). Yahweh confirmed that
Solomon's prayer was 'heard', picking up the many pleas that
God would hear from heaven (see 6:19, 21, etc.). The prayer
had mentioned God's choice of Jerusalem and of David (6:5-6,
34, 38) and Yahweh now adds that He had chosen the temple
as the place of sacrifice. This is the place Moses urged the
people to seek which Yahweh their God would choose out of
all their tribes to make His name to dwell there (Deut. 12:5, 11,
14, 18; etc.). Not only is it a house of prayer but of sacrifice, the
two being very closely associated (see Pss. 107:22; 116:17; Heb.
13:15). Both David and Solomon saw the temple as a place to
offer sacrifices (1 Chron. 22:1; 2 Chron. 2:6). It is the mountain
of God's inheritance, the sanctuary of which Moses and all
Israel sang on their deliverance at the Red Sea (Exod. 15:17).

Chronicles includes important material missing in the Kings account. It deals first with the responsibilities of God's people in general (vv. 13-16) before joining Kings in setting out the king's obligations (vv. 17-22). Yahweh's response picks up on points raised in Solomon's prayer concerning lack of rain, devastation by locusts and pestilence (v. 13; see 6:26, 28). God promises to 'hear from heaven' (v. 14; see 6:22-39) and not only to meet the request for the forgiveness of sins (see 6:21, 25, 27, 30, 39) but to undo any damage to the land. The prophet probably had this in mind when he speaks of God restoring the years that the locusts had eaten (Joel 2:25). At the fall of Jerusalem it is stated that there was to be no 'healing' (2 Chron. 36:16). Physical healing of the people occurred through the humble prayers of Hezekiah (2 Chron. 30:20). But there is one big condition on God's people, on those who are chosen and owned by Yahweh. Similar phraseology concerning God's name is used for Yahweh's ownership of the temple (see 6:33). If they are to receive forgiveness there must be true repentance. Four terms are used to express this sincere inner change of direction and they are important in the Chronicler's whole work. They must humble themselves, pray, seek God's face and turn. What was not seen at the beginning in the life of king Saul or in king Zedekiah at the end of the history, is urged upon the people at the start of this new stage in the life of the nation.

Examples are given of kings, princes of Judah and people humbling themselves (2 Chron. 12:6-7, 12; 30:11; 32:26; etc.) as well as of those who refused (2 Chron. 33:23; 36:12). It is the kind of humble prayer that Solomon had offered and before him, Jabez (1 Chron. 4:10). More examples of prayer follow including those by Hezekiah and Manasseh (2 Chron. 32:20, 24; 33:12-13). There are two words (*bqš* and *drš*) for seeking God or His presence ('His face'). To 'seek' God is sometimes used for worshipping Him especially at a place of worship (Amos 5:5-6) but here and in many other places it means to desire God, while to seek His face means to set oneself to experience God's favour. The verb employed here (*bqš*) was found earlier in David's psalm (1 Chron. 16:10-11) and is used in the case of those from the northern tribes who refused to follow Jeroboam but came to Jerusalem seeking Yahweh

(2 Chron. 11:16; see also 15:4, 15; 20:4). As for the synonymous term *drš*, sometimes translated 'to enquire', it was first used of Saul when he sought the medium instead of Yahweh and especially interesting is its use when David urged Israel's leaders to set their mind and heart to seek Yahweh and similarly in his charge to Solomon (1 Chron. 10:13-14; see 13:3; 15:13; 16:11; 21:30; 22:19; 28:8-9; etc.). As for the verb 'turn' (*šûḇ*), this is an important term for 'repent' in the Hebrew Bible and was used a number of times in Solomon's prayer (6:24, 26, 37, 38), and is found later in the time of Asa, Hezekiah and Zedekiah (2 Chron. 15:4; 30:6, 9; 36:13).

Verse 15 is a direct promise arising out of Solomon's plea in 6:20 and 40, while the following verse repeats Yahweh's commitment to the place He has chosen, adding what is paralleled in 1 Kings 9:3, that He had sanctified the temple in order that His name might dwell there for ever. Most wonderfully, Yahweh speaks of His 'heart' being there always, which goes beyond the idea of 'name' to suggest the inner being of God (Jer. 31:20; 32:41). For the post-exilic community, this must have been very encouraging to know that God was committed to the temple. The future is associated with all for which that temple stood.

Solomon and the whole Davidic dynasty also had responsibilities (vv. 17-18). As a direct response to Solomon's prayer (6:16-17), God committed Himself to the Davidic covenant (1 Chron. 17). There is a condition, however. The Davidic king must follow the example of David in living in obedience to God's law. This law is set out particularly in the book of Deuteronomy which the king was required to possess, read and obey (Deut. 17:18-20; Josh. 1:8; Ps. 1:2). The Davidic covenant never guaranteed that a king would always sit on the throne in Jerusalem, but it did guarantee that David would not lack a man to rule over Israel (see Micah 5:2[1]) and it was to that promise, encouraged by the prophets and psalmists, that the post-exilic community looked.

In the remaining verses of God's reply, a solemn warning is given to both king and people (vv. 19-22). Failure to meet the conditions by rejecting God's commandments and through apostasy by worshipping other gods, would result in king and people being destroyed. There is a 'turning' (*šûḇ*) that is opposite to the 'turning' involved in repentance. The word 'forsake' (*'āzaḇ*) is another of the Chronicler's key terms (see v. 22; 2 Chron. 12:1, 5; 13:10-11; 21:10; 24:20, 24; 28:6; 29:6; 34:25). Both king and people would be removed from Yahweh's land which He had given to Israel as a gift (6:27). Apostasy forfeits their right to the land. In addition, even the temple, which had been set apart as holy by Yahweh and was the very means of gaining God's ear, would be cast away out of Yahweh's sight so that not only Israel as in the Kings account, but the temple itself would become 'a proverb' and a 'taunt' or 'byword'. These latter terms are typical expressions of covenant curses (Deut. 28:37; Jer. 24:9). The temple is described as 'exalted' (v. 21; see 6:2) for it was a fine, imposing structure and yet, as part of the final curse of the Mosaic covenant, it would be destroyed and become an object of ridicule to all who passed by. Yahweh is prepared to see His name dishonoured by bringing devastation to land and temple in order to discipline His people. The question asked by onlookers about the reason for the ruins is one found when the curses of the covenant were first stated, and it would be raised by Israel itself (Deut. 29:24-28[23-27]; Jer. 5:19; 13:22; 16:10-13; 22:8-9). It is the same non-Israelite onlookers who give the correct answer. It is forcefully presented in terms of forsaking Yahweh, the God of Abraham and his descendants and the God of the exodus, in order to 'take hold of' other gods and worship them. It is seen to be a staggering, unbelievable thing to do. Furthermore, it is the God whom Israel abandoned who is seen as the one who had brought about the calamity.

Application

The glory cloud is a reminder of the Son of God who tabernacled among us and who was transfigured in the heavenly cloud. After His atoning death, He ascended in His resurrected body, hidden by that heavenly cloud, and he yet will appear a second time with the clouds of heaven. Also Jesus is associated with the heart of God when John states that 'No one has seen God at any time; the only begotten Son who is in the bosom of the Father, he has declared him' (John 1:14, 18). It is in Jesus that the fulfilment of God's presence, associated with the temple, His name and His heart, is to be found and remains for ever. The Chronicler shows little enthusiasm for the restoration of the kind of monarchy that the history of Israel reveals, but this did not mean he did not encourage his people to look for the kind of king idealised under the rule of David and Solomon.

The biblical examples make it all too obvious that God is willing for His reputation to be tarnished in order to punish His people. The same has happened throughout church history. Places in the Middle East, Asia Minor and North Africa that once named the name of Christ are now dominated by a religion that considers the gospel to be blasphemous.

The Chronicler's message was a prompt for his people, following the exile, to pray earnestly at the house of prayer and sacrifice that God would fulfil the outstanding promises relating to the Davidic and Abrahamic covenants. It encouraged prayer that God would present Himself among them, that the latter temple would be more glorious than the former, and that the true anointed king of David's line would reign over them. Humble prayer from a contrite heart has often been an early indication of spiritual awakening among Christians resulting in whole communities being transformed by God's Spirit through gospel ministry.[15]

Solomon's international fame (8:1–9:31)

In some respects this whole section is a mirror image of 2 Chronicles 1:1–5:1 with its emphasis on Solomon the builder, his international relations and his wealth and wisdom. It covers the final years of Solomon's reign much more succinctly than the first twenty years but, very importantly, it is still viewed within the context of the temple (8:1, 16). Chapter 8 deals with further building projects of Solomon, his use of Canaanite forced labour, a house for Pharaoh's daughter, his concern for temple worship and his sea-trading exploits. It begins and ends with Solomon's relations with Hiram of Tyre (vv. 1-2, 17-18). While the text follows the parallel version in 1 Kings 9:10-28, there are again some significant omissions (1 Kings 9:15-16) and additions (vv. 11b, 13-16). With the

---

15. See Murray, 'Retribution and Revival', pp. 77-99.

Kings text already available to his readers, the Chronicler is not seeking to contradict Kings or to invent an account for theological reasons as some scholars suppose. His object is to present Solomon in idealistic terms and therefore he presents supplementary material and omits what does not suit his purpose.

Solomon's political and military projects (8:1-18)

> 8:1. And it was at the end of twenty years, during which Solomon had built the house of Yahweh and his own house, 2. that he built the cities that Huram had given to Solomon, and he settled the sons of Israel there. 3. And Solomon went to Hamath-zobah and seized it. 4. He also built Tadmor in the wilderness, and all the storage cities which he built in Hamath. 5. He also built Upper Beth-horon and Lower Beth-horon, fortified cities *with* walls, double gates and bars. 6. Also Baalath, and all the storage cities that Solomon had, and all the chariot cities and the cities of the cavalry, and all that Solomon desired to build in Jerusalem, in Lebanon, and in all the land of his rule.

Solomon reigned for forty years and during the first twenty years of his reign he had built the temple and his own house. The beginning of the second half of his reign continues with more building projects. Again, the Chronicler brings together Yahweh's house and Solomon's (v. 1; see 2:1; 7:11). While Yahweh's house witnessed to God's presence among His people, the king's house symbolised God's rule among them through His representative. In this way the kingdom of God on earth was portrayed.

Verse 2 leaves out Hiram's displeasure at the cities Solomon gave him in payment for the material he had received in order to build the temple (1 Kings 9:11-13). Some think that Hiram gave these cities back to Solomon in disgust while others suggest that Hiram gave, on another occasion, twenty different cities from territory he owned. This latter position seems more likely and that is why Solomon settled Israelites in these places. Other areas that Solomon possessed in the north are mentioned including Tadmor, known later as Palmyra, which lay over a hundred miles (161 kilometres) north of Damascus in the Syrian wilderness. Uniquely, despite being seen as a man of peace (1 Chron. 22:9), Solomon is credited with having gained a military victory over Hamath-zobah, a place otherwise unknown, but perhaps implying the Aramean area that extended from Zobah to Hamath on the river Orontes. Only during the David–Solomon era was it under Israelite authority (1 Chron. 18:9-10), but it was considered the ideal northern boundary of Israel (see Num. 34:8; Josh. 13:5; Amos 6:14). Upper and Lower Beth-horon were strategic sites controlling an important pass northwest of Jerusalem that led down to the coast at Joppa. These Solomon fortified (1 Chron. 7:24). Baalath is probably to be identified with the Danite city near Gezer (Josh. 19:44). Over all Solomon's dominion there were as many building projects as the king desired and cities to house his stores (see Exod. 1:11), his chariots and horsemen.

> 8:7. All the people who were left of the Hittites and the Amorites and the Perizzites and the Hivites and the Jebusites, who were not of Israel, 8. from their descendants who were left after them in the land, whom the sons of Israel did not destroy, Solomon raised forced labour to this day. 9. But of the sons of Israel that Solomon did not make slaves for his work, for they were men of war, and commanders of his captains, and commanders of his chariots and his cavalry. 10. And these were the chiefs of the officials which belonged to king Solomon, two hundred and fifty, who governed the people.

Reference is made to the forced labour for Solomon's continuing building projects from among the descendants of the pre-Israelite inhabitants whom Israel was not able to destroy. Only five of the seven are named (see Deut. 7:1). Those non-Israelites conscripted for this work were state slaves and different from the levy of forced workers from among the Israelites that 1 Kings 5:13-14 mentions. It was from the Israelites alone that Solomon appointed soldiers and officers to engage in military service and administrative duties. The figure of 250 governors at first sight, contradicts the 550 in 1 Kings 9:23 but interestingly, this difference of 300 matches a similar difference earlier where Chronicles has the higher figure of 3,600 (2:18) and 1 Kings 5:16 the lower figure of 3,300, and thus making the total number of governors (the word 'chief officials' can be translated 'garrisons' as in 2 Chron. 17:2) the same in both texts, 3,850, even though they have been added up in a different way.[16]

> 8:11. Now Solomon brought the daughter of Pharaoh up from the city of David to the house he had built for her, for he said, 'My wife shall not live in the house of David king of Israel, because these are holy where the ark of Yahweh is.' 12. Then Solomon offered burnt offerings to Yahweh on the altar of Yahweh which he had built in front of the porch, 13. in accord with the daily requirement, offering according to the commandment of Moses, for the sabbaths and for the new moons and for the appointed festivals, three times in the year – the feast of Unleavened Bread, the feast of Weeks and the feast of Tabernacles. 14. And, according to the ruling of David his father, he appointed the divisions of the priests for their service, and the Levites for their duties to praise and serve before the priests according to the daily requirement, and the gate-keepers in their divisions for each gate; for so was the commandment of David the man of God. 15. And they did not turn aside from the command of the king concerning the priests and Levites relating to any matter or relating to the treasuries. 16. And all the work of Solomon was finished from[17] the day of the foundation of the house of Yahweh and until it was finished. So the house of Yahweh was completed.
>
> 17. Then Solomon went to Ezion-geber and to Eloth on the sea coast, in the land of Edom. 18. And Huram sent to him ships by the hand of his servants, and servants who knew the sea. And they went with servants of Solomon to Ophir, and took from there four hundred and fifty talents of gold, and brought it to king Solomon.

The Chronicler takes the diplomatic marriage of Solomon to Pharaoh's daughter as read as well as other references to the Pharaoh and his daughter (see 1 Kings 3:1; 7:8; 9:16; 11:1). Both 1 Kings 9:24 and Chronicles state that Solomon moved the queen from the city of David to new quarters specially built for her, presumably near to Solomon's own palace

---

16. See J. Wenham, 'Large numbers in the Old Testament,' p. 49. Note that there is no mention in 2 Chronicles 2:18 that the overseers over the aliens were non-Israelites. The phrase 'to this day' is probably taken from the Chronicler's source.

17. The MT has 'until' ('aḏ) both here and in the last phrase of the sentence. English and ancient versions translate it as 'from' in order to make sense. Normal Hebrew practice would be to use 'from' (min) rather than 'aḏ, but we must allow for different usages in later Hebrew.

(1 Kings 7:8). Unique to Chronicles is the reason for the move: to keep her away from areas associated with the holiness of the ark (v. 11b). Ritual purity is a concern of the Chronicler as the Mosaic law of Leviticus emphasised (see 1 Chron. 13:9-13). The palace of David is likely to have been next to the temple site and Solomon may well have been worried about his foreign pagan bride's safety as well as about maintaining the holiness of the sacred areas where sexual relationships were prohibited (see Exod. 19:15; 1 Sam. 21:5-6).

After the note concerning the need to preserve ritual purity at the temple site, the Chronicler continues to add significant details missing in the text of 1 Kings 9:25 to indicate Solomon's care that the worship at the temple followed correct procedure as his father David had directed and as Moses had commanded. After a brief mention of Solomon's burnt offerings on the bronze altar in front of the porch (v. 12; see 2 Chron. 3:4; 4:1), the Chronicler sets out the main temple worship rituals that Yahweh had revealed to Moses (v. 13). These included the daily morning and evening sacrifices, the extra sacrifices offered on the sabbath day and other sabbaths as well as the new moon sacrifices and those associated with the three annual pilgrim festivals (Num. 28:1-31; 29:12-38; Deut. 16:16). Interestingly, nothing is said about the Passover or new year sacrifices nor the sacrifices on the Day of Atonement (see Num. 28:16; 29:1-11). It remains a mystery why, in particular, the Day of Atonement finds no mention in the rest of the Old Testament.

After detailing the sacrificial system instituted by Moses, the Chronicler proceeds to show how the priests were organised according to their divisions along with the supporting role of the Levites who offered praise with musical instruments. The gatekeepers made sure only the right people entered the various parts of the temple (vv. 14-15; see 1 Chron. 16:4-6, 37-42; 23:1-26:19). They had the added responsibility of the 'treasuries' where the people's dedicated gifts were placed (1 Chron. 26:20-32). All this organisation was carried out precisely as king David had commanded. Not only does the Chronicler lay emphasis on the authority of Moses both here and elsewhere (1 Chron. 6:49; 15:15; 21:29; 22:13; 2 Chron. 1:3; 5:10; 23:18), but he also considers David a second Moses. He is given the title 'man of God' which was first used to describe Moses and then the prophets (v. 14; see 1 Chron. 23:14; 2 Chron. 11:2; 25:7, 9). The temple ministry commenced during Solomon's reign according to God's word revealed both to Moses and David. While the actual building process was completed earlier (2 Chron. 5:1), it is only after the regular worship was set up and running that it could be said to be finally finished just as David promised with God's help (v. 16; 1 Chron. 28:20). Two Hebrew words are used to indicate the accomplishment of the work. In the first half of the verse, the word 'finish' is used twice. In the second half, the verb 'completes' (*šalēm*) is employed probably with a play on Solomon's name (*šᵉlōmōh*) where the same root letters are used.

The final paragraph (vv. 17-18), paralleled in 1 Kings 9:28, has some relevance to what has gone before in terms of the wealth associated with the temple 'treasuries' (v. 15) but it certainly prepares for a consideration of Solomon's international relations and wealth that follow. More clearly than Kings, Solomon takes the responsibility for the maritime venture but again has the help of the sea-faring nation of which Hiram was king. Ships were built in Edomite territory near the modern city of Eilat, at the head of the Gulf of Aqaba, and Hiram brought further ships from Tyre, probably carrying them overland where necessary, and his sailors assisted Solomon's men who had little knowledge of the sea. The expedition by this combined naval fleet brought back gold in abundance for Solomon. It was imported from Ophir, a location still unknown, but which may refer either to somewhere in the horn of Africa or the south west of Arabia (see 1 Chron. 29:4). There may be a very good reason for the difference between the 420 talents of gold in the Kings account and the 450 given here to which we are not privy. The amount is large, some fifteen tons, but such amounts were not unknown in the ancient world.[18]

Application

The depiction of Solomon's rule over this large area of land from the banks of the Orontes to the borders of Egypt is a picture of the future worldwide rule of the Messiah (see Ps. 72).

---

18. See Alan R. Millard, 'Does the Bible Exaggerate King Solomon's Wealth?' *Biblical Archaeology Review* (15:3), May/June 1989, pp. 20-34.

As for the reference to the nations in subservience to Israel, this would have been of encouragement to the post-exilic community who considered themselves still exiles under the governance of Persia. The prophets and psalmists looked to a time when the nations would be in submission to the God of Israel (Isa. 60; Micah 4:1-5; Zeph. 3:9-11; Zech. 8:20-23; 9:9-10; 14:9; Ps. 72:8-11).

Worship under the new covenant is not bound by the rules and regulations of David or Moses because all that is associated with the temple has its fulfilment in Christ's once for all sacrifice at Calvary. God announced this when the veil of the temple was miraculously torn from top to bottom and when providentially the temple was destroyed by the Romans in A.D. 70. There is much more freedom now that we live in the age of the Holy Spirit. Nevertheless, there are principles we derive from the Scriptures when Christians meet for public worship and fellowship. All things are to be done decently and in order, but that principle is subject to wide interpretation due to denominational and cultural traditions. What is considered stuffy to some may be the height of reverence to others, while a more relaxed and informal style may be viewed as disrespectful and irreverent. The elements that ought to be present include the reading, preaching and teaching of the Word of God. These are central concerns along with the ordinances of baptism and the Lord's Supper, prayer and singing. This is supplemented by communal exhortations and encouragements as the Spirit prompts under the supervision of the church leaders with all things being done for building up the people of God and the conversion of young and old from both within and outside the church environment.

Solomon's wisdom, wealth, influence and death (9:1-31)

The chapter covers the visit of the queen of Sheba (vv. 1-12), Solomon's wealth and international fame (vv. 13-28), and a concluding summary (vv. 29-31). It balances the opening to his reign (2 Chron. 1). The final verses of chapter eight act as a bridge to the account of Solomon's international recognition and wealth.

> 9:1. Now when the queen of Sheba heard the fame of Solomon, she came to test Solomon with riddles in Jerusalem, with a very

great retinue, and camels bearing spices and gold in abundance and precious stones. And she came to Solomon and spoke with him about all that was on her heart. 2. So Solomon answered all her questions; there was nothing hidden from Solomon that he did not explain to her. 3. And when the queen of Sheba saw the wisdom of Solomon and the house that he had built, 4. and the food of his table and the seating of his servants and the service of his attendants and their clothing and his cup-bearers and their clothing, and his upper room by which he went up to the house of Yahweh, there was no more breath in her. 5. Then she said to the king: 'The report *was* true which I heard in my land concerning your words and your wisdom, 6. but I did not believe their words until I came and my eyes saw them; and indeed, the half of the greatness of your wisdom was not told me; you exceed the report that I heard. 7. How fortunate *are* your men and how fortunate *are* these your servants, who stand before you continually and listen to your wisdom! 8. Blessed be Yahweh your God, who has delighted in you, to put you on his throne as king for Yahweh your God! Because your God has loved Israel, in order to establish it for ever, so he made you king over them, to do justice and righteousness.' 9. Then she gave the king one hundred and twenty talents of gold, spices in great quantity and precious stones; there were no spices like those that the queen of Sheba gave to king Solomon.

10. And also the servants of Huram and the servants of Solomon, who had brought gold from Ophir, brought almug wood and precious stones. 11. And the king made walkways of the almug wood for the house of Yahweh and for the king's house, also lyres and harps for the musicians; and there was not seen the like of them before in the land of Judah. 12. Now king Solomon gave to the queen of Sheba every desire for which she asked, besides that which she had brought to the king. Then she turned and went to her own land, she and her servants.

The account of the queen of Sheba's visit follows closely the parallel passage in 1 Kings 10:1-13. Having dealt with the naval activities of Solomon and Hiram's sailors in the south (8:17-18) and before mentioning further trips to Ophir, again accompanied by Hiram's servants, which resulted in more costly materials appearing in Jerusalem (vv. 10-11), attention is drawn to this special visit of a queen from the south (vv. 1-9, 12). It provides an example of Solomon's international standing, especially in terms of his wisdom and wealth. What

connection the two descendants of Cush named Seba and
Sheba in the introductory genealogical lists (1 Chron. 1:9; see
Gen. 10:7, 28) have with the land of Sheba is uncertain. Both
names appear in Psalm 72:10 and many scholars regard the
places bearing these names as either synonymous or related.
Both places are considered to be the home of the Sabeans who
mainly occupied southern Arabia. However, there are signs
that while Sheba may be identified with what is known as
Yemen today, Seba is more closely associated with north east
Africa, south of Egypt (see Isa. 43:3), and there are evidences
of traders and colonists regularly crossing from Arabia to
the horn of Africa. Ancient inscriptions also witness to the
presence of queens in Arabia as early as the eighth century
B.C. Even so, the north of Africa cannot be ruled out as the
area from where this queen came.[19]

Wisdom involved the ability to solve riddles (Prov. 1:6;
Dan. 5:12). This not only included clever brain teasers
(Judg. 14:12-18) but the deeper mysteries of life (Ps. 78:2). The
queen's main purpose in making the long journey of well over
a thousand miles (1609 kilometres) was to see for herself this
king who had such influence and power in the region and to
ply him with difficult questions. Her information could well
have arisen from the sailors who had gone to Ophir or from
local merchants who had traded with Solomon's men. She
came with an impressive retinue of her own that included
camels loaded with spices, gold and precious stones, items
mentioned elsewhere as associated with Sheba (Isa. 60:6;
Jer. 6:20; Ezek. 27:22). Solomon passed all the testing questions
which may well have included any political and economic
concerns the queen had on her mind (v. 2). Not only Hiram
(see 2 Chron. 2:12[11]) but now the queen recognised Solomon's
wisdom (v. 3). The 'house' probably refers to his palace in view
of what is said in verse 4. She was so impressed by the food, the
seating arrangement along with all the attendants and their
clothing as well as the room that led from the palace to the
temple that it left her overwhelmed (v. 4). The idiom 'no more
breath in her' or 'breathless' is found elsewhere in Joshua 2:11;

---

19. See Kenneth A. Kitchen 'Sheba and Arabia' *Age of Solomon* (Leiden: E J
Brill, 1997) pp. 127-153.

5:1 and again it describes non-Israelites and their reaction to Israel's God. In 1 Kings 10:5 the text reads 'burnt offering' instead of 'upper room' and many modern translations follow the ancient versions in changing the text to agree with Kings. Other scholars emend or accept the traditional text and render it 'his ascent' or 'his stairs'. Not only the answers to his questions but all the grandeur of his palace displayed the wisdom of Solomon and seeing it all for herself far surpassed the reports she had heard in her own land (vv. 5-6). The queen acknowledged that Israel was in a most privileged or fortunate position (v. 7). Like Hiram, she also worshipped Yahweh for placing Solomon over the kingdom and acknowledged God's love for Israel (2 Chron. 2:11-12[10-11]).

Instead of the reference to 'the throne of Israel' (v. 8; 1 Kings 10:9), the Chronicler makes a characteristic change to stress that this throne was Yahweh's throne, and that Solomon was Yahweh's king. This same point concerning the Davidic king has been made several times before (1 Chron. 17:14; 28:5; 29:23) and coupled with it is the added thought that it is through Yahweh's king that Israel would be established for ever. It is an expression of God's love for Israel which is another theme often stressed by Moses (Deut. 4:37; 7:8, 13; 10:15; 23:5[6]). The justice and righteousness that characterised David's rule (1 Chron. 18:14) is here said to be the reason why Solomon had been made king. These two qualities of the David–Solomon era reflect Yahweh's own character (Ps. 99:4) and become a type of God's rule over His people through the future anointed one of David's line (Ps. 72:1-2; Jer. 23:5; 33:15; Isa. 9:6-7). The queen's gifts to Solomon included about four tons of gold, which was equivalent to the amount of gold received from Hiram (1 Kings 9:14), precious stones and a quantity of spices the like of which had never been seen before. On the other hand, Solomon is not viewed as being obligated in any way to this foreign queen for verse 12 suggests that she went home with far more than she had brought.

Application

It was good for the post-exilic community to appreciate that God was the real king of Israel especially as they no

longer had any Davidic monarch reigning over them. The
'throne of Israel' (1 Kings 10:9) was Yahweh's throne (v. 8)
and Solomon was there to fulfil God's purposes. When
Solomon and all the Judaean kings were gone, God still
ruled. God's promise is that the kingdom will endure for
ever. The Psalms likewise move the focus to Yahweh as king
and away from the type of Davidic kings who were exiled
(Pss. 90–99), but at the same time they do not lose sight of
the Davidic ideal who will be one with Yahweh (Pss. 2; 110).
With the coming of Jesus, the greater than Solomon has
arrived in whom are hid all the treasures of wisdom and
knowledge (Matt. 12:42; Luke 11:31; Col. 2:3).

9:13. Now the weight of gold that came to Solomon in one year
was six hundred and sixty-six talents of gold, 13. besides what
the merchants and traders were bringing; and all the kings of
Arabia and the governors of the land were bringing gold and
silver to Solomon. 15. And king Solomon made two hundred
large shields of beaten gold; six hundred *shekels* of beaten gold
went into each shield. 16. And *he made* three hundred small
shields of beaten gold; three hundred *shekels* of gold went into
each shield; and the king put them in the House of the Forest
of Lebanon. 17. Also the king made a large throne of ivory, and
overlaid it with pure gold. 18. The throne had six steps and a
footstool in gold fastened to the throne and hand-rests on each
side of the seat and two lions standing each side of the hand-
rests. 19. And twelve lions were standing there, one either side
of the six steps; nothing like it was made for any kingdom. 20.
And all the drinking vessels of king Solomon *were* gold and all
the vessels of the House of the Forest of Lebanon *were* pure gold;
silver was not considered as anything in the days of Solomon.
21. For the king's ships were going to Tarshish with the servants
of Huram. Once every three years the ships of Tarshish would
come bringing gold and silver, ivory and apes and peacocks.
22. So king Solomon surpassed all the kings of the earth
in riches and wisdom. 23. And all the kings of the earth were
seeking the presence of Solomon to hear his wisdom which God
had put in his heart. 24. And they were each bringing a present:
articles of silver and articles of gold, and garments, weapons
and spices, horses and mules, so much year by year. 25. And
Solomon had four thousand stalls for horses and chariots and
twelve thousand horsemen whom he stationed in the chariot
cities and with the king in Jerusalem. 26. And he was reigning

over all the kings from the River to the land of the Philistines and up to the border of Egypt. 27. And the king made silver as common in Jerusalem as stones, and cedars he made as plentiful as the sycamores in the Shephelah. 28. And they were bringing horses from Egypt for Solomon and from all the lands.

Verses 13-28 describe Solomon's wealth and influence. The extent of his empire meant that he controlled all the overland trade routes from Mesopotamia to Egypt, Arabia and Africa and this made him very rich. His annual income in gold was colossal amounting to about fifty thousand pounds or twenty-five metric tons in weight, but this was no more astounding than the claims of other ancient kings of Mesopotamia and Egypt. This yearly sum probably represented the total amount generated from his naval expeditions and the tribute money from the Arab rulers and the governors of the various Aramaean states, and from Edom and other lands conquered by David (1 Chron. 18-20; 2 Chron. 8:3, 17). Income also came from taxes received from the traders (vv. 13-14). From all this gold, Solomon made large rectangular body shields and the smaller round shields and both types were placed in the 'House of the Forest of Lebanon' for display and ceremonial occasions (vv. 15-16; see 2 Chron. 12:9-11). The parallel account refers to the construction of this house, a hall larger than the temple, and named after the rows of cedar columns that would have given the impression of a forest (1 Kings 7:2-5; see Isa. 22:8).

Further indication of his impressive status, wealth and power was the construction of the royal throne (v. 17-19). It probably would have been a wooden structure overlaid with 'fine' gold and with ivory panels. Lion figures were beside the arms of the throne. There was a gold footstool attached to the throne with six steps leading to the throne and a pair of lions flanked either side of each step. There are examples of such thrones in the ancient world, but this throne surpassed them all in magnificence. Remembering that Solomon reigned as viceregent on God's throne over Israel, it is to be expected that that status should be expressed visibly in the uniqueness of the king's royal chair. Even the drinking vessels and other utensils were made of gold, as silver was considered too common for displaying the king's wealth. The Chronicler, in rounding off this description of Solomon's display of wealth, returns to note the cooperation of Hiram's men in the maritime trade that resulted in the provision of various rich and exotic items including monkeys and possibly peacocks (v. 21; see 8:17-18). Tarshish is usually identified with a city in south west Spain, colonised by the Phoenicians (see Jon. 1:3), and it is unlikely that such a trip would have commenced from the Red Sea port of Ezion-geber. Some have thought the phrase literally translated as 'ships going of Tarshish' is an idiom for 'ocean-going trading ships' (NIV translates as 'trading ships'), acceptable in 1 Kings 10:22 and Isaiah 2:16, but unlikely in this context where the participle 'going' suggests travelling to Tarshish (see 2 Chron. 20:37). It is better to consider the name Tarshish as a popular name for a far-away place (see Ps. 72:10), much as 'Timbuktu' became in more modern times.

Solomon's superiority in terms of riches, wisdom and international standing (vv. 22-24; see 1 Chron. 29:30) brings to realisation Yahweh's promise in 2 Chronicles 1:11-12. Hyperbolic language is used to express his greatness and presents him almost as a godlike figure, especially with the use of a phrase normally associated with Yahweh – 'seeking the presence of' (v. 23; see 1 Chron. 16:11; 2 Chron. 7:14; Pss. 24:6; 27:8). Nowhere else is it employed of a human being. Like the queen of Sheba, other monarchs came to have first-hand knowledge of his wisdom and like her each brought a 'present', with the phrase 'year by year' suggesting that it was tribute payment. The gifts included much of what had been brought by others (vv. 9-11, 14, 21). Garments, weapons, horses and mules are extra items not listed previously (see 1 Kings 10:25[29]).

The following verses (25-28) continue to press home the incomparable riches and influence of Solomon, repeating what had been said earlier (2 Chron. 1:14-17; see 1 Kings 10:26-29[30-33]). There were possibly two or three horses to one chariot. The 'River' is the Euphrates and the border of Egypt is probably the wadi mentioned in 2 Chronicles 7:8. This statement neatly rounds off the whole account of Solomon's reign.

Application

Solomon was on God's throne and again he is viewed as God's viceregent, with kings of the earth coming before his presence, as God's representative. It is a picture of the one greater than Solomon. The magi from the east who came with gifts to give the infant Jesus point to the fulfilment of Psalms 72:10, 15; 76:11 and Isaiah 60:6 of which this picture of Solomon is a foretaste. It would have been an inspiration to the post-exilic community. Instead of looking back wistfully and nostalgically they were to see this as a foretaste of all that the prophets and psalmists wrote.

> 9:29. Now the rest of the acts of Solomon, the first and last things, are they not written in the words of Nathan the prophet and in the prophecy of Ahijah the Shilonite and in the visions of Iddo the visionary concerning Jeroboam the son of Nebat? 30. And Solomon reigned forty years in Jerusalem over all Israel. 31. And Solomon slept with his fathers and he was buried in the city of his father David and his son Rehoboam reigned in his place.

The Chronicler moves quickly from the glowing depiction of Solomon to the concluding statement concerning his death, citing three prophetic sources for further material on the king's life and activities, sources not mentioned in the parallel account in 1 Kings. Similarly, three prophetic sources are cited at the close of David's reign (1 Chron. 29:29). Unlike the parallel account, there is no report of Solomon's apostasy through marrying many foreign wives or of the difficulties in the empire and the divisions within his own kingdom (see 1 Kings 11:1-40). The Chronicler was not seeking to suppress such material as is clear from his references to the prophecy of Ahijah the Shilonite and Jeroboam (see 1 Kings 11:26-40). It did not suit his purpose to present any of the negative features of Solomon's reign. It was enough for a reference to Jeroboam to be brought into close proximity to Rehoboam who succeeded his father Solomon as king. The prophet Nathan was influential during David's reign (1 Chron. 17; 29:29). As for Iddo the visionary (actually spelt 'Jeddo' or 'Jeddi' here, but Iddo later), his visions provided information not only for Solomon's reign but also for the reigns of Rehoboam and Abijah (2 Chron. 12:15; 13:22). It is over 'all Israel' that Solomon reigned for forty years, and although this is noted by the compiler of Kings, it is especially significant to the Chronicler who uses the phrase much more often. Only of David and Solomon was it true that they actually reigned over 'all Israel'

(1 Chron. 29:26). It was that ideal unity that existed during the David–Solomon period that the Chronicler sought to highlight. Death is euphemistically referred to as 'sleeping'. The phrase 'slept with his fathers' is an idiom for dying a non-violent death and, like David, Solomon was buried in Jerusalem (v. 31; 1 Kings 2:10).

Application

Solomon's reign completed the work and concerns of his father David so that together they present a picture of God's rule on earth through His anointed one. The unity of God's people from all nations under the rule of King Jesus is the reality of which the golden age of the Israelite monarchy was but an imperfect copy.

PART THREE:
The Judean Kingdom and its failure
(2 Chron. 10–36)

Chronicles contains three main parts: an introduction (1 Chron. 1–9), the central concern (1 Chron. 10–2 Chron. 9) and a conclusion (2 Chron. 10–36). At the heart of the whole work is the David–Solomon rule, providing a dim glimpse into God's future earthly kingdom. In this concluding part, the events leading to the breakup of that symbolic kingdom are recounted, followed by a more rapidly moving narrative tracking the Davidic kings down to their exile, with a hint of a new beginning. The introduction has already indicated that the Davidic dynasty, Jerusalem and the temple with its Levitical ministry were to be the chief concerns of the Chronicler's work, so it comes as no surprise to find that, after the schism, the northern kingdom, its rulers and its apostate worship are only mentioned when they directly impact the Judean kingdom. It is also in the introductory genealogies and the brief account of king Saul's demise that the Chronicler first alludes to the later failures, unfaithfulness and exile as well as to the encouragements to pray and trust God and his revealed word.

7

The Davidic monarchs
(2 Chron. 10–35)

Of the nineteen kings of Judah that followed Solomon, attention is drawn to the first four with little recorded about the final four. Hezekiah, as in Kings, is given pride of place but whereas in the Kings' account Jehoshaphat and Josiah are joint second in the amount of space given to them, in Chronicles Jehoshaphat almost equals Hezekiah in what is recorded of him, while Josiah by contrast though given more verses than Kings has only a slightly longer text than that allotted to Rehoboam. More important than the length of text assigned to each monarch is the content unique to Chronicles that seeks to drive home the Chronicler's message.

Rebellion and Rehoboam's reign (10:1-12:16)
The material divides into two main sections: the division of the kingdom (10:1-19) and the reign of Rehoboam (11:1–12:16).

The kingdom divides (10:1-19)
The narrative progresses as follows: the introduction sets the scene (vv. 1-3); the people confront Rehoboam (vv. 4-5); Rehoboam consults the old counsellors (vv. 6-7); Rehoboam consults the young counsellors (vv. 8-11); Rehoboam confronts the people (vv. 12-16); and the results of the decision (vv. 17-19). Apart from minor differences, the Chronicler's account closely follows the parallel narrative in 1 Kings 12:1-19 and assumes

that the reader is familiar with the material relating to
Solomon's idolatry and Jeroboam's escape to Egypt following
Ahijah's prophecy (1 Kings 11:1-40).

> 10:1. And Rehoboam went to Shechem because all Israel had
> come to Shechem to make him king. 2. And it happened that
> when Jeroboam the son of Nebat heard – and he was in Egypt
> where he had fled from the presence of Solomon the king –
> that Jeroboam returned from Egypt. 3. So they sent and called
> him, and Jeroboam and all Israel came and spoke to Rehoboam
> saying, 4. 'Your father made our yoke hard; now therefore
> lighten the hard service of your father and his heavy yoke that
> he placed on us and we will serve you.' 5. So he said to them,
> 'Return to me again in three days.' So the people went.

Following the final words of the previous chapter where
Rehoboam is said to rule on the death of his father Solomon
(2 Chron. 9:31), it comes as something of a surprise to find that
he had to travel to Shechem to be made king. Rehoboam was
already the rightful successor to Solomon and is referred to
as 'king' (v. 6). Why then was it necessary for this investiture
or coronation to take place in Shechem? When Solomon
was made king during the final period of David's life, the
installation took place in Jerusalem with 'all Israel' subservient
to the new monarch (1 Chron. 29:22-25). The phrase 'all Israel'
(v. 1) is often used, especially in Chronicles, for the whole
nation comprising all twelve tribes. Here and in the parallel
Kings text, however, it more likely refers to representatives
of the northern tribes. Those belonging to Judah would have
received the descendant of David without question but not
so the northerners. Under the strong leadership of David
the old divisions between north and south had been kept
in check (see Judg. 12:1; 2 Sam. 2:8-9; 19:43; 20:1-2), but by the
end of Solomon's reign discontent simmered as a result of
the administrative burdens felt especially by the Ephraimites
(1 Kings 11:28). David had originally made a covenant with the
elders of Israel at Hebron and was anointed king by them and
this was obviously continued with David's involvement in
Solomon's accession to the throne (1 Chron. 11:1-3; 2 Sam. 3:21;
5:1-3), but the northern tribes now felt the need for a new
covenantal agreement, similar perhaps to that arranged later
with Joash (2 Chron. 23:3).

A question mark still lies over the king's need to travel to Shechem. This ancient settlement lay in the centre of the country, about thirty miles (forty-eight kilometres) north of Jerusalem. Both Abraham and Jacob are associated with the place (Gen. 12:6-7; 33:18-20). It was also where Joshua had gathered the tribes to deliver his farewell address and renew the covenant, and Joseph's coffin was eventually placed there. (Josh. 24:1, 25, 32). It was in this settlement that Abimelech's abortive rule was centred (Judg. 9). Shechem became one of the cities of refuge in the hill country of Ephraim just below mount Gerizim (Josh. 20:7; 21:21; 1 Chron. 6:67[51]; 7:28). Ephraim, a descendant of Joseph, was the dominant tribe of the north (Gen. 48:13-20) and his name often occurs as a synonym for the whole northern kingdom of Israel (Hosea 4:17; 5:3, 12, 14; etc.). Jeroboam, the son of Nebat, was from this tribe (1 Kings 11:26).

Though the reasons why Rehoboam needed to travel to Shechem are not given by the Chronicler, the event was certainly significant. David had received the northern representatives in his temporary capital at Hebron, whereas Rehoboam journeyed to their territorial centre. This is more than a hint that the northern tribes sat loosely to the importance of Yahweh's rule through His Davidic representative in Jerusalem where Yahweh's temple had been erected. Subsequent events would make this very clear. They had a sympathetic spokesman in Solomon's enemy, Jeroboam, who had returned from Egypt on hearing of the death of Solomon (vv. 2-3; 1 Kings 11:26-40; 2 Chron. 13:6). Grievances can be exaggerated in initial negotiations and here they are expressed using agricultural language associated with beasts of burden and reminiscent of Israel's oppression under Pharaoh: 'hard service'; 'heavy yoke' (v. 4; Exod. 5:9; 6:6-9; Lev. 26:13). The sons of Israel were not treated in the same harsh way as the descendants of the Canaanites (see 2 Chron. 8:7-11; 1 Kings 9:20-22); nevertheless, there were some legitimate complaints. Their petition is stated in a remarkably conciliatory and positive way, and they promise to serve the king if their demands are met. Rehoboam's inexperience is admitted later (2 Chron. 13:7) and already reveals itself in not being able to give a decisive reply at the time. In addition, unlike David in such situations, there is no indication that Rehoboam looked to Yahweh. The only mention of God is when the Chronicler adds his comment (see v. 15).

> 10:6. Then king Rehoboam took counsel with the elders who had stood before Solomon his father while he was alive, saying, 'How do you advise to answer this people?' 7. And they spoke to him saying, 'If you will be kind to this people and please them and speak good words to them, they will be your servants all the days.' 8. But he rejected the advice of the elders that advised him and took counsel with the youths that grew up with him, who stood before him. 9. And he said to them, 'What do you advise that we answer this people who have spoken to me saying, "Lighten the yoke that your father placed on us"?' 10. Then the youths who had grown up with him spoke to him saying, 'Thus you shall say to the people who spoke to you saying, "Your father made our yoke heavy, but you make it lighter for us"; thus you shall say to them, "My little thing is thicker than my father's thighs! And now, my father loaded on you a heavy yoke, but I will add to your yoke; my father disciplined you with whips, but I with scorpions."'

The elders whom Rehoboam first consulted were those who had served Solomon and therefore they were men with considerable experience and political wisdom. Rehoboam himself showed wisdom in seeking their advice for they would have been present at the royal court when Jeroboam rebelled. They urged the king to show kindness (literally 'good') and a conciliatory spirit (v. 7) which would result in the people being the king's loyal servants always. But that was not what the king apparently wanted to hear and so he turned to his contemporaries, to 'the youths' (v. 8), those with little experience in affairs of state, perhaps other younger sons of Solomon at court (see 2 Sam. 13:23-27). Rehoboam was aged forty-one when he came to the throne (2 Chron. 12:13). These inexperienced advisers gave him the kind of reply he wanted and the repetition in the text emphasises that this was their considered position. The people needed to be put in their place and told who was boss. If they thought his father was demanding and harsh, Rehoboam was urged to be even harsher and more demanding by adding to their heavy yoke and disciplining them with more painful, prickly whips

(vv. 10-11). It was this kind of tyrannical answer that Pharaoh gave when Moses and Aaron requested he let the Israelites go (Exod. 5:7-8). The rare term 'little thing' has been traditionally rendered 'little finger,' but could be a reference to the male sexual organ especially as a comparison is made between it and the 'thighs' or 'waist'.

> 10:12. So Jeroboam and all the people came to Rehoboam on the third day as the king had spoken saying, 'Return to me on the third day.' 13. Then the king answered them harshly, and king Rehoboam rejected the advice of the elders, 14. and he spoke to them according to the advice of the youths saying, 'My father made your yoke heavy, but I will add to it; my father disciplined you with whips but I with scorpions.' 15. So the king did not listen to the people, for it was a turn of events from God in order that Yahweh might establish his word that he had spoken by the hand of Ahijah the Shilonite to Jeroboam the son of Nebat 16. and all Israel, for the king did not listen to them. Then the people replied to the king saying, 'What portion do we have in David, and what inheritance in the son of Jesse? Each one to your tents, O Israel! Now see to your own house, David.' So all Israel went to their tents.

No doubt the northerners expected some concessions after this short consultation period but instead they received harsh and uncompromising words. Rehoboam was devoid of his father's wisdom: 'A gentle answer turns away wrath, but a harsh word stirs up anger' (Prov. 15:1). For a second time, the text informs the reader that the wise counsel of the elders was rejected (vv. 8, 13) and the king merely mouthed the advice of the 'youths' but without their crude introduction (v. 14).[1] It is then, at this point, that the Chronicler reveals the underlying purpose of God in the whole sorry affair. He employs a term only found here: 'a turn' (*nᵉsibbāh*), in the sense of 'a turn of events' (v. 15; a similar word from the same root is used in 1 Kings 12:15), seeing it as another example of God's sovereign purposes in the affairs of Israel (see 1 Chron. 10:14; see also 2 Chron. 11:4). It was not the Chronicler's purpose to draw attention to the part that Solomon's sins played in the division

---

1. My father made your yoke heavy' is the reading of many Hebrew MSS, editions, versions and the text of 1 Kings 12:14, but the MT of the Leningrad Codex has 'I have made your yoke heavy'.

of the kingdom. The reference to Ahijah's prophecy was enough
to remind his readers of this (1 Kings 11:29-39; 2 Chron. 9:29).
It is Rehoboam's folly in not listening to the people that is
brought to our attention in this chapter (vv. 15-16), while it is
the rebellious attitude of Jeroboam and his northern followers
that is stressed later (see 13:1-20). All three, Solomon, Rehoboam
and Jeroboam, bore responsibility for the permanent division
but the important point for the Chronicler, made even stronger
than by the compiler of Kings if the Masoretic Text is accepted
in verse 16a, was the certainty of God's revealed Word which
applied to 'all Israel' as well as to Jeroboam.[2]

The people's reply to Rehoboam is in the form of pithy
and familiar aphorisms. The saying about 'inheritance' (v. 16)
calls to mind the concern of Jacob's wives about the 'portion'
and 'inheritance' that was due to them from Laban their
father, as well as the position of the tribe of Levi who had no
'portion nor inheritance' with the rest of the tribes (Gen. 31:14;
Deut. 10:9) when Canaan was shared out among the other
tribes (Josh. 13:7). But in more recent times a similar saying
had been heard when Sheba had rebelled against David, with
the addition of 'each' making it even closer than the parallel
account (2 Sam. 20:1; see 1 Kings 12:16). By referring to David
as 'the son of Jesse' they were possibly belittling him and
putting him on a par with Jeroboam 'the son of Nebat'. In
the same way, Nabal had enquired in a derisive way: 'Who is
David? Who is the son of Jesse?' (1 Sam. 25:10). The cry of the
northerners was in stark contrast to Amasai's prophetic words:
'We are yours, David, and we are with you, son of Jesse ...'
(1 Chron. 12:18[19]), as well as the testimony of 'all Israel' who
came to David at Hebron and announced: 'Here we are, your
bone and your flesh!' (1 Chron. 11:1). Their rejection of the
Davidic dynasty ('now see to your own house, David', v. 16)
meant rebellion against Yahweh's rule (see 2 Chron. 13:5-7).

10:17. And as for the sons of Israel who lived in the cities of
Judah, Rehoboam reigned over them. 18. Then king Rehoboam

---

2. This is the MT and LXX reading. Many Hebrew MSS and some versions
begin a new sentence at verse 16 and add 'saw' (*rā'û*) as in 1 Kings 12:16 and read
'When all Israel saw that the king had not listened...' It is also possible to treat 'and
all Israel' as *casus pendens*: 'As for all Israel, since the king would not listen...' (see
Johnstone, *1 and 2 Chronicles*, vol. 2, p. 28).

sent Hadoram, who was over the forced labour, but the sons of
Israel stoned him with stones and he died; and king Rehoboam
hastened to go up to *his* chariot to flee to Jerusalem. So Israel has
been in revolt against the house of David until this day.

While the 'Israel' or 'all Israel' of the northern tribes returned,
each individual to his own home and wanting nothing more
to do with the Davidic dynasty (v. 16), there were Israelites
who remained loyal to the king, for they lived in what was
now to become the southern kingdom of Judah, but defined
here as 'the cities of Judah'. The phrase is found thirteen times
in Chronicles but is used even more frequently in Jeremiah.

Before all the northern tribes disbanded and presumably
in an endeavour to negotiate further, Rehoboam foolishly sent
the chief officer of the forced labour, the elderly Hadoram (also
spelled 'Adoram' and 'Adoniram' if he is the same person who
served under David; see 2 Sam. 20:24; 1 Kings 4:6; 5:14[28];
11:28; 12:18). Whether the stoning was a case of mob violence
or a deliberate judicial act is not made clear. What is clear is
that by the use of the expression 'sons of Israel', the stoning
of Hadoram was not something done by the whole nation but
by the breakaway tribes of the north. The account ends with
Rehoboam completely humiliated as he fled for his life back
to Jerusalem. While 1 Kings 12:20 goes on to describe how
Jeroboam became king of the northern tribes, the Chronicler
had no wish to give that rebellious segment of Israel any
status for its revolt against Yahweh's legitimate Davidic ruler.
It was a situation that still existed either when it was first
recorded in the Chronicler's source or in the Chronicler's own
day ('to this day,' v. 19; see 1 Chron. 4:43; 5:26).

Application

Rehoboam becomes a type of all who reject wise counsel and
seek to bolster their own prejudices by consulting people who
will agree with them. For his first readers, the Chronicler's
account of the northern revolt presented the kind of political
situation in which they found themselves in the Persian
period. Though the hostility between Jews and Samaritans
intensified later, there is clear evidence that there was no love
lost between the returned exiles in the province of Judah and

the colonists who had settled in Samaria after the deportation of the people of the north to Assyria in 721 B.C. The people are to see in this event the working out of Yahweh's sovereign purposes – purposes that continued through to the post-exilic period. Chronicles encourages the Old Testament people of God to look with anticipation to the coming of Messiah who would heal such divisions between north and south, between Jerusalem and Samaria (Ezek. 37:15-28; Hosea 3:5). Jesus, who grew up in the north, first ministered in Galilee and then in Jerusalem and Judea as well as among the Samaritans (Mark 1:9, 14-15; 10:1; John 2:1-12, 13-23; 4:3-4, 39-42). Until the right moment for Him to die, Jesus even went to live in a city called Ephraim with His disciples (John 11:54).

God's sovereign purposes, of course, in no way excused either Rehoboam's folly or the northerners' rebellion against Yahweh's rule through His anointed king. In the same way, the crucifixion of Jesus, though fulfilling the eternal plan of God, did not exonerate those who put Him to death. It was 'wicked hands' that killed Him (Acts 2:23). There was no sin or folly in great David's greater Son, and yet people from that day to this will not have Jesus to reign over them. He was rejected and disparagingly dismissed as merely 'the son of Joseph'. Yet, unlike Rehoboam, Jesus is the good, kind shepherd of His people who invites all who are weary and heavy laden to find rest in Him, for His burden is easy and His yoke is light (Matt. 11:28-30).

Rehoboam's reign (11:1–12:16)
The account of Rehoboam's reign is much longer than in Kings and provides further illustrations of lessons the Chronicler wished his readers to learn. It becomes a paradigm of God's relations with all the following kings of Judah, where blessing follows obedience and disobedience leads to disaster. But this pattern is not followed in any mechanical or inflexible way, for warnings are given, and where they are heeded, trouble is averted. The narrative begins with Rehoboam's attempt to win the north back by force (11:1-4), then describes the cities he fortified (11:5-12), his support from other tribes (11:13-17), and a statement concerning his wives and children (11:18-23). Chapter 12 focuses on Rehoboam's sin and the account of the

Egyptian attack (12:1-4), his repentant response and its results (12:5-12), and closes with a summary statement concerning his reign (12:13-16).

> 11:1. Now Rehoboam came to Jerusalem, and he assembled the house of Judah and Benjamin, one hundred and eighty thousand chosen ones who were warriors, to fight against Israel to return the kingdom to Rehoboam. 2. But the word of Yahweh came to Shemaiah, the man of God, saying, 3. 'Speak to Rehoboam the son of Solomon, king of Judah, and to all Israel in Judah and Benjamin saying, 4. Thus says Yahweh, You shall not go up and you shall not fight against your brothers; return each to his house, for this thing is from me.' So they listened to the words of Yahweh and returned from going to Jeroboam.

This account is similar to the parallel text in 1 Kings 12:21-24 with some slight differences. Rehoboam still seemed to think that a show of force would quash the rebellion and 'win back' the kingdom for himself. But the 'kingdom' did not belong to Rehoboam, it belonged to Yahweh (1 Chron. 10:14; 29:11, 23). The kingdom over which Rehoboam now ruled is described as 'the house of Judah and Benjamin' (v. 1). For the first time in Chronicles we learn that the tribe of Benjamin remained loyal with Judah to the Davidic dynasty and these two geographical areas are viewed as one political entity ('house') under Rehoboam who is referred to as 'the king of Judah' (v. 3; 1 Chron. 4:41; 5:17). The Chronicler is also careful to show that both north and south can be called 'all Israel' (v. 3; 2 Chron. 10:3, 16) while at the same time referring to the northern kingdom as 'Israel' (v. 1). It is also significant that the northern tribes are called 'brothers' (v. 4; 2 Chron. 28:8-15). They were fellow Israelites with ties that united them as descendants of Jacob (Israel) and the covenant promises initially made to Abraham.

The Chronicler refers to the mustering of Rehoboam's troops as an 'assembled' gathering, which often suggests that it was a religious meeting (see 1 Chron. 13:5; 15:3; 28:1; 2 Chron. 5:2-3). For the first time, it would appear, Rehoboam had God in mind and it is at that point that Yahweh graciously sent a prophet to speak to him. The phrase 'the word of Yahweh came to' is found over eighty times in the Old Testament to introduce direct revelatory messages from God to His prophets (Isa. 38:4; Jer. 1:11; 2:1; Ezek. 11:14; Jonah 1:1; Zech. 7:4; etc.). On this occasion, it is the prophet Shemaiah who is used to bring God's word to king and people, and he is given the title 'man of God' (see 1 Chron. 23:14; 2 Chron. 8:14). His only other appearance is in the following chapter (2 Chron. 12:5, 15). The messenger formula, 'Thus says Yahweh', is used to introduce his oracle (see Amos 1:3, 6, 9, 11, etc.) which consists of commands and reasons. First, they are instructed not to go up and fight and the reference to 'brothers' provides them with one important implied reason: they are family members of God's covenant with them. Secondly, they are each one to 'return' home and in this case the reason is spelled out: Yahweh's purposes are being realised in this split (see 2 Chron. 11:4). The troops obeyed Yahweh's will and did as they were told, with the Chronicler adding an interesting detail that they turned back 'from attacking Jeroboam' (v. 4b). Although one hundred and eighty thousand soldiers from Judah and Benjamin appears large it is certainly smaller than later army numbers from the south. Jehoshaphat's army was twice the size (see 2 Chron. 13:3; 14:8; 17:14-18). The number 'thousand' could be a technical term and refer in this instance to eighteen military units (see 1 Chron. 5:18; 12:24).

> 11:5. And Rehoboam lived in Jerusalem and he built cities for defence in Judah. 6. So he built Bethlehem and Etam and Tekoa, 7. and Beth-zur and Soco and Adullam, 8. and Gath and Mareshah and Ziph, 9. and Adoraim and Lachish and Azekah, 10. and Zorah and Aijalon and Hebron, which are fortified cities in Judah and in Benjamin. 11. He also strengthened the fortresses and put leaders in them and stores for food and oil and wine. 12. And in every city *he placed* shields and spears and strengthened them very greatly. So Judah and Benjamin belonged to him.

Jerusalem was not far from the border with the breakaway kingdom and therefore vulnerable to attack from the north with much of the territory of Benjamin lying within the disputed area between north and south. The fifteen cities that Rehoboam fortified, however, all lay within Judah and were presumably meant to help defend the heartland of the kingdom from attacks from every direction but the north. Again Judah and Benjamin are mentioned first as

geographical areas (v. 10) and then as a political unit under
Rehoboam's rule (v. 12).

As Solomon had built fortified cities so Rehoboam did the
same (2 Chron. 8:5). 1 Kings 12:25 states that Jeroboam built
Shechem in the hill country of Ephraim and 'lived' there
and then went on to build Penuel. The Chronicler makes
no mention of Jeroboam's activities but, as if to parallel that
account, he states that Rehoboam 'lived' in Jerusalem but built
far more cities than Jeroboam's two cities. The first four places,
Bethlehem to Beth-zur, defended the eastern border from
north to south; the second four, Soco to Mareshah, defended
the western border from attacks coming from the Philistian
coastal plain; the following three, Ziph to Lachish, defended
the southern border from east to west; another three, Azekah
to Aijalon, protected further up the western border, while
Hebron to the north of Ziph was the main stronghold in the
south and thus mentioned last. The Gath mentioned in verse
8 may well be Moresheth-Gath rather than the Philistine city
of Gath. It was important to secure the south for Simeonite
territory lay within the southern border of Judah and people
of the north did make pilgrimages to the important city of
Beersheba that belonged to Simeon (Amos 5:5; 1 Chron. 4:28).
In addition, the very real threat from Egypt, which had
sheltered Jeroboam when he fled from Solomon, would have
also reinforced the need to protect the southern border from
east to west (1 Kings 11:14-25; see 2 Chron. 12:1-12).

Rehoboam 'strengthened' (v. 11; see v. 17) the defences
of the Judean cities and placed commanders, provisions
and armaments in them; all of these would be important in
the event of a siege. Shields and spears could be used for
defensive and offensive action (1 Chron. 12:8).

> 11:13. And the priests and the Levites who were in all Israel
> stood with him from all their territory. 14. For the Levites left
> their pasture lands and their possessions and came to Judah and
> Jerusalem, for Jeroboam and his sons had rejected them from
> serving as priests to Yahweh, 15. and set up for himself priests
> for the high places, and for the goat-demons and for the calves
> that he had made. 16. And after them, from all the tribes of
> Israel, they who had set their hearts to seek Yahweh the God of
> Israel, came to Jerusalem to sacrifice to Yahweh the God of their

fathers. 17. And they strengthened the kingdom of Judah and made Rehoboam the son of Solomon secure for three years for they walked in the way of David and Solomon for three years.

As a result of Jeroboam's apostasy in which he set up his own syncretistic religion, which the Chronicler only mentions in passing (v. 15; see 1 Kings 12:26-33), those loyal to Yahweh from all areas of the north made their way south to worship at the Jerusalem temple. Some individual Israelites probably came on a temporary basis to sacrifice (v. 16; see 2 Chron. 15:9) while others, particularly the Levitical priests and Levites who were not priests, were forced to abandon their property and the pasture lands which would have included the Levitical cities (Num. 35:2-5; 1 Chron. 6:54-81[39-66]) and move permanently to the south (vv. 13-14). The reason is given: Jeroboam prevented them from fulfilling their ministries and the reference to his sons suggests that this expulsion was a lasting policy. Furthermore, they had been replaced by a new set of priests to operate at the 'high places' that Jeroboam had appointed for worship. Mention is briefly made of the 'calves' that had been made to represent Yahweh, not unlike the one set up in the wilderness (Exod. 32:4; 1 Kings 12:28-29). The 'goat-demons' or 'satyrs' were seen as hairy creatures that inhabited desolate places (Isa. 13:21; 34:14) and Israel was directed away from such creatures associated with idolatrous worship (Lev. 17:7). Paul regards such religion as devilish (1 Cor. 10:19-20).

The move by the priests and Levites encouraged other Israelites from 'all the tribes' in the north to follow their example. They are described as people who had with their innermost being set themselves to seek Yahweh the God of Israel. The phrase 'set their heart to seek Yahweh' is similar to the one used by the Chronicler in David's exhortation to the leaders (1 Chron. 22:19) with the important term 'seek' (bāqaš rather than the synonymous word dāraš) employed for consulting God. It emphasises that the true kingdom of God is made up of those who acknowledge Yahweh and seek His will for their lives. These people came to sacrifice to Yahweh, the God of their fathers at the true place of worship. The paragraph suggests that it was more for religious than political reasons that these northerners moved to the south.

Jeroboam and the representatives of 'all Israel' in the north were justified in rebelling for they had prophetic support, but they were not free to set up their own religion. At any rate, it was in this way that Rehoboam's kingdom, described as 'the kingdom of Judah', was strengthened and made secure and the Chronicler uses a familiar term to make the point ('strengthen'; see v. 11; see 1 Chron. 22:13; 28:20; 2 Chron. 1:1). The David–Solomon era is held up as the ideal by which their descendants were to be judged. Rehoboam 'the son of Solomon' is said to be secure while the kingdom of Judah continued in the pattern ('walked in the way') set by the joint rule of David and Solomon. This meant living according to the requirements of God's law (see 2 Chron. 12:1-2). But the repeated phrase 'for three years' sounds an ominous note.

> 11:18. Then Rehoboam took as his wife Mahalath the daughter of Jerimoth the son of David *and the daughter of* Abihail the daughter of Eliab the son of Jesse. 19. And she bore sons to him: Jeush, and Shemariah and Zaham. 20. And after her he took Maacah the daughter of Absalom and she bore to him Abijah and Attai and Ziza and Shelomith. 21. And Rehoboam loved Maacah the daughter of Absalom more than all his wives and concubines, for he had taken eighteen wives and sixty concubines and fathered twenty-eight sons and sixty daughters. 22. And Rehoboam appointed Abijah the son of Maacah as the head for a ruler among his brothers, for *he intended* to make him king. 23. And he acted with understanding and distributed some of his sons to all the lands of Judah and Benjamin, to all the fortified cities; and he gave them food in abundance, and requested many wives *for them*.

This account of Rehoboam's wives and sons is reminiscent of the record concerning David's wives and sons that followed a similar statement concerning the establishment of his kingdom (1 Chron. 14:2-7). A flourishing royal court was a symbol of power (see 2 Chron. 13:21) and many sons were regarded as a sign of divine blessing (1 Chron. 26:5; Pss. 127:3-5; 128:3-4). Two of Rehoboam's eighteen wives are mentioned and seven of his twenty-eight sons. He also fathered sixty daughters. The Chronicler makes no mention of the many wives and concubines of Solomon, assuming that readers will be well aware of 1 Kings 11, but he seems to present Rehoboam as a kind of second Solomon with his stress both on his wives and secondary wives (mentioned twice in verse 21), which again sounds a warning note. No other king in Chronicles is mentioned as having more wives than Rehoboam and, apart from the introduction (1 Chron. 3:9), he is the only monarch mentioned to have had concubines. The king kept the Davidic line strong through his first marriage, as his first wife, Mahalath, was the granddaughter of David on his father's side and the granddaughter of David's oldest brother Eliab on his mother's side (1 Chron. 2:13).[3] Mahalath's mother Abihail was the wife of Jerimoth. His second wife, Maacah, was the daughter of Absalom. If this is the Absalom who rebelled against David his father, then her mother, who had the same name, was a foreigner (2 Sam. 3:3). But it is likely that David's son, Absalom, sometimes spelt Abishalom, is not intended (see 2 Chron. 13:2), as his only daughter was Tamar (2 Sam. 14:27), unless it is assumed that 'daughter' means 'granddaughter' (see 2 Chron. 13:2). Appointing Maacah's son as chief prince over his brothers with a view to him succeeding his father as king flouted the Mosaic law which laid down that the rights of the firstborn son should be maintained even though he was not the son of the favourite wife (Deut. 21:15-17). In patriarchal times there are similar examples where the rights of primogeniture were set aside (Gen. 17:19-21; 48:13-20). In this Rehoboam was acting like David who appointed Solomon instead of Adonijah (2 Sam. 3:3-5; 1 Kings 1:5-6, 29-30). Placing his sons in the fortified cities was considered to be a perceptive move by the Chronicler (v. 23). It would enable the favoured son to take over the kingdom on Rehoboam's death more easily and by providing the rest of the family with 'abundant provisions' and marriage partners, he ensured they were all well satisfied.

Application

As the passage encouraged the first readers to live in obedience to God's word through His prophets and to seek to worship God sincerely as He had directed, so it continued to urge God's people to be faithful to God's revealed will in the written word.

---

3. 'Daughter' is the Qere reading and LXX. The Kethibh reads 'son'.

God does reward those who diligently seek Him (Heb. 11:6) and He graciously blesses in ways that far exceed what we deserve. Interestingly, the Chronicler is keen to show that it was the people themselves who obeyed Yahweh's words (v. 4) and that it was the laity from the north who 'set their hearts to seek Yahweh' (v. 16). It is the duty of all God's people to be sincere in their worship and walk with God.

The chapter also makes clear that false religion, however much it is dressed up to resemble the true faith, is devilish. When the Samaritan woman questioned Jesus about the right place to worship, He informed her that her religion did not lead to saving knowledge. It was the worship of the true God in the Jerusalem temple according to Moses and interpreted by prophets and psalmists that pointed the people to Jesus the Saviour of the world and not the worship at Jeroboam's Bethel and Dan or that of the Samaritans on Mount Gerizim (John 4:20-26).

When Christians have been persecuted and forced to become exiles, it has often led to the impoverishment of their own countries and to the benefit of the places where they finally settled. This was true, for instance, in the case of the French Huguenots.[4]

12:1. And it happened when the kingdom of Rehoboam had established itself and was strong, he and all Israel with him forsook the law of Yahweh. 2. So it was that in the fifth year of King Rehoboam, Shishak the king of Egypt came up against Jerusalem, for they had acted unfaithfully toward Yahweh, 3. with one thousand two hundred chariots and sixty thousand horsemen, and of the people who came with him from Egypt they were without number: Libyans, Sukkiim and Cushites. 4. And he captured the fortified cities which belonged to Judah and came up to Jerusalem.

5. Then Shemaiah the prophet came to Rehoboam and to the officials of Judah who had gathered together at Jerusalem because of Shishak and said to them, 'Thus says Yahweh, You have abandoned me and so I have abandoned you into the hand of Shishak.' 6. Then the officials of Israel and the king humbled themselves and said, 'Yahweh is righteous.' 7. And when Yahweh saw that they had humbled themselves, the word of Yahweh

---

4. See Wilcock, *The Message of Chronicles*, p. 169.

came to Shemaiah, saying, 'They have humbled themselves; I will not destroy them but I will give them a little deliverance and my wrath will not be poured out on Jerusalem by the hand of Shishak. 8. Nevertheless, they will become his servants that they may know my service and the service of the kingdoms of the lands.'

9. Then Shishak the king of Egypt went up against Jerusalem and he took the treasures of the house of Yahweh and the treasures of the house of the king. He took all! He also took the golden shields that Solomon had made. 10. And in their place king Rehoboam made shields of bronze and he entrusted *them* into the hand of the officials of the runners who guarded the entrance to the house of the king. 11. And it was that as often as the king entered the house of Yahweh, the runners came and carried them, then brought them back to the chamber of the runners. 12. And when he humbled himself, the anger of Yahweh turned from him so as not to destroy *him* completely and also in Judah there were good things.

While 1 Kings 14:22-28 mentions Judah's apostasy in some detail before reporting Shishak's attack, it does not actually indicate any link between the sin and the invasion. The Chronicler, on the other hand, makes it clear that the invasion was a punishment for infidelity and holds the king as well as the 'all Israel' of the southern kingdom responsible. More information is provided in Chronicles about the Egyptian invasion and new material is included about a prophetic word from Shemaiah.

The language in verse 1 is typical of the Chronicler but it is interesting that no mention is made of God's involvement in establishing and strengthening the kingdom as in the case of David and Solomon which would also be true in the case of Jehoshaphat (1 Chron. 14:2; 17:11; 2 Chron. 17:5). Earlier it was noted that the northern refugees had strengthened the kingdom and the king (2 Chron. 11:17). Like Uzziah later (2 Chron. 26:16), pride in his own strength led Rehoboam away from God (see Deut. 8:10-17). He forsook or abandoned Yahweh's law, a serious sin that deserved exile (2 Chron. 7:19-22). To 'forsake' Yahweh and His law is the opposite of seeking God which was expressed in a love for Jerusalem and its temple worship (2 Chron. 11:16; see 12:14). Solomon was warned by David that if he forsook Yahweh then Yahweh would forsake him (1 Chron. 28:9).

Another key term in Chronicles is the verb 'to act unfaithfully' (*mā'al*) and its associated noun 'unfaithfulness' (*ma'al*). The words are used in the case of Achan's sin and in the concern over the altar erected by the Transjordanian tribes (Josh. 7:1; 22), but it does not appear in Samuel or Kings. It expresses the idea of treacherous disloyalty, a breach of faith, and often occurs in contexts that suggest breaking covenant relationships (Lev. 26:40; Ezek. 14:13; 17:20; etc.). The Chronicler employs the term toward the beginning and end of his introduction (1 Chron. 2:7; 9:1), at the beginning and end of his narrative concerning the monarchy using both verb and noun (2 Chron. 10:13; 36:14), and here to describe the first king of the divided monarchy period (v. 2; see also 1 Chron. 5:25; 2 Chron. 21:11, 13; 26:16, 18; etc.).

Shishak, whom Egyptologists spell as Shoshenq, was the founder of Egypt's Twenty-Second Dynasty (945–924BC). The extra authoritative material that the Chronicler adds finds some confirmation in Shishak's own record of the event written on the walls of a temple of Amun at Karnak and a fragment of a stele of Shishak found at Megiddo which speaks of his Palestinian military campaign. The large numbers are typical of Chronicles, and it may be that here as elsewhere sixty cavalry divisions are to be read rather than sixty thousand horsemen (v. 3). Shishak was a Libyan and on this occasion the Egyptian king had the support of Libyan and Sukkiim forces from the oasis in the western desert, as well as Cushites from those parts south of Egypt that are today known as Ethiopia and the Sudan.[5] How many of Rehoboam's fortified cities the Egyptians captured is not given in Chronicles, whether all or some, and in the Karnak inscription only Aijalon is mentioned, although many other places in the coastal region and the north are named. Jerusalem was clearly in a vulnerable position (v. 4). Whereas Rehoboam 'came to Jerusalem' to establish his kingdom (2 Chron. 11:1), Shishak 'came up to Jerusalem' to threaten it.

The prophet Shemaiah is again given a prophetic word for Rehoboam and his officers who had gathered together in the capital. Interestingly, the officers are first described as

---

5. See Kenneth A. Kitchen, *The Third Intermediate Period* (Warminster: Aris & Phillips, 1973), p. 295.

'of Judah' (v. 5), meaning the southern kingdom, whereas in verse 6 they are referred to as 'of Israel' to indicate that, like the people of the north, they had a common origin and could look back to the Israel of the David–Solomon era. Shemaiah's meeting with the Judean leaders is in two phases. First, there was a word of judgment. It is one of a number of messages from God that are found only in Chronicles (v. 5; 1 Chron. 12:18[19]; 2 Chron. 15:2-7; 16:7-9; 19:2-3; 20:15-17, 37; 21:12-15; 24:20; 25:7-9, 15-16; 28:9-11; 35:21). Using the messenger formula, 'Thus says Yahweh,' the prophet confronted them with their guilt and then pronounced the sentence. The punishment fitted the crime: they had abandoned God so God abandoned them, and this kind of link between sin and sentence, using similar phraseology, is emphasised by the Chronicler on other occasions (1 Chron. 28:9, 20; 2 Chron. 15:2; 24:20). Such dire pronouncements were given by God as warnings to lead to repentance (see Jonah 3:4-10). God is seen as gracious and slow to anger. On this occasion the announcement led to king and officers humbling themselves, as 2 Chronicles 7:14 encourages, and acknowledging that Yahweh was 'just' or 'righteous' in His sentence. At one stage in the clash between the king of Egypt and Yahweh, the Pharaoh had made a similar confession (Exod. 9:27; see also Ezra 9:15; Neh. 9:33; Dan. 9:14). Amon would be an example of a king who did not humble himself (2 Chron. 33:23), and as the history of Israel headed toward the tragedy of exile, further examples are presented of those who humbled themselves in order to indicate that this was the only way to avert the disaster (2 Chron. 30:11; 32:26; 33:12; 34:27).

True humility meant confession of guilt and a repentant spirit, and this led to the second stage in Shemaiah's encounter with Rehoboam and his officers (vv. 7-8; see Lev. 26:40-42). Yahweh indicated through His prophet that He would not destroy but grant them a 'little' deliverance, either in the sense of deliverance 'in a short time' or 'some small' deliverance (v. 7; see v. 12). It is reminiscent of Yahweh's grace toward David and Jerusalem (1 Chron. 21:15-17). Yes, they would experience something of God's displeasure, but God's wrath would not be poured out on Jerusalem by Shishak as was to happen when the city with its temple was destroyed by the Babylonians (2 Chron. 34:25; 36:16; Jer. 44:6). It is ironic that the descendants of those who were originally redeemed from Egyptian slavery to be formed into the Israelite nation should find themselves servants to this Egyptian king, if only partially. Verse 8 seems to be saying that this disciplining experience with Shishak would serve to show the difference between being God's servants and becoming slaves to earthly rulers. Israel was called to be Yahweh's servant (Isa. 41:8). The phrase 'kingdoms of the lands' is found in relation to David (1 Chron. 29:30; see also 2 Chron. 36:23 in relation to Cyrus).

The first half of verse 9 repeats verse 2 concerning Jerusalem and proceeds to describe how the city escaped through a one-off payment of tribute. It was a humiliating experience which left Judah greatly weakened with treasures taken from both the palace and the temple, including the golden shields, all items that David and Solomon had acquired (1 Chron. 26:22; 2 Chron. 5:1; 9:16). The substitution of bronze shields to replace the gold ones (v. 10) emphasised Rehoboam's reduced position. His rule remained but a shadow of the glory of the David–Solomon era although the ceremonies that indicated importance and power continued (v. 11). Those described as 'runners' seem to be a kind of 'rapid response' force who had the responsibility of not only acting as the king's bodyguards (v. 10b; see 2 Sam. 15:1; 1 Kings 1:5) but also protecting those shields by storing them not in the 'House of the Forest of Lebanon' (2 Chron. 9:15-16), where the golden shields had been kept, but in their own guard room ('chamber', vv. 10-11). In the Chronicler's summarising statement (v. 12), he picks up what has been said in verses 5-7 about the king's humility, God's wrath and the partial destruction. But an enigmatic note is added that there were still some 'good things' in the southern kingdom. Such 'good things' would have included those who were committed to the temple worship in Jerusalem (2 Chron. 11:13-17; see 19:3).

Application

God is a gracious God. We deserve the full extent of His wrath to fall on us for our sins and unfaithfulness, but He is faithful and just to forgive sins and to cleanse from all unrighteousness. To be in God's service is perfect freedom while service to the devil is abject slavery (John 8:30-36; Rom. 6:6-23). The exile had certainly taught the Chronicler's first readers what Rehoboam had learnt. And now under Persian rule they were being encouraged to continue to humble themselves and repent of their sins and remain faithful. Only in this way would come freedom and rest. The passage points us to Christ who alone can deliver from the deep slavery to sin and Satan and bring true freedom to serve God. God disciplines His people both through His word and circumstances that He might bring us to confess that we are at fault and that God is in the clear. It is the height of rebellion against Him when we blame God for troubles that come our way when often they are the result of our own waywardness.

> 12:13. So king Rehoboam strengthened himself in Jerusalem and he reigned. Now Rehoboam was forty-one years old when he became king, and he reigned seventeen years in Jerusalem, the city which Yahweh had chosen from all the tribes of Israel to put his name there. And the name of his mother was Naamah the Ammonitess. 14. And he did evil because he did not establish his heart to seek Yahweh. 15. Now the acts of Rehoboam, from first to last, are they not written in the words of Shemaiah the prophet and Iddo the visionary, for a genealogical record. And the wars of Rehoboam and Jeroboam *were* all their days. 16. But Rehoboam slept with his fathers and was buried in the city of David and Abijah his son reigned in his place.

While this closing section bears some similarity to the parallel account in 1 Kings 14:21-22a, 29-31, the Chronicler adds significant material that highlights his theological concerns. First, Rehoboam 'strengthened himself,' the verb being used in a more positive sense than in verse 1 (v. 13; see 2 Chron. 1:1). Reference to 'in Jerusalem' ('Judah' in 1 Kings 14:21) already draws attention to the Davidic capital, which is then described as the chosen city and the place where Yahweh had put his name (see 2 Chron. 6:6, 34, 38; 7:12, 16). This is the place where Yahweh's wrath had not been poured out (v. 7; see 1 Chron. 21:15). Rehoboam's age at his accession indicates that he was born before Solomon's accession. Naamah, his mother, was one of Solomon's foreign wives (see 1 Kings 11:1, 5).

Rehoboam's whole reign can be described as doing 'evil' (v. 14) because he did not sincerely seek Yahweh, unlike those from the north who came to Jerusalem (see 2 Chron. 11:16). Future kings who did 'seek' God included Asa, Jehoshaphat, Uzziah, Hezekiah and Josiah (2 Chron. 14:4; 20:3-4; 26:4-5; 30:19; 34:3). The opposite of to 'seek' is to 'forsake' and 1 Kings 14:22-23 shows the full extent of Judah's apostasy with Chronicles holding Rehoboam personally responsible.

While Kings refers to the annals of the Judean kings, the Chronicler's sources for the whole of Rehoboam's life from first to last included the prophetic works of Shemaiah (v. 15; 2 Chron. 11:2; 12:5, 7) and Iddo (2 Chron. 9:29). A 'visionary' or 'seer' (*hōzeh*) is another name for a prophet, but perhaps with more stress on the method of receiving revelation from God (see 1 Kings 22:17, 19; Isa. 30:9-10). The reference to the genealogical record (the Hebrew word is unique to Chronicles, Ezra and Nehemiah; see 1 Chron. 9:1) is not easy to interpret in this context but may refer to the genealogical material in Iddo's prophetic work that is used in 2 Chronicles 11:18-23. The reference to 'wars' or 'battles' between north and south during Rehoboam's reign probably refers to skirmishes in the border region, for the king had been prevented from engaging in all-out war with Jeroboam (2 Chron. 11:4).

The concluding formula concerning the death and burial of Rehoboam uses idiomatic language (v. 16). To sleep with one's ancestors suggests a peaceful death while burial in the city of David denotes a dignified resting-place in the royal city (see 2 Chron. 9:31). It is reading too much into the text that the omission of the phrase 'with his fathers' after 'was buried' (unlike 1 Kings 14:31) implies a negative assessment.[6] Rehoboam's son who reigned in his stead, is given as 'Abijah' ('my father is Yahweh') while in 1 Kings 14:31 he is called 'Abijam' ('my father is Yam'). Such variant spellings of names are common, especially in Chronicles, but it is of interest that the Chronicler prefers an ending that speaks of Yahweh than of the Canaanite sea god, 'Yam'.

---

6. Williamson, *1 and 2 Chronicles*, p. 249; Selman, *1 and 2 Chronicles*, p. 377.

Application

Up to this point, Chronicles may have suggested a more ambivalent attitude toward Rehoboam, but in the summary statement it is clearly stated that the king bears the greater responsibility for the sad state of the kingdom. Nevertheless, there were some 'good things' in Judah (v. 12) and this served as an encouragement to the remnant in the post-exilic community who feared God (see Mal. 3:16-18; 4:2). Seeking God is not only an Old Testament sign of true commitment to God or something that non-Christians are urged to do. Christians are directed to draw near to the Lord (James 4:8).

Christians do not sleep with their fathers; they sleep in Jesus who Himself died and was buried but then rose from the dead. Sleep is a reminder that God's people will arise with glorified bodies like our Lord's to live with Him in the new creation (Acts 7:59-60; 1 Cor. 15:18-22, 51-57; 1 Thess. 4:13-18).

Abijah and Asa (13:1–16:14)

The Hebrew text of Chronicles suggests viewing these two kings together. As scholars admit, it is difficult to see where the chapter division should end (see 14:1[13:23]). In bringing the account of Abijah's reign to a close, the Chronicler sees a clear link between his victory over the north and the 'quiet' that existed when his son Asa became king. Abijah and Asa parallel the David–Solomon era where David overcame his enemies so that Solomon could reign in peace (see 1 Chron. 22:9), and significantly the same terms for 'quiet' or 'quietness' (*sqt*) reappear when describing Asa's reign (2 Chron. 14:1[13:23]; 14:5-6[4-5]). In addition, a contrast is drawn in these chapters between Jeroboam's 'forsaking' God (13:10-11) and Asa's 'seeking' God (14:4, 7; 15:2, 4, 12, 15; also 16:12). Coupled with this theme of trust in God, is the Chronicler's use of the verb 'rely' (*š'n*) which appears only in these chapters in Chronicles. In the days of Abijah and Asa, examples are given to indicate that Judah relied on God (13:18;14:11;16:8). Later, Asa relied on Aram rather than God and ended his days seeking physicians rather than Yahweh (16:7, 12). A further reason for linking the two reigns is the reference to the queen mother, Maacah/Micaiah (2 Chron. 13:2; 15:16).

Abijah's reign (13:1-14:1[13:23])

While 1 Kings 15:1-8 has nothing good and little to say about Abijah, the Chronicler allows a whole chapter to his reign and presents him in a favourable light. There is no contradiction because the two works have different aims in view. In Kings, Abijah is compared with David and is seen to fall far short of the ideal king by following in the steps of his father Rehoboam and not 'wholly' devoted to Yahweh, whereas the Chronicler indicates that in comparison with Jeroboam Abijah had not totally rejected God's promises to David or openly forsaken the worship of Yahweh at the central sanctuary in Jerusalem. It is emphasised twice in Kings that there was war between Abijah (Abijam) and Jeroboam whereas the Chronicler reports one serious battle which he uses to stress his own theological message.

The passage divides into two main parts. Part one (vv. 1-20) includes the introduction to Abijah's reign (vv. 1-3), his speech to Jeroboam (vv. 4-12) and the battle account (vv. 13-20). Part two (13:21-14:1[13:23]) provides a summary of Abijah's reign.

> 13:1. In the eighteenth year of king Jeroboam, Abijah became king over Judah. 2. Three years he reigned in Jerusalem and his mother's name was Micaiah the daughter of Uriel from Gibeah. And there was war between Abijah and Jeroboam. 3. And Abijah joined the battle with an army of valiant fighters, four hundred thousand chosen men, while Jeroboam set in battle order against him with eight hundred thousand chosen men, valiant warriors.

Unlike the book of Kings, this is the only place in the introduction to a new king's reign where the Chronicler includes a cross-reference to a reigning king in the north (v. 1; 1 Kings 15:1). It is appropriate in this context as the bulk of the chapter concerns Abijah's war with Jeroboam. It was on account of Rehoboam's love for Abijah's mother, Micaiah (a variant of Maacah), that Abijah became king (see 2 Chron. 11:21-22). The exact identity of Micaiah ('Who is like Yahweh') is problematic, especially her relationship to Asa (see 2 Chron. 15:16; 1 Kings 15:2, 10, 13), but as in other cases, apparent irreconcilable statements are compatible when further evidence comes to light. While Kings prefers to spell the name of Rehoboam's son as 'Abijam' ('My father is Yam') to emphasise the negative assessment of his reign, Chronicles appropriately uses the name Abijah ('My father is Yah') to stress the positive aspects of his kingship (see 2 Chron. 12:16; 1 Kings 14:31). His mother's father, Uriel ('My light is God'), is from Gibeah, a city in Benjamin (v. 2a) and this may suggest the marriage was a diplomatic means of bringing the tribe of Benjamin closer to the Davidic crown.[7]

A general state of enmity existed between north and south for control of the border region and this seems to have flared up into actual fighting from time to time (v. 2b; 2 Chron. 12:15; 1 Kings 15:6-7). While abiding by God's word through Shemaiah that Judah should not seek to reunite the kingdom by force (2 Chron. 11:1-4), it was necessary for the south to maintain its frontiers against northern aggression. One such battle, unique to Chronicles, is described which effectively put an end to further hostile attacks during Jeroboam's lifetime. At face value, the number of men involved is staggering (v. 3) but is similar to David's census (1 Chron. 21:5; 2 Sam. 24:9). It is possible that hyperbole is being employed or that a 'thousand' stands for a military unit, but the main point of the statistics is to indicate that Judah was outnumbered two to one.

The king's speech (vv. 4-12) is seen by the Chronicler as marking an important moment in the history of Israel. Both David and Solomon had made significant orations during the united monarchy period (1 Chron. 28:1-10; 2 Chron. 6:1-11) and now for the first time since the kingdom was divided it was given to king Abijah to make a similar theological statement, addressed to 'all Israel' who had made Jeroboam their king. At the close of the divided monarchy period, an analogous call was made to the northern tribes by king Hezekiah and his officials (2 Chron. 30:6-9).

> 13:4. Then Abijah stood on Mount Zemaraim, which is in the hill country of Ephraim and said: 'Listen to me, Jeroboam and all Israel. 5. Do you not know that Yahweh the God of Israel gave the kingship over Israel to David forever, to him and to his sons by a covenant of salt? 6. Yet Jeroboam the son of Nebat, the servant of Solomon the son of David, rose up and rebelled against his lord. 7. And worthless men gathered to him, sons of

---

7. Johnstone, *1 and 2 Chronicles*, vol. 2, p. 51.

Belial, and they strengthened themselves against Rehoboam, the son of Solomon, when Rehoboam was young and weak of heart and could not hold out against them. 8. And now, you think you can hold out against the kingdom of Yahweh *that is* in the hand of the sons of David; and you are a great multitude and with you *are* the calves of gold that Jeroboam made for you for gods. 9. Have you not forced out the priests of Yahweh, the sons of Aaron and the Levites, and made for yourselves priests like the peoples of the lands? Whoever comes to consecrate himself with a young bull or seven rams then becomes a priest to no gods. 10. But as for us, Yahweh is our God, and we have not forsaken him; and the priests who minister to Yahweh *are* the sons of Aaron and the Levites *are* in the work. 11. And they burn to Yahweh burnt offerings and sweet incense every morning and evening, and the rows of bread *are set* on the pure table and the gold lampstand and its lamps to burn every evening, for we keep the charge of Yahweh our God but you have forsaken him. 12. And God is actually with us at the head and his priests and the battle-cry trumpets to sound the battle-cry against you. O sons of Israel, do not fight against Yahweh the God of your fathers, for you will not succeed.'

There is uncertainty about the identity of Mount Zemaraim (v. 4), but it may be associated with a city in Benjaminite territory (Josh. 18:22). If this is right then the 'hill country of Ephraim' in this context refers to a region within Benjamin rather than to land belonging to the tribe of Ephraim (see Judg. 4:5). It was a spot where the king's voice would carry far and wide. George Whitefield, the Methodist preacher, had such a voice that could be heard by thousands in the open air. Abijah's 'sermon on the mount', as some commentators have been quick to describe it, consists of two main accusations (vv. 5-8a, 8b-12a) and an appeal (v. 12b).

The first major charge concerned the Davidic kingship (vv. 5-8a). Abijah introduces his sermon by reminding Jeroboam and 'all Israel' that Yahweh is the 'God of Israel' and that He is the one who gave the kingship to David and his descendants 'for ever'. God had established with David a 'covenant of salt' which meant that the promises made to David were not subject to change but permanent (Lev. 2:13; Num. 18:19; Ezek. 43:24). David's dynasty was to rule over God's people for ever (1 Chron. 17:14; 28:4-5; 2 Chron. 7:18).

Though Jeroboam's kingship over the north had prophetic support, including the promise of his own perpetual dynasty, it was dependent on his obedience (1 Kings 11:38). In the case of the Davidic dynasty, God indicated He would discipline descendants who were disobedient but that the covenant itself was everlasting and unconditional. Jeroboam was no 'son of David' like Solomon but a mere 'son of Nebat' and is referred to as if he were not present. He is humiliated further by being called a servant who had rebelled against his master (v. 6). This could be a reference first to his initial rebellious intentions under Solomon, then to his actual revolt under Rehoboam's rule (1 Kings 11:11, 26-27; 2 Chron. 10), and in the current crisis, to his continuous rebellious stance in resisting the present occupant of the Davidic throne (v. 8a). Yes, the division was the result of the divine will and prophetic announcement in order to discipline the Davidic king (2 Chron. 10:15) but that did not absolve him from his treacherous act in rebelling against Yahweh's kingdom and anointed king.

There is a difference of opinion concerning verse 7. Some recent scholars have followed Josephus[8] and believe that the verse refers to the wicked inexperienced advisers who prevailed over Rehoboam. However, the more obvious interpretation would suggest that some low-life ruffians gathered around Jeroboam so that genuine concerns and justifiable complaints by the northern tribes were utilised to present an intimidating situation to the vulnerable Rehoboam who is described as weak and inexperienced. As in the case of Solomon, Rehoboam was young not in age but in terms of experience or courage and he was also weak-willed and could not withstand them (v. 7; 1 Chron. 22:5; 29:1; 1 Kings 3:7). Jeroboam's 'worthless men' (see Judg. 9:4; 11:3) are described as 'sons of Belial', an expression that Chronicles only uses here but which is often found in the earlier biblical books (Deut. 13:13[14]; Judg. 19:22; 20:13; 1 Sam. 1:16; 2:12; 10:27; 1 Kings 21:10, 13). It denoted morally corrupt people deserving condemnation and eventually came to express all that was evil and demonic and was later used as another term

---

8. Josephus, *Antiquities* 8.277.

for the devil (2 Cor. 6:15). Using an ironic wordplay, Abijah challenged the assumptions of the northern tribes in their attempt to 'hold out against' or 'withstand' God's rule even though his weak father had failed to 'withstand' Jeroboam and his allies (vv. 7-8). Unlike Rehoboam, Abijah had a strong sense that he ruled over Yahweh's kingdom and that meant that those who fought against the Davidic king were rebelling against God (1 Chron. 17:14; 28:5; 29:23; 2 Chron. 9:8).

The second major accusation related to worship (vv. 8b-12). Abijah acknowledged that Jeroboam had superiority in numbers and an impressive display of religion, but the truth was that the northern tribes had forsaken Yahweh, so that any attempt to defeat Judah would be in vain, for God was with them. The phrase 'great multitude' is often used by the Chronicler for forces arrayed against the Davidic king (2 Chron. 14:11[10]; 20:2, 12, 24; 32:7). Reference has already been made to the golden calves that Jeroboam set up at his new worship-centres in Bethel and Dan (2 Chron. 11:15; 1 Kings 12:28-29). Even though Jeroboam intended to continue worshipping Yahweh using the calves as symbols, it ran counter to God's direct command and repeated the idolatry in which Israel had engaged at the foot of Sinai and for which they were severely punished (Exod. 32). The northern kingdom had abandoned the Jerusalem temple and its Aaronic priesthood and had expelled the Levites from the north (2 Chron. 11:13-15); in their place Jeroboam had set up his own system of worship with priests of any background and no different from their non-Israelite neighbours. The price of consecration[9] to this priesthood was raised from one bull and two rams in the Mosaic law to one bull and seven rams (Exod. 29:1, 35). Despite their belief that they were still sacrificing to Yahweh, Abijah condemned their religion as worship offered to what were 'no-gods' (v. 9; Hosea 8:5-6).

Whatever failings were present in Judah and in the king's own devotion to Yahweh, of which the Chronicler and his readers would have been very well aware (1 Kings 15:3), Abijah was right to point out the stark contrast between the worship of the north and the south. Verses 10 and 11 are framed by

---

9. The Hebrew idiom for 'consecrate' is 'fill the hand' (see 1 Chron. 29:5).

the verb 'forsake'. Judah had not abandoned Yahweh whereas the northerners had abandoned Him and invented a new type of religion. Unlike the north, Judah had continued what Yahweh had commanded ('the charge of Yahweh,' v. 11; see 1 Chron. 23:32), having priests belonging to Aaron's line and Levites to support them. Furthermore, in the Jerusalem temple they followed the rituals that were first introduced under Moses in the tabernacle: offering burnt offerings and sweet incense every morning and evening (Exod. 29:38-42; 30:7-10; Num. 28:3-8; 2 Chron. 2:4[3]); setting out the 'showbread' and preparing the golden lampstand to burn every evening (Exod. 25:30-40; Lev. 24:1-9; 2 Chron. 2:4[3]). Mentioning only one golden lampstand may refer to the original Mosaic lampstand that was placed among the others that Solomon introduced (2 Chron. 4:19-20).

Though Judah only had half the military strength of the north, God was 'with' them at the head of their army and the priests were ready with their trumpets to sound the ritual battle cry (v. 12a; see v. 14; Num. 10:8-9; 31:6). Abijah therefore urged the north not to fight against Yahweh for they would not 'succeed' or 'prosper' (vv. 12b; 1 Chron. 29:23; 2 Chron. 14:7; 20:20; 24:20). He appealed to them as 'sons of Israel' and reminded them that Yahweh was the God of their fathers, no doubt with the hope that they would desist and perhaps even return to the fold (see 2 Chron. 15:9).

Application

Worship of God rests on divine revelation and not on human preferences. It became an important question in the post-exilic and intertestamental period as to where exactly true worship was to be centred: Jerusalem or Gerizim. The Jerusalem temple was the designated place for worship until Jesus fulfilled all that it typified.

Though the temple worship had been reinstated, the post-exilic community still awaited the re-establishment of the Davidic rule and the evidence of God's presence. Chronicles encouraged them to go on waiting and, as in the Psalter, to be assured of Yahweh's overall kingship and that the promises made to David would be fully realised. That Davidic rule belongs now to King Jesus. Although Satan and his human associates plotted against Yahweh and His anointed, they could not win (Ps. 2). Christians, too, are encouraged to look expectantly for the return of King Jesus in order to judge the world and bring about the eternal state of peace and righteousness on a renewed earth.

Those who seek to persecute God's people fight against the living God and they cannot win (v. 12). Gamaliel was to reason in a similar way with fellow members of the Jewish Council, warning that they might find themselves fighting against God in continuing to persecute the apostles and, interestingly, Peter in his defence speaks like Abijah of 'the God of our fathers' (see v. 12; Acts 5:30, 34-39).

> 13:13. But Jeroboam had set the ambush to come from behind them so they were in front of Judah and the ambush was behind them. 14. So when Judah turned, to their surprise the battle was in front of them and behind and they cried out to Yahweh and the priests were blowing with the trumpets. 15. Then each man of Judah shouted, and it happened when each man of Judah shouted that God struck Jeroboam and all Israel before Abijah and Judah. 16. And the sons of Israel fled before Judah and God gave them into their hand. 17. Then Abijah and his people struck them with a great slaughter so five hundred thousand chosen men from Israel fell slain. 18. Thus the sons of Israel were subdued at that time and the sons of Judah grew strong because they leaned on Yahweh the God of their fathers. 19. And Abijah pursued after Jeroboam and seized from him cities: Bethel and its villages, Jeshanah and its villages, and Ephrain and its villages. 20. So Jeroboam did not regain strength again in the days of Abijah. And Yahweh struck him and he died.

Abijah's warning was not heeded and Jeroboam, adept in the art of war and taking nothing for granted, seized his opportunity, using the strategy of an ambush to obtain victory (v. 13; see Josh. 8:9-13; Judg. 9:35, 43-44; 20:29). 1 Chronicles 19:10 describes a previous example of an ambush. Finding themselves surrounded by the enemy, the men of Judah cried out to God in their desperation, a response which the Chronicler often draws attention to when people find themselves in distress (v. 14; 1 Chron. 5:20). The blowing of the trumpets by the priests and the battle shouts by each member of Judah's army recalls the capture of Jericho (Josh. 6:16). As Selman explains, the term 'holy war' for such an occasion where God intervenes in war on behalf of His people is misleading, and so he prefers 'Yahweh's war'.[10] This was Yahweh's kingdom and Abijah sat on Yahweh's throne and when His anointed is attacked Yahweh acts. On this occasion the victory belonged to God, who 'routed' the enemy, causing them to flee and the elite men of Jeroboam's army were slain by Abijah's troops. The number of soldiers left after the slaughter was three hundred thousand (v. 17). While the 'sons of Israel' were humiliated (1 Chron. 20:4), the 'sons of Judah' were 'strengthened' (v. 18; see v. 7). The Chronicler is quick to show that this was because of Judah's dependence ('leaned/relied,' *š'n*) on Yahweh, using a verb that is applied again in the life of Abijah's son, Asa (2 Chron. 14:11[10]; 16:7-8). Judah's reliance on the God of their fathers was in marked contrast to the 'sons of Israel' who had fought against the God of their fathers (vv. 12, 18).

It was not Judah's intention to reunite the divided kingdom by force for that had been disallowed (2 Chron. 11:4), but they did gain important Benjaminite territory from the north including Bethel, one of Jeroboam's newly designated worship centres, along with its 'daughter' communities (v. 19). In the same border area lay Jeshanah, possibly to be identified as Shen or Zemaraim (v. 4; Josh. 18:22; 1 Sam. 7:12). The third city captured by Judah was 'Ephrain' or 'Ephron' (depending on which Masoretic reading is correct, the *Qere* or *Kethibh*), a settlement to the west of Jerusalem (see Josh. 15:9).

Though Jeroboam outlived Abijah, his death through the direct intervention of God is recorded at this point (see 1 Chron. 10:14), after stating that he was unable to regain the power he once wielded (v. 20).

13:21. But Abijah grew strong and married fourteen wives and fathered twenty-two sons and sixteen daughters. 22. Now the rest of the acts of Abijah and his ways and his words are written in the midrash of the prophet Iddo. 14:1[13:23]. And Abijah slept with his fathers and they buried him in the city of David and Asa his son reigned in his place. In his days the land was quiet for ten years.

10. Selman, *2 Samuel*, p. 382.

The contrast with Jeroboam could not be greater. While the northern king lost strength and came under God's curse, Abijah gained in strength and was blessed, the most obvious indications of which were the many sons he fathered as well as daughters (v. 21; see 1 Chron. 26:5; 2 Chron. 11:18-21). As he only reigned three years (v. 2), it is clear that he had obtained most of his fourteen wives and thirty-eight children before he came to the throne.

Only one prophetic source is mentioned, that of Iddo the prophet, from where the Chronicler gleaned the additional information not found in Kings of Abijah's 'words and ways' (v. 22). Josephus identified Iddo with the unknown prophet who prophesied against Jeroboam's altar at Bethel, but this is very unlikely in view of what happened to the prophet later (1 Kings 13). Iddo was one of the sources for the reigns of Solomon and Rehoboam, where he is called a 'visionary' (2 Chron. 9:29; 12:15). The prophet's material is termed 'midrash' (2 Chron. 24:27), not in the later sense of the rabbinical commentaries or interpretations of the Hebrew Scriptures, but of prophetic expositions of Israel's history. The historical writings in the Bible are God's authoritative interpretation of Israel's past through His prophets.

Like Solomon and Rehoboam, Abijah had a peaceful death ('slept with his fathers'; see 2 Chron. 9:31;12:16) and as a member of the Davidic line he was buried in the city of David. While 1 Kings 15:3 states that Abijah's heart was not wholly devoted to Yahweh like David, the Chronicler indicates that in comparison with Jeroboam he did remain true to the God of his fathers. The lack of war that existed between north and south after Abijah's victory spilled over into his son's reign and lasted ten years. This note gives a further indication of God's overall blessing on Abijah's kingship. Various forms of the word translated 'quiet' or 'tranquil' (*šqṭ*) appear throughout Chronicles commencing with Solomon where it is coupled with the term 'rest' (*nûaḥ*; 1 Chron. 22:9, 18; 23:25; 28:2; 2 Chron. 14:5-6[4-5]; 15:15; 20:30).

Application

As Judah gained the victory that day because they relied on 'the God of their fathers' (v. 18; Acts 5:30) so the Church's trust

must be in the God of Abraham who is the God and Father of
our Lord Jesus Christ. Abijah is a reminder of the Solomonic
peace and tranquillity that pertain to the reign of King Jesus.

Asa's reign (14:2[1]–16:14)

While Abijah only reigned for three years, Asa was king for
forty-one years, one of the longest reigning monarchs of Judah.
Compared to the report of Asa's reign in 1 Kings 15:9-24, the
account in Chronicles is nearly three times as long. Four main
periods of Asa's life are highlighted, and they alternate between
peace and war: peace through seeking Yahweh (14:2-8[1-7]);
victory through trust in Yahweh (14:9-15[8-14]); peace through
obedience to Yahweh (15:1-19); and war and illness through
lack of trust and obedience (16:1-14). Chronological notices
are a feature of this account (2 Chron. 15:10, 19; 16:1, 12, 13),
continuing what began with the comment about Asa's ten-
year period of quiet which the Chronicler adds as he makes
the switch from Abijah to Asa (14:1[13:23]). Some of the
dating is not easy to reconcile with Kings (see 1 Kings 15:33;
2 Chron. 16:1). The Chronicler is keen to indicate where
similarities exist between the various kings in Judah's history.
In the case of Asa, there are noteworthy parallels between
Asa and Hezekiah including references to their religious
reforms, to the gathering of the people and entering into a
covenant with God, to their piety, heart religion, obedience
to God's laws, reforms, their welcoming of northerners, their
faith in God in times of national emergency, their lack of faith
during illnesses as well as the special honours they received
on their deaths (see 2 Chron. 29:10; 30:11, 13; 31:1, 20-21; 32:7-8,
24-26, 33). In addition, both resemble Solomon, but Hezekiah
even more so.

> 14:2[1]. Now Asa did good and *what was* upright in the eyes of
> Yahweh his God, 3[2]. for he removed the foreign altars and high
> places, and broke in pieces the pillars, and cut down the Asherim.
> 4[3]. And he commanded Judah to seek Yahweh the God of their
> fathers and to observe the law and the commandments. 5[4]. He
> also removed from all the cities of Judah the high places and the
> shrines, so the kingdom was quiet before him. 6[5]. And he built
> fortified cities in Judah, for the land was quiet, and he had no
> war in these years because Yahweh had given him rest. 7[6]. And

he said to Judah, 'Let us build these cities and surround them with a wall and towers, double gates and bars. The land is still before us because we have sought Yahweh our God, we have sought *him*, and he has given us rest on every side.' So they built and prospered. 8[7]. Now Asa had an army of three hundred thousand from Judah bearing large shields and spears, and from Benjamin bearing shields and drawing bows were two hundred and eighty thousand; all of them were mighty warriors.

The Chronicler begins with a statement about Asa's piety (see 1 Kings 15:11). He did what was 'good and upright' in Yahweh's sight (Deut. 12:28; 2 Chron. 31:20), meaning that he pleased God by being faithful to God's law and not deviating from it. Rehoboam, on the other hand, had done what was 'evil' (2 Chron. 12:14). This right conduct showed itself in his religious reforms and concern for the defence of his people. The 'foreign altars' (3[2]) were probably those that Solomon had erected for his foreign wives (1 Kings 11:7-8). These 'high places' were perhaps houses where pagan worship took place. The 'pillars' refer to stones erected in dedication to particular deities. The Mosaic law called for the destruction of such pagan objects including also the wooden Asherah poles that represented the Canaanite fertility goddess Asherah, Baal's consort (Exod. 23:24; 34:13; Lev. 26:1; Deut. 7:5; 12:3; 16:21-22). His religious zeal extended to removing from the cities of Judah the 'high places' where perhaps, unlike verse 3[2], people continued to worship Yahweh locally (v. 5[4]; see further 2 Chron. 15:17 and 1 Kings 15:14). In addition, tall pagan 'shrines' (*ḥammānîm*), a meaning now considered more likely than 'idols' or 'incense altars', were taken away (see Lev. 26:30; Isa. 17:8; 27:9; Ezek. 6:4, 6; 2 Chron. 34:4, 7).

To direct the people away from pagan or idolatrous practices, Asa ordered his people to 'seek Yahweh' (v. 4[3]) and this positive directive is similar to what is said about Jehoshaphat, Hezekiah and Josiah (2 Chron. 17:7-9; 30:6-9; 34:29-32). David had set this example (1 Chron. 22:19; 28:8), whereas Rehoboam was remiss in this (2 Chron. 12:14). To 'seek' (*dāraš*) God is one of the Chronicler's key themes and is referred to numerous times in relation to Asa's reign (14:7[6]; 15:2, 12, 13; 16:12), along with the synonym *bāqaš* (15:4, 15). It includes the idea of worship and especially prayer which is more obviously associated with reliance on God (see v. 11[10]). The God of 'their fathers' would have included not only king David but their ancestor Israel. Obedience to God's law is another important theme in Chronicles. Asa's desire to seek God and keep His commandments was expressed in the steps he took to remove from his kingdom all that was contrary to the worship of Yahweh at the one legitimate sanctuary in Jerusalem.

The 'quiet' mentioned earlier (2 Chron. 14:1[13:23]) is emphasised as a mark of the initial period of Asa's reign. It had commenced with his father's victory over the northern kingdom, but it continued with Asa's own faithfulness to Yahweh (vv. 5-7[4-6]). It is now clear that this time of 'quiet' meant an absence of war and it is highlighted twice that Yahweh was the one who has given them 'rest' all around. The terms 'quiet' (*šāqaṭ*) and 'rest' (*nûaḥ*) are here brought together and are a reminder of the rest from war that came to Canaan after the conquest (Josh. 11:23; see Deut. 12:8-10; 1 Chron. 22:9, 19). This time of peace enabled Asa to encourage Judah to build the fortified cities and thus to prepare for any unforeseen crisis. They had been eager to 'seek' Yahweh and He had blessed them by enabling them to build and prosper (see 1 Chron. 22:11, 13; 2 Chron. 32:30). It is another of the Chronicler's interests to show that building activities were a sign of divine blessing. The projects undertaken by David and Solomon are prime examples (1 Chron. 11:8; 14:1; 15:1; 2 Chron. 7:11; 8:1-6) and instances continue throughout the divided monarchy period (2 Chron. 11:5-11; 14:6-7; 16:6; 17:12; 26:2, 6, 9-10; 27:3-4; 33:14). In view of this, the building undertaken by the Ephraimites and Benjaminites is probably to be seen similarly as early and introductory cases of God's blessing (1 Chron. 7:24; 8:12).

References to strengthening the kingdom's army sometimes follow building projects and provide further indications of divine blessing (v. 8[7]; see 2 Chron. 17:12-19; 26:9-15). Asa's army is composed of three hundred-thousand foot soldiers from Judah and two hundred and eighty thousand bowmen from Benjamin. The Chronicler mentioned a vast army of such valiant men when he introduced the Transjordanian tribes (1 Chron. 5:18), while the first 'valiant' man the Chronicler named was Nimrod (1 Chron. 1:10). These notifications about the fortified cities and army prepare for the next scene.

> 14:9[8]. Now Zerah the Cushite came out against them with an army of a thousand thousands and three hundred chariots and he came to Mareshah. 10[9]. So Asa went out to meet him and they drew up in battle formation in the valley of Zephathah at Mareshah. 11[10]. Then Asa cried out to Yahweh his God and said, 'Yahweh, it is nothing with you between helping the many and those who have no strength. Help us, Yahweh our God, for we lean on you, and in your name we come against this multitude. Yahweh, you are our God, do not let a mortal man prevail against you.' 12[11]. So Yahweh struck the Cushites before Asa and before Judah, and the Cushites fled. 13[12]. And Asa and the people who were with him pursued them as far as Gerar; and some Cushites fell and could not recover, for they were broken before Yahweh and before his camp and they carried away very much spoil. 14[13]. And they attacked all the cities around Gerar, for the dread of Yahweh was on them; and they plundered all their cities for there was much plunder in them. 15[14]. They also attacked the tents of livestock, and they carried away sheep in abundance and camels, and they returned to Jerusalem.

Zerah, a common Hebrew name (1 Chron. 1:37, 44; 2:4; 4:24; 6:21[6]), is not of Semitic stock but a Cushite and therefore a descendant of Ham and closely associated with Egypt. Interestingly, Cush was the father of 'mighty' Nimrod (1 Chron. 1:9-10; Gen. 10:6-12), but geographically it is the name for the area south of Egypt called Nubia and known today as Sudan. The Cushites are associated with the Libyans (2 Chron. 12:3; 16:8). At this time, Cush was under Egyptian rule, and it is possible that the old Pharaoh Osorkon I who was of Libyan origin appointed Zerah as his general to invade Canaan in an attempt to copy Shishak's successes (see 2 Chron. 12). At any rate, a massive army invaded the south of Judah, outnumbering Asa's army by almost two to one (see vv. 8-9[7-8]). It was a similar situation to that experienced by his father in his clash with Jeroboam (2 Chron. 13:3). The battle site was perhaps the Mareshah that lay about twenty-two miles (thirty-five kilometres) southwest of Jerusalem and one of Rehoboam's garrison cities (2 Chron. 11:8), but there is no certainty about the valley of Zephathah.

Asa's threefold use of God's personal name, Yahweh, to introduce the three parts of his prayer, reveals the seriousness of the situation and the urgency of his plea (v. 11[10]). Though he spoke directly to God he did so against the background of Solomon's dedicatory prayer which encouraged all to direct their petitions via the Jerusalem temple to the God who hears from His heavenly dwelling place (2 Chron. 6:34-35; 13:4-12). He first made a declaration of assurance concerning God's ability or His uniqueness. Though the syntax is difficult it suggests that Asa is confident that divine 'help' will come to intervene on behalf of Judah's weakness against the enemy's strength. Then the king appealed for 'help' (see 1 Chron. 5:20; 15:26), expressing the nation's reliance on God ('we lean on you'; see 2 Chron. 13:18; Isa. 10:20; 50:10) and their complete confidence in all that Yahweh's name meant (see 1 Sam. 17:45). In this battle, God's reputation was at stake, and it was in the Jerusalem temple that God had placed His name (2 Chron. 6:10, 20). The enemy is again described as a 'great multitude' (see 2 Chron. 13:8). Finally, Asa appealed once more for God to demonstrate His superiority over mere mortals ('ᵉnôš), based on the conviction that Yahweh was their God.

Unlike Abijah's battle (2 Chron. 13:14-15), no details of the encounter are given; rather the Chronicler emphasises that it was Yahweh who totally defeated the Cushites. Asa and his men are depicted as simply spectators (v. 12[11]), almost like Israel's victory over the Egyptians (Exod. 14:14). All that was left for Judah to do was to chase the enemy to the southern border of Canaan at Gerar (see Gen. 10:19). Some Cushites 'fell' wounded and could not be revived, having been 'broken' in the presence of Yahweh and Judah's troops, but the majority escaped over the frontier leaving a vast amount of spoil for Judah's army to collect. The context does not favour taking 'his camp' to mean Yahweh's angelic host (v. 13[12]), but certainly Asa's army camp had become like 'an army of God' (1 Chron. 12:22). It would appear that the cities around Gerar and the herdsmen of that region had supported Zerah, and this led Asa and his troops to attack them and plunder their possessions. The 'tents of livestock' (v. 15[14]) is probably an elliptical phrase for the 'tents of the livestock herdsmen'. All the emphasis on plundering and carrying off much spoil including sheep and camels is in preparation for what is said about the offerings made to Yahweh or the gifts that were dedicated for temple use (2 Chron. 15:11, 18). As this part of the narrative closes, the reader is left with the unmistakable impression that it was Yahweh who had given Judah victory. Yahweh is the one who had struck the Cushites, with some of them 'broken' before Yahweh, and it was the 'fear of Yahweh' that came upon the cities around Gerar (v. 14[13]; see 2 Chron. 17:10; 20:29). Nothing is said about what happened to Zerah, but Asa and his men, who had prayed for Yahweh's help and who had gone out against the enemy in Yahweh's name, returned unscathed to Jerusalem.

Application

The victory spoke to the Chronicler's post-exilic people, encouraging them to pray and trust God. To seek to fight against God's people is to fight against God (Acts 5:29, 39). The Christian's warfare is spiritual and only the spiritual weapons which God has supplied are appropriate against the unseen forces of evil. But in every battle we are to go forward in the name of the Lord, trusting Him to give us the victory through Jesus Christ. Edith Cherry's hymn, based on Asa's words, remind us that

> We go in faith, our own great weakness feeling,
> And needing more each day Thy grace to know;
> Yet from our hearts a song of triumph pealing:
> We rest on Thee, and in Thy name we go.[11]

15:1. Now upon Azariah the son of Oded the Spirit of God came 2. and he went out before Asa, and said to him, 'Hear me, Asa, and all Judah and Benjamin; Yahweh is with you when you are with him, and if you seek him he will be found by you; but if you forsake him, he will forsake you. 3. Now for many days Israel was without the true God and without a teaching priest and without law. 4. But when in their distress they turned to Yahweh the God of Israel and sought him, he was found by them. 5. And in those times there was no peace to anyone who went out or came in, but much turmoil was upon all the inhabitants of the

---

11. The hymn begins, *We rest on Thee, our shield and our Defender!*

lands. 6. And they were broken in pieces, nation against nation, and city against city, for God troubled them with every kind of distress. 7. But as for you, take courage! And do not let your hands drop, for your work shall be rewarded.'

This section of Asa's reign concerns Azariah's prophecy (15:1-7) and the king's good response (15:8-19). Only the final four verses show any similarity with what is found in 1 Kings 15:13-16.

The prophet Azariah ('Yahweh has helped'), the son of Oded (see v. 8), is mentioned nowhere else but he was endowed with God's Spirit (see 1 Chron. 12:18; 2 Chron. 20:14) and suddenly appeared before Asa as he returned from his victory over the Cushites. He addressed both king and people. Often in Chronicles, the compiler introduces sermon-like messages that illustrate from Israel's history the great principle of Yahweh's rule among His people (see 1 Chron. 22:17-19; 28:2-10; 2 Chron. 13:4-12). The prophetic message is in three sections: the basic principle is stated (v. 2); it is then illustrated from Israel's history (vv. 3-6); and this is followed by a closing exhortation (v. 7).

The opening call to both king and the two tribes that made up the southern kingdom (v. 2; 2 Chron. 11:1) is reminiscent of the beginning of Abijah's speech to the north (2 Chron. 13:4). Azariah expresses the fundamental principle in its fullest form. The first two clauses concern the importance of being 'with Yahweh'. This will include walking 'before' or 'with' God and keeping His commandments (2 Chron. 7:17) and the promise is that Yahweh will be with them to prosper and protect them (see 1 Chron. 11:9; 2 Chron. 13:12). Then follows the even more familiar conditional promise first used by Moses in his sermon to the Israelites (Deut. 4:29) but also employed by David as he encouraged his son (1 Chron. 28:9). God is gracious and committed to the promises made to their fathers, so that even when they have sinned and experienced God's judgment, there is hope for His people if they repent and return to God. It was on the basis of this truth that Jeremiah could present a message of hope after judgment (Jer. 29:13-14). God is sovereign, however, and it is not automatic that those who decide to seek God will necessarily find Him (Isa. 55:6; 65:1). He remains in control which is why in place of the straightforward active verb 'you will find Him', the passive is used: 'He will be found by you' or 'He will allow Himself to be found by you'. To 'forsake' or 'abandon' God is the direct opposite of to 'seek' Him and is associated with violating Yahweh's law and His way of worship (2 Chron. 7:19; 12:1; 13:10-11). Abandoning God results in God abandoning His people which leads in turn to the covenant curses falling on them, the final and most severe punishment being exile (2 Chron. 7:19-21;12:5; 24:20, 24; 34:25).

Azariah then illustrated his message by referring to a period of great trouble and ignorance of the true God and his law (v. 3-6). He is probably describing the period of the judges when Israel 'abandoned' Yahweh, the God of their fathers and worshipped the Baals and other gods (Judg. 2:11-13). The priests and Levites who were instructed to teach the law (Lev. 10:11; Deut. 33:10; 2 Chron. 17:7-9) failed in their duties as was witnessed by Micah's shrine and the Levite whom he dedicated to be his priest (Judg. 17; see Hosea 4:6-7). Interestingly, no mention is made about being without a king (Judg. 17:6; 18:1; 21:25). The period of the judges expressed the amazing patience and mercy of God after repeated episodes of apostasy and repentance (Judg. 2:14-19; 3:7-11, 12-15). When Israel sinned they were punished, and when in their distress they repented and turned back to 'seek' Yahweh, He 'was found' by them, which meant that He forgave and delivered them (v. 4; see v. 2). The pre-exilic prophets in their canonical writings, following the words of Deuteronomy 30:1-10, announced the disaster of the exile but also spoke of a repentant people seeking Yahweh (see Hosea 3:5). For the post-exilic community, such reminders would have served both as a warning and an encouragement (see Mal. 2:4-7).

In verse 5, Azariah returns to the time of the judges and instead of peace (šālôm) the very opposite existed. People were afraid to go out or come in, suggesting they could not engage in their regular business (Judg. 5:6; 6:2). It was a time of 'much turmoil' or 'great panic' (mᵉhûmōṯ rabbôṯ; see Amos 3:9; Ezek. 22:5; Zech. 14:13). The plural form intensifies the meaning suggesting much destructive confusion. It not only affected the different tribal regions but nearby nations, as verse 6 suggests. Azariah's words become reminiscent of end time events (Hag. 2:22; Zech. 8:10; 11:6; 14:13) with inhabitants 'broken in pieces' as God 'troubled' nations and cities with all kinds of 'distress' (see Isa. 19:2). After these terrifying reminders of Israel's past troubles, Azariah concluded with an exhortation to king and people (v. 7). They are urged to be courageous (see 1 Chron. 19:13; 22:13; 28:10, 20; 2 Chron. 32:7). After the victory over Zerah, it might have been tempting to sit back and take it easy, but they are urged not to become complacent or weak-willed (see Isa. 35:3-4; Zeph. 3:16). Asa and the whole southern kingdom were assured that their work would be rewarded (see Jer. 31:16).

Application

For the post-exile people who felt that they were still in bondage under foreign rule, the principle presented here proclaimed the need to repent and to seek God for the fulfilment of all God's promises for His people. God goes one step further, for He seeks and is found by those who have not sought Him (Isa. 65:1; Rom. 3:11) and also invites all to seek Him (Acts 15:17; 17:27). We are urged to seek if we would find (Matt. 7:7). God is a rewarder of those who seek Him (Heb. 11:6). As the returned exiles were in danger of losing heart and letting their hands become weak (Neh. 6:9) so the same can happen to Christians. We are urged to discipline ourselves in the Christian life and to 'strengthen the hands that are weak' (Heb. 12:12-13).

> 15:8. And when Asa heard these words even the prophecy *by the son of* Oded the prophet, he took courage and put away the abominable items from all the land of Judah and Benjamin and from the cities which he had captured in the hill country of Ephraim; and he restored the altar of Yahweh that was before the vestibule of Yahweh. 9. Then he gathered all Judah and Benjamin and those who sojourned with them from Ephraim, Manasseh and Simeon, for many defected to him from Israel when they saw that Yahweh his God was with him. 10. So they gathered at Jerusalem in the third month of the fifteenth year of Asa's reign. 11. And they sacrificed to Yahweh on that day from the booty they had brought, seven hundred oxen and seven thousand sheep. 12. Then they entered into a covenant to seek Yahweh the God of their fathers with all their heart and with all their soul.

13. But all who did not seek Yahweh the God of Israel were put to death, whether small or great, whether man or woman. 14. Then they swore an oath to Yahweh with a loud voice and with shouting and with trumpets and with rams' horns. 15. And all Judah rejoiced over the oath, for they had sworn with all their heart and they had sought him with all their desire; and he was found by them, and Yahweh gave them rest all around.

16. And also Maacah, the mother of Asa the king, he removed her from being great lady, because she had made an abominable image of Asherah; and Asa cut down her abominable image, crushed it and burned it by the wadi Kidron. 17. But the high places were not removed from Israel. Nevertheless, the heart of Asa was faithful all his days. 18. He also brought into the house of God the dedicated items of his father and his own dedicated items: silver and gold and utensils. 19. And there was no war until the thirty-fifth year of the reign of Asa.

Asa took immediate action after hearing Azariah's message and continued the reforms that he had already begun. Seeking and trusting God meant accepting God's word through His prophets (see 2 Chron. 20:20). While many omit 'Oded the prophet', imagining it to be a marginal gloss that at an early stage was mistakenly thought to be part of the biblical text, it is better, with Matthew Poole, to understand the words as a Semitic way of referring to a descendant of the named father.[12] As 'David' is used in prophecy to mean the future son of David (Hosea 3:5; Jer. 30:9), so 'Oded' is short for 'the son of Oded,' and the LXX rightly explains the ellipsis by adding 'Azariah the son of.'

Azariah had urged king and people to 'be strong' and now Asa shows himself strong by removing those detestable practices that the parallel text in 1 Kings 15:12 highlights such as male cult prostitutes and other evidences of pagan worship (see 2 Kings 23:13, 24). This reforming zeal extended not only throughout the southern kingdom of Judah and Benjamin but into Ephraimite territory that he had probably captured during his skirmishes with Baasha (2 Chron. 16:1; 1 Kings 15:16, 32). It was the bronze altar for the burnt offerings that was renovated (v. 8). No doubt it needed

---

12. Matthew Poole, *A Commentary on the Holy Bible*, Vol. 1 (Edinburgh: The Banner of Truth Trust, 1962), p. 835.

attention if no repairs had been done to it since Solomon's time (2 Chron. 8:12; see also 29:18; 33:16).

Asa 'gathered' (qbṣ; another key term: see 1 Chron. 11:1; 13:2; 2 Chron. 20:4; 32:4) a religious assembly that consisted of the two tribes from his own kingdom and many northerners who had defected to the south (v. 9; see 2 Chron. 11:13-17). Ephraim and Manasseh, the dominant tribes of the north, are mentioned several times by the Chronicler to express the unity that did exist between north and south especially during the reigns of reforming kings (2 Chron. 19:4; 30:1, 11, 18; 31:1; 34:6, 9). The mention of the Simeon tribe is interesting for though they belonged to the ten tribes of the north their territory lay to the south of Judah and included Beersheba, the southernmost city of Israel (Josh. 19:1-9; 1 Kings 11:31; 1 Chron. 4:28-33; 6:65). Northerners journeyed to Beersheba on pilgrimage during the divided monarchy period (Amos 5:5; 8:14). The 'third month' (v. 10) is associated with the one-day harvest festival of Weeks (Exod. 23:16; 34:22; Lev. 23:15-21; etc.), but whether the assembly met on that day is not stated. The sacrifices offered are from the booty taken in the mopping up campaign near Gerar (2 Chron. 14:14-15[13-14]).

The climax to this assembly came when they 'entered' (v. 12; the more common verb 'cut/made' is not used) into a covenant together to seek (dāraš) Yahweh wholeheartedly, as the prophet Azariah had urged (v. 2) and also commanded by Asa (2 Chron. 14:4[3]). Three more covenants by the people are mentioned in Chronicles (2 Chron. 23:16; 29:10; 34:31-32). Entering into such an agreement was taken seriously. Those not 'seeking' God were to be executed, whatever their age or gender (v. 13), for they were breaking the group solidarity. Anyone's refusal to 'seek' would mean they were intent on worshipping other gods. The penalty for such apostasy was death (Deut. 13:6-11; 17:2-7). Taking an oath was part of the covenant ceremony (see Deut. 29:12, 14; 1 Chron. 16:15-17; Neh. 10:29[30]). Despite its solemn and serious nature, the covenant ceremony ended on a note of joy and enthusiasm, expressed by the same kind of shouting and use of trumpets and horns that occurred when the ark was brought into Jerusalem (v. 14; 1 Chron. 15:28). Verse 15 emphasises the joyous nature of the event, the unity that is implied and the earnest desire of all to keep the oath. Azariah's message is taken to heart: they had sought Yahweh and he was found by them, and He rewarded them with a period of 'rest' (see v. 7; 2 Chron. 14:1, 6-7[13:23; 14:5-6]). Instead of anarchy and turmoil (see v. 5), there was the kind of rest that was promised for Israel in Canaan and symbolised by the ark at rest in the Jerusalem temple (Deut. 12:5-12; 2 Chron. 6:11), a reminder of the original paradise where God was present with His people.

The final verses of the chapter parallel the account in 1 Kings 15:13-15. They include one further reform that related to the most powerful woman in the royal household, namely, the 'great lady' (gᵊḇîrāh) or more traditionally translated as the 'queen mother', although not all those designated 'great' ladies at court were queen mothers (2 Kings 10:13; Jer. 13:18; 29:2). The mother of Israelite kings often had great influence at court (1 Kings 2:19; 2 Kings 10:13). This 'Maacah' could be Abijah's mother and therefore Asa's 'mother' in the sense of 'grandmother' (2 Chron. 13:2; 1 Kings 15:2, 10), but it is impossible to be dogmatic and it could equally be Asa's actual mother. In keeping with the covenant that had been entered into, the king took the bold though perhaps painful step of deposing Maacah, but she was spared the death penalty (see v. 16). Her image of Asherah (2 Chron. 14:3-5) was cut down, crushed and burned in the Kidron valley, that infamous dumping spot for such items (2 Chron. 29:16; 30:14). The description of the image as abominable or horrifying uses a term from the same family of words for expressions of trembling horror and the shuddering terror of an earthquake (Isa. 21:4; Ps. 55:5[6]; Job 9:6).

Asa's failure to remove 'the high places' (v. 17) is not a contradiction of the earlier statement (2 Chron. 14:2, 5[3, 6]), but an acknowledgement that he had no such reforming success in the 'Israel' he had gained from the northern kingdom (v. 8; 2 Chron. 17:2). Despite Asa's sinful behaviour in the next chapter, the king's heart was basically 'sound' or 'whole' in his devotion to Yahweh. Like David and Solomon, Asa brought his own dedicated articles and those of his father Abijah into the temple (v. 18; see 1 Chron. 18:11; 26:20-28; 28:12; 2 Chron. 5:1). These gifts will have included spoil taken from the enemy (see 2 Chron. 14:9-15[8-14]).

The final verse 19 seems to contradict the text of 1 Kings 15:16 but whereas Kings is probably referring to 'cold war' or to the skirmishes that continued along the border with the north, Chronicles stresses that there was no major incident until Asa's conflict with Zerah (2 Chron. 14:9-15) and the war with Baasha that occurred the following year (see 2 Chron. 16:1). The word 'more' is added in some translations, but this is not in the Hebrew text.

Application

Faithfulness to God cuts across family ties. Jesus stated that any who would be His disciples must be willing to part with all that is dear to them (Luke 14:25-27). Nothing must come before our commitment to Christ. He must have first place in our lives.

> 16:1. In the thirty-sixth year of the reign of Asa, Baasha the king of Israel went up against Judah and built the Ramah, that he might let no-one go out or come in to Asa the king of Judah. 2. Then Asa brought out silver and gold from the treasuries of the house of Yahweh and of the king's house and sent to Ben-hadad the king of Aram, who lived in Damascus, saying, 3. 'Let there be a treaty between me and you, even as there was between my father and your father. I have actually[13] sent to you silver and gold. Go, break your treaty with Baasha king of Israel so that he will withdraw from me.' 4. So Ben-hadad listened to king Asa and sent the commanders of his troops to the cities of Israel and they attacked Ijon, Dan, Abel-maim, and all the store place of the cities of Naphtali. 5. And it was that when Baasha heard, he stopped building the Ramah and ceased his work. 6. Then king Asa took all Judah and they carried away the stones of the Ramah and its timber with which Baasha had been building, and with them he built Geba and Mizpah.

The final chapter concerning Asa's reign covers his war with Baasha (vv. 1-6), his angry reaction to Hanani's rebuke (vv. 7-10), and his illness and death (vv. 11-14). There are some close parallels between this account and the one in 1 Kings 15:17-22 but also with noticeable differences

---

13. The translation 'actually' conveys the immediacy of the action better than the traditional 'Behold' (hinnēh).

underlining the Chronicler's theological message. His account reveals how this period of Asa's life ran so counter to the earlier part of his reign.

There is no completely satisfactory solution to the Chronicler's dating of this major incident with the northern kingdom (vv. 1-6). Matthew Henry was 'at a loss' to reconcile the date. According to the chronology in Kings, Baasha died several years before the thirty-sixth year of Asa's reign (1 Kings 15:33; 16:8). A long-held view[14] understands the references to the thirty-fifth and thirty-sixth years not to Asa's actual period as king but to the time from the division into two kingdoms. Rehoboam reigned seventeen years and Abijah three years (2 Chron. 12:13; 13:2). When these are added to the first fifteen years of Asa's reign (2 Chron. 15:10) the result is the thirty-fifth year mentioned in the final verse of the last chapter. Baasha engaged in hostilities, no doubt as a result of the defections to Asa from the north, following his victory over Zerah (2 Chron. 15:9). Thus it was in Asa's sixteenth year that full-scale war broke out with the north. But why would the Chronicler have calculated the year back to the division of the kingdom when his normal practice was to date events according to the actual years of Asa's reign (vv. 12 and 13)? Perhaps it was to remind readers of the division and Shemaiah's prophetic word that the south was not to regain the breakaway region by force (2 Chron. 11:1-4). Others consider that the Chronicler wished to give the impression that war occurred during the latter years of Asa's reign in order to stress his message that peace is associated with the king's faithfulness, and war related to his unfaithfulness.

According to the Kings account, Baasha came to the throne in the third year of Asa's reign. He assassinated Nadab, Jeroboam's son, and exterminated the entire family (1 Kings 15:25-29, 33) and went on to rule the northern kingdom from Tirzah his capital for twenty-four years, with his son Elah succeeding him in the twenty-sixth year of Asa (1 Kings 15:33; 16:8). It looks as if Baasha was trying to regain control of territory lost through the actions of Abijah and Asa (2 Chron. 13:19; 15:8).

---

14. See Matthew Poole's commentary, p. 836. It was revived by Edwin Thiele, *The Mysterious Numbers of the Hebrew*, 3rd edition (Grand Rapids: Zondervan/Kregel, 1983).

The building work at Ramah[15] was for fortification purposes, and as it lay just five miles (eight kilometres) north of Jerusalem on the main access route from the north to the south, Baasha wished to cut off an easy highway for commerce and more especially defectors from the north (v. 1; see 2 Chron. 15:9). On this occasion, it seemed a good idea for Asa to contact the Aramean king, Ben-hadad I of Damascus (see 1 Kings 15:18) and persuade him with a large monetary incentive to break the treaty he already had with Baasha and instead enter into a fresh treaty with him. Apparently their fathers had had such an agreement in the past (vv. 2-3). The word for 'treaty' (*bᵉrît*) is the same as that used for the people's 'covenant' to seek Yahweh in the previous chapter (15:12). Instead of a covenant that encouraged him to seek God, Asa turned to a pagan king for protection. He broke covenant with Yahweh and pressed Ben-hadad to break covenant with Baasha. In addition, he not only used his own wealth to seal this treaty, but raided the temple treasures, taking the 'silver and gold' that had recently been dedicated to God (2 Chron. 15:18).

Ben-hadad agreed to the terms and invaded the far north of Israel along one of the international highways. Among the places attacked were the store cities of Naphtali and other border cities of Ijon and Dan and Abel-maim, the latter place probably being the post-exilic name for the Abel-beth-maacah of 1 Kings 15:20. All this had its desired effect so that Asa and 'all Judah' were able to take the building materials that Baasha had left at Ramah and used them instead to strengthen two of his own border cities that lay close by, namely, Geba and Mizpah (vv. 5-6; 2 Kings 23:8; 25:23; Jer. 41:9-10).

> 16:7. At that time Hanani the seer came to Asa the king of Judah and said to him, 'Because you have relied on the king of Aram and have not relied on Yahweh your God, therefore, the army of the king of Aram has escaped out of your hand. 8. Were not the Cushites and the Libyans a huge army with very numerous chariots and horsemen? But when you relied on Yahweh, he gave them into your hand. 9. For, as for Yahweh, his eyes move to and fro in all the earth to strengthen those whose heart is

---

15. The article often appears with this place name, as it does with some Welsh towns and villages!

completely his. You have acted foolishly in this, so from now
on you will have wars.' 10. Then Asa was provoked to anger
with the seer and put him in the house of the stocks for he was
in a rage with him about this. And Asa oppressed some of the
people at that time.

The prophecy begins and ends with 'at that time'. It was with
gracious intent that God sent His prophet to Asa as the name
Hanani ('my gracious one' or 'Yahweh is gracious') suggests
(see 2 Chron. 19:2; 20:34). 'Seer' (rō'eh) is a term used by the
Chronicler for Samuel (1 Chron. 9:22; 26:28; 29:29). The related
term 'visionary' (ḥōzeh) has been used for Heman, Gad and
Iddo (1 Chron. 21:9; 25:5; 29:29; 2 Chron. 9:29; 12:15). Far from
congratulating Asa, Hanani appeared before the king as
Shemaiah had once confronted Rehoboam (2 Chron. 12:5-8).
Whereas in the previous chapter Azariah had brought a
message of encouragement and exhortation that Asa had
accepted and acted upon, Hanani brought a message which
contained a reprimand and judgment that Asa angrily rejected.

The key word 'rely' or 'lean upon' (š'n, vv. 7-8; 2 Chron. 13:18;
14:11) is repeated to emphasise the importance of trusting
God rather than human beings. Asa was reminded of how
he had relied on Yahweh in his victory over the Cushites
(v. 8; 2 Chron. 14:11[10]). There is every encouragement to
be wholly committed to God (something that is said of Asa
in the previous chapter, v. 17) because He can view what is
going on throughout the entire world, as one of the post-
exilic prophets made clear (v. 9; Zech. 4:10). Yahweh is no
local god but sovereign over the whole earth. Now it is the
king who is accused of unfaithfulness and of acting foolishly.
Unlike David who, with God's help, had been able to bring the
Arameans to submission (1 Chron. 18:6), Hanani indicates that
the Arameans had escaped defeat as a result of Asa's alliance
with the Damascus king and therefore they would be a threat
to the kingdom (v. 7). In addition, when David was rebuked
he acknowledged his foolishness (1 Chron. 21:8), whereas Asa
showed no sorrow and was so enraged at the prophet's word,
that he put him in the prison-house stocks (v. 10). This is the
first instance in Chronicles of a king persecuting a prophet
(see 2 Chron. 18:25-26; 24:20-22). Jeremiah was similarly put in
the stocks for faithfully proclaiming God's word. As is often

the case, a lack of godly fear in Asa led him to oppress some of his people in a brutal way, probably including those who sympathised with Hanani.

> 16:11. And here are the acts of Asa, the first and the last, here they are written in the books of the kings of Judah and Israel. 12. And in the thirty-ninth year of his reign, Asa became ill in his feet until his illness became severe; yet even in his illness he did not seek Yahweh but the healers. 13. So Asa slept with his fathers and died in the forty-first year of his reign. 14. And they buried him in his own burial chambers which he had dug for himself in the city of David, and they laid him on the bier that was filled with spices of various sorts blended by the perfumer's art; and they kindled a very great fire for him.

In concluding Asa's life, the Chronicler rephrases the parallel account in 1 Kings 15:23-24 and includes more detail. Instead of citing a prophetic work, for the first time he refers in a rather excited way ('now', 'here they are')[16] to the 'Book of the kings of Judah and Israel' (see 2 Chron. 25:26; 28:26; 32:32). With reference to this source, 1 Kings 15:23 only mentions 'Judah'. In fact, in comparison to Kings, Chronicles always adds 'Israel' which suggests that this is the Chronicler's way of showing that the kingdom of Judah was still a part of the people of Israel (2 Chron. 11:3; 12:1). For the phrase 'first and last', see 1 Chronicles 29:29 and 2 Chronicles 9:29; 12:15.

Chronicles gives the more precise date of 'the thirty-ninth year' of Asa's personal reign for his illness than the indefinite 'old age' in the Kings text. Despite much speculation by scholars, the specific illness in Asa's feet which grew ever more severe is not explained but what is clearly stressed is his reaction. It might have been thought that such a serious affliction would have humbled the king (see 2 Chron. 12:6). But instead of seeking (*dāraš*, a synonym of *bāqaš*) Yahweh, as he had done when his kingdom was in danger from the Cushites (2 Chron. 14:11[10]), he still, 'yet even in his illness', remained stubbornly self-reliant (vv. 7-10) and resorted to healers (v. 12). The Chronicler is not condemning physicians as such but Asa's reliance on human aid rather than on Yahweh's help.

---

16. In both instances the particle *hinnēh* is employed, traditionally translated 'behold', the second occurrence with a third person plural suffix.

Overall, Asa was a 'good' king who did 'right'
(2 Chron. 14:2[1]; see 20:32; 21:12), having a long life and
a peaceful end (v. 13; see 2 Chron. 14:1[13:23]). Despite the
negative note, the elaborate detail concerning his burial in
the city of David suggests that the Chronicler did not wish in
the end to detract from the positive assessment of his reign.
The report of his burial is the longest recorded for any of the
kings (v. 14). While he slept with his fathers, nothing is said
about being buried with his fathers (2 Chron. 12:16). Instead,
it is noted that Asa had dug out his own special tomb and
his body was placed on some kind of base that was full of
spices and perfumes. His body was not cremated but an
enormous fire was lit in his honour (see 2 Chron. 21:19-20).

Application

It spoke to the post-exilic situation. People can start well
and even though there is no apostasy there can be a lack of
trust and humble reliance on God, preferring rather to seek
what might appear easy human solutions. Wholehearted
commitment to the Lord is urged. It is not that physical
remedies are to be dismissed. God has given, in His gracious
providence, all good things for the benefit of people's health
and wellbeing, whether in terms of the balm of Gilead or oil
and wine (Jer. 8:22; 46:11; 1 Tim. 5:23). Paul even describes
Luke as 'the beloved physician' (Col. 4:14). But medics and
medicines are never meant to take the place of reliance on
God and a commitment to Him. Ultimately, it is the Lord
who delivers us from harm and danger (Ps. 121; 2 Cor. 1:10).

Jehoshaphat's reign (17:1–21:1)
Chronicles gives more space to Jehoshaphat than any other
king who reigned over Judah during the divided monarchy
period apart from Hezekiah. For the compiler of Kings, the
reign is more noteworthy for Jehoshaphat's associations
with the Omri dynasty in the north (1 Kings 15:24; 22:1-36,
40-51; 2 Kings 3:4-27), whereas for the Chronicler the king is
presented as one of the great reforming monarchs of Judah.
There are a number of similarities between this account
of Jehoshaphat and that of his father Asa and it provides a
preview of what will be drawn out from the reign of Hezekiah.

The material can be divided as follows: an introduction to the reign (17:1-6); Jehoshaphat's faithfulness (17:7-19); Jehoshaphat and Ahab (18:1–19:3); Jehoshaphat's judicial reforms (19:4-11); Jehoshaphat's victory over his enemies (20:1-30); and the conclusion to his reign (20:31–21:1).

Introduction to Jehoshaphat's reign (17:1-6)

In these first verses, the Chronicler introduces a number of his key themes that will be fleshed out with examples from Jehoshaphat's life.

> 17:1. And Jehoshaphat his son reigned in his place, and strengthened himself over Israel. 2. And he placed a force in all the fortified cities of Judah, and set garrisons in the land of Judah, and in the cities of Ephraim that Asa his father had captured. 3. And Yahweh was with Jehoshaphat because he walked in the first ways of David his father and did not seek the Baals, 4. but he sought the God of his father and walked in his commandments and not like the practices of Israel. 5. So Yahweh established the kingdom in his hand and all Judah brought tribute to Jehoshaphat, so that he had riches and honour in abundance. 6. And his heart was exalted in the ways of Yahweh and again he removed the high places and the Asherim from Judah.

Jehoshaphat immediately consolidated ('strengthened himself,' see 2 Chron. 1:1; 12:1, 13) his position with regard to the northern kingdom now ruled by Ahab (1 Kings 22:41), securing the border region by stationing troops in the fortified cities that previous kings of Judah had built (2 Chron. 8:5-6; 11:5-11; 14:6-7[5-6]), and by placing smaller 'garrisons' (see 1 Chron. 11:16) in other parts of Judah and those cities in the hill country of Ephraim that his father had captured (2 Chron. 15:8).

Yahweh was 'with' the king as he was with David, Solomon, Abijah and Asa (1 Chron. 11:9; 2 Chron. 1:1; 13:12; 15:9). We have the earlier example of Jabez who prayed that God's hand would be 'with' him (1 Chron. 4:10). Later in this chapter the preposition 'with' is used a number of times to show the people's support for Jehoshaphat as was once the case in David's time (1 Chron. 12:18). Jehoshaphat had God's blessing because of his faithfulness to Yahweh in that he 'walked' (2 Chron. 6:16) in the 'first' ways of his father David. Some scholars prefer the reading of a few Hebrew MSS and the LXX in dropping 'David' so that 'his father' refers to Asa and his earlier good period in contrast to the later period of his reign. But though David's reign is not divided clearly into an earlier good and a later bad period, the traditional text should remain, with the Chronicler probably thinking of his presentation of David's early life prior to his numbering the people (1 Chron. 21) or to the Samuel account where there is a much clearer distinction between David's early and later reign resulting from his sin with Bathsheba (2 Sam. 11-12; see 1 Kings 15:5). David is depicted in Chronicles as the ideal king.

Interestingly, reference is made for the first time to the pagan 'Baals' (v. 3).[17] 'Baal' was the chief Canaanite god, and during Ahab's reign his wife Jezebel had introduced the Phoenician Baal worship into Israel (1 Kings 16:31-32). The Chronicler expects his readers to be aware of these Baal cults in the northern kingdom and hence the plural form is used. By the negative statement that Jehoshaphat did not 'seek' (*dāraš*, v. 3) these 'Baals', a clear contrast is implied and made more obvious in the following verse which states that he did not follow what was being done in the north ('the practices of Israel', v. 4). Positively, the king 'sought' (*dāraš*) Yahweh, the God of his father David. In other words, he was committed to worshipping Yahweh, and this was indicated by ordering his life according to God's will as revealed in the Mosaic law (see v. 9).

Jehoshaphat's devotion to God was recognised by both Yahweh and his subjects. The kingdom was still Yahweh's, and He rewarded the king by confirming him in his position as He had previously done for David (v. 5; 1 Chron. 10:14; 14:2; 17:11; 22:10; 28:7). His people brought gifts so that, like David and Solomon, the king had an abundance of 'riches and honour' (1 Chron. 29:12, 28; 2 Chron. 1:12). Unusually, the phrase 'his heart was exalted' (v. 6) is used positively for Jehoshaphat's zeal to follow Yahweh. In all the other places where the expression is found, the phrase has the negative

---

17. Prior to this a person's name 'Baal' was found in 1 Chronicles 5:5; 8:30; 9:36.

sense of being haughty (2 Chron. 26:16; 32:25-26; Ps. 131:1; etc.). His enthusiasm for God is expressed in his removal of the high places and the Asherim (v. 6; see 2 Chron. 14:3[2]). Such items associated with Canaanite paganism could re-emerge quite quickly in local communities away from the centralised worship in Jerusalem.

Jehoshaphat's faithfulness (17:7-19)

Two examples are provided: his teaching of Yahweh's law in the cities of Judah and the attitude of neighbouring states (vv. 7-11) and his military measures (vv. 12-19).

> 17:7. And in the third year of his reign he sent his officials, Ben-hail and Obadiah and Zechariah and Nethaniel and Micaiah, to teach in the cities of Judah. 8. And with them the Levites: Shemaiah and Nethaniah and Zebadiah and Asahel and Shemiramoth and Jehonathan and Adonijah and Tobijah and Tob-adonijah, the Levites; and with them Elishama and Jehoram, the priests. 9. And they taught in Judah and with them was the book of the law of Yahweh; and they went around in all the cities of Judah and taught the people. 10. Now the terror of Yahweh came upon all the kingdoms of the lands that were around Judah, so they did not fight with Jehoshaphat. 11. And some of the Philistines brought to Jehoshaphat gifts and silver as tribute; the Arabians also brought him flocks: seven thousand seven hundred rams and seven thousand seven hundred male goats.
>
> 12. So Jehoshaphat was continually growing greater still, and he built fortresses and store cities in Judah. 13. And he had many works in the cities of Judah, and men of war, valiant warriors, in Jerusalem. 14. And these are their numbers according to the house of their father. Belonging to Judah: the commanders of thousands, Adnah *was* the commander, and with him three hundred thousand valiant warriors. 15. And next to him was Jehohanan the commander, and with him were two hundred and eighty thousand. 16. And next to him *was* Amasiah the son of Zichri, who volunteered for Yahweh, and with him two hundred thousand valiant warriors. 17. And from Benjamin: Eliada a valiant warrior, and with him *were* two hundred thousand armed with bow and shield. 18. And next to him Jehozabad, and with him *were* one hundred and eighty thousand equipped for war. 19. These were in the service of the king, besides those whom the king put in the fortified cities through all Judah.

It is possible that Jehoshaphat's third year was the first where he was in sole charge, having served as co-regent for a couple of years when his father was ill and dying.[18] To wean the local people away from idolatrous practices, the king commissioned a set of five lay officials, eight Levites and two priests to instruct them in God's law. It was the duty of the Levites to teach the people (Deut. 33:10) along with the priests who would have had the added responsibility of making clear the sacrificial rituals and purity laws (2 Chron. 15:3; Lev. 10:11; Hag. 2:11; Mal. 2:7). Yahweh's lawbook is comprised of the five books of Moses. Many modern scholars suppose this 'book of the law' to be an anachronism for Jehoshaphat's time, due to the Chronicler's 'pre-critical view of the date of the Pentateuch,'[19] but their criticism indicates the presumptuous views that still exist in some academic circles.

Peace is one of the results of faithfulness to God (v. 10; 2 Chron. 14:6-7[5-6]). The 'kingdoms of the lands' have been mentioned earlier (see 1 Chron. 29:30; 2 Chron. 12:8; see also 'peoples' and 'inhabitants of the lands,' 2 Chron. 13:9; 15:5). These neighbouring lands had a dread of Jehoshaphat's God and acknowledged that he ruled as Yahweh's viceroy (1 Chron. 14:17; 2 Chron. 14:14[13]; 20:29). Far from being in fear of God, the pagan nations were later to mock God and His people (Ps. 115:2) and there were those in the post-exilic period who doubted God's love because they were still under foreign domination. Both prophet and Chronicler sought to challenge and encourage their people (Mal. 1:2, 11, 14; 3:8-12). Evidence of the respect received from other lands and the existence of peace in Judah was the bringing of presents to Jehoshaphat (v. 11). Not since Solomon's day had such tribute been given (2 Chron. 9:14, 24, 28). The Philistines (1 Chron. 1:12; 18:1, 11), who had caused such problems in the days of Samuel, Saul and David become symbolic of former enemies submitting to the Davidic king. While the kings of Arabia had brought gold and silver to Solomon (2 Chron. 9:14), the Arabian nomads appropriately brought flocks of sheep and goats.

Both Rehoboam and Asa had built forts (v. 12; 2 Chron. 11:5-12; 14:6-7[5-6]). The extensive 'works' (v. 13) is often thought to refer

18. Thiele, *The Mysterious Numbers*, pp. 96-97.

19. Klein, *2 Chronicles*, p. 252.

to the supplies the king gathered into the storage cities, but it is more likely a reference to the building works mentioned in the previous verse.[20]

The rest of the chapter (vv. 13b-19) gives details of the king's army. Some scholars distinguish between a standing army in Jerusalem (vv. 13b and 19a) and conscripts composed of three units from Judah and two from Benjamin (vv. 14-18), but the text reads better if the whole passage is about a citizen force of conscripts who 'served the king' (v. 19a; 1 Chron. 27:1; 28:1) and were mustered according to their households. The professional army is probably the one mentioned in verse 2 and referred to again in verse 19b that the king stationed in the fortified cities of Judah. The term 'thousand' in the phrase 'commanders of thousands' (v. 14) may well mean a military unit of far less than a thousand men. Nevertheless, it is made clear that Jehoshaphat's army was very large, twice the size of Asa's (2 Chron. 14:8[7]). Only David had a larger one (1 Chron. 21:5). An interesting detail is the note that the commander Amasiah 'volunteered' for Yahweh's service (v. 16). The verb *nāḏaḇ* in the *hithpael* (literally 'offered himself freely') is used by the Chronicler a number of times to indicate the willingness of the people in bringing their offerings for the temple (1 Chron. 29:5, 6, 9, 14, 17; see also the adjective *nāḏîḇ* in 1 Chron. 28:21; 2 Chron. 29:31). Concerning the Benjaminite contingents, one group had weapons specially associated with that tribe ('bows and shields,' v. 17; 2 Chron. 14:8[7]; 1 Chron. 8:40; 12:2), while the other was well prepared for army service (v. 18; 1 Chron. 12:24[25]).

The whole chapter indicates how Jehoshaphat's piety was blessed by God and stands in stark contrast to what follows.

Application

For the encouragement of the post-exiles and for Christians seeking God, wholehearted commitment is promoted rather than the 'anything will do' for God mentality of Malachi's day. Knowing the truths of God's word and living in the light

---

20. The exact phrase 'continually going greater' (*hōlēḵ weḡāḏēl*) only occurs elsewhere in the Bible in 1 Samuel 2:26 and '*aḏ-ləmā'lāh* ('still', literally 'up to above') is one of the Chronicler's idioms (2 Chron. 16:12; 26:8).

of it is emphasised. Like the king, Christians are urged to be fervent in spirit, serving the Lord. Do we serve for the right reasons? Do we volunteer to serve in the local church or in other capacities for selfish reasons or in a half-hearted way? (See Ps. 110:3; Eph. 6:7).

When the Spirit of God is at work among His people, fear comes on the people at large (Gen. 35:5; Acts 5:11). We are always only one generation away from falling into paganism. Pagan practices are hard to stamp out completely. This was so even when the Methodist revival transformed nearly every local community in Wales. Superstitions of various kinds continued. The alternative to paganism and superstition is the faithful teaching of God's word. As the post-exilic community was encouraged to pray and to be familiar with God's written word, so prayer and the ministry of the word remain the essential elements in the ongoing life of the Christian Church.

Jehoshaphat and Ahab (18:1–19:3)

This is one of the best examples of Hebrew narrative in the Bible. Most of the material finds a parallel in 1 Kings 22 but it contains some small significant changes that reveal the Chronicler's own concerns (see 18:31b). The text also contains an introduction (18:1-2) and conclusion (19:1-3) that is new and focuses the reader's attention on Jehoshaphat rather than on Ahab. In Kings, the account shows the fulfilment of prophecies against Ahab (1 Kings 20:42; 21; 18:18-19) whereas in Chronicles the narrative emphasises the folly of Jehoshaphat in aligning himself with Ahab. Following the introduction, the account covers the endorsement of the war by Ahab's prophets (18:3-11), Micaiah's prophecy (18:12-27), the battle account (18:28-34) and Jehu's prophecy (19:1-3).

> 18:1. Now Jehoshaphat had riches and honour in abundance; and he became related by marriage to Ahab. 2. And some years later he went down to Ahab at Samaria. And Ahab slaughtered sheep and cattle in abundance for him and for the people who were with him and induced him to go up to Ramoth-gilead.

The chapter begins by reiterating Jehoshaphat's blessed position (v. 1a; see 17:5b), and this is followed by the abrupt statement without comment that he had entered into a marriage alliance with Ahab (v. 1b). It is implied that Jehoshaphat did not need to be allied to the northern kingdom and verse 1 could be translated: 'Though Jehoshaphat had riches … he allied himself in marriage …'. The marriage was between Jehoshaphat's son Jehoram and Ahab's daughter Athaliah (2 Chron. 21:6; 22:2, 10-12). It has already been shown that Asa's military alliance with Ben-hadad had met with God's disapproval (2 Chron. 16:2-4, 7).

Instead of 'in the third year' (1 Kings 22:1) which relates to the peace between Israel and the Arameans (1 Kings 20:26-43), the Chronicler is viewing the following event from a Judean perspective 'after some years' (v. 2), and further differences to the Kings text emphasises the Chronicler's interests. Jehoshaphat's state visit 'down' from Jerusalem to the new capital of the northern kingdom at Samaria (1 Kings 16:24) was in order to meet Ahab who gave him and his retinue a right royal reception. This put the Judean king in a good mood to be cajoled or seduced into agreeing to support Ahab's desire to recapture Ramoth-gilead in Gilead, a strategic city about sixty miles (ninety-six kilometres) northeast of Samaria. Unlike 1 Kings 22:3, the Chronicler omits the reason behind the plan to take this city, for his interest is not in the north's political affairs as such except when they impact Judah. The verb 'to induce' or 'incite' (sûṯ) is used to describe David's temptation by Satan (1 Chron. 21:1; see 2 Chron. 32:11, 15), but sometimes it has a more neutral sense (see v. 31 below). It must not be forgotten that the Davidic king was by this alliance legitimising an Israelite state that had rebelled against the Davidic rule and had set up an administration and worship that ran counter to God's will. It was equivalent to being in league with the devil.

> 18:3. And Ahab the king of Israel said to Jehoshaphat the king of Judah, 'Will you go with me *to* Ramoth-gilead?' And he said to him, 'I am as you are and my people as your people, and *we will be* with you in the battle. 4. But Jehoshaphat said to the king of Israel, 'Seek now today the word of Yahweh.' 5. Then the king of Israel assembled the prophets, four hundred men and said to them, 'Shall we go to Ramoth-gilead to battle, or shall I refrain?' And they said, 'Go up, and may God give *it* into the hand of the king.' 6. But Jehoshaphat said, 'Is there not here

yet a prophet of Yahweh that we may seek from him?' 7. And
the king of Israel said to Jehoshaphat, 'There is still one man
from whom we may seek Yahweh, but I hate him, for he does
not prophesy for good concerning me but always for evil. He
is Micaiah, the son of Imlah.' But Jehoshaphat said, 'Let not the
king say so.' 8. Then the king of Israel called one eunuch and
said, 'Bring quickly Micaiah, the son of Imlah.' 9. Now the king
of Israel and Jehoshaphat the king of Judah were sitting each on
his throne, arrayed in robes, and sitting at the threshing floor
at the entrance of the gate of Samaria while all the prophets
were prophesying before them. 10. And Zedekiah the son of
Chenaanah made horns of iron for himself and said, 'Thus says
Yahweh, With these you shall gore the Arameans, until they
are destroyed.' 11. And all the prophets were prophesying thus,
saying, 'Go up to Ramoth-gilead and be successful, for Yahweh
will give *it* into the hand of the king.'

Unlike the Kings text, both kings are given their names and
titles (v. 3). Chronicles omits the reference to horses but adds
instead 'we will be with you …' (1 Kings 22:4), thus making
clear that Jehoshaphat 'speaks as an equal'.[21] Though he had
committed himself to the venture, the pious Jehoshaphat still
politely urged Ahab to 'seek' (*dāraš*) a word from Yahweh
(v. 4). It was customary to gain divine approval before a battle
(Judg. 1:1; 1 Sam. 23:3-4). There were many Yahweh prophets
in the northern kingdom beside the Baal prophets that Jezebel
had introduced (1 Kings 18:4, 13, 19, 22). These prophets
that Ahab summoned turned out to be false prophets who
may well have succumbed to the syncretistic worship that
Jeroboam had set up (2 Chron. 13:8-9). They told Ahab what
he wanted to hear, using all the right religious language (v. 5;
see 2 Sam. 5:19).

Jehoshaphat was not impressed with the united voice of
these prophets and asked for another Yahweh prophet from
whom they could seek an answer (v. 6). The difference between
a true and false prophet became a big issue in the days of
Jeremiah and one of the reasons for the exile was the people's
treatment of the true prophets (2 Chron. 36:16). Like Elijah,
Micaiah ('who is like Yahweh') did not tow the party line
and, for this, Ahab hated him (v. 7). Micaiah had obviously

---

21. Japhet, *I & II Chronicles*, p. 759.

been consulted on many occasions previously and had only proclaimed disaster ('evil') rather than 'good' (2 Chron. 10:7). The king preferred prophets who agreed with his wishes than whether their words were true or false. Jehoshaphat gently reproved Ahab for being so negative toward him and so Ahab agreed to call Micaiah.

While the court official hurried to fetch Micaiah (v. 8), a vivid account is given of these prophets excitedly repeating their positive message in front of the two kings as they sat on their thrones by the city gate (v. 9). Their 'prophesying' may well have turned into the kind of ecstatic behaviour that was sometimes witnessed in true prophets of Yahweh (Num. 11:25-27; 1 Sam. 10:5-13; 19:20-24). Zedekiah ('Yahweh is righteous') may have been the leader over this band of prophets (see 1 Sam. 10:9-13; 19:20) and he produced a visual aid using a pair of iron horns that he must have made some time before (v. 10). Had he used them on previous occasions? Prophets often engaged in symbolic actions to confirm their messages (Isa. 20:2-4; Jer. 27:2; Ezek. 4:1-17; etc.). Zedekiah accompanied his action using words reminiscent of Moses' oracle concerning the descendants of Joseph's sons, Ephraim and Manasseh, now the dominant tribes of the northern kingdom (Deut. 33:13-17). The same verb for 'gore' with the horns of an ox is employed for the destruction of their enemies. Zedekiah's action implied that the blessing which belonged to Joseph would come to Ahab in the battle. This visual aid encouraged all the prophets to repeat their original message (v. 11; see v. 5). In the battle, the kings were assured they would 'succeed' or 'prosper'. This verb is another important term for the Chronicler, but success would only happen if there was obedience to Yahweh's revealed will (see 1 Chron. 22:13).

> 18:12. Then the messenger who went to call Micaiah spoke to him saying, 'The words of the prophets are indeed unitedly favourable for the king, so now let your word be like one of them and speak favourably.' 13. But Micaiah said, 'As Yahweh lives, what my God says, that I will speak.' 14. And he came to the king, and the king said to him, 'Micah, shall we go to Ramoth-gilead to the battle, or shall I refrain?' And he said, 'Go up and be successful, for they will be given into your hand.' 15. Then the king said to him, 'How many times must I make you

swear that you will not speak to me anything but truth in the name of Yahweh?' 16. So he said, 'I saw all Israel scattered on the mountains, like sheep that have no shepherd; and Yahweh said, These have no masters, let each return to his house in peace.' 17. Then the king of Israel said to Jehoshaphat, 'Did I not tell you that he would not prophesy good concerning me, only evil?' 18. Then he said, 'Therefore, hear the word of Yahweh, "I saw Yahweh sitting on his throne and all the host of heaven standing on his right and on his left. 19. And Yahweh said, Who will deceive Ahab the king of Israel so that he will go up and fall at Ramoth-gilead? And one said saying this while another *was* saying that. 20. Then the spirit came forward and stood before Yahweh and said, I will deceive him. And Yahweh said to him, How? 21. And he said, I will go out and be a lying spirit in the mouth of all his prophets. Then he said, You are to deceive him and be successful also. Go out and do so. 22. And now Yahweh has indeed put a lying spirit in the mouth of these your prophets, for Yahweh has spoken evil against you."' 23. Then Zedekiah the son of Chenaanah came near and struck Micaiah on the cheek and said, 'Which way did the Spirit of Yahweh pass from me to speak to you?' 24. And Micaiah said, 'You will certainly see on that day, when you enter an inner room to hide yourself.' 25. Then the king of Israel said, 'Take Micaiah and return him to Amon the governor of the city and to Joash the king's son; 26. and you shall say, "Thus says the king, Put this one in the prison and feed him food of oppression and water of oppression until I return in peace."' 27. And Micaiah said, 'If you really do return in peace, Yahweh has not spoken by me.' And he said, 'Hear, peoples, all of them.'

The royal messenger kindly informed Micaiah what the prophets were unanimously saying and advised him to be one with them and give a favourable message (v. 12). Micaiah's response was uncompromising, swearing by Yahweh's life (see Judg. 8:19; Ruth 3:13; 1 Sam. 14:45; etc.) that he would only speak what God gave him to say (v. 13). Yahweh was his God and therefore the prophet was under orders from a higher authority than an earthly monarch (see Amos 3:8). Ahab presented the same question to the prophet as to the other four hundred, calling him by the shortened form of his name, 'Micah' ('who is like'), and the prophet replied sarcastically by agreeing with the prophets (v. 14). Judging

by Ahab's response, Micaiah had acted like this previously
(v. 15). It was a way of bringing the king to appreciate that
this prophet spoke the true word of God. Though Ahab hated
the truth he still wanted to hear the truth and in this he acted
in a manner similar to Herod in his dealings with John the
Baptist (Mark 6:17, 20). Another way of treating Micaiah's first
message to Ahab would be to understand it as Micaiah's way
of indicating that it was indeed God's will for the king to be
deceived and thus be killed (see vv. 19-22).

Micaiah presented God's word in the form of two visions
he had received, the first revealing that Israel would lose their
king in the battle (v. 16) and the second explaining why the false
prophets spoke as they did (vv. 18-22). The picture of the nation
like sheep scattered with no one to lead them is a familiar one
(see Num. 27:16-17; Isa. 13:14; Nah. 3:18; Zech. 10:2; 13:7), with
shepherds a common Ancient Near Eastern metaphor for kings,
and there are a number of examples of this found in the Bible
(2 Sam. 5:2; Ps. 78:72; Ezek. 34; Matt. 9:36; Mark 6:34). There is
irony in the final words where each returns home 'in peace'
(v. 16) whereas there was to be no peaceful return for Ahab even
though he stubbornly believed he would return 'in peace' (v. 26).

The second vision follows Ahab's reaction to the first vision.
For Ahab, Micaiah's words only confirmed what the king
had previously said to Jehoshaphat (vv. 7, 17). The prophet
saw a heavenly scene with Yahweh seated on His throne,
surrounded by the heavenly host of counsellors (v. 18; see Isa.
6:1-3; Ps. 103:21; Luke 2:13). It counterbalances the earthly scene
of the two kings sitting on their thrones at the city gate with
the prophets shouting their advice (v. 9). While 1 Chronicles
21:1 in contrast to 2 Samuel 24:1 attributes to Satan rather
than Yahweh David's temptation to number the people, here
Yahweh is depicted as directly involved in calling for Ahab to
be deceived (v. 19). A spirit from Yahweh became a 'false spirit'
that possessed Ahab's prophets and by that means deceived
Ahab. Calvin believed that this spirit was a reference to Satan,
but this is unlikely as he is not named as such. It seems that
this lying spirit is 'the personified spirit of prophecy itself'[22]

22. Edward J. Young, *My Servants the Prophets* (Grand Rapids: Eerdmans, 1961), p. 141.

(see Zech. 13:2; 1 John 4:6; 2 Thess. 2:11). Yahweh guaranteed success to this spirit. So these Yahweh prophets in the service of king Ahab had unknowingly been deluded in order that Ahab might be deceived and killed (vv. 20-22). And yet, the fact that Yahweh's faithful prophet Micaiah was revealing this deception to the earthly kings and the prophetic advisers presented a final opportunity for repentance. The passage teaches both divine sovereignty and human responsibility.

There was an immediate response first from Zedekiah (v. 23) and then the king (vv. 25-26) and to both Micaiah made reply (vv. 24, 27). Zedekiah again appears as the spokesman for the band of prophets (see vv. 9-11) and sought to humiliate Yahweh's true prophet by using physical force and questioning his integrity. His question could be a sarcastic comment on how an alleged false spirit could go from himself and then give such a contradictory false message through Micaiah. Micaiah's reply is brief but direct: 'Wait and see!' (v. 24). One way by which true prophecy could be assessed was in its fulfilment (Deut. 18:21-22) and Micaiah indicates that all would be revealed when the disaster ('evil') happened, and the discredited Zedekiah would be forced to hide in fear for his own life.

The response of Ahab was to call for Micaiah's arrest and for the city governor and one of the king's sons to incarcerate him with prison rations until the king returned 'in peace', flatly contradicting Micaiah's word (vv. 25-26; see v. 16). Asa, the Davidic king, had also imprisoned a prophet of Yahweh (2 Chron. 16:10). Micaiah's reply to the king is similar to the one he gave Zedekiah. The fulfilment of the prophecy would show who was right (vv. 27). Micaiah's final bold word was for the different people groups that crowded around the gate of this cosmopolitan city to watch the spectacle. The canonical prophet Micah or Micaiah (Jer. 26:18) used exactly the same words as his name's sake in the opening to his prophecy where it literally reads 'Hear, peoples, all of them' (Micah 1:2a).

> 18:28. And the king of Israel and Jehoshaphat the king of Judah went up to Ramoth-gilead. 29. So the king of Israel said to Jehoshaphat, 'I will disguise myself and go into the battle but you put on your robes.' So the king of Israel disguised himself, and they went into the battle. 30. Now the king of Aram had

ordered the commanders of his chariots, saying, 'Do not fight
with small or great but with the king of Israel alone.' 31. So it
was when the commanders of the chariots saw Jehoshaphat, that
they said, 'He is the king of Israel'; and they surrounded him to
fight. But Jehoshaphat cried out and Yahweh helped him, and
God lured them away from him. 32. Then it happened when
the commanders of the chariots saw that it was not the king
of Israel, that they turned back from pursuing him. 33. And
a man drew his bow in his innocence and struck the king of
Israel between the scale armour and the breastplate. So he said
to the charioteer, 'Turn your hand, and take me out of the camp,
for I am wounded.' 34. And battle erupted on that day, and the
king of Israel propped himself up in his chariot in front of the
Arameans until the evening; and at sunset he died.

Jehoshaphat naively followed Ahab into battle despite having
heard the words of Yahweh's faithful prophet and even
though Ahab informed him of his scheme to play safe in case
there was any truth in Micaiah's prophecy. The Judean king
was also prepared to put his own life at risk as he submitted
to this cunning plan to dupe the enemy. The royal robes
had been mentioned earlier (v. 29; see v. 9). Jehoshaphat was
clearly shown to be the weak partner in this alliance with the
northern king, and this was totally out of keeping with his
status as a Davidic ruler over God's kingdom. The Aramean
king's tactic was to seek to engage with Ahab himself but as
his presence in the battle was not obvious due to his disguise,
the cavalry went for the obvious target, the one dressed in
his royal robes! Jehoshaphat was only saved because God
providentially intervened and 'lured them away' (v. 31; the
same word is translated 'induced' in v. 2; see 1 Chron. 21:1). The
Chronicler's addition to the Kings account provides another
illustration of divine aid in answer to a desperate cry for help
(see 1 Chron. 5:20; 2 Chron. 6:34-35; 14:11[10]). God's purposes
are not thwarted, and an innocent or random shot reached
its divinely ordained target, at a vulnerable point in Ahab's
armour (v. 33). The Israelite king asked to be taken out of the
heat of the war camp, but remained propped up in his chariot
facing the enemy, probably to give his troops the courage to
fight on, but by the end of the day his own life came to an end
(v. 34). No further details are given in Chronicles of Ahab's
death as is found in 1 Kings 22:35b-40. The Chronicler's

concern is ultimately not with what happened in the north but with the consequences for Jehoshaphat.

> 19:1. And Jehoshaphat the king of Judah returned to his house, to Jerusalem, in peace. 2. Then Jehu the son of Hanani the visionary came out to confront him, and he said to the king Jehoshaphat, 'Should you help the wicked, and love those who hate Yahweh? On account of this, wrath from the presence of Yahweh *is* upon you. 3. However, good things were found in you for you have taken away the Asheroth from the land and you have set your heart to seek God.'

The Chronicler is not concerned with the prophecies of Elijah concerning Ahab (1 Kings 21:19; 22:38) but only with those relating to Jehoshaphat. The following scene, unique to Chronicles, presses home the compiler's message. First, it is noted that, unlike Ahab whose end was as Micaiah had predicted, Jehoshaphat returned home 'in peace' (18:16, 26-27). All seemed well until another prophet came out to 'confront him' (literally 'before him'). The aged visionary, Jehu, the one who had announced judgment against Baasha some forty years earlier (1 Kings 16:1, 7, 12; see 2 Chron. 20:34), is the son of the prophet who was imprisoned for rebuking Asa (2 Chron. 16:7-10). The term 'visionary' (*ḥōzeh*) is, like 'seer' (*rō'eh*), another term for a prophet (see 1 Chron. 29:29).

Jehu's terse oracle first rebuked the king using a couple of rhetorical questions that led to the announcement of God's 'wrath' (*qeṣep*; see 1 Chron. 27:24; 2 Chron. 19:10; 24:18; 29:8; 32:25-26) upon him, but this was followed by a message that implied that the judgment he deserved would be mitigated. What that wrath entailed is not made clear and the Hebrew verb-less sentence could point to past, present or future punishment. The enemy invasion could be one example of God's wrath (2 Chron. 20) and certainly the results of the marriage alliance that led later to great trouble for the Davidic line would be a further example (2 Chron. 22:10-12). Jehoshaphat had aligned himself to the powerful Omri dynasty and had given 'help' to a king who was described as 'wicked'. The Chronicler no doubt expected his readers to have read the account of Ahab's unrighteous rule (1 Kings 16:25-33; 21:1-26). Solomon defined 'wicked' as the opposite of 'righteous' (2 Chron. 6:23, 37; see 20:35; 24:7). It is activity that is contrary to God's norm as revealed in His law. In addition, Jehoshaphat is accused of showing 'love' to those who 'hate' Yahweh (v. 2). Ahab showed his hatred for God by hating Yahweh's prophet (2 Chron. 18:7). The marriage alliance that involved Jehoshaphat in a joint military action showed an attachment (2 Chron. 18:3) that was completely unacceptable for a Davidic ruler (see Pss. 97:10; 139:21-22).

God's wrath is not averted but it is allayed on account of the 'good things' (see 2 Chron. 12:12) that were found in Jehoshaphat (v. 3). Two evidences of good are recorded, one negative and one positive. There were the reforms he had already carried out such as the removal of the 'Asheroth', those objects that represented the female counterparts to the Baals (see 2 Chron. 14:3; 17:6). Then there was his whole-hearted commitment ('set his heart'; 1 Chron. 29:18; 2 Chron. 12:14) to 'seek' (*dāraš*) God (2 Chron. 17:4; 18:4, 6; 20:3; 22:9). Jehoshaphat was no apostate, and his basic desire was to please and serve Yahweh.

Application

The passage spoke to the post-exilic people, that though the Jews must be winsome toward all descendants of Israel, there was to be no compromise with those who had departed from God. It is a reminder that unity must be in the truth as revealed in God's word. There can be no alliances with unbelievers (2 Cor. 6:14-18). The Christian is urged not to love the world while, on the other hand, we are encouraged to love our enemies but not in the sense of uniting with them in their wicked ways. Augustine considered that God's enemies could be hated for their wickedness but loved as human beings.

As there were false as well as true prophets of the Lord in Israel, so there are church leaders who follow the thinking of the world and lead people away from the truth. We have God's word to help us discern the true from the false. Giving people over to deception is part of God's righteous judgment of the ungodly (Matt. 24:23-24; 2 Thess. 2:9-11; Rev. 13:13-14; 19:20). On the other hand, God is gracious toward His people, and although they are chastised for disobedience, God knows His own and He is faithful and just to forgive their sins as they confess and return to Him.

Jehoshaphat's judicial appointments (19:4-11)

The king's name, Jehoshaphat (Yahweh judges), may have prompted the inclusion of this material unique to the Chronicler but it also served his purpose in pressing home important themes and in giving fresh evidence of the king's piety. A characteristic feature of the early charismatic leaders in Israel, known as judges, was not so much their role in considering judicial cases but the part they played as deliverers from the enemies of Israel. This aspect of judgment appears in the Chronicler's account of Jehoshaphat (2 Chron. 17:10; 20:29). It was also the judge's function to rally the people to serve Yahweh and this Jehoshaphat was keen to do by teaching the law, removing pagan worship from the land, and bringing the people back to Yahweh (2 Chron. 17:6-9; 2 Chron. 19:4). In this section, however, the dominant note is the king's desire to see that justice was maintained in accordance with Israel's covenant obligations.

After a brief introduction (v. 4), the chapter divides into two neatly organised paragraphs: the appointment of judges in the fortified cities and the king's address to them (vv. 5-7) and the appointment of judges in Jerusalem and his address to them (vv. 8-11).

> 19:4. Now Jehoshaphat lived in Jerusalem. But again he went out among the people from Beersheba to the hill country of Ephraim and he brought them back to Yahweh the God of their fathers.

The first sentence is a reminder, especially in the light of Jehoshaphat's disastrous associations with the northern kingdom and its ruler, that the Davidic king reigned from Jerusalem (v. 1; 2 Chron. 11:5). His throne did not belong alongside apostate Ahab at the city gate of Samaria. Jehoshaphat's throne was Yahweh's throne and belonged in the city where Yahweh had caused His name to dwell. Yahweh's house and the king's house belonged together in the same city (1 Chron. 29:23; 2 Chron. 7:11-16; 8:1; 18:9).

When Jehoshaphat again left the city, it was to walk the length of his kingdom from Beersheba in the south to the border region with the north that had been gained by Asa (2 Chron. 17:2). As was his custom, the Chronicler reverses the usual way of referring to the limits of the land (1 Chron. 21:2; 2 Chron. 30:5). Jehoshaphat's purpose was to encourage the people to repent of their idolatrous backsliding by turning them back to Yahweh (2 Chron. 7:14), thus reinforcing the teaching that had already been given (2 Chron. 17:7-9). In this Jehoshaphat was following his father's good policy of returning the people to 'Yahweh the God of their fathers', another favourite expression of the Chronicler, found twenty-seven times in his whole work (see 1 Chron. 5:25[6:16]; 2 Chron. 15:12). The verse indicates that unlike Asa his father, Jehoshaphat humbly received Jehu's rebuke and repented of his own wrong.

> 19:5. And he appointed judges in the land in all the fortified cities of Judah, city by city. 6. And he said to the judges, 'See what you are doing, for you do not judge for humankind but for Yahweh and he is with you in the matter of judgment. 7. Now then let the dread of Yahweh be upon you; observe and act, for with Yahweh our God there is no injustice, or respecting of persons or the taking of a bribe.'

Moses chose men from the tribes to deal with day-to-day issues, leaving difficult cases to be referred back to himself (Exod. 18:13-26). During the judges' period, local charismatic leaders acted both as judges and deliverers. Jehoshaphat's appointment of permanent judges is limited to the fortified cities of Judah (2 Chron. 17:2), leaving intact the legal system that operated in the other cities (Deut. 16:18).

The king's exhortation to these newly appointed royal judges was to remind them that all judgment comes from Yahweh (v. 6). For similar contrasts between Yahweh and humanity (*'āḏām*), see 1 Chronicles 21:13 and 29:1. Yahweh is the ultimate judge (Gen. 18:25) and they were to judge on behalf of God. They had a God-given authority and were responsible ultimately to God. As the Davidic king acted as God's viceroy among the people, so these judges acted as Yahweh's representatives in matters of justice, and they too were assured of God's presence in all the judicial decisions they made (v. 6; Deut. 1:17). The kind of divine 'dread' (*pahaḏ-Yāhweh*) that fell on cities and surrounding nations was to be felt by these judges (2 Chron. 14:14; 17:10). The justice they were to exercise was based on God's justice and is described in negative terms: no injustice, no favouritism and no corruption (see Deut. 16:19; 10:17).

> 19:8 And also in Jerusalem Jehoshaphat appointed some of the Levites and priests and some of the heads of the fathers of

Israel for the judgment of Yahweh and for disputes; and they
returned to Jerusalem. 9. Then he commanded them, saying,
'Thus you shall act in the fear of Yahweh, with fidelity and
with a perfect heart. 10. And every dispute that comes to you
from your brothers who live in their cities between bloodshed
and bloodshed, between law and commandment, statutes and
rulings, you shall also warn them so that they may not be guilty
before Yahweh, and wrath be upon you and upon your brothers.
Thus you shall act and not incur guilt. 11. And here is Amariah
the chief priest over you for all matters of Yahweh and Zebadiah
the son of Ishmael, the leader of the house of Judah, for all
matters of the king. Also the Levites will be officers before you.
Be strong and act and may Yahweh be with the good.'

As in the previous paragraph, a brief report about the setting
up of a legal system, this time in Jerusalem, is followed by an
exhortation from the king. Moses had legislated concerning
priests alongside lay judges (Deut. 17:9, 12) and David and
Solomon had appointed Levitical judges (1 Chron. 23:4; 26:29;
2 Chron. 1:2). The 'heads' of Israelite families also served as
judges and in difficult cases they could appeal to the priests and
judges at the central sanctuary (Deut. 19:15-18). Jehoshaphat's
appointments followed the general Mosaic ruling with Levites,
priests and lay heads of families discharging justice on behalf
of Yahweh ('for the judgment of Yahweh', v. 8) and settling
disputes. He undertook to reform this Jerusalem court of law
which, as the king's appeal suggests, needed an overhaul. The
traditional pointing of the text ('they returned to Jerusalem', v. 8b)
suggests peripatetic judges, which seems unlikely. A proposed
repointing of the text reads 'they lived in Jerusalem'[23] which
would indicate that the priests and Levites who normally lived
in the countryside remained in the capital to hear difficult cases.
    These judges were urged to act in the 'fear of Yahweh' (yir'at-
Yāhweh, v. 9; see Ps. 34:11[12]), with 'fidelity' (1 Chron. 9:26, 31)
and 'a perfect heart' (1 Chron. 29:19). The Jerusalem court
system is not so much a higher court of appeal as a court
of reference to help the local courts in complex cases (v. 10).
Jethro had advised his son-in-law that only problematic
cases should come to Moses (Exod. 18:22, 26). An example
of such cases is described, similar to the ones set out in

---

23. See Dillard, *2 Chronicles*, p. 146.

Deuteronomy 17:8-9. They included whether a death (literally 'blood') was caused deliberately or accidentally, and therefore whether the crime was murder or manslaughter. Discernment was also needed where written instruction or law (*tôrāh*), commandment (*miṣwāh*), statutes or decrees (*ḥuqqîm*) and judgments or rulings (*mišpāṭîm*) might seem unclear. All these terms are used for God's revealed Word (see Ps. 119).

Besides helping people in the provincial courts, the Jerusalem judiciary was to be involved in 'warning' them (v. 10; see Exod. 18:20; Deut. 17:10-11). The law needed to be taught and kept (2 Chron. 17:7-9) so that they would be free from guilt and God's wrath would be averted (for *qeṣep*, 'wrath,' see 2 Chron. 19:2).

A distinction is made between affairs relating to the temple and those relating to the crown (v. 11). Such a division between cultic and non-cultic matters existed under David's rule (1 Chron. 26:30, 32) and was apparent in post-exilic times under the leadership of Zerubbabel the governor and Joshua the high priest (Hag. 1:1, 12, 14). The expression 'head priest' (*cōhēn hāro'š*; see 2 Chron. 24:11; 26:20) is used instead of the more familiar 'chief priest' (*cōhēn haggāḏôl*, literally 'great priest'). Of the Amariahs named in the list of priests in 1 Chronicles 6:1-15[5:27-41], perhaps he is to be identified with the one mentioned in verse 11[37]). Nothing is known of Zebadiah the son of Ishmael, apart from the fact he is described as 'leader of the house of Judah,' and therefore a most appropriate person to deal with the Davidic king's issues. Again, his name is a common one appearing seven times in Chronicles. The Levites who were appointed to serve as officers alongside the judges are similar to those grouped with the judges in David's time (1 Chron. 23:4).

Jehoshaphat concluded his instructions with a word of encouragement (see 1 Chron. 28:10, 20) and a prayer wish that Yahweh would be with the 'good' (see v. 3), which is probably an elliptical phrase meaning all the God-like activity urged on those involved in this beneficial reform work (see 1 Chron. 11:9).

Application

Despite the fact they were still under foreign domination, God's people, after the exile, were able to have a governor appointed by the Persians who was of their own race and religion in the person of Zerubbabel, a descendant of David, and again later when Nehemiah was appointed. In addition, they had a high priest such as Joshua who also had a significant place in the community. The Chronicler's inclusion of this unique material relating to Jehoshaphat's judicial reforms sets a good example of an orderly society that was more concerned to please and honour God than to engage in corrupt practices to gain human approval.

In societies where the rulers are anti-Christian or pagan, Jesus made an important distinction when He ruled that God's people should give to the secular authorities what belonged to them and to God what belonged to Him (Mark 12:13-17). God is the supreme judge, and all human justice is at best but a pale reflection of His perfect justice. He has given the state responsibilities for enforcing law and order, that good might be rewarded and evil punished (Rom. 13:1-7; 1 Pet. 2:13-14). However, even under one of the best judicial systems of the time, Jesus was denied justice and so committed Himself to Him who judges justly. Christians, innocent of accusations made by their enemies, are not guaranteed fair trials in this world but they have a Saviour who is the perfect example to follow (1 Pet. 2:18-25).

In the Christian church, believers are not perfect and so provision is made for truth to be ascertained and offenders called to book or to be disciplined (Matt. 18:15-17; 1 Cor. 1:1-11; 1 Tim. 5:21). Christian masters and slaves are also to behave well toward one another, knowing they have a God in heaven who judges impartially (Eph. 6:9).

The cry for justice to be done is universal. Jehoshaphat's desire for God-like justice in His kingdom is but a pointer to the future Davidic ruler and Servant of Yahweh who will truly bring in that perfect justice (Ps. 72:4-5, 12-14; Isa. 11:3-5; 42:1-4). He also is the one appointed to judge the living and the dead (Acts 17:31).

Jehoshaphat's victory over his enemies (20:1-30)
This passage gives an example of what happens when nations who have no fear of Yahweh decide to attack God's anointed king (see 2 Chron. 17:10) and it is full of themes emphasised throughout the book including prayer, worship, Levitical music, a prophetic message, seeking God and dependence on Him. It can be divided in the following way: Jehoshaphat's reaction to the enemy invasion (vv. 1-4); Jehoshaphat's prayer

(vv. 5-13); Jahaziel's oracle and the response (vv. 14-19); and the victory and its effects (vv. 20-30).

> 20:1. Now it was afterwards that the sons of Moab and the sons of Ammon, and with them some from the Ammonites, came against Jehoshaphat for battle. 2. Then some came and reported to Jehoshaphat, saying, 'A great multitude is coming against you from beyond the sea, from Aram and there they are in Hazazon-tamar' (that is En-gedi). 3. And Jehoshaphat was afraid and set his face to seek Yahweh; and proclaimed a fast for all Judah. 4. So Judah gathered together to seek from Yahweh; even from all the cities of Judah they came to seek Yahweh.

Sometime after the events of chapters 18 and 19, Jehoshaphat was faced with an enemy attack from the east and southeast. The Moabites were last mentioned when David gained a notable victory over them (1 Chron. 18:2, 11) and the Ammonites were neighbours to the north of Moab. There was certainly a third group which the Hebrew traditional text associates with the Ammonites, and these are identified in verses 10 and 22-23 as people from Mount Seir, which is generally assumed to be in the area of Edom, south of Judah. The LXX identifies this third contingent as 'Meunites' (see 1 Chron. 4:41; 2 Chron. 26:7; Ezra 2:50; Neh. 7:52), who are thought to be a nomadic group on the southern borders of Judah. It seems clear that the Chronicler considered this third group to be distinct from the Edomites who were at this time subject to Jehoshaphat (see 1 Kings 22:47[48]; 2 Kings 8:20-22). The Aramaic Targum reads 'Edomites who had joined themselves to the Ammonites'. All three groups, Ammon, Moab and those associated with Mount Seir who were supporting Ammon, attacked from the Transjordan region, from across the 'sea', that is, the Dead Sea. En-gedi lies midway along the western shore of the Salt Sea. In the only other reference in the Bible to Hazazon-tamar, it is again the site of military conflict in the Dead Sea area (see Gen. 14:7). It is not unlikely that Aram (v. 2)[24] had some influence over these Transjordan peoples to incite them to rise up against Judah.

---

24. Edom is almost universally suggested as a more likely reading from the context than a reference to Aram. In the Hebrew consonantal text, *resh* (r) *'rm* (Aram) is similar to *daleth* (d) *'dm* (Edom) and this confusion of letters occurs in other parts of the Old Testament as well. Williamson, *1 and 2 Chronicles*, p. 294, prefers the MT text.

Having set the scene, the Chronicler is concerned to present Jehoshaphat's reaction to these hordes who had invaded his kingdom (v. 3). First, his fear at the situation is noted, a not unnatural response when faced with enemies from north, south and east. But instead of immediately summoning his army to attack, Jehoshaphat set himself 'to seek (*dr*š) Yahweh'. This is the kind of response the Chronicler wished his readers to appreciate (see 2 Chron. 17:4; 19:3). Proclaiming a 'fast' (see 1 Chron. 10:12 for the only other observance of a fast in Chronicles) indicated the serious nature of the situation and the king's earnestness and utter dependence on God. Fasts are recorded elsewhere in the Bible especially in association with repentance and in times of deep trouble and need (1 Sam. 7:6; Joel 2:12-17; Zech. 8:19; Ezra 8:23; Neh. 1:4; Esther 4:16; Dan. 9:3). The only fast or self-affliction mentioned in the Mosaic law was the one connected with the Day of Atonement (Lev. 16:29, 31).

The people acted appropriately by assembling together to 'seek' help from Yahweh (v. 4, where the verb *bqš* is used twice as a synonym of *dr*š). It was the kind of religious gathering and united action witnessed in the days of David where 'all' participated (vv. 4, 13, 15, 18; see 1 Chron. 11:1-3; 13:2; 15-16; 2 Chron. 5). In this, Jehoshaphat and his people responded according to God's directive to Solomon, where the same verb for 'to seek' (*bqš*) is employed (2 Chron. 7:14).

20:5. Then Jehoshaphat stood in the assembly of Judah and Jerusalem, in the house of Yahweh before the new court, 6. and he said, 'Yahweh, the God of our fathers, are you not God in the heavens? And do you not rule over all the kingdoms of the nations? Also power and might are in your hand so that no one can withstand you. 7. Did you not, our God, drive out the inhabitants of this land before your people Israel, and give it forever to the seed of Abraham, your friend? 8. And they lived in it and have built for you in it a sanctuary for your name, saying, 9. "If evil come upon us, sword, judgment or pestilence or famine, we will stand before this house and before you, for your name is in this house, and we will cry to you in our distress and you will hear and save." 10. And now, here are the sons of Ammon and Moab and Mount Seir, whom you did not let Israel to enter when they came out of the land of Egypt, but they turned aside from them and did not destroy them. 11.

But here they are repaying us by coming to drive us out from your possession which you have given us to possess! 12. Our God, will you not judge them? For we are powerless before this great multitude that is coming against us, and we do not know what we should do, but our eyes are on you.' 13. And all Judah was standing before Yahweh, also their infants, their wives and their sons.

Again, the unity of the assembled company is emphasised with this reference to 'Judah and Jerusalem' (v. 5; see vv. 15, 17, 18, 20, 27). Jehoshaphat stood with his people in that part of the temple where the people were allowed to gather, the 'new court' being perhaps the post-exilic second temple term for Solomon's 'great court (2 Chron. 4:9). The situation which led to this prayer being offered was exactly the kind Solomon had in mind in his dedicatory prayer (2 Chron. 6:12-40). As for the prayer, it takes the form of a national lament, such as we find in the Psalter (see Ps. 44). It begins with invocation and a confession of faith (v. 6) and is followed by a recital of past blessings (v. 7) and a statement of innocence and trust (vv. 8-9), and closes with the grievance and appeal (10-12).

Jehoshaphat calls on 'the God of our fathers' (v. 6). Similar expressions appear often in this book (1 Chron. 5:25; 12:17; 28:9; 2 Chron. 7:22; 11:16; 13:12, 18; 14:4[3]; 19:4; 24:18, 24; etc.). King David or the early patriarchs like Abraham are usually in mind (1 Chron. 29:10, 18, 20; 2 Chron. 21:12). The rhetorical questions concerning Yahweh's almighty and unique sovereignty expressed both their desperate plight out of which only God could bring them and also their strong belief in all that God had revealed concerning Himself and His promises. Yahweh is the absolute ruler not only in heaven but over all the earthly kingdoms (see v. 29; 2 Chron. 12:8; 17:10) which included those attacking Judah. While they were powerless (see v. 12), God is all-powerful (v. 6b). His prayer echoes the language of David's prayer (1 Chron. 29:10-12).

The king then appealed to Yahweh's promises and actions associated with God's covenant with Abraham concerning the land of promise as a permanent possession and His assurances in the Sinai covenant concerning the conquest of the land (v. 7; Gen. 12:7; Exod. 33:1-2; Deut. 4:37-39; Judg. 11:14-27; Ps. 44:2[3]). Abraham is called God's 'friend' (literally God's 'lover'; Isa. 41:8; James 2:23; see 2 Chron. 19:2). That close intimacy is revealed in Genesis 18:17-19. The king continued by referring to the fact that God's people lived in the land, had built the temple there, and was quick to refer to it as the 'holy place' or 'sanctuary' for Yahweh's 'name' (see 2 Chron. 6:20, 34, 38), and that their present predicament met the kind of condition where earnest prayer for deliverance was to be made (vv. 8-9; 2 Chron. 6:28-31). Also in mind was the assurance that God would hear such cries and act on behalf of His people (2 Chron. 7:12-14).

Unlike so many of the situations described in Solomon's prayer, there is no mention of any particular sin having been committed that had led to this emergency. The king's prayer on this occasion is more like other laments in the Psalter which protest the suppliant's innocence (Ps. 44) and that go on to express the details of the complaint (vv. 10-11). Despite the fact that Israel had spared the Transjordanian nations, these were the very people who were now repaying such kindness by invading Judah and threatening to deprive Israel of its inheritance. Moab and Ammon were descendants of Lot, Abraham's nephew, while Seir had been given by Yahweh to Esau, Jacob's brother (Gen. 19:30-38; 25:19-26; Num. 20:14-21; Deut. 2:5, 9, 19). Jehoshaphat legitimately drew God into the argument by not only pointing out that the nations were spared on Yahweh's orders but that the land from which they were seeking to drive out God's people belonged to Yahweh. It was God's 'possession' which He had given to Israel as a gift to possess (v. 11; Lev. 25:23-24; Deut. 11:31; 12:1; etc.).

The king's impassioned plea reaches its climax in verse 12 with the call for Yahweh to judge these nations. Only He could right the injustice. Acknowledging God's covenant with Israel, he appealed to Yahweh as 'our God', recognising their own weakness and inability and confirming that their trust was in God. The prayer is similar to Asa's forceful plea (2 Chron. 14:11[10]) and the phrase 'our eyes are upon you' recalls the psalmist's words in Psalm 123:2. Verse 13 describes in a powerful way the desperate nature of the situation and the utter dependence of the people upon God. Not only did the congregation consist of the male members of the kingdom, but it included their little ones, their wives and sons (see

2 Chron. 31:18; Ezra 10:1; Neh. 8:2-3). This made the occasion even more poignant as king and people stood before Yahweh. For the Chronicler, the concluding words of the paragraph concerning all Judah 'standing' before Yahweh (v. 13) provided a fitting end to what began with the king standing in the congregation before the new court of the temple (v. 5).

Application

The prayer is an example of humble submission to the Lord in testing times. In desperate situations, the people of God must look in faith to the living God and wait patiently for Him. It is very often the case that God brings His people to the position where, becoming aware of their utter inability to do anything, they have been thrown completely on God for help. The disciples were brought to see this when they were powerless to help a father in his distress over his son (Mark 9:28-29).

> 20:14. Now upon Jahaziel the son of Zechariah, the son of Benaiah, the son of Jeiel, the son of Mattaniah, the Levite of the sons of Asaph, the Spirit of Yahweh came in the middle of the assembly, 15. and he said, 'Listen, all Judah and the inhabitants of Jerusalem and king Jehoshaphat. Thus says Yahweh to you, Do not fear or be dismayed because of this great multitude, for the battle is not yours but God's. 16. Tomorrow go down against them. There they are, coming up at the ascent of Ziz, and you will find them at the end of the wadi in front of the wilderness of Jeruel. 17. You will not fight in this; station yourselves, stand and see the salvation of Yahweh on your behalf, Judah and Jerusalem. Do not fear or be dismayed; tomorrow go out to face them for Yahweh is with you.' 18. And Jehoshaphat bowed face to the ground and all Judah and the inhabitants of Jerusalem fell down before Yahweh, to worship before Yahweh. 19. And the Levites from the sons of the Kohathites and of the sons of the Korahites, stood up to praise Yahweh the God of Israel, with an exceedingly loud voice.

Yahweh responded by giving a prophetic message through a Levite belonging to the line of Asaph. It seems it was not uncommon for oracles of salvation to be received when prayers of lament were offered (see Ps. 60:6). What is unusual is the emphasis on the prophet's family background. The linear genealogy of Jahaziel is traced back four or five generations to the David–Solomon era (see 1 Chron. 9:15; 15:17-18, 21; 16:5). Prominence is also given to this Levite through placing his name at the head of the Hebrew sentence. Unlike the Levitical prophesying that involved singing praises to God with musical instruments (vv. 19, 21-22; 1 Chron. 25:1-6), this was similar to the prophecies given by recognised prophets such as Nathan and Isaiah where messages were received from God for king and people to hear. Jahaziel was endowed with the Spirit of Yahweh (see 2 Chron. 15:1; 24:20), whereas in 2 Chronicles 18:20-22 lying spirits empowered the false prophets.

The message begins not unlike the kind of encouragement the priests were to deliver to the people before they went out to battle against their enemies (Deut. 20:1-4). Following the Levite's call for king and people to pay attention (see 2 Chron. 13:4), the divine communication is introduced with the familiar prophetic messenger formula, 'Thus says Yahweh' (see Amos 1:3, 6, etc.). The command not to fear and its accompanying words of comfort and preparation for battle are reminiscent of Moses' speech to the people at the Red Sea (Exod. 14:13-14; see Isa. 41:10-13 and 1 Chron. 22:13; 28:20). David also confronted Goliath in the certainty that 'the battle is Yahweh's' (1 Sam. 17:47). In answer to Jehoshaphat's confession that they were at a loss what to do (v. 12), Jahaziel instructs them on the battle strategy which is backed up by another word of encouragement (v. 16-17). There is no certainty about the precise location of the confrontation, but Ziz may lie somewhere along the descent from Tekoa to En-gedi, about fifteen miles (twenty kilometres) south of Jerusalem (see vv. 2, 20). The plan, according to one commentator, turns out to be an occasion where 'Israel has only to take her place in the spectator's gallery!'[25] Well, not quite. They do participate in that they are required to find the enemy, to go out to face them as if to engage them in battle and position themselves (v. 17). The whole oracle is framed with the exhortation not to fear and the encouragement of Yahweh's presence (vv. 15, 17).

The response of king and 'all' his people following the message of assurance was both an act of worship and

25. Selman, *2 Chronicles*, p. 426.

an indication that they accepted the oracle (vv. 18-19; see Exod. 4:31; 1 Chron. 29:20). It was given to the Levitical musicians, as David had appointed, to lead in enthusiastic joyful praise to God (see 1 Chron. 25:1-7). The Korahites were a subdivision of the wider branch of Kohathites, Korah being a grandson of Kohath (1 Chron. 6:22, 33-38; see Exod. 6:16-24). It is possible that the Chronicler was seeking to be more specific by his reference to the Korahites, so that instead of two groups of Levites as the conjunction 'and' suggests, it would be better to translate as 'even' or 'that is': 'even the Korahites.' The main duty of the Korahites seems to have been as temple gatekeepers, but as a number of the Psalm titles suggests, some were also singers and musicians (1 Chron. 9:19; 26:1; Pss. 42–49; 84; 85; 87; 88).

> 20:20. And they rose early in the morning and went out to the wilderness of Tekoa; and when they went out, Jehoshaphat stood and said, 'Listen to me, Judah and inhabitants of Jerusalem, trust in Yahweh your God and you will be established; trust in his prophets and you will succeed.' 21. And when he had consulted with the people, he then appointed those who were to sing to Yahweh and those who were to praise for holy splendour when they went out before the army and they said, 'Give thanks to Yahweh, for his steadfast love is forever.' 22. And at the time they began with a joyful cry of praise, Yahweh set ambushes against the sons of Ammon, Moab, and Mount Seir, who were coming against Judah; so they were struck down. 23. And the sons of Ammon and Moab stood up against the inhabitants of Mount Seir to exterminate and destroy, and when they had put an end to the inhabitants of Seir, they helped to destroy one another. 24. When Judah came to the wilderness lookout, they turned toward the multitude; and there they were, corpses fallen to the ground and no one had escaped. 25. And when Jehoshaphat and his people came to take their plunder, they found much among them: goods, corpses, and precious utensils and they took for themselves until they could carry no more. And they were three days taking the plunder because there was much. 26. Then on the fourth day they assembled in the valley of Beracah, for there they blessed Yahweh. Therefore they call the name of that place the Valley of Beracah until today. 27. And every man of Judah and Jerusalem returned and Jehoshaphat at their head, to return to Jerusalem with joy, for Yahweh had

made them to rejoice over their enemies. 28. And they came to Jerusalem with harps and lyres and trumpets to the house of Yahweh. 29. And the dread of God was on all the kingdoms of the lands when they heard that Yahweh had fought against the enemies of Israel. 30. So the kingdom of Jehoshaphat was quiet, for his God gave him rest all around.

They made an early start and when they reached the appointed place Jehoshaphat himself addressed his people with a mini sermon, similar to the stirring words of the priest before Israel went into battle (Deut. 20:1-4). There are a number of occasions where the Chronicler records speeches prior to a battle (1 Chron. 19:12-13; 2 Chron. 13:4-12; 25:7-9; 32:7-8). This address bears close resemblance to a couplet in Isaiah's message to king Ahaz except that the prophet's words to the king are stated negatively – 'If you will not trust then you will not be established' (Isa. 7:9) – whereas king Jehoshaphat's message to the people is stated positively – 'trust … and you will be established' (v. 20). Resemblance, however, does not mean dependence on Isaiah's words as some scholars maintain. King Ahaz is six kings later than Jehoshaphat. It is more likely that similar wording and phraseology developed quite naturally over time among the true prophets of Yahweh. Both 'trust' and 'established' are from the same Hebrew verb and indicate even more the close correlation between the people's faith in God and their being firmly established. Their secure state would be the result of their firm faith.

The second part of the couplet indicates that the people would 'succeed' or 'prosper' if they trusted the prophetic word. The verb 'prosper' is another of the Chronicler's favourite terms (1 Chron. 22:11, 13; 29:23; 2 Chron. 7:11; etc.). It should not be thought surprising that the words of Yahweh's true prophets are put on a par with Yahweh Himself. They were spokesmen for Yahweh and spoke under the influence of God's Spirit. The Chronicler shows how refusal to believe Yahweh's prophets had disastrous consequences, while obedience to God's word through His prophets brought success (2 Chron. 26:5; 36:15-16). Yahweh's true prophets follow in the tradition of Moses and the Sinai covenant legislation with its blessings for obedience and curses for disobedience (see Exod. 14:31).

As David consulted the people before bringing the ark to Jerusalem, so Jehoshaphat included the people in his decision-making (v. 21; 1 Chron. 13:1). One scholar speaks of a 'thread of democratization' that runs through Chronicles.[26] The people are partners with the king and all feel something of the weight of responsibility. In this crucial situation there was unity of purpose and action. Singers, presumably from among the Levitical musicians, were then appointed to accompany Jehoshaphat and his army to the front line to face the foe. They were to praise Yahweh and the phrase 'holy splendour' probably relates to the majesty of God's holiness. The alternative translation, 'in holy attire', is less convincing as there is no reference to any holy garments worn by the Levitical singers (see 1 Chron. 16:29; Pss. 29:2; 96:6-9). Their song was the substance of a refrain that often appears in Chronicles and the Psalter (1 Chron. 16:34, 41; 2 Chron. 5:13; 7:3, 6; Pss. 106:1; 118:1, 29; 136:1). It expressed their trust in Yahweh.

No sooner had they begun to sing and praise their God for His faithful love than He acted to give them victory (v. 22). It is not entirely clear by what means the enemy was at first ambushed which then led to the defeat. The unusual form of the word translated 'ambushes', literally 'ones lying in wait', may well suggest a supernatural army of angelic beings was involved (see 1 Chron. 14:15). After the initial consternation and panic that would have ensued, the Chronicler records how the enemy was finally defeated by self-destruction, without the involvement of God's people. Previous examples of self-destruction are recorded in Judges 7:22; 1 Samuel 14:20; and 2 Kings 3:23. First, the Ammonites and Moab attacked the inhabitants of Seir and destroyed them by devoting them to destruction ('exterminate,' v. 23), as Israel had been directed to do to the Canaanites (Deut. 2:34; Josh. 2:10; 10:28; etc.). Then the Ammonite and Moabite soldiers helped to destroy themselves by killing each other.

From a notable vantage point ('watchtower') in the wilderness, Judah's army saw not a 'great multitude' (vv. 2, 12, 15) but a 'multitude' of dead bodies with no survivors (v. 24; see 2 Kings 19:35). All that was left for them to do was to pick up

---

26. Japhet, *I & II Chronicles*, p. 47.

the spoil which was so great that it took three days to complete. The following day they lost no time in acknowledging who deserved the credit for the enemy's total defeat. Jehoshaphat and his army 'blessed' or 'bowed the knee in worship to' Yahweh (v. 26). The valley was thereafter renamed the 'Valley of Beracah' (blessing), or its name was given a fresh association through this incident. In the place where God had 'blessed' His people by giving victory to them, they in turn 'blessed' or 'paid homage' as an expression of their appreciation. They 'assembled' in a communal act of worship, and this was followed by a victory parade led by the king back to Jerusalem and the temple where Jehoshaphat had first prayed to Yahweh and had received the message of salvation (vv. 27-28; see vv. 5-19). The 'joy' of the occasion was due to Yahweh having granted them this joy and the musical instruments helped to express their enthusiasm and relief (see 1 Chron. 15:25, 28). No cymbals were used on this occasion. The divine gift of joy is also found in the post-exilic period (Ezra 6:22; Neh. 12:43).

The whole war narrative ends by noting its effects both nationally and internationally. Verse 29 is almost a repetition of what is said near the introduction to Jehoshaphat's reign (2 Chron. 17:10), where it is stated that the fear of God fell on the neighbouring kingdoms so that they did not attack the Judean kingdom. The intervening material has related how the king showed weakness and lack of faith in Yahweh through his alliance with Ahab (18:1-19:3). Despite his subsequent reforms within Judah that witnessed to Jehoshaphat's continued trust in Yahweh (19:4-11), the surrounding nations had no longer possessed that same fear of God and His anointed king. However, as a result of this episode against the Transjordanian alliance, 'all the kingdoms of the lands' (1 Chron. 29:30; 2 Chron. 36:23) feared God once more. Yahweh's reputation and, by implication, that of His king were restored to the state that existed before Jehoshaphat's disastrous alliance with the northern kingdom of Israel. The kingdom of Judah was again quiet and at rest with no battles to wage against foreign nations. It is emphasised that these peaceful conditions were due to God. Rest is one of the indications of Yahweh's blessing as was seen under the reigns of Solomon and Asa (1 Chron. 22:9; 2 Chron. 14:4-5[5-6]). The Chronicler demonstrates how on a number of occasions faithful reliance on God causes foreign nations to fear both Yahweh and His king and to cease waging war on God's people (1 Chron. 14:17; 2 Chron. 14:14[13]; 26:8).

Application

The messages of the true prophets of God were delivered by divine inspiration so that to trust God meant also trusting what God had spoken through His prophets. Likewise, for the Christian, the written words of the apostles and the evangelists associated with them are as authoritative as the words of Jesus recorded in the Bible. The Hebrew Scriptures were to become as important as prayer for the Jews living in the intertestamental period. Jesus and the apostles used the Holy Writings which Christians call the Old Testament as God's authoritative and infallible written word (Matt. 5:17-18; 7:12; Luke 24:27, 44-46; John 5:39; Rom. 15:4; 2 Tim. 3:15-17; 2 Pet. 1:20-21).

Our prayer, like that of Isaiah's, should be that God would rend the heavens and come down that the nations might tremble at His presence (Isa. 64:1-4).

Concluding remarks to Jehoshaphat's reign (20:31–21:1)
This short section first presents a summary of Jehoshaphat's reign (vv. 31-34), gives another example of the king's close ties with the apostate northern kingdom with disastrous results (vv. 35-37), and closes with Jehoshaphat's death (21:1).

> 20:31. So Jehoshaphat reigned over Judah. He was thirty-five years old when he began to reign, and he reigned in Jerusalem twenty-five years. And his mother's name was Azubah the daughter of Shilhi. 32. And he walked in the way of his father Asa and did not turn from it, doing right in the sight of Yahweh. 33. However, the high places were not removed; the people had not yet set their hearts to the God of their fathers. 34. Now the rest of the acts of Jehoshaphat, first and last, there they are written in the words of Jehu the son of Hanani, which are taken up in the book of the kings of Israel.

This and the following paragraph find some resemblance to 1 Kings 22:41-50[51] but with some significant differences. No synchronization with Ahab's kingship of Israel is found here. It builds on the summary already given of Jehoshaphat's reign

in 2 Chronicles 17:3 and again compares him with his father
Asa. However, the Chronicler does not state that he followed
in 'all' things, on account of the negative aspects of Asa's reign
in 2 Chronicles 16. The apparent contradiction concerning
the king's removal of the 'high places' (2 Chron. 17:6) and the
statement here that he did not remove them (v. 33) would seem
to be due to the people's persistence in following old traditions
rather than being truly devoted to Yahweh. In the same way,
Jehoshaphat sought to remove the 'high places' even though
his father is said to have removed them (2 Chron. 14:3, 5; 15:17).
Unlike their king's commitment to seek God (2 Chron. 19:3), the
people had still not fixed their hearts on God. With the best
will in the world central government cannot change people's
hearts. For further information, the Chronicler directs his
readers to a written account by the prophet Jehu, the son of
Hanani (see 2 Chron. 16:7; 19:2-3), which is to be found in the
larger work concerning the 'kings of Israel' (v. 34). Interestingly,
in 1 Kings 22:45 this source is called 'the chronicles of the kings
of Judah'. For the Chronicler the kingdom of Judah is again
viewed as the true Israel (see 2 Chron. 16:11; 27:7).

> 20:35. And after this Jehoshaphat king of Judah joined himself
> with Ahaziah king of Israel who acted to do wickedly. 36. So he
> joined himself with him to make ships to go to Tarshish, and
> they made the ships in Ezion-geber. 37. Then Eliezer the son
> of Dodavahu from Mareshah prophesied against Jehoshaphat
> saying, 'Because you have joined yourself with Ahaziah,
> Yahweh has broken up your works.' So the ships were broken
> in pieces, and they were not able to go to Tarshish.
> 21:1. And Jehoshaphat slept with his fathers and was buried
> with his fathers in the city of David, and Jehoram his son reigned
> in his place.

In this final paragraph, the Chronicler includes a shortened and
apparently different version of what is found in 1 Kings 22:44,
48-50. While no mention is made of the extermination of the
male cult prostitutes or of conditions in Edom, Jehoshaphat's
relations with Ahaziah the son of Ahab are recorded and,
as in Kings, appear just before the account of Jehoshaphat's
death. The text in Kings, however, only briefly recounts how
the ships were broken up at Ezion-geber, whereas Chronicles
gives more details of why they were destroyed.

Jehoshaphat was the first Judean king to make a peace settlement with the northern kingdom of Israel as 1 Kings 22:44 suggests and it was to have devastating consequences after his death. Chronicles has already noted that the Judean king had 'allied himself by marriage' to Ahab (ḥtn, 2 Chron. 18:1). A similar intensive reflexive verb, 'to join oneself,' occurs here three times (ḥbr, vv. 35-37) in connection with Ahab's son, Ahaziah, to draw attention to the continuing ill-judged close relationship with the north. In addition, Ahaziah is morally no better than his father, for they both acted 'wickedly' (v. 35; 2 Chron. 19:2). With help from Ahaziah, Jehoshaphat built ships at Ezion-geber on the Gulf of Aqaba that were capable of going as far as Tarshish, possibly a sea-port on the Spanish coast (v. 36; Jonah 1:3, but see 2 Chronicles 9:21). However, these vessels were broken to pieces before they even set sail (v. 37b). This outcome was predicted by an otherwise unknown prophet, Eliezer, who made clear that it was a judgment from Yahweh. The prophet was from Mareshah (see 1 Chron. 2:42; 4:21; 2 Chron. 11:7-9; 14:9-15[8-14]). The verb translated 'broken in pieces' is one of the Chronicler's favourite terms and with God as the subject suggests that His wrath brought about an end to sinful human schemes (see 1 Chron. 13:11; 14:11; 15:13). As Matthew Henry suggests, Kings picks up where Chronicles ends by indicating that Jehoshaphat had learnt his lesson so that when the northern king suggested a further attempt, the Judean king declined.

Cooperating with the head of another kingdom was not considered an act of infidelity. Solomon's maritime ventures were undertaken with the help of Hiram, and this Phoenician king had previously been of considerable assistance to David and Solomon in the construction of Yahweh's temple (1 Chron. 14:1; 2 Chron. 2:3-16; 4:11-16; 8:17-18). What was wrong with this commercial enterprise was that it involved collaborating with the head of a breakaway, apostate kingdom whose head was guilty of flagrant breaking of God's covenant.

The account of Jehoshaphat's reign ends with the familiar formula (see 2 Chron. 9:31; 12:16; 14:1[13:23]). It also serves to begin the reign of his son, Jehoram. It parallels exactly the statement in 1 Kings 22:50[51] except for the omission of 'his father' after David.

Application

The alliance between Jehoshaphat and Ahaziah and its outcome would have spoken powerfully to the post-exilic people. It underlined what Ezra and Nehemiah had been seeking to impress upon their people, namely, how contrary to the will of God was their joining in marriage with those who practised abominable acts (Ezra 9:13-14). To be unequally joined to unbelievers, to those who worship other gods, is to court disaster (2 Cor. 6:14-18; Rev. 18:4).

Genealogical Table of the House of David during the Omri and Jehu Dynasties

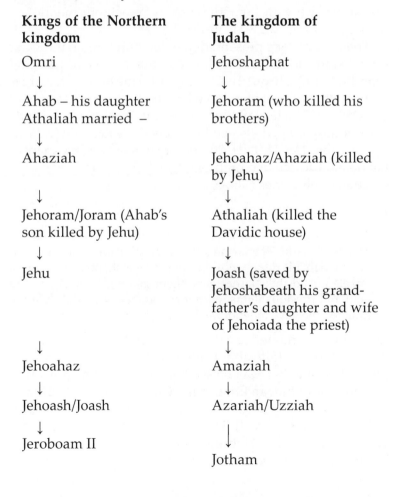

Kings of the Northern kingdom	The kingdom of Judah
Omri	Jehoshaphat
↓	↓
Ahab – his daughter Athaliah married –	Jehoram (who killed his brothers)
↓	↓
Ahaziah	Jehoahaz/Ahaziah (killed by Jehu)
↓	↓
Jehoram/Joram (Ahab's son killed by Jehu)	Athaliah (killed the Davidic house)
↓	↓
Jehu	Joash (saved by Jehoshabeath his grandfather's daughter and wife of Jehoiada the priest)
↓	↓
Jehoahaz	Amaziah
↓	↓
Jehoash/Joash	Azariah/Uzziah
↓	↓
Jeroboam II	Jotham

Jehoram's reign (21:2-20)

All three monarchs who reigned after Jehoshaphat belonged by marriage to the Omri dynasty that ruled in the north and to which the Chronicler refers as the 'house of Ahab' (21:6, 13; 22:3, 4, 7, 8). The alliance with Ahab, Omri's son, not only tarnished Jehoshaphat's reign, but it also brought into the Judean kingdom the kind of internal troubles that were often a feature of the north, and it resulted in a very real threat to the Davidic dynasty. In comparison to the brief account of Jehoram's reign in 2 Kings 8:16-24, where he is also known as Joram, the Chronicler gives much more information, although the overall narrative is far shorter than for his father. Elijah's letter is placed in a central position in the narrative (vv. 12-15) with reports of rebellions mentioned before and after (vv. 8-11, 16-17).

The Chronicler's presentation of Jehoram's reign indicates how he undid all the achievements of his father and grandfather (2 Chron. 21:12b). He lost control of those areas to the south and east of Judah where they had been successful (vv. 8-10), and instead of Philistines and Arabs paying tribute to the Judean king, they rebelled under his leadership (v. 16-17; see 2 Chron. 14:9-14; 17:11; 20). Whereas Asa and Jehoshaphat had sought to remove high places, Jehoram encouraged the erection of new ones (14:2-5; 17:6).

Jehoram's accession (21:2-3)

21:2. And he had brothers, the sons of Jehoshaphat: Azariah and Jehiel and Zechariah and Azaryahu and Michael and Shephatiah; all these were the sons of Jehoshaphat the king of Israel. 3. And their father gave them many gifts of silver and gold and precious items, with fortified cities in Judah; but the kingdom he gave to Jehoram, because he was the firstborn.

Jehoram was named as the successor to Jehoshaphat in verse 1. More details about this heir to the throne are now given. Jehoshaphat was blessed with seven sons (for other named sons of Judean kings, see 2 Chron. 11:18-22; 13:21) and interestingly, he is described as the 'king of Israel' (see also 'officials of Israel' in v. 4). This is not a mistake as the ancient versions and some Hebrew manuscripts have assumed, but it is one of at least ten instances that clearly reveal the

Chronicler's desire to emphasise that the Judean kingdom is the Israel that has remained true to the Israel of David's time (see 2 Chron. 12:6; 28:19, 23, 27). For the post-exilic people of God it was important to show that the Jews were the true successors of the united Israel. Like Rehoboam, Jehoshaphat had provided his many sons with provisions and fortified cities, but the firstborn was appointed as king (2 Chron. 11:5-12, 18-23).

Jehoram's atrocities and Yahweh's faithfulness (21:4-7)

> 21:4. Now when Jehoram was raised over the kingdom of his father, he strengthened himself and killed all his brothers with the sword and also some of the officials of Israel. 5. Jehoram was thirty-two years old when he became king and he reigned eight years in Jerusalem. 6. And he walked in the way of the kings of Israel, as the house of Ahab had done, for the daughter of Ahab was his wife; and he did evil in the sight of Yahweh. 7. Yet Yahweh was not willing to destroy the house of David, on account of the covenant that he had made with David and since he had promised to give a lamp to him and to his sons for ever.

Previous Davidic monarchs had 'strengthened' themselves (2 Chron. 1:1; 12:13; 13:21; 17:1), but only Jehoram felt the need to remove all possible rivals to the throne, and in such a violent way. It was typical of northern rulers to do this (v. 6; see 1 Kings 15:29; 16:11-12) and of pagan kings who possessed no fear of God and lacked respect for human life (see Judg. 9:5, 56). From the start, Jehoram is shown to be the evil king that he was. He is the first Davidic monarch to be charged by the Chronicler as having done evil in Yahweh's sight (v. 6).

The Chronicler frames the rest of the account by noting the king's age when he became king and the length of his reign (vv. 5, 20a). As in the text of 2 Kings 8:17-19, there follows a theological evaluation of his kingship. It is assumed that the history of the northern kingdom is known from reading Kings. Nothing worse could be said about a southern king than to be compared with the kings of northern Israel and especially with Ahab, whom the book of Kings regards as having done more evil than all before him (1 Kings 16:30-33). The influence of his wife, Ahab's daughter, is reckoned to be the reason for this assessment, not in order to excuse Jehoram but to indicate the effects of a marriage with apostates who had introduced Tyrian Baal worship into Israel. While Kings states that Yahweh was not willing to destroy 'Judah', Chronicles has 'house of David', and in place of 'for the sake of David', reference is made explicitly to the Davidic 'covenant' (v. 7). God's special promise to David and his descendants which was first mentioned in 1 Chronicles 17:4-14 was referred to as a 'covenant of salt' (2 Chron. 13:5) when Judah and the Davidic king were under threat from the north. Here again it is underlined. Though Yahweh indicated that He would discipline kings who were unfaithful (2 Sam. 7:14, but not included in 1 Chron. 17), He was committed for ever to the Davidic covenant (see 2 Sam. 23:5; Isa. 55:3; Jer. 33:21; Pss. 89; 132:11-12). As a 'lamp' (nîr) continues to shine in the darkest of places so the Davidic light in the sense of 'lineage' would not be snuffed out. Some scholars have understood the Hebrew word to mean 'yoke' rather than 'lamp' and given it, in this context, the metaphorical meaning of 'dominion',[27] but the arguments are weak, and the traditional meaning has strong support in other Ancient Near Eastern languages and the ancient versions and interpreters (see 1 Kings 11:36; 15:4; 2 Kings 8:19; Prov. 21:4). The more common word for 'lamp' (nēr), from the same Hebrew root (nwr), is also used figuratively for David as the 'lamp of Israel', meaning that the prosperity of Israel was embodied in him (2 Sam. 21:17; see also Ps. 132:17).[28] Jehoram and his son who succeeded him on the throne were ripe for judgment but God's covenant with David saved the dynastic line from disappearing altogether as the following chapters will reveal.

Application

This was an encouragement to the first readers to look forward to the Davidic king. In the light of the coming of the Son of God, all these promises of God concerning David have found their affirmative in Him (2 Cor. 1:19-20). The Lord God gave to Him 'the throne of his father David' (Luke 1:31-33).

---

27. See Pratt, *1 and 2 Chronicles*, p. 352.

28. See Deuk-Il Shin, 'The Translation of the Hebrew Term Nīr: "David's Yoke?"', *Tyndale Bulletin* 67.1 (2016), pp. 7-21.

Edom and Libnah rebel (21:8-11)

21:8. In his days Edom revolted from under the hand of Judah and set up a king to rule over themselves. 9. Then Jehoram passed over with his commanders and all the chariots with him and it happened he arose by night and struck Edom who had surrounded him and the chariot commanders. 10. So Edom revolted from under the hand of Judah until this day. Then Libnah at that time revolted from under his power because he had forsaken Yahweh the God of his fathers. 11. He also made high places in the mountains of Judah and caused the inhabitants of Jerusalem to commit prostitution and made Judah go astray.

This paragraph highlights the revolt of Edom on the southeastern border and Libnah in the southwest region of Judah near Philistine territory (Josh. 10:29-30; 12:15; 15:42; 1 Chron. 6:57[42]). These rebellions are seen as the beginning of divine discipline for Jehoram's unfaithfulness. Edom seems to have been subservient to Judah during Jehoshaphat's reign (2 Kings 3:9, 12, 26), but they asserted their independence especially as they had a king instead of a deputy (v. 8; 1 Kings 22:47[48]). The Chronicler reports the night attack that Jehoram and his men made on the Edomites who had surrounded them (v. 9), and that Edom had remained in revolt through to the Chronicler's times (v.10a), but no mention is made that Judah only narrowly escaped in the battle (2 Kings 8:21).

What is implicit in the Edomite revolt against the power of Judah ('from under the hand of Judah') is made explicit in Libnah's revolt (v. 10b). It was because Jehoram had 'forsaken' or abandoned Yahweh 'the God of his fathers' that they had rebelled, a reason not mentioned in the text of Kings. The language is typical of the Chronicler (see 2 Chron. 12:1; 15:2). To stress that it was on account of Jehoram's infidelity that divine judgment had occurred, the Chronicler adds further evidence of his sins (v. 11). While Jehoshaphat and Asa had sought to remove 'high places', Jehoram became the first Davidic king that the Chronicler mentions who erected 'high places' and these would have been far more syncretistic than those that his father and grandfather had failed to remove. Walking in the way of the kings of the north meant following

Jeroboam who, as the earlier history emphasised, first made Israel to sin (1 Kings 15:26, 34; etc.). The term 'prostitution' is used metaphorically for spiritual unfaithfulness. Judah had been encouraged to worship false gods. Israel was seen as God's bride and Yahweh is described as like a jealous husband (Exod. 34:14; Hosea 1:2-7).

Elijah's prophetic letter (21:12-15)

21:12. And a letter came to him from Elijah the prophet, saying 'Thus says Yahweh the God of your father David: Because you have not walked in the ways of Jehoshaphat your father, or in the ways of Asa the king of Judah, 13. but have walked in the way of the kings of Israel and have caused Judah and the inhabitants of Jerusalem to commit prostitution as the house of Ahab caused prostitution, and also have killed your brothers, of your father's house, who were better than yourself, 14. Yahweh will indeed strike with a great plague your people, and your sons and your wives and all your possessions. 15. And you will be with many illnesses, with an illness of your bowels until your bowels come out day after day from the illness.'

The prophetic compiler of Kings reveals the significance of the prophet Elijah during the time that Ahab and his sons ruled the northern kingdom (1 Kings 17-19; 2 Kings 1-2). None of this is recorded by the Chronicler. In its place, he introduces correspondence that Elijah had with Ahab's son-in-law, Jehoram of Judah. This letter is a prophetic word, similar to those unique messages that the Chronicler often includes (2 Chron. 13:4-12; 15:1-7; 16:7-9). Elijah must have sent his letter shortly before his ascension. As Jehu, a prophet from the north, had been used by God to speak to Jehoshaphat (2 Chron. 19:2), so the most powerful of Yahweh's prophets in the north was used to deliver this message of doom to Jehoshaphat's son. The prophetic word begins with the familiar messenger formula, 'Thus says Yahweh' (v. 12). Jehoram, the one who by his actions seemed more at home with the house of Ahab than the house of David, is reminded that Yahweh is the God of his father David (see 1 Chron. 28:9). The following accusation highlighted the close affiliation that the Judean king had with the north. Instead of adhering to the path set by his father and grandfather who despite failures did seek to be faithful to Yahweh, Jehoram's life and actions indicated that he had abandoned Yahweh to follow the way of the northern kings (v. 12b-13a; see v. 6). More precisely, he had led the whole southern kingdom ('Judah and the inhabitants of Jerusalem'; see 2 Chron. 20:17) into spiritual prostitution (v. 13a; see v. 11). The final indictment concerns the murder of his brothers, who are regarded as better than he (v. 13b; see v. 4). Again, this action was typical of his wife's family who treated human life as cheap and disposable. His brothers are considered better in that they were not guilty of apostasy and murder.

While the accusations looked to what the Chronicler has mentioned in previous verses (vv. 4, 6, 11), the punishments that are threatened in the letter find their fulfilment in the remaining verses of the chapter (vv. 16-20). First, the punishment would involve his people, that is, those near and dear to him. Like a plague, everything belonging to him, including his close family, would be struck. Secondly, he himself would suffer from a severe illness that would affect his bowels (vv. 14-15). As Jehoram had committed fratricide, so the punishment affected his own family as well as himself. Elijah had a similar message of judgment sent to Ahab's son Ahaziah (2 Kings 1). This letter of doom came before the judgment fell on the king. Retribution is often preceded by gracious warnings of impending doom. However, in this instance, we do not read that it humbled Jehoram in any way.

Jehoram's demise (21:16-20)

21:16. And Yahweh stirred up against Jehoram the spirit of the Philistines and of the Arabs who were near the Cushites. 17. And they came up against Judah and invaded it and carried away all the possessions that were found in the king's house and also his sons and his wives, and there was not a son left to him except Jehoahaz, the youngest of his sons. 18. And after all this, Yahweh struck him in his bowels with an illness for which there was no cure. 19. Then it was, in the course of time, and about the time of his demise, for two days his bowels came out because of his illness and he died with horrible illnesses. And his people did not make for him a fire like the fire for his fathers. 20. He was thirty-two years old when he became king, and he reigned eight years in Jerusalem. And he departed with no attractiveness, and they buried him in the city of David but not in the graves of the kings.

The remaining verses indicate the way Elijah's prophecy was fulfilled. First, God used the Philistines and Arabs to punish the king. In 2 Chronicles 17:11 these two groups brought tribute to Jehoshaphat and later Uzziah engaged them in war (2 Chron. 26:6-7). With Libnah having already rebelled against Judah (v. 10), it may have encouraged the Philistines into action as they lived nearby. The Arabs may be either associated with a Cushite bedouin tribe south of Judah or with those south of Egypt (see 2 Chron. 14:12-13). It was probably a king's house in one of the fortified cities that was attacked where Jehoram had placed those members of his family that were captured. The king's wife, Athaliah, and youngest son were probably with Jehoram in Jerusalem and thus escaped the exile. It was this remaining son, referred to as Jehoahaz but better known as Ahaziah, who ascended the throne on the death of his father (v. 17; see 2 Chron. 22:1; 2 Kings 8:25). The God who had 'stirred up' the spirit of these enemies against Jehoram later 'stirred up' the Assyrian king to carry the northerners into exile and later 'stirred' up the spirit of Cyrus to return the Jewish exiles to their land. It was this same God who was to keep His promise to keep a 'lamp' to David (v. 16; see 1 Chron. 5:26; 2 Chron. 36:22-23; 21:7).

The second part of the punishment sees the king brought to his grave in great agony with an incurable illness. Speculations concerning the nature of his bowel complaint abound, but it is impossible to be specific except to say that it was terribly painful and unpleasant. But again, the Chronicler shows that it was Yahweh who struck him. The 'evil' that Jehoram did in the eyes of Yahweh relating to his apostasy and barbarity during his comparatively short life (v. 6) is reflected in the 'evil' or 'horrible illnesses' with which God punished him, leading to the gruesome way he finally died (vv. 18-19). Echoing Elijah's words 'day by day' (v. 15), the word 'day' is repeated three times in verse 19 (*yāmîm*, translated twice as 'time'), with the third occurrence referring to the final couple of days before his death. The Hebrew sentence construction of verse 19a is difficult but the general sense is clear. It reads

literally, 'then it was, to days from days and as the time of
the going out of the end, for two days his bowels came out …
and he died with evil illnesses.' Though in some contexts the
plural word for 'day' can occasionally denote a whole 'year'
(Lev. 25:29; Judg. 17:10; 1 Sam. 1:3; 27:7; etc.), that is not how it
is normally translated despite what is found in the majority
of English versions (see AV, NKJV, NIV, ESV, etc.).

Jehoram's unpopularity is revealed by the fact that he was
not honoured at his funeral with a customary bonfire (v. 19b;
2 Chron. 16:14) and he was not buried in the royal cemetery
(v. 20b). Though he was a descendant of David, his whole
reign set him apart from the Davidic kings who had preceded
him, and this was recognised at the time. As the condition
of his body and manner of his death were repulsive so the
difficult phrase 'with no attractiveness' or 'without desire'
could mean that he himself was considered by the people as
unattractive. Another suggested translation is 'without any
interest' or 'to no one's regret', which perhaps would then
explain why the Chronicler, for the first time, saw no need to
direct readers to other sources.[29]

Application

When the returnees from exile rebuilt the temple and the
walls of Jerusalem, the reference to the Davidic 'lamp'
would have been an encouragement to look with hope to
the re-establishment of the Davidic monarchy (Ps. 132:17), a
hope that was realised in the announcements to Zechariah
and Mary (Luke 1).

The passage is a warning to those who think that they
can unashamedly disregard all the spiritual good they
have received from their parents without suffering any
consequences. What people sow they reap. 'Do not be
deceived: God is not mocked' (Gal. 6:7-8). We can be assured
that in the gravest of situations, God's promises are secure
and though the devil and his minions seem to do their worst
(Rev. 12:17), their end is assured, and the people of God will
triumph (Rom. 8:35-39; 16:20).

29. See Peter Ackroyd, *I & II Chronicles, Ezra, Nehemiah*, Torch Bible
Commentary (London: SCM Press, 1973), p. 155.

Ahaziah's reign (22:1-9)

Ahaziah's reign is recounted briefly and his close links with the northern kingdom are more clearly emphasised than Kings. The Chronicler would have expected his readers to be conversant with the text of Kings so that the apparent problems that exist between the two accounts must have a resolution that rests beyond our present knowledge.

Introduction to Ahaziah's reign (22:1-4)

> 22:1. Then the inhabitants of Jerusalem made Ahaziah his youngest son king in his place, for the marauding band that came with the Arabs to the camp, had killed all the older ones. So Ahaziah the son of Jehoram, the king of Judah, reigned. 2. Ahaziah was forty-two years old when he became king and he reigned one year in Jerusalem and his mother's name was Athaliah, the granddaughter of Omri. 3. He too walked in the ways of the house of Ahab, for his mother was his counsellor to cause him to act wickedly. 4. And he did evil in the sight of Yahweh, like the house of Ahab; for they were his counsellors after the death of his father, to his destruction.

Chronicles parallels the text of 2 Kings 8:24b-27 but with some significant additions. The Chronicler's presentation suggests a close similarity between the situation that existed with the death of Jehoram and the circumstances surrounding Saul's death (1 Chron. 10:6). As it fell to the people of Israel to make David king (1 Chron. 11:10), so it was the people of Jerusalem who appointed Ahaziah king (v. 1). In another crisis situation, the people of Judah made Uzziah king (2 Chron. 26:1; see also 33:25; 36:1). In one sense the inhabitants of Jerusalem had no choice because Jehoram had killed all his brothers and the Arab raiders had not only taken away all Ahaziah's older brothers but had killed them as well, a fact not mentioned in the previous chapter (v. 1; 2 Chron. 21:4, 17).[30]

The reign was short and tragic, and the following verses indicate the reasons. This youngest son is given an age that is practically double what it should be and would make him older than his father who was forty when he died (see 2 Chron. 21:20). It is difficult to account for this even

---

30. As in 2 Chronicles 18:33 the Hebrew word 'camp' or 'host' could be a synonym for 'battle'; see Japhet, *I & II Chronicles*, p. 817 and 2 Samuel 1:2, 3, 4.

as an error in transmission.[31] Judging by the emphasis in Chronicles concerning his mother's influence on his life (see v. 3), it may be, on Matthew Henry's proposition, that the Chronicler is suggesting that this twenty-two-year-old king (see 2 Kings 8:26) who is described as 'forty-two years old' (literally 'a son of forty and two year') is really a son of a mother who is forty-two, taking the idiomatic Hebrew phrase 'son of' in a more literal way. It was the queen mother, Athaliah, a descendant (literally 'daughter') of the Omri dynasty[32] in the north and daughter of Jezebel, who was the brains and power behind the throne and who would eventually usurp the Davidic throne. She had infected both her husband and her son with all the depravity that belonged to the 'house of Ahab' (v. 3). Like his father, Ahaziah 'did evil' in God's sight and again the influence of the Ahab dynasty is highlighted (v. 4). Instead of the Davidic kings influencing the north for good, the north's religious and political policies were meekly accepted by the south and so the north's counsellors became Ahaziah's 'destruction' (v. 4), a word used of the 'destroyer' at the time of the exodus from Egypt (Exod. 12:23).

Ahaziah's downfall and death (22:5-9)

> 22:5. He too walked in their counsel and went with Jehoram the son of Ahab king of Israel to war against Hazael the king of Aram at Ramoth-gilead; and the Arameans wounded Joram. 6. So he returned to Jezreel to recover because of the wounds which struck him at Rama, when he fought against Hazael the king of Aram. And Azariah the son of Jehoram, the king of Judah, went down to see Jehoram the son of Ahab in Jezreel, because he was ill.
> 7. But the downfall of Ahaziah was from God, by coming to Joram, for when he came, he went out with Jehoram to Jehu the son of Nimshi, whom Yahweh had anointed to cut off the house of Ahab. 8. And it happened when Jehu was executing judgment on the house of Ahab, that he found the princes of Judah and the sons of Ahaziah's brothers who served Ahaziah, and he killed them. 9. Then he searched for Ahaziah, and they caught him as he was hiding in Samaria, and brought him to

---

31. 2 Kings 8:26 reads 'twenty-two' and the main LXX texts read 'twenty'.

32. As 'son' can mean 'grandson' or 'descendant' in some contexts, so 'daughter' can mean 'granddaughter' or 'descendant' in this verse (see 2 Chron. 21:6).

Jehu and killed him and buried him, for they said, 'He is the son of Jehoshaphat, who sought Yahweh with all his heart.' And there was no one belonging to the house of Ahaziah to retain the power of the kingdom.

The first two verses find a parallel in 2 Kings 8:28-29 but with significant additions but then the account in Chronicles becomes but a summary of the fuller narrative in 2 Kings 9–10. In Chronicles, the reason is given for Ahaziah's folly in joining Jehoram in military action against the Arameans. Like Jehoshaphat before him ('He too,' v. 5; see v. 3), he followed the advice that came from the 'house of Ahab', no doubt through his mother. This is the third occurrence of the reference to evil counsel (vv. 3-5). Jehoram was a son of Ahab and succeeded his brother Ahaziah as king of Israel. It is very possible that as a result of Jehoshaphat's marriage alliance with Ahab, the descendants of Jehoshaphat who occupied the Davidic throne, Jehoram his son and Ahaziah his grandson, were purposely given the same names as those sons of Ahab who had succeeded him in the northern kingdom. First, Ahaziah reigned in the north for two years and because he had no son, his brother Jehoram/Joram followed him (1 Kings 22:31; 2 Kings 1:17).

Ramoth-gilead was in the territory allotted to Gad and made a city of refuge (1 Chron. 6:80[65]; Deut. 4:41-43). It was a strategic place and the scene of frequent conflicts between Israel and the Arameans. At some point it had been annexed by the Arameans of Damascus and the alliance between Jehoshaphat and Ahab had brought them into a joint venture against the city which resulted in Ahab's death and Jehoshaphat fleeing for his life (2 Chron. 18). The Judean king Ahaziah did not learn from his grandfather's experience because his mind had been made up for him by the northerners so that he meekly followed king Jehoram to battle against the Aramean king Hazael at Ramoth-gilead (v. 5). As in the case of Ahab, his father, Jehoram was severely wounded[33] and headed home to Jezreel, where his father had his winter palace (1 Kings 18:45-46; 21:1). This northern king

---

33. The traditional text lacks an *aleph* at the beginning of the name which might have suggested 'archers' as translated in the LXX, but the pointing assumes that the word meant 'Arameans', as in 2 Kings 8:28 and two Hebrew MSS.

was the brother of Athaliah, the wife of the southern king, so it is understandable that king Ahaziah/Azariah of Judah, having accompanied Jehoram in battle, should now, as a family member, visit him in his Jezreel home (v. 6).[34]

At this point the Chronicler summarises what is recorded in more detail in 2 Kings 9–10 and makes his own assessment of the events. Readers are expected to be conversant with the earlier account, and the apparent differences in Chronicles, such as the chronology of events, are there to draw attention to the divine judgment on the Judean king, Ahaziah. It was ordained by God that Ahaziah should meet his 'downfall'[35] through a sick-visit. Jehu, an officer in Ahab's army at Ramoth-gilead, had been anointed to succeed to the Omri dynasty and to be God's agent in executing judgment on the house of Ahab. As the king of Judah was a puppet of the northern regime he shared its fate at this time, receiving the punishment he deserved.

Ahaziah found his relative much better and accompanied Joram, who is also called Jehoram, in an attempt to meet up with Jehu. The killing of Ahaziah's relatives and officers are mentioned first so as to end with the death and burial of the Judean king. Ahaziah's brothers were killed during the Philistine–Arab attack and now their sons were murdered. Nothing is said about Joram's death for the Chronicler's interest is in what happened to Ahaziah. Jehu searched for the Judean king who fled south from Jezreel to hide in Samaria, but Ahaziah was eventually brought to Jehu who fatally wounded him near Ibleam, according to Kings, a place between Jezreel and Samaria. The Kings account then tells us that he fled by chariot north west to Megiddo where he died. Chronicles does not mention that his body was carried by Ahaziah's servants to Jerusalem where he was buried, only that he was given a decent burial on account of his grandfather's piety.

The Chronicler continues to emphasise the need to seek God with all one's heart (dṛš, 'to seek', v. 9; 2 Chron. 17:3-4;). Ahaziah,

---

34. The MT reads Azariah while some Hebrew MSS and LXX read 'Ahaziah' as in 2 Kings 8:29. Maybe he was known by both names.

35. Literally 'crushed' or 'downtrodden', a unique word in the Hebrew Bible.

like Saul, failed in his behaviour (see 1 Chron. 10:13-14) and received the same kind of divine retribution. The king whose life and actions were governed by Ahab's house, ended his days, not in Jerusalem, but in the northern kingdom, hiding in Samaria, and then caught and killed by the same divine agent who had destroyed the rest of the apostate family. His was an exile that prefigured the exile of the whole nation. As in the case of his father Jehoram (2 Chron. 21:20), no sources are cited, and the account closes with a state of affairs that resembled the situation after Saul's death. The Chronicler explains that the 'house of Ahaziah' had no one left capable of ruling. He uses one of his key expressions 'to retain strength' or 'to retain the power'. Ahaziah's line had become 'powerless' like Jeroboam's whom Yahweh also killed, and the very opposite to the enabling given in the time of David and Solomon (1 Chron. 29:14; 2 Chron. 2:6[5]; 13:20; see also 14:11-13[12-14]; 20:37).

Application

The sovereignty of God is clearly revealed in judgment and in grace. God's judgment had brought the Davidic line to the verge of extinction. The message would not have been lost on the post-exilic readers who were living without a Davidic king. It was divine judgment that had brought about the end of the Davidic rule because it had become like the north. But that did not mean that God's promises to David were annulled. God has wonderfully brought to realisation those promises through the coming into the world of His Son. It was also a reminder to the Jews of the post-exilic period that they had no cause to despise the northerners. Their king Ahaziah was no better than the families of Jeroboam or Ahab. It called for a humble acknowledgment of their own sinfulness but gave hope in the mercy of God toward repentant sinners. Paul uses similar teaching to warn Gentile believers and to encourage his own Jewish nation (Rom. 11:17-24).

Jesus experienced a greater exile outside the city though He had no sins of His own. He endured the judgment of God for the sins of His people. Ahaziah's bad example is a reminder to each of us to walk 'not in the counsel of the wicked,' but like our Lord Himself, the true anointed one, to love God's law and to meditate on it always (Ps. 1).

Athaliah and Joash (22:10–24:27)

Though most of the narrative finds a parallel in 2 Kings 11:1-20, the Chronicler highlights that Joash's right to be king had the support of the people and how the priest and Levites played such a crucial part in the unprecedented events that took place in the temple and its vicinity. There are two main sections: the first concerns Joash's succession to the throne in place of Athaliah the usurper (22:10-23:21), and secondly, Joash's reign (24:1-27). The account of Joash's life begins with him hidden in a bedroom and ends with him assassinated in his bedroom (22:11 and 24:25).

Athaliah seizes power (22:10-12)

These verses are paralleled in 2 Kings 11:1-3 with slight differences.

> 22:10. Now when Athaliah the mother of Ahaziah saw that her son was dead, she arose and destroyed all the royal seed of the house of Judah. 11. But Jehoshabeath, the daughter of the king, took Joash the son of Ahaziah, and stole him away from among the king's sons who were being put to death and put him and his nurse in the bedroom. Thus Jehoshabeath, the daughter of king Jehoram, the wife of Jehoiada the priest, because she was a sister of Ahaziah, hid him from Athaliah so that she did not put him to death. 12. And he was hidden with them in the house of God six years, while Athaliah was reigning over the land.

Athaliah's murderous action (v. 10) ensured that this influential queen mother would have no rival claimants to the throne. This was the final step in a series of killings relating to the Davidic royal seed that had begun when king Jehoram of Judah murdered his six brothers (2 Chron. 21:4). It was a step that immediately followed Jehu's ferocious activity in the north and led to the death of Ahaziah and his officers and relatives (2 Chron. 22:8-9). We are not informed what ideas Athaliah had about who would succeed her on the throne. She had 'destroyed'[36] for her own self-seeking ends the royal

---

36. The MT has the word normally rendered 'and she spoke' (*wātəḏabēr*) instead of 'and she destroyed' (*watə'abēr*) as found in 2 Kings 11:1. But it is just

seed of the 'house of Judah,' whereas Jehu had received divine warrant to cut off all the 'house of Ahab' (v. 10; 2 Chron. 22:7).

However, there was one son of Ahaziah who, by the providence of God, escaped the clutches of Athaliah. This was baby Joash, who was rescued by his aunt, Jehoshabeath (spelt Jehosheba in 2 Kings 11:2). She was the daughter of Jehoram and Ahaziah's sister, and the Chronicler adds that she was the wife of the priest Jehoiada, and this made it easier for the child to be reared in 'the house of God' without suspicion even after he was weaned, much like Samuel who grew up from an infant with Eli the high priest (v. 12; 1 Sam. 1:22-28; 3:1). Joash would have been no more than one at the time and so he was put with a wet nurse into a concealed room with a bed (v. 11). What had happened to his mother is not revealed (see 2 Chron. 24:1).

The contrast could not be starker; on the one hand, there is a brave woman of faith who hid the legitimate heir to the throne in the house of God, and on the other, a wicked woman of Ahab stock who ruled the land as a devotee of Baal (see 2 Chron. 24:7). Jehoshabeath's part in protecting the infant is emphasised more in Chronicles ('she put …' and 'she hid …' v. 11; see 2 Kings 11:2). Athaliah ruled for six years in Judah (v. 12). Ironically, she was the one remaining member of the Ahab dynasty who had not been wiped out by Jehu in the north but was found ruling in the south. Everything about it was illegitimate and neither the text of Kings nor Chronicles refer to her as the queen or give the usual accession formula or any summary of her reign. She was to be the only non-Davidic ruler over the kingdom of Judah and, in fact, the only female to reign over Israel.

The account bears some resemblance to the early life of Moses where male offspring were being killed, a baby destined to lead God's people was hidden, and a princess came to the rescue and provided a nurse.

Application

This account of a future king being hidden as a baby from the murderous intent of a foreign queen is not only a reminder of

---

possible that in this context following the hostile sense of 'she arose' immediately before it, that the MT means 'she destroyed' from a root cognate with the Akkadean 'to overthrow' (see Williamson, *1 and 2 Chronicles*, p. 314).

baby Moses hidden from Pharaoh's policy of infanticide but points forward to the infant Jesus who needed to be smuggled to Egypt while still an infant on account of king Herod's rage. The six years when there was no visible evidence of any offspring of David to ascend the throne was similar to the intertestamental period before Jesus was eventually revealed. David's 'lamp' would not be snuffed out and the godly remnant continued to hope. God is in control and will fulfil His purposes and promises. What humans cannot see, God has purposed and brings to pass in His own time.

The paragraph is also the tale of two women: one a self-seeking cruel oppressor and the other an example of unselfish heroism. It is a glaring reminder of the horrors committed by those who have never known or who have turned their backs on the biblical revelation concerning the sanctity of human life. It also provided encouragement to God's people to hold on to God's promises concerning the royal seed of the woman who would be victorious over the old snake and his brood.

Joash's rise to power (23:1-21)
This passage again finds a close parallel in 2 Kings 11:4–12:22 but with some significant differences that underline the Chronicler's concerns. It can be divided into three parts: the true king is crowned (23:1-11), the usurper is killed (23:12-15), the kingdom is quiet (23:16-21).

1. Now in the seventh year Jehoiada strengthened himself, and he took with him into the covenant the commanders of the hundreds: Azariah the son of Jeroham, and Ishmael the son of Jehohanan, and Azariah the son of Obed, and Maaseiah the son of Adaiah, and Elishaphat the son of Zichri. 2. And they went around through Judah and gathered the Levites from all the cities of Judah, and the heads of fathers of Israel and they came to Jerusalem. 3. Then all the assembly made a covenant in the house of God with the king. And he said to them, 'Here is the king's son; he shall reign as Yahweh spoke concerning the sons of David. 4. This is the thing you must do: one third of you, of the priests and of the Levites, who come on the Sabbath, *shall be* gatekeepers of the thresholds, 5. one third in the king's house, and one third at the Gate of the Foundation. And all the people *shall be* in the courts of the house of Yahweh. 6. But let no one come into the house of Yahweh except the priests and those of

the Levites who serve. They may come in for they are holy; but all the people shall keep the watch of Yahweh. 7. And the Levites shall surround the king, everyone with his weapons in his hand; and whoever comes into the house, let him be put to death. And be with the king when he comes in and when he goes out.' 8. So the Levites and all Judah did according to all that Jehoiada the priest commanded; and each took his men, who were coming *on duty* on the Sabbath with those who were going *off duty* on the Sabbath, for Jehoiada the priest did not dismiss *any* of the divisions. 9. Then Jehoiada the priest gave to the commanders of the hundreds the spears, and the large shields, and the small shields which belonged to king David, and which *were in* the house of God. 10. And he stationed all the people round about the king, and each with his weapon in his hand, from the right side of the house to the left side of the house, from the altar and from the house. 11. And they brought out the king's son and put the crown on him and *gave him* the testimony, and they made him king and Jehoiada and his sons anointed him and said, 'May the king live.'

In the overthrow of Athaliah, the Chronicler emphasises more than the compiler of Kings the role of the temple personnel and that the coup meant the restoration of the Davidic monarchy. The paragraph begins by dating the action of Jehoiada, the husband of Jehoshabeath, to the seventh year of Athaliah's reign. By the use of the verb 'to strengthen himself,' Jehoiada the priest is portrayed as if he were a Davidic ruler who had just succeeded to the throne (v. 1; see 2 Chron. 1:1; 12:13; 13:7, 21; etc.). He clearly took the initiative in bringing the rightful monarch to the throne and acted as regent during Joash's early years as king (2 Chron. 23:18-20; 24:1-2). Interestingly, it is noted later that the priest was buried in the city of David among the kings (2 Chron. 24:16). Jehoiada made careful plans that involved entering into a binding agreement with five commanders of military units ('the hundreds') that included the Carites and bodyguards mentioned in 2 Kings 11:4. These commanders are named, and though many of their names are common in Levitical lists, they should not be identified as Levites. Rather, these commanders were sent throughout Judah to convene a special assembly in Jerusalem of Levites from all Judah's cities as well as the heads of Israel's families (v. 2). This plot had more support from the start than the text

of Kings would have led us to believe. At this assembly that
had gathered in the temple precincts, the people entered into
a covenant with the boy king. Jehoiada produced the young
prince to the assembly and indicated why the revolution was
necessary by emphasising that it was according to Yahweh's
promise concerning David's family line (see 2 Chron. 21:7).
Yahweh's covenant with the house of David, which Athaliah's
reign had temporarily disrupted, was re-established.

At the same time, the priest informed the gathering how
the plan was to be executed (vv. 4-7; see 2 Kings 11:5-7). The
most important concern was the safety of the king. Again,
in contrast to the Kings' account, the deployment of guards
and the order in which they are introduced are seen from
the Chronicler's perspective with his interest in the Levites
and their special qualifications in this area of duty. It was the
Levites who were to protect the king and they were well-armed
for the task of preventing anyone entering the temple area (v. 7;
see Exod. 32:27-29). The changing of the guard at the temple
gates and palace on the Sabbath provided the ideal time for
staging the coup, for it allowed for double the number of priests
and Levites to be present in the temple area without arousing
suspicion with no off-duty allowed (v. 8) and more people
would be around worshipping than on an ordinary working
day, while Athaliah's interests would be centred on worship
at the temple to Baal (see v. 17). Chronicles makes clear the
distinction that had to be made between the priests and Levites
who could enter the holy parts of the temple and the rest of the
people who were to remain in the temple courts. Even in this
emergency situation the temple was not to be defiled. Yahweh's
'watch' (v. 6), in the sense of commandment, emphasises their
religious obligation to abide by the Mosaic law. The 'Foundation
Gate' (v. 5) cannot be identified. Some suppose it to be the
same as the unknown 'Sur Gate' (2 Kings 11:6). All the duty
guards and the gathering of the people on the Sabbath gave
the impression of 'business as usual'.

The plan was executed precisely as Jehoiada had
commanded. Again, the Chronicler underlines the role of
the Levites and also of the people ('all Judah', v. 8) to show
the unanimous support for a true successor to David. On
this occasion, no guards were allowed to go off duty, and

spears and shields kept in the temple as tokens of David's victories over his enemies were handed out (1 Chron. 18:7-11; 2 Chron. 9:15-16; 12:9-10). Significantly, it is David's weapons that are used to defend the Davidic dynasty (v. 9).

The king is shielded by 'all the people' in a semi-circle round the entrance area to the sanctuary courtyard where the altar of burnt offering stood (v. 10). Ironically, this would be the very spot where Jehoiada's son Zechariah would be killed on the orders of the very person whom Jehoiada was protecting (see 2 Chron. 24:21). At this point, the young king was brought out again (v. 11; see v. 3), this time for the coronation ceremony which involved three key components. Joash first received a royal crown or diadem that symbolised being set apart to this special office. Such a head-piece was worn by the high priests as well as the kings of Israel (Exod. 29:6; Lev. 8:9; 21:12; 2 Sam. 1:10; Pss. 89:39[40]; 132:18). Secondly, he was presented with the 'testimony'. This term suggests a connection with the Mosaic law which the king was required to possess (Deut. 17:18-19). The Ten Commandments, that symbolised the whole law, is referred to as the 'two tablets of the Testimony' (Exod. 31:18; Deut. 4:13). Because it contained those tablets, the ark of the covenant is sometimes called the 'ark of the testimony' (Exod. 25:22; 39:35; 40:20). This testimony, therefore, that was given to the king is most probably Yahweh's covenant law as set out in the book of Deuteronomy (see 2 Chron. 17:9). The final ceremonial act was the anointing. The account suggests that Jehoiada was the high priest with his sons serving alongside him (v. 11). In Chronicles the only record of other kings being anointed apart from Joash are David, Solomon and the northern king Jehu (1 Chron. 11:3; 14:8; 23:1; 29:22; 2 Chron. 22:7). The traditional cry of acclamation, 'May the king live!', brings the scene to an end and, interestingly, all such recorded cries, as here, occur in contexts where there are some question marks over the succession (see 1 Sam. 10:24; 2 Sam. 16:16; 1 Kings 1:25, 34, 39). At that moment there were two ruling over Judah: the rightful king and the usurper.

> 23:12. When Athaliah heard the sound of the people running and praising the king, she came to the people in the house of Yahweh. 13. And she looked and there was the king standing

by his pillar at the entrance, and the commanders and the trumpeters *were* by the king, and all the people of the land were rejoicing and blowing on the trumpets, and the singers with musical instruments and giving the instruction to praise. Then Athaliah tore her clothes and said, 'Treason! Treason!' 14. And Jehoiada the priest brought out the commanders of hundreds who were in charge of the army, and he said to them, 'Bring her out from within the ranks; and anyone who follows her is to be put to death with the sword.' For the priest said, 'Do not kill her in the house of Yahweh.' 15. So they laid hands on her and she came to the entrance of the Gate of Horses in the king's house and they killed her there.

In his attempt to succeed David, Adonijah had heard the loud noise of people rejoicing at Solomon's coronation and in fear had run toward the temple and taken hold of the horns of the altar (1 Kings 1:39-41, 45-50). Athaliah, likewise, came to the temple at the noise of the people and to her complete surprise she saw a seven-year-old lad by one of the temple pillars, surrounded by bodyguards and with all the people honouring him as king (vv. 12-13). The singers and the instrumentalists added to the joy of the celebration as the Chronicler especially notes on numerous other occasions. Athaliah signified her shock and horror by ripping her clothes and calling it an act of treachery, with the hope perhaps that some would come to her support. Jehoiada again took the lead and instructed the military commanders to seize her and to put to death anyone attempting to follow her. The phrase 'they laid hands on her' could perhaps be translated more idiomatically 'they made space for her' in view of the following verb which suggests she went willingly (v. 15). She was brought through the ranks of soldiers away from the temple area and killed near the entrance to her own royal palace. The 'horses' gate' must be clearly distinguished from the gate of the same name in the city wall (Jer. 31:40; Neh. 3:28). A clear distinction is made between the holy and the common (Lev. 10:10). Jehoiada's efforts to protect the sanctity of Yahweh's temple did not concern king Joash when he later had Jehoiada's son stoned to death in the temple court (2 Chron. 24:21). The Chronicler's view of Athaliah is shown by the absence of the usual summary statements concerning her reign and burial, and of any source material.

23:16. Then Jehoiada made a covenant between himself and all the people and the king that they should be Yahweh's people. 17. Then all the people came to the house of Baal and tore it down. And they shattered its altars and its images and they killed Mattan the priest of Baal before the altars. 18. And Jehoiada set the oversight of the house of Yahweh into the hand of the priests the Levites, whom David had assigned to the temple of Yahweh to offer Yahweh's burnt offerings as written in the law of Moses with rejoicing and singing, according to the order of David. 19. And he set the gatekeepers at the gates of the house of Yahweh, so that no one who was unclean in any way could enter. 20. Then he took the commanders of the hundreds, the nobles, the governors of the people, and all the people of the land and brought the king down from the house of Yahweh and they went through the upper gate in the king's house and set the king on the throne of the kingdom. 21. So all the people of the land rejoiced and the city was quiet and they had put Athaliah to death with the sword.

The high point of the counter-revolution was the covenant that the high priest initiated that bound together temple, palace and country (v. 16). By this solemn act the entire nation renewed its commitment to God. It was one great covenant with two main elements to it as the earlier account makes clear: the covenant between Yahweh, the king and the people and the covenant between the king and the people (see 2 Kings 11:17). Because the Chronicler has already mentioned a covenant between the congregation and the king (v. 3), it is the kingdom's allegiance to Yahweh that is emphasised at this point. Echoes of that fundamental element in the covenant relationship can be detected in the words 'they should be Yahweh's people' (see Lev. 26:12; Jer. 32:38; Ezek. 37:27). Jehoiada is seen to represent Yahweh in this covenant that was in effect a renewal of the Sinai agreement (Exod. 19:1-8; 24:1-8). A similar covenant was made during Asa's kingship (2 Chron. 15:12-13).

Athaliah and her son Ahaziah had introduced into Judah the kind of Baal worship that Jezebel, the wife of Ahab, had imposed on the northern kingdom (see 2 Chron. 22:4; 24:7). It had been Jehu's task to rid the country of such pagan worship, and this same kind of purge was now carried out in Judah, not initially by those at the top but by the ordinary citizen ('the

people of the land', v. 17; see 1 Chron. 5:25). This was evidence
of the whole nation's desire to abide by the demands of the
covenant (see Deut. 12:1-4). The purge was not as bloody as in
the north, with only Mattan, the priest of Baal, put to death
(v. 17). Where the temple to Baal was situated is not known.

The Chronicler adds further information not found
in Kings concerning Jehoiada's restoration of the temple
worship according to the Mosaic legislation. It concerned the
burnt offerings (see 1 Chron. 6:48-49[33-34]; 16:40) and the
instructions that David gave concerning the responsibilities
of the priests and Levites for the oversight of the temple and
its music, and as keepers of the gates (1 Chron. 23:6; 24:3;
26:1-19). David's authority in the orderly worship of the temple
is equal to that of Moses and is expressed by the way David's
name encircles that of Moses (v. 18). The ritual purity of the
temple area has been a particular concern of the Chronicler
in this account and verse 19 is a reminder of the importance
of the gatekeepers (1 Chron. 26:1-19; see Pss. 15; 24:3-4).

Again, in the procession of the young king from the temple
to the palace for his enthronement, the Chronicler stresses how
the whole kingdom was one in its support of the king (v. 20).
The true king of David's line sat once more on 'the throne
of the kingdom' (see 1 Chron. 29:23; 2 Chron. 9:8). Instead
of 'the gate of the guards' (2 Kings 11:19), the 'upper gate' is
mentioned and may be a different name for the same gate.
It must not be confused with the upper gate built by Jotham
(2 Chron. 27:3). The people generally showed their acceptance
of the coup by their joyful spirits (v. 21; see 1 Chron. 12:40).
Athaliah is again mentioned with the extra information given
that it was by the sword she was killed (v. 21; see vv. 14-15).
After the violence and upheaval of the usurper's reign, there
was 'quiet' in the city, the kind of ideal state that witnessed
to God's blessing for faithful obedience (1 Chron. 4:40; 22:9;
2 Chron. 14:1[13:23]; 14:4-5; 20:30).

Application

We have in Joash a picture of the one whom Isaiah describes as
a shoot out of the stem of Jesse (Isa. 11:1). All seemed lost and
yet a child emerged to carry on the seed of David. In Athaliah

we have one of Satan's brood who sought to annihilate the seed of the woman. The enemies of the Son of God thought they had destroyed Him through His death on the cross, but God raised and vindicated Him so that all authority in heaven and earth has been given to King Jesus.

The emphasis on the need to keep the purity of the holy place intact is a reminder that nothing unclean can enter God's city and holy presence (Rev. 21:27; 22:15).

Joash's reign (24:1-27)

The chapter parallels the text of 2 Kings 12:1-21 but with a number of significant variations. In Chronicles, Joash's reign divides into two clearly marked periods: one indicates his concern for Yahweh and the temple during the high priest Jehoiada's life, and the other how, following Jehoiada's death, the king turned away from God (note the various forms of the verb 'zb, 'to forsake'; vv. 18, 20, 24, 25), and how he was brought to a sad end. The final verse (v. 27) summarises the whole of his reign with the reference back to his many sons (v. 3) as well as to the two contrasting periods of his kingship. Three main items are covered in the chapter: Joash's temple renovations (24:1-14), Jehoiada's death and Joash's apostasy (24:15-22), and Joash's punishment (24:23-27). In Kings, Joash's name is usually spelled 'Jehoash'.

> 24:1. Joash was seven years old when he became king, and he reigned forty years in Jerusalem and his mother's name was Zibiah from Beersheba. 2. And Joash did what was right in the sight of Yahweh all the days of Jehoiada the priest. 3. And Jehoiada took two wives for him, and he fathered sons and daughters.
>
> 4. Now it happened after this Joash had his heart on restoring the house of Yahweh. 5. So he assembled the priests and the Levites and said to them, 'Go out to the cities of Judah, and gather from all Israel money to strengthen the house of your God from year to year, and you should do the matter quickly.' However the Levites did not do *it* quickly. 6. So the king called Jehoiada the chief *priest*, and said to him, 'Why have you not sought the Levites to bring from Judah and from Jerusalem the tax *levied by* Moses the servant of Yahweh and of the assembly of Israel, for the tabernacle of witness?' 7. For the sons of Athaliah, that wicked one, had broken into the house of God and had also made all the sacred things of the house of Yahweh for the

Baals. 8. Then the king commanded and they made a chest, and put it outside at the gate of the house of Yahweh. 9. And they made a proclamation in Judah and Jerusalem to bring to Yahweh the tax levied by Moses the servant of God on Israel in the wilderness. 10. Then all the officials and all the people rejoiced and brought *it* in, and cast *it* into the chest until it was full. 11. So it was, at the time when the chest was brought to the king's administrators by the hand of the Levites, and when they saw that there was much money, the king's scribe and the high priest's representative came and emptied the chest and took it and returned it to its place. Thus they did day by day and collected money in abundance. 12. Then the king and Jehoiada gave it to those who did the work of the service of the house of Yahweh and they hired masons and carpenters to restore the house of Yahweh and also those who worked in iron and bronze to strengthen the house of Yahweh. 13. So the workmen laboured and the restoration work flourished in their hand; and they restored the house of God to its original condition and made it firm. 14. When they had finished they brought the rest of the money before the king and Jehoiada, and they made utensils for the house of Yahweh, utensils for serving and burnt offerings, and ladles, and utensils of gold and silver. And they offered burnt offerings in the house of Yahweh continually all the days of Jehoiada.

The first part of Joash's long reign is marked by his loyalty to Yahweh. For this reason, the Chronicler at this point makes no negative reference, as in 2 Kings 12:3, about the high places. Judging by the number of references to his name (vv. 2, 3, 6, 12 and twice in v. 14), Jehoiada remained a significant influence on the king and continued for some time to act as a surrogate father by arranging two of the king's marriages (v. 3). The phrase, 'all the days of Jehoiada,' frames this section (vv. 2, 14) and sounds an ominous note in that it suggests the king only did what was right in God's sight during the lifetime of the high priest. But the introductory paragraph also emphasises that after the upheaval of the previous reigns and the near decimation of the Davidic line (see 2 Chron. 21:4, 17; 22:1, 8, 10), the kingdom enjoyed a period of stable rule with a king who produced numerous sons and daughters (see also v. 27). All this indicated God's blessing on king and people. Nothing is known of the king's mother other than that she came from the southernmost border of Canaan that belonged to the tribe of Simeon. Beersheba seems to have continued to be a place of pilgrimage by people from the north even after the northern breakaway (see Amos 5:5).

Joash's good idea concerning the temple renovations is a reminder of David's plan to build the temple (1 Chron. 22:7; 28:2). The word 'renew' or 'restore' (vv. 4, 12) is used for personal renewal (Pss. 51:10[12]; 103:5; Lamentations 5:21) as well as for 'renewing' the kingdom, repairing cities and the altar of the temple (1 Sam. 11:14; Isa. 61:4; 2 Chron. 15:8). Previous years of neglect plus the activity of Athaliah's agents (referred to as 'sons' in v. 7) had left the building in need of immediate attention. Joash 'assembled' the Levites as well as the priests to collect the annual funds from the people to 'repair' or 'strengthen' (vv. 5, 12) the decaying structure. The Chronicler uses the term 'Israel' for the people of Judah, not to make a contrast between Judah and the northern kingdom for political reasons, but rather to indicate that in Judah was to be found that continuity with the Israel of earlier generations.

The Levites, for some unknown reason, turned out to be too slow in collecting the money so it became necessary for the king to devise a second plan. It was the king who took the initiative and summoned the chief priest and rebuked him for the failure of the scheme through his mismanagement of the Levites (v. 6). The funds that were to have been collected are described as the tax that was originally imposed on the people by Moses for the tabernacle (vv. 6, 9). Everyone aged twenty and over was required to give half a shekel (Exod. 30:12-16; 38:25-26). Here only in Chronicles is the tabernacle called 'the tent of the testimony' (v. 6; see Num. 9:15; 17:7-8[22-23]; 18:2). Athaliah is described as the embodiment of wickedness (v. 7), and it is on account of her 'brood' ('sons') that it was necessary to restore the holy vessels (see v. 14) in addition to repairing what they had vandalised.

Under the new scheme, a chest was made, and it was placed at the temple entrance where the people came with their sacrifices to the altar of burnt offering (v. 8; 2 Kings 12:9[10]). Such cash boxes were a common feature of pagan temples in first millennium Mesopotamia. By drawing attention again to the tax that Moses levied, a parallel continues to be drawn by the Chronicler between the temple and the wilderness tabernacle. The same applies to the way the

joyful giving by the people and their leaders is highlighted
(v. 10; see Exod. 35:21-36:7; 1 Chron. 29:1-9, 17; 2 Chron. 7:10;
15:15), after the proclamation concerning the collection was
made throughout the kingdom ('Judah and Jerusalem', v. 9).
The Chronicler draws attention to the joy of the people,
for it expressed the ideal, united response of the covenant
community (see 1 Chron. 12:40). Money poured in on a daily
basis and it was the duty of the Levites to carry the box first
to the king's special administrators where a representative
of both crown and temple counted the money and returned
the box to its place (v. 11). In this way, everything was done
decently and above board and avoided corrupting influences.

Cooperation between king and priest continued in that
they saw to the distribution of the funds for repairing the
temple. Masons, carpenters and craftsmen were employed.
The two verbs 'restore' and 'strengthen' (v. 12) echo their use
in verses 4 and 5 and mark the end of the restoration work. The
completed work is summarised by the Chronicler employing
a term for restoration that is associated with the healing of
wounds (v. 13; see Jer. 8:22). It is used of Israel's restoration
and for the rebuilding of Jerusalem's walls (Isa. 58:8; Jer. 30:17;
33:6; Neh. 4:7[1]). The work 'flourished' so that the temple was
restored to its 'original condition'[37] revealed by God's Spirit
to David (1 Chron. 28:11-12; see Exod. 25:9, 40; Ezek. 43:11).
Chronicles adds that money, surplus to requirements, was
used to make various ritual utensils for the temple. This again
draws a parallel with the tabernacle (see Exod. 31:1-10).

The final sentence of verse 14 includes the phrase 'all the
days of Jehoiada' which forms an *inclusio* with verse 2 and
ends the first part of Joash's reign. It summarises his piety
in his concern for Yahweh's temple and its proper worship,
which is expressed particularly in the regular presentation of
the burnt offerings (see Exod. 29:38-42; 2 Chron. 2:4; 8:12-13).

Application

The close link between the king and the temple that
Chronicles has emphasised from the time of David and
Solomon continues in this narrative. Haggai and Zechariah

---

37. Literally 'according to its measurement'.

show a similar interest as do so many of the psalms. The tangible evidence of a restored temple after the exile was a small but significant encouragement to the people as they looked for a new Davidic king.

The people's obligation to contribute the annual temple tax is mentioned in Nehemiah 10:32[33], and the account of the tax in Matthew 17:24-27 implies that Jesus is one with God the Father who first ordained it and that with Him the old temple rituals and service were being superseded by something far better.

Paul encourages Christians to give cheerfully and generously remembering God's indescribable gift to them (2 Cor. 8–9). When gifts for God's work are received, they need to be handled with care. Transparency and accountability were ensured by Paul in collecting and transporting the funds donated by the Gentile believers for the poor saints in Jerusalem (Acts 24:17; Rom. 15:25-27, 31; 1 Cor. 16:1-4).

> 24:15. But Jehoiada grew old and was full of days, and he died. *He was* one hundred and thirty years old when he died. 16. And they buried him in the city of David with the kings, for he had done good in Israel, both with regard to God and his house.
> 17. Now after the death of Jehoiada, the officials of Judah came and prostrated themselves before the king. Then the king listened to them. 18. And they forsook the house of Yahweh the God of their fathers, and served the Asherim and the idols; so wrath was upon Judah and Jerusalem because of this their guilt. 19. Yet he sent prophets among them, to bring them back to Yahweh; and they testified against them but they did not listen. 20. Then the Spirit of God endued Zechariah the son of Jehoiada the priest, and he stood above the people, and said to them, 'Thus says God: Why do you transgress the commandments of Yahweh, so that you will not prosper? Because you have forsaken Yahweh, he also has forsaken you.' 21. But they conspired against him and by the commandment of the king they stoned him with stones in the court of the house of Yahweh. 22. And Joash the king did not remember the loyalty that Jehoiada his father had done to him, but killed his son, and as he was dying he said, 'May Yahweh see and avenge!'

Only the Chronicler gives these details about Jehoiada, and they mark the end of the first period of the king's reign. This statement about the death and burial of the high priest is unprecedented in the Bible and uses phraseology that echoes what is said at the close of David's life (v. 15; see 1 Chron. 29:27-28). Jehoiada is presented as a royal figure (see 2 Chron. 23:1) who is buried, in sharp contrast to Joash, 'with' the Davidic rulers in 'the city of David' (v. 16). Not only is he honoured with a state burial, but his long and full life is evidence of God's favour and blessing (Gen. 25:8; Job 42:17). His age at death puts him among the patriarchs. The last age given for Jacob before his death was one hundred and thirty years (Gen. 47:9). In this, Jehoiada is like the father of the nation. He is also described as one who had 'done good' in Israel (see 2 Chron. 7:10; 10:7; 12:12; 19:3) in that his concerns were for God, the Davidic king and the temple, as evidenced in his involvement in the temple renovations and his risky and dangerous actions in preserving the Davidic line. Jehoiada must have been a hundred years old when he crowned Joash as king.

The Chronicler again mentions Jehoiada, only this time to introduce the king's apostasy, a matter not mentioned in the Kings account (v. 17; see v. 2). Comparing the various ages and lengths of reign, it is probable that Joash had by this time reigned about thirty years and was about thirty-six years of age. Not for the first time a Davidic king accepts bad advice (see 2 Chron. 10:8-10; 22:3-5). He was flattered by the 'officials of Judah' who bowed down before him (v. 17). They may have been among a remnant of former leaders who had supported Athaliah and who saw, with the high priest's death, an opportunity to change the moral and religious stance of the king that had been based on Mosaic traditions, for the more generally accepted Canaanite practices. Thus the king and his advisers 'forsook' Yahweh, their ancestral God, by abandoning His temple, the place which the king had recently renovated and where he had been kept safe as an infant and later crowned (v. 18). 'Forsake' is one of the characteristic terms for abandoning God and is the antithesis of 'seeking' God (1 Chron. 28:9; 2 Chron. 15:2). The 'Asherim' were sacred poles or idolatrous forms of the Canaanite fertility goddess Asherah (see 2 Chron. 14:3[2]; 15:16; 17:6). Worshipping these representations of a pagan deity and other 'idols' (see 1 Chron. 10:9) incurred 'guilt' (1 Chron. 21:3) and led to the kingdom being under Yahweh's 'wrath' (2 Chron. 19:2). But that judgment did not fall immediately for God sent them prophets (v. 19, and see 'many oracles' in v. 27), as He had done under previous Davidic rulers, to warn them and call them to repentance (2 Chron. 12:5-8; 16:7-10; 19:2-3; Neh. 9:26, 29-30). It was their refusal to listen and repent that led to the deserved punishment (see 2 Chron. 16:7-10). The Chronicler often emphasises the importance of obeying the prophetic word and shows that rejection of the prophet's warnings leads eventually to exile (2 Chron. 20:20; 36:15-16).

The Chronicler gives one example of a prophetic voice raised against the nation and it is a particularly poignant one, for it is none other than the recently deceased high priest's son, Zechariah, who is killed for his faithful witness (vv. 20-22). There is no indication that Zechariah had succeeded his father as high priest. Like Amasai, the chief of the Thirty, God's Spirit 'clothed' him (v. 20; 1 Chron. 12:18[19]; and the same is said of Gideon in Judges 6:34). Other references in Chronicles where the Spirit of God 'comes upon' individuals who then proclaim a message to king and people include Azariah and Jahaziel (2 Chron. 15:1-7; 20:14-17). In order to gain a better hearing he 'stood above the people'. Abijah had stood on a mountain to deliver his prophetic message to Jeroboam and his people, whereas Solomon had stood on a specially made platform to give his dedicatory prayer (2 Chron. 6:13; 13:4; see also Neh. 8:4-5). Zechariah introduced his brief message with the usual messenger formula, 'Thus says God.' The prophet's pointed question is the nub of the accusation. They had disobeyed Yahweh's explicit command against worshipping other gods and making idolatrous images (Exod. 20:3-6). The result would be that they would not 'prosper' or 'succeed', which is another word frequently found in Chronicles (1 Chron. 22:11, 13; 29:23; 2 Chron. 13:12; 14:7[6]; 18:11, 14; 20:20; etc.). Zechariah's words are similar to those of Moses to rebellious Israel (Num. 14:41). As is often stated in this book, the punishment fits the crime: they had abandoned Yahweh and so He abandons them (2 Chron. 12:5; 15:2; 21:10). Like all true prophets of God, Zechariah's message of doom followed that set by Moses in the covenant curses (see Deut. 29:25-26; 31:16-17).

For his faithfulness to God, Zechariah was stoned to death (see 2 Chron. 10:18). Instead of obeying the commandments of Yahweh, the people obeyed the command of the king (vv. 20-21). Joash showed his ingratitude by silencing the son of the man whose 'loyalty' had brought him to the throne (v. 22). The verb 'to conspire' from the same word family as Athaliah's cry of 'treason' or 'conspiracy' (*qšr*) is used in relation to the prophet and ironically of Joash himself (vv. 21, 25, 26; 2 Chron. 23:13). Furthermore, the killing took place at the very spot where Joash had been anointed (2 Chron. 23:10-11) and indicated the king's entire rejection of Jehoiada's policy of keeping the temple area holy (2 Chron. 23:14). Zechariah's dying words are not evidence of a vengeful spirit; they are a prophetic announcement that leaves God to do the avenging as the Mosaic law indicated (v. 22; see Deut. 32:35, 41, 43). The word for 'avenge' (*drš*), often used by the Chronicler for 'seeking' God, is here employed with God as subject. In this context, it has the sense of 'seeking out' for revenge (see Deut. 18:19; Pss. 9:12[13]; 10:4, 15). It is probable that the phrase, 'Joash the king did not remember' (v. 22), is a play on Zechariah's name, 'Yahweh has remembered'. The prophet's final words indicated his belief that Yahweh would not forget the shed blood of His servant.

Application

The high priest's growing influence in the post-exilic period when they had no king may account for the Chronicler's special interest in Jehoiada. It is however Jehoiada's kingly recognition that particularly stands out and calls to mind the depiction of Joshua the high priest in Zechariah's prophecy. An elaborate crown was placed on Joshua's head so that he became a type of the coming priest-king (Zech. 6:9-15). The priest-king after the order of Melchizedek in Psalm 110 provided yet further encouragement to the people to look forward to the future king who would exercise both priestly and kingly functions (Heb. 6:20–7:22).

Brave Zechariah who proclaimed God's word to the wayward king at the cost of his life is mentioned by Jesus in His condemnation of the scribes and Pharisees (Matt. 23:35;

Luke 11:51). He looked to God to avenge the taking of his life as do all God's persecuted people (Rev. 6:10). Like Jesus Himself, he committed himself to the one who judges justly, as David the type of Christ does in many of the psalms. Such a position in no way contradicts the prayers of Jesus and Stephen for the forgiveness of their persecutors (Luke 23:34; Acts 7:60). Praying for our persecutors and trusting God to avenge wrongs are both right responses and must not be played one against the other.

It is tragic when leaders, who have been used by God to build up the church of Jesus Christ, later fall grievously or even end their lives denying the faith. We are not only given encouragements to faith through the exploits of men and women who completed their earthly course well, but we are also warned through the failures of those who showed at first every indication of being fully committed to God. The fall of respected leaders can unsettle Christians. How necessary it is to point people to the perfect Leader and Saviour, our Lord Jesus Christ.

> 24:23. So it happened at the turn of the year an army of Aram came up against him; and they came to Judah and Jerusalem, and they destroyed all the officials of the people from the people and sent all their spoil to the king of Damascus. 24. Though the army of Aram came with a few men, Yahweh gave a very large army into their hands, because they had forsaken Yahweh the God of their fathers. So they executed judgment on Joash. 25. And when they had withdrawn from him, for they had left him with many wounds, his servants conspired against him because of the blood of the sons of Jehoiada the priest, and they killed him on his bed. So he died and they buried him in the city of David, but they did not bury him in the tombs of the kings. 26. And these are the ones who conspired against him: Zabad, the son of Shimeath the Ammonitess, and Jehozabad, the son of Shimrith the Moabitess. 27. Now concerning his sons, the many oracles about him and the fixing of the house of God, there they are written in the midrash of the book of the kings. Then Amaziah his son reigned in his place.

The reign had begun so well. With Joash, the Davidic line had been re-established and Yahweh's temple had been renovated. But his apostasy brought its inevitable consequences as

God had indicated in the original Sinai covenant that included blessing for obedience and curses for disobedience. Throughout the account, the Chronicler has presented his theological message that rebellion against God leads to disaster, whereas faithfulness to God, witnessed most notably in the life of Jehoiada, leads toward a long and fulfilled life and an honourable death. It is this theological evaluation of the events that marks out the significant difference to the otherwise similar narrative in Kings.

The Aramean invasion (vv. 23-24) is seen as a direct punishment for forsaking Yahweh, their ancestral God. Whether this was part of the same attack as the one mentioned in 2 Kings 12:17-19 is unclear. There are some noticeable differences. The invasion in Kings is not related to Joash's death as it is in Chronicles, which suggests that a later incident is recorded here. It was in the spring ('turn of the year'), the dry season, when kings went out to war (see 1 Chron. 20:1; 2 Sam. 11:1; 1 Kings 20:26), that the Arameans of Damascus attacked the south. They took advantage of the weak state of the northern kingdom of Israel at this time (2 Kings 13:3-7). The account presses home the point that this was a judgment from God on Joash and the kingdom of Judah, which is referred to as 'Judah and Jerusalem'. The 'officials of the people', the ones who had influenced the king (vv. 17-18), were punished by being 'destroyed' (see 2 Chron. 12:7; 25:15-16; 26:16; 27:2; 36:19 where it is sometimes translated 'corrupted') and their goods carried off to the royal palace in Damascus. Whereas God's people might have expected to take the spoils of war, the opposite was the case. Instead of Yahweh fighting on behalf of His people when often their numbers were much smaller than that of the enemy (see 2 Chron. 13:3, 13-18; 14:8-14[7-13]; 20:2, 20-23), on this occasion, though they had a much larger force than the Arameans, Yahweh gave the victory to the enemy.

In this Aramean attack, Joash was 'left' ('zb), a possible play on one of the Chronicler's favourite words 'forsake'. God had forsaken him and the enemy had 'forsaken' him. Suffering wounds in battle is another of the Chronicler's thematic terms that suggest the person was not in a wholesome condition before God (see 1 Chron. 10:3; 2 Chron. 16:12; 21:15, 18; 35:23). There is further irony in the account. Just as people 'conspired' against

Zechariah (v. 21), so his own servants 'conspired' against Joash, killing him on his sick bed (v. 25). It was in a bedroom that Joash had been hidden when a baby (2 Chron. 22:11) and he ends his days in a bedroom. Kings reports that Joash's servants conspired to kill him but gives no reason, whereas Chronicles states that it was God's revenge for the killing of Zechariah.[38] In contrast to Jehoiada's burial, Joash was not buried with the kings although his tomb was in the city of David (v. 25; see 2 Chron. 21:19-20; 28:27). The assassins are named and identified as sons of Ammonite and Moabite women which only added to the king's humiliation. Both men's names are similar, Zabad and Jehozabad, and the difference that appears between the spelling of Zabad's name in Chronicles and its form in Kings (Jozacar) may be due to the confusion over the similar-looking Hebrew letters: ב (b) and כ (k), ד (d) and ר (r).

The Chronicler, in his closing review (v. 27), is not unmindful of the king's earlier divine blessings such as his many sons, only one of whom is named, namely Amaziah who reigned on the death of his father. Also appreciated is Joash's efforts in 'fixing' or 'establishing' the temple. But the abstract also re-emphasises the 'oracles' of judgment that were delivered 'to' or 'against' the king through the many prophets sent by God (vv. 19-20). The term translated 'oracles' is more literally 'burden' and denotes the prophet's heavy sense of duty.[39] However unacceptable to king and people, the true prophets of Yahweh had no option; they were under constraint (see Isa. 13:1; 15:1; etc.; Zech. 9:1; 12:1; Mal. 1:1; Jer. 20:9; Amos 3:8).

For a second time the Chronicler employs the word 'midrash' to describe his source (v. 27; see 2 Chron. 13:22). The term, as before, is not to be taken in the much later rabbinical sense of a commentary on the Hebrew Scriptures. As for 'the book of kings' this is not the canonical book of Kings but probably a stylistic variation of the fuller 'the book of the kings of Israel and Judah' (see 2 Chron. 16:11; etc.) or 'the

---

38. The plural 'sons' in the MT used for the singular is not uncommon in Chronicles. Rabbi David Kimḥi (Radak), the medieval Jewish commentator, suggested that the rest of Jehoiada's sons were killed when they murdered Zechariah.

39. The translation 'many' oracles follows the *Kethibh* rather than the *Qere* reading 'may it increase', which would result in the literal translation, 'may the burden about him increase.'

book of the kings of Israel' (2 Chron. 20:34; see 1 Kings 14:29; 22:45[6]; 2 Kings 12:19[20]; etc.). Like the 'midrash' of Iddo the prophet, the work may have contained prophetic expositions relating to the nation's kings.

Application

The Chronicler preached to his own day and generation to be forward in their support of the temple. Their commitment to the temple would be an indication of their commitment to God. For Christians, their commitment to God is to be seen in their love for Christ and His people. For this reason we are not to forsake the coming together as a local assembly of God's people for worship, edification and evangelism, and to offer tangible expressions of love. Preachers who are called by God have a heavy responsibility as proclaimers of God's word. 'Woe is me,' said the apostle Paul, 'if I do not preach the gospel' (1 Cor. 9:16).

Sickness and death can be indications of God's disciplinary rod on His people (1 Cor. 11:30; 1 John 5:16). Sudden death powerfully demonstrated God's judgment on people who lied to the Holy Spirit (Acts 5:1-11). All such judgments are warnings of the second death (Rev. 21:6-8). The physical healing of Jesus pointed to the need for spiritual healing from sin and its evil effects as well as to the future when the people of God will be whole in body, mind and spirit. God often uses human instruments to carry out His purposes of judgment on people (Isa. 10:5-7; Deut. 32:30-31). Jesus spoke of the death of Zechariah as an example of hatred for God's truth and likewise pronounced judgment on his contemporaries, a judgment that came to fulfilment in the events that led to the destruction of Jerusalem by the Romans in A.D. 70. Jesus Himself, of course, experienced a conspiracy against Him (Mark 12:1-12), but through His death and resurrection He has restored the true temple making it beautiful with living stones (John 2:14-22; 1 Pet. 2:4-10).

Amaziah's reign (25:1-28)

The account of Amaziah's reign parallels fairly closely the wording in 2 Kings 14:1-20 especially relating to the beginning

(vv. 1-4) and end (vv. 17-28) of his kingship but substantially expands the brief statement in 2 Kings 14:7 relating to his war with Edom (vv. 5-13) and also introduces his resulting apostasy (vv. 14-16). For the Chronicler, the reign is yet another illustration of the themes he wishes to stress. He provides a theological basis both for the victory over Edom and the later defeat against Israel. Though at first glance the king seemed to be following the pattern of his father's reign where he began well but ended badly, the account suggests a less than wholesome attitude evident toward God from the beginning that revealed itself more obviously later. The narrative covers the introduction to Amaziah's reign (vv. 1-4), war with Edom (v. 5-13), Amaziah's apostasy (vv. 14-16), war with Israel (vv. 17-24), and the conclusion to Amaziah's reign (vv. 25-28). This chiastic arrangement highlights at the centre the king's idolatry.

Introduction (25:1-4)

> 25:1. Amaziah was twenty-five years old when he became king, and he reigned twenty-nine years in Jerusalem. His mother's name was Jehoaddan of Jerusalem. 2. And he did what was right in the sight of Yahweh but not with a whole heart. 3. Now it was when the kingdom was established upon him, that he killed his servants who had slain his father the king. 4. However, their sons he did not put to death, but according to what was written in the law in the book of Moses, which Yahweh commanded, saying, 'Fathers shall not die for their sons, nor shall sons die for their fathers, but each shall die for his own sin.'

Though he reigned twenty-nine years, it is the first fourteen years that concern the Chronicler when Joash king of the northern kingdom was alive. In order to make sense of the chronological details concerning the length of the kings who reigned during this period in both kingdoms, a number of co-regencies is suggested.[40] It is calculated that the last fourteen years of Amaziah's rule, or even longer on some reckonings, [41] was shared with his son Azariah and probably resulted from his defeat at the hands of the northern

---

40. See Thiele, *The Mysterious Numbers*, pp. 106-16.
41. Dillard, *2 Chronicles*, p. 198.

kingdom's ruler (vv. 23-25). There was probably also a co-regency with Amaziah's father, Joash, at the beginning of his reign. Jehoaddan, his mother, hailed from Jerusalem (see also 2 Chron. 26:3). Her name means 'Yahweh took pleasure in'.

Like the book of Kings, the Chronicler could state that to all outward appearances Amaziah began by doing what was right in the eyes of Yahweh, but the rider indicates, his heart was not in it from the beginning. The Kings text makes it clear that he was more like his father Joash and unlike king David. The phrase a 'whole heart' has been found earlier in a positive sense (1 Chron. 12:38[39]; 28:9; 29:9, 19; 2 Chron. 15:17; 16:9; 19:9).

Only after the king had consolidated his position after the assassination of Joash, did he take action to bring to justice those involved in his father's murder. Blood vengeance is allowed in the Mosaic law (Num. 35:19), but it is never meant to be indiscriminate, and both Kings and Chronicles quote from Deuteronomy 24:16. This is to be distinguished from the divine wrath that could involve the descendants being punished for the sins of their parents (Exod. 20:5; Deut. 5:9; Josh. 7:24). There are corporate repercussions on societies that violate basic divine moral standards. Jeremiah in 31:29-30 and Ezekiel 18 had special reason for emphasising individual responsibility in their day, but they were certainly not calling for the kind of individualism expressed in many modern societies. The call for personal responsibility rejects fatalistic views or the opinions of those who would blame others for their own sins or those who would seek to accuse God of capriciousness and lack of love.

Application

The rebellious effect of one generation on future generations is well-known. On an individual level it occurs when a parent has misused their bodies through drugs, drink or tobacco and it can lead to long-term effects on children. More serious rebellion against God in one generation can result in damage that lasts for a number of generations. On the other hand, God's mercy, as Exodus 20:5 indicates, can have beneficial effects for countless future generations. We see this in the lasting benefits of the Protestant Reformation and the long-lasting consequences of spiritual revivals that have affected communities and even nations.

Though all the atrocities that happen fulfil God's plan, that does not justify the wickedness that is expressed in such acts of violence and their perpetrators themselves deserve to be punished. It was in God's purposes that Jesus should die the death of the cross, but it was 'wicked hands' that crucified our Lord (Isa. 53:10; Acts 2:23).

War with Edom (25:5-13)

25:5. And Amaziah gathered Judah together and stationed them according to the house of *their* fathers under commanders of thousands and commanders of hundreds, for all Judah and Benjamin; and he numbered them from twenty years old and above, and found them to be three hundred thousand select men, ready for war, who could handle spear and shield. 6. He also hired from Israel a hundred thousand valiant warriors for a hundred talents of silver. 7. But the man of God came to him saying, 'King, do not let the army of Israel go with you, for Yahweh is not with Israel – all the sons of Ephraim. 8. But if you go, act, be strong in the battle! God will cause you to stumble before an enemy; for there is strength with God to help and to cause to stumble.' 9. Then Amaziah said to the man of God, 'But what *shall I* do about the hundred talents which I gave to the Israel troop?' And the man of God answered, 'Yahweh is able to give you much more than this.' 10. So Amaziah separated the troop that had come to him from Ephraim, in order to go to their place, but their anger burned greatly against Judah, and they returned to their place in burning anger. 11. Then Amaziah strengthened himself, and he led his people and went to the Valley of Salt and killed ten thousand of the sons of Seir. 12. And the sons of Judah took ten thousand alive and brought them to the top of the rock, and threw them from the top of the rock so that all of them were dashed to pieces. 13. But the band of troops that Amaziah had turned back from going with him to battle, raided the cities of Judah from Samaria to Beth-horon, and killed three thousand of them and took much spoil.

The southern kingdom of Judah was made up of the tribes of Judah and Benjamin and the king mustered an army of three hundred thousand, a smaller number than those given during

Asa's and Jehoshaphat's reigns (v. 5; 2 Chron. 14:8; 17:14-19). His military enrolment is similar to those carried out by previous Davidic kings from David to Jehoshaphat, the minimum age of twenty being in line with Mosaic practice (Num. 1:3, 18). Perhaps it was on account of the reduced numbers revealed by the census that Amaziah decided to hire a hundred thousand mercenaries from the northern kingdom of Israel. Again, as with all figures that include the term 'thousand', a literal number may not be intended but there remain problems with all such totals in the Old Testament and until further light becomes available, interpreters must humbly admit their limitations. The main point is that a substantial mercenary force was hired and paid well for their services (v. 6).

The title 'a man of God' indicated how prophets were generally regarded by the people (v. 7; 1 Sam. 9:6-10; 2 Kings 4:9). It is also used of Moses, David and Shemaiah (1 Chron. 23:14; 2 Chron. 8:14; 11:2; 30:16; see 2 Tim. 3:17) who are also called prophets. This anonymous prophet called on the king to disband the hired force for the very good reason that Yahweh was not with the northern kingdom of Israel, otherwise known by its principal tribe, Ephraim (see Isa. 7:2; Hosea 4:17; 5:3; etc.). Previous prophetic words have implied that Yahweh was 'with' the Davidic king and not 'with' the political kingdom of Israel (2 Chron. 13:12). The northern kingdom therefore could not prosper and any kind of alliance with it by Judah was considered sinful (2 Chron. 18:1–19:3; 20:35-37). That did not mean that individuals and groups from the north could not know God's presence and help if they repented (2 Chron. 11:4; 28:9-15). The Hebrew of verse 8 is difficult but it suggests a strong ironic note, similar to Micaiah's prophecy (2 Chron. 18:14), that if the king went out for battle with the mercenaries, they would be soundly defeated. A second reason why the king was not to employ the northerners is that it would indicate a lack of faith in God's ability to save by few or many (2 Chron. 13:3-18; 14:8-15; and see Judg. 7). It was a call for Amaziah to trust God who had the power both to help as well as to overthrow (1 Chron. 29:12; 2 Chron. 20:6).

The king accepted the prophet's warning but was worried about the financial loss, having already paid the mercenaries for their services. To this concern, the prophet assured

Amaziah of a much greater reward (v. 9). By discharging the mercenaries, the king showed why it could be said of him that he did what was right in the sight of Yahweh (v. 10; see v. 2). The response of the dismissed northern troops is one of extreme outrage and it resulted in action that tested the king's faith (see v. 13).

The reason for gathering together choice soldiers for war is only given in verse 11. Amaziah strengthened himself to attack Edom, Judah's neighbour to the south. Edom had invaded Judah during Jehoshaphat's reign (2 Chron. 20:10-23) and in Jehoram's reign they had regained the independence they had lost under David (1 Chron. 18:11-13; 2 Chron. 21:8-10). The terms 'Edom' and 'sons of Seir' are used interchangeably for the same people group.

Expanding on the brief account in 2 Kings 14:7, the Chronicler tells not only of the ten thousand Edomites killed in the Valley of Salt (see 1 Chron. 18:12) but of a second slaughter of another ten thousand who had been captured (vv. 11-12). The 'rock' (sela') is not to be identified with what became Petra, the city cut out of rock, but a reference to some suitable cliff in the area. Amaziah's military campaign was devastatingly successful and reasserted Israel's dominion over Edom (see Gen. 27:29, 37). The narrative concerning the Edomite war closes, not on a high note, but by describing the rampage of the disgruntled and hopping-mad mercenaries who were probably hoping for a share in the spoils of war. They seized the opportunity, while Amaziah was in the south against Edom, to gather in Samaria and move down to the border city of Beth-horon, raiding cities in Ephraim that Judah had taken in skirmishes with the northern kingdom (v. 13; see 2 Chron. 13:19). The booty they were deprived of in Edom they obtained from the three thousand they killed.

Application

The gloating pleasure of Edom when Jerusalem was destroyed in 587 B.C. (see Obadiah, Lamentations and Ezekiel 35) may be the reason why the Chronicler spends time on this campaign.[42] Edom symbolised all opposition to God and His people. The description

---

42. See Johnstone, 1 and 2 Chronicles, vol. 2, p.156.

of those taken captive being thrown to their destruction is a vivid and gruesome reminder of the final end of all who remain in rebellion against God (Pss. 2:9; 137:7-9). Christians are never to engage in vindictive actions but are encouraged to pray for their enemies, to overcome evil with good and to look to God Himself to take vengeance (Rom. 12:14, 17-20).

The Lord is no man's debtor. God can make up for all loss be it in money and property or even in the loss of loved ones. Jesus states that Christians are to deny self and take up their cross and He promises that no one who has left house and family for His sake will lose out (Mark 8:34-35; 10:28-31).

Amaziah's apostasy (25:14-16)

> 25:14. Now it was after Amaziah came from the slaughter of the Edomites, that he brought the gods of the sons of Seir, set them up *to be* his gods and bowed down before them and burned incense to them. 15. Then the anger of Yahweh was aroused against Amaziah, and he sent him a prophet who said to him, 'Why have you sought the gods of the people that did not deliver their people from your hand?' 16. So it was, while he spoke to him, that he said to him, 'Have we made you the king's counsellor? Stop! Why should you be struck down?' Then the prophet stopped and said, 'I know that God has taken counsel to destroy you because you have done this and have not listened to my counsel.'

Amaziah returned from his resounding victory over the Edomites but laden among the booty were images of their gods. Instead of burning them as David had done with the idols taken from the Philistines (1 Chron. 14:12; see Deut. 7:5; 12:3), Amaziah accepted them as representations of real gods and began to pay homage and offer sacrifice to them and by so doing he was probably acknowledging that they had played some part in his conquest of Edom (v. 15). He may even have been encouraged in this apostasy through hearing of the raid by the mercenaries, believing that God had not been true to His word (see v. 9). This change in his religious devotion was an indication of how half-hearted he really was in seeking to please Yahweh (v. 2).

Yahweh's anger burned against Amaziah but instead of immediate punishment, an unnamed prophet was graciously sent to challenge him (v. 15). Whether it was the same one who had spoken to him earlier is not stated (see v. 7). The message appealed to reason: why was the king worshipping gods who were impotent to save their people? In contrast to 'seeking' God, which is one of the main themes of Chronicles, Amaziah was 'seeking' (*drš*) pagan gods. Prophets were raised up by God to be the conscience of the nation and particularly to confront and question the activities of Israel's kings. Amaziah, like previous occupants of the throne, resented the prophet's intervention and sarcastically enquired whether the prophet had become a royal counsellor. He called for him to desist or be killed, which was exactly what his father had ordered in the case of the prophet Zechariah (2 Chron. 24:20-21). False prophets at court were expected to agree with whatever the king wished (see 2 Chron. 18:5-13). On this occasion the prophet stopped but not before issuing God's word of judgment. The term 'counsellor' (v. 16), used in the king's ironic reprimand, is used by the prophet as a play on words. Because the king refused 'counsel', God 'has counselled' the destruction of the king. The word for 'destroy' (*šḥt*) is another of the Chronicler's important terms (2 Chron. 12:12; 21:7; 26:16; 36:19).

Application

Matthew Henry helpfully comments that if the king had thrown the idols off the cliff rather than the people he would have shown more of a godly spirit. He also suggests that it was because of 'that barbarous inhumanity', that the king was 'given up' by God's wrath to the kind of foolish idolatry which often led to such atrocities in the first place (Rom. 1:18-25).

The prophet graciously reasoned with the king as he does generally with sinners (Isa. 1:18-20). To harden oneself after being given reproof and warning is to be in a dangerous position (Prov. 29:1).

War with Israel (25:17-24)

25:17. Then Amaziah the king of Judah took counsel and sent to Joash, the son of Jehoahaz, the son of Jehu, the king of Israel, saying, 'Come, let us face each other.' 18. And Joash the king of Israel sent to Amaziah king of Judah saying, 'The thistle that was in Lebanon sent to the cedar that was in Lebanon saying, "Give your daughter to my son as wife"; and a wild animal that was in Lebanon passed by and trampled the thistle. 19. Indeed, you say that you have struck Edom and your heart is lifted up to boast. Now, stay in your house; why should you engage with trouble and fall, you and Judah with you?' 20. But Amaziah did not listen, for it was from God that he might give them into *their* hand, because they sought the gods of Edom. 21. So Joash the king of Israel went up; and he and Amaziah king of Judah faced each other at Beth-shemesh, which belongs to Judah. 22. And Judah was defeated before Israel, and each one fled to his tent. 23. Then Joash the king of Israel captured Amaziah the king of Judah, the son of Joash, the son of Jehoahaz, at Beth-shemesh, and he brought him to Jerusalem and broke down the wall of Jerusalem from the Gate of Ephraim to the Corner Gate – four hundred cubits. 24. And he took all the gold and silver and all the utensils that were found in the house of God with Obed-edom, and the treasuries of the king's house, also hostages and returned to Samaria.

At this point, the Chronicler's account parallels the text of Kings but not before introducing the narrative with another play on the 'counsel' word family (v. 17; see v. 16). In this way, the compiler unifies the two paragraphs to show how God punished Amaziah for his idolatry. Instead of consulting God he made up his own mind to pick a fight with the northern kingdom of Israel. No doubt his success over the Edomites in the south and his desire to win back what the mercenaries had taken, bolstered his ego to take on the enemy to the north.

There are only two fables in the Old Testament: the one by Jotham, Gideon's youngest son, and this one by Joash (also spelled Jehoash in 2 Kings 14), the king of Israel (see Judg. 9:7-15; 2 Kings 14:9). While the cedar of Lebanon was proverbial for its grandeur in the forest and the quality of its fragrant wood, the thorn was mere vegetation of the wilderness which a wild animal could easily trample down. The northern king likened himself to the cedar for he was in a strong position at this time and reckoned that his southern neighbour was like a thorn and no match for him, despite the southern king having gained a notable victory over Edom. But Amaziah, who had refused to accept the counsel of one of Yahweh's prophets, was in no mood to listen to the advice of his enemy, especially as it was introduced by such an undiplomatic and highly insulting moralistic tale. The patience of God is clear in using the northern king to underline what the unnamed prophet had said. Amaziah's pride prevented him from seeing how foolish his plan was. The Chronicler adds that it was in God's purposes to use the king's arrogant stupidity to punish him and those who followed him for their idolatry (see 2 Chron. 10:15; 22:7 for the same phrase 'from God'). Again, Judah's guilt consisted in 'seeking' the gods of Edom (v. 20; see v. 15).

Amaziah had his way, and the two kings faced each other in battle at Beth-shemesh, a strategic point on the Judah–Israel border which guarded a major route from the west to Jerusalem. The reference to 'Judah' distinguishes this Beth-shemesh from cities of the same name in Issachar and Naphtali (v. 21; Josh. 15:10; 19:22, 38). It was a humiliating defeat for Judah and its king, for Amaziah was captured, other hostages were taken, Jerusalem's northern wall was breached, and the temple and palace treasures were plundered. On the other hand, the all-conquering northern king, Joash, was able to return safely and triumphantly to his own capital in Samaria (vv. 23-24).

The Ephraim Gate (see Neh. 8:16; 12:39), as the name implies, faced the north while the Corner Gate (26:9; Jer. 31:38; Zech. 14:10) was situated at the north west corner. A length of wall of about six hundred feet (two hundred metres) was damaged, leaving the city defenceless at its weakest point. The Chronicler adds a note not found in Kings about an Obed-edom who had care of the temple treasures. No doubt this man was a descendant of the illustrious Levite who had charge of the temple treasures in David's day (v. 24; 1 Chron. 13:13-14; 26:15). It was David who had dedicated to Yahweh silver, gold and other utensils that he had brought back from his defeat of Edom and other nations (1 Chron. 18:11).

The 'hostages', literally 'sons of pledges', occurs only here and in the parallel text of Kings, and probably refers to important officials who were taken as a guarantee of future loyal behaviour. If it included temple officials, Donald Wiseman surmises that this might have been the occasion for those Levites exiled in the north to have composed such Psalms as 42 and 43 that express the longing to be back in

God's house.[43] At all events, what the house of Ahab had tried and failed to achieve during the period of the Omri dynasty in gaining the ascendancy over the Davidic throne and all it represented, Joash of the Jehu dynasty had accomplished. The success over Edom to the south in reasserting the status of the Davidic line was undermined by this catastrophic defeat.

Conclusion (25:25-28)

25:25. And Amaziah, the son of Joash the king of Judah, lived fifteen years after the death of Joash the son of Jehoahaz, the king of Israel. 26. Now the rest of the acts of Amaziah, the first and the last, are they not indeed written in the book of the kings of Judah and Israel? 27. And from the time that Amaziah turned from following Yahweh, they plotted a conspiracy against him in Jerusalem and he fled to Lachish; but they sent after him to Lachish and put him to death there. 28. Then they carried him on horses and buried him with his fathers in the city of Judah.

These closing verses also parallel the text in Kings including, uniquely, the synchronism with the northern regime. It witnesses to the southern kingdom's dependence on the northern kingdom and, more particularly, Amaziah's final years are viewed in relation to the northern king Joash's death (v. 25). Some commentators believe that the reference also implies that Amaziah was not released from captivity until the death of Joash, while others believe he would have been released earlier when the hostages were taken to Samaria (v. 24). The statement that Amaziah 'lived' rather than 'reigned' after the death of Joash may well suggest that a co-regency was operating in Judah, which is, in any case, necessary for the chronology of the kings to fit (see v. 1). It is also important to distinguish between Joash the father of Amaziah of the southern kingdom and Joash who is usually given the longer form, 'Jehoash', in the Kings' account. In fact, the Chronicler himself seeks to avoid any confusion in this course of the narrative by providing the parentages of both kings, north and south (vv. 17, 23, 25).

Why the conspiracy took so long to remove Amaziah is not given unless the clause beginning 'And from the time ...'

---

43. See Donald J. Wiseman, *1 and 2 Kings* (Leicester: Inter-Varsity Press, 1993), p. 246.

(v. 27) has more to do with the ultimate cause than the exact timing of the plot. Unlike Kings which gives no reason for Amaziah's assassination, the Chronicler clearly indicates that it was due to his apostasy. But God was in no hurry to bring about the king's death. It must have been some twenty-four years after Amaziah's humiliating defeat, and for the last fifteen of those years since the death of king Joash of Israel, he had been given further opportunities to repent. No information is furnished as to why or when Amaziah fled to Lachish, one of Judah's most important fortified cities some thirty miles (fifty-five kilometres) southwest of Jerusalem (see 2 Chron. 11:9). Maybe the plot to kill him grew over time and when it became too hot for him to remain in Jerusalem he fled to a city where he thought he would have more support. But it was in that very city where Amaziah had sought sanctuary that the anonymous assassins eventually caught up with him and killed him. He was carried unceremoniously on horses with no mention of a chariot (v. 28; see 2 Chron. 35:24) and was buried with his fathers. Instead of the usual 'city of David' (2 Kings 14:20), the traditional text reads 'city of Judah,' and though this is a unique name for Jerusalem in the Old Testament, it is attested in extra-biblical records. The fact that Amaziah's son, Uzziah, the co-regent, is not said to have punished the conspirators as Amaziah had done in the case of his father's assassins (see v. 3) may suggest that he was at least acquiescent.

Application

Exclusive loyalty to Yahweh is again emphasised by this account. Early success for faithfulness is no guarantee that we shall continue to be true to the Lord. Many who have committed themselves to Christ in their formative years and even pastors who have been very successful in their early ministries have tragically fallen away in later life. 'Let him who stands take heed lest he fall,' warns Paul and adds 'flee from idolatry' (1 Cor. 10:12-14). Pride comes before a fall (see Prov. 29:23). When the faithful preaching of God's messengers is not received, God in His mercy will sometimes use other means such as the rebukes and criticisms of those who are not Christian.

Whole-hearted service was what was required post-exile; Amaziah's life was a warning but also an exhortation to loyal service.

Uzziah's reign (26:1-23)

For the account of this reign, Chronicles consistently uses the name Uzziah ('Yahweh is my strength'), while in 2 Kings 14:21 and 15:1-8 the same king is called Azariah ('Yahweh has helped'). In other references to the king, the Chronicler uses the name 'Azariah' only once (1 Chron. 3:12), whereas there are four occurrences in Kings where 'Uzziah' is used (2 Kings 15:13, 30, 32, 34). The Chronicler's use of the name 'Uzziah' certainly avoided any confusion with Azariah the priest who is mentioned in verses 17 and 20. In the prophetic writings, the king is generally known as 'Uzziah' (Isa. 1:1; 6:1; Hosea 1:1; Amos 1:1; Zech. 14:5) and this may suggest that this was his throne name while 'Azariah' was his birth name. Some scholars assume that the two forms are variants of the same name (the root letters are 'zr for Azariah and 'zz for Uzziah).

The parallel to this reign is found in 2 Kings 14:21-22 and 15:1-7 but Chronicles adds far more detail both to indicate the divine blessing he experienced at the beginning of his reign and the reason why Yahweh later struck him down with 'leprosy'. There are four main sections to the account. The introduction (26:1-5) and conclusion (26:22-23) frame the two main parts to Uzziah's life, namely, the years of blessing for faithfulness (26:6-15) and the years of curse for unfaithfulness (26:16-21).

Introduction (26:1-5)

The traditional Hebrew text suggests that verses 1 and 2 should be taken with the previous chapter as part of the conclusion to Amaziah's reign. There is a close parallel with the Kings text, with the first two verses paralleling 2 Kings 14:21-22 and the following two verses paralleling 2 Kings 15:2-3. The Chronicler's omission of 2 Kings 14:23–15:1 which deals with the reign of Jeroboam II, is due to his policy of only mentioning the northern kingdom when it had direct contact with the southern kingdom of Judah. While in 2 Kings 15:2 the account picks up again on Uzziah in a natural way, the parallel words in Chronicles (v. 3) that repeat the king's age so soon after its mention in verse 1 seem unnecessary. Nevertheless, it does indicate that the Chronicler is keen to stick close to his sources. As with the previous king, the Chronicler makes no mention of the high places so as to concentrate on the positive elements in the first half of the reign.

> 26:1. Now all the people of Judah took Uzziah, and he was sixteen years old, and they made him king instead of his father Amaziah. 2. And he built Eloth and restored it to Judah after the king slept with his fathers. 3. Uzziah was sixteen years old when he became king, and he reigned fifty-two years in Jerusalem and the name of his mother was Jecoliah from Jerusalem. 4. And he did what was right in the sight of Yahweh according to all that Amaziah his father had done. 5. And he sought God in the days of Zechariah, who was skilled in the seeing of God; and as long as he sought Yahweh, God made him prosper.

The opening phrase 'all the people of Judah' is unique (but see 2 Sam. 19:41; 2 Chron. 23:13) and suggests that the plot to kill Amaziah, his father, had popular support. It also implies that Uzziah was at least compliant. By the time his father was assassinated, it is calculated that Uzziah would have already been co-regent for twenty-four years, [44] perhaps from the time that Amaziah had been taken prisoner. This means that he became the sole king when he was forty. What his father had failed to achieve in his campaign against Edom, namely, retaking the fortified port of Eloth or Elath, his son succeeded in capturing. It was of immense importance to Judah for it opened up trade with south Arabia, Africa and India. The city lay on the north west of the Gulf of Aqaba near to Ezion-Geber where Solomon and Jehoshaphat had each kept a fleet of ships (2 Chron. 8:17-18; 20:36).

Uzziah's reign, including the co-regencies, is the second longest reign of the Davidic kings and occurred at the time when the north had a similar long and stable period under the rule of Jeroboam II. The first half of the eighth century was a time when Egypt was damaged by internal strife, Assyria was preoccupied with enemies to their north, and Damascus was

---

44. Dillard, *2 Chronicles*, p. 207.

in a weakened position. This providential situation enabled both Israelite kingdoms to become prosperous.

Like his father, Uzziah had a mother from Jerusalem (2 Chron. 25:1). The Masoretic Text provides two ways of spelling her name. It is spelt Jekiliah ('Yahweh is able') with the *Kethibh* (the consonantal text) or Jecoliah ('May Yahweh sustain') with the *Qere* (the reading in the margin explaining the Masoretic pointing). The Chronicler begins by giving Uzziah a general statement of approval (v. 4; see 2 Kings 15:3-4). Doing 'right' in God's sight meant that the king set himself to 'seek' God (*drš*; see 1 Chron. 10:13-14) and this enabled him to 'prosper' or 'succeed' (another key term associated with the Chronicler's theology of blessing for obedience; see 1 Chron. 22:11, 13; 29:23; 2 Chron. 13:12; 14:7[6]; 24:20) in contrast to his father whose reign was marred by 'seeking' the gods of Edom and whose life ended in tragedy (2 Chron. 25:15, 20, 21-24, 27). To seek 'God' is to seek 'Yahweh', the God of Moses and the exodus. Uzziah had an adviser in Zechariah during his youthful years who kept him humble, in much the same way as Jehoiada the priest influenced Joash (v. 5; 2 Chron. 24:2). Who Zechariah was is not revealed but he may well have been one of the witnesses named by Isaiah (Isa. 8:2). Most scholars emend the traditional text to read with the LXX 'in the fear of God'. In Hebrew, the words for seeing (*r'h*) and fearing (*yr'*) can sometimes be confused. If, however, Zechariah was himself a 'seer' or prophet and like Isaiah 'saw' his visions, then the unusual phrase 'seeing of God' is not surprising. This man instructed the king in the prophetic word (see Isa. 1:1; 6:1, 5; 13:1; 29:18).

Secure and prosperous (26:6-15)

> 26:6. Now he went out and fought against the Philistines and broke down the wall of Gath, the wall of Jabneh and the wall of Ashdod; and he built cities *by* Ashdod and among the Philistines. 7. And God helped him against the Philistines and against the Arabs who lived in Gur-baal and against the Meunites. 8. Also the Ammonites gave tribute to Uzziah, and his name went as far as the entrance of Egypt, for he was exceedingly strong. 9. And Uzziah built towers in Jerusalem at the Corner Gate, and at the Valley Gate and at the Angle and he fortified them. 10. He also built towers in the wilderness

and dug many cisterns, for he had much livestock, both in the Shephelah and in the plain; *he had* farmers and vinedressers in the mountains and in the fertile area, for he loved the soil. 11. And Uzziah had an army for doing battle who went out to war by divisions, according to the number of their enrolment by the hand of Jeiel the scribe and Maaseiah the officer, under the direction of Hananiah, one of the king's officials. 12. The total number of the heads of fathers belonging to the valiant men *was* two thousand six hundred. 13. And under their hand was a valiant army of three hundred and seven thousand five hundred, that made war with valiant power, to help the king against the enemy. 14. Then Uzziah prepared for them, for the entire army, shields and spears and helmets and body armour, and bows and stones for slinging. 15. And he made devices in Jerusalem, invented by skilful men, to be on the towers and corners, to shoot with the arrows and with the stones, large ones. So his name spread out far, for he was marvellously helped until he was strong.

The paragraph divides into two with similar comments referring to the king's fame and power at the close of each part (vv. 8, 15). First, an example is provided of Uzziah's success in war (vv. 6-8), followed by details of his building projects (vv. 9-10), agricultural concerns (v. 10b), and improvements in military organisation and equipment (vv. 11-15).

In subduing the neighbouring nations, Israel's arch enemy to the west, the Philistines, is mentioned first (see 1 Chron. 1:12; 10:1-11; 14:15; 18:1). As the wall of Jerusalem had been breached by the northern kingdom of Israel (2 Chron. 25:23), so Uzziah was able to do the same to Gath, to Jabneh to the north (see Jabneel in Josh. 15:11), and to Ashdod which seems to have become by this time a separate entity from the other Philistine places (see Isa. 20). This whole Philistine area was part of Judah's allotted territory and Uzziah was even able to build settlements there (v. 6; Josh. 15:45-47). In this enterprise, the king had God's 'help' which is another of the Chronicler's key terms as witnessed in this chapter (vv. 7, 13, 15; see 1 Chron. 12:18; 2 Chron. 14:11[10]; 18:31). Divine help also came to Uzziah in his victory over nomadic groups such as the Arabs and Meunites to the south of Judah (see 1 Chron. 4:41; 2 Chron. 21:16). In an inscription of the Assyrian king, Tiglath-Pileser III, some Meunites were located near the

Egyptian border, southwest of Judah. The place-name 'Gur-baal' does not occur elsewhere in Scripture but it may be the same as Jagur, one of the cities on the southern border of Judah (Josh. 15:21). Instead of being any threat to Judah, the Ammonites to the east of Judah paid tribute as a token of their submission (v. 8; see 1 Chron. 18:11; 2 Chron. 27:5). Like David, Uzziah's 'name', that is his fame or reputation, spread over the whole area (vv. 8, 15; 1 Chron. 14:17; 17:8). Just as Solomon was strengthened in the kingdom (2 Chron. 1:1) so Uzziah, whose name is from another verb meaning 'to be strong' ('zz), became very strong (ḥzq). This strength was the result of his faithfulness in 'seeking' God (vv. 5, 15).

The second half of this paragraph concerns the domestic activities of Uzziah. Building projects were a further sign of God's blessing. Fortifying the walls of Jerusalem was necessary after they were broken by Jehoash of the northern kingdom during Amaziah's reign, and which may have been made worse by the severe earthquake that happened during Uzziah's reign (2 Chron. 25:23; Amos 1:1; Zech. 14:5). Building the walls of Jerusalem was a major concern during Nehemiah's governorship (Neh. 1:3; 2:3, 11-17; 3:1-6:15). The gates mentioned include the 'Corner Gate' (2 Chron. 25:23; Zech. 14:10), the 'Valley Gate' (Neh. 2:13, 15; 3:13) and the 'Angle' ('buttress' in older English versions; see Neh. 3:19-20, 24-25). Many towers and cisterns in the desert from this period have been excavated and in one cistern a seal was found bearing the name of Uzziah. The desert towers were not only for defensive purposes but served as storehouses (v. 10; see 1 Chron. 27:25; 2 Chron. 27:4). Cisterns were dug for all the cattle that the king owned (see Jer. 2:13). Besides the Negev desert area, the Shephelah or foothills and the coastal plain, the king placed farmers and vinedressers in the hilly regions and fertile valleys. Uzziah was a king who 'loved' working the ground and all this royal agricultural interest was a reminder of the situation under David (1 Chron. 27:25-31). The prophets revealed the kind of lifestyle enjoyed by those whose wealth had increased during this period at the expense of the poor (Isa. 5:8-12), but for the Chronicler the pastoral picture of peace and prosperity was a sign of divine blessing during this early part of the king's reign.

The rest of this second section of the account, illustrating the marks of blessing, is a description of the king's army. Previous examples describing the sizes of royal armies are confined to Judean kings who were at the time faithful to God (2 Chron. 14:8[7]; 17:14-19; 25:5). An adequate, well-equipped fighting force was essential to secure the nation's peaceful state and continuing safety. Nothing is known of the individuals named but the scribe and officer assigned in mustering the troops were under the overall supervision of the king's commander (v. 11). The census and the organisation of the army is based on the traditional system of ancestral houses but for the first time no mention is made of the two tribal units, Judah and Benjamin (v. 12; see 2 Chron. 14:8[7]; 17:14-18; 25:5). While the heads of families numbered two thousand six hundred, the size of the army of conscripts amounted to three hundred and seven thousand five hundred. The total number is larger than Amaziah's army (v. 13; 2 Chron. 25:5). Again, the terms 'hundred' and 'thousand' may be referring to particular units. The purpose of this powerful force was to 'help' the king against the enemy (v. 13b). The royal conscripts were provided with government armour, whereas previously, soldiers usually brought their own weapons (v. 14; Judg. 20:8-17; 1 Sam. 13:19 22; 1 Chron. 12:2). Some of the equipment was defensive like the shields, helmets and coats of mail ('body armour'; see 1 Sam. 17:5, 38; 2 Chron. 18:33), while the spears, bows and stone-slings were for attack. As for the specially invented devices for the walls 'of Jerusalem (v. 15), they are unlikely to have been catapults at this time in Judah's history but rather coverings on the walls and towers to give more protection to the archers and slingers from enemy arrows and stones.

The paragraph ends by repeating the three terms mentioned in verses 7 and 8, namely 'help', 'name' and 'strength'. These words express the kind of ideal situation to which every Davidic king should attain. Uzziah's reputation extended further because he was 'marvellously helped' (v. 15). The word family associated with 'marvellously' or 'wonderfully' (*pl'*) usually suggests a supernatural element (see Exod. 3:20; Judg. 13:19; Isa. 9:6[5]; 28:29; 29:14) and this would parallel the earlier statement that God helped him (v. 7). It was divine aid that made him strong. The time reference at the end of the sentence ('until he was strong') sounds an ominous note and it prepares for the next paragraph.

Application

This part of Uzziah's reign is a reminder of David, his victories over the enemies of God and His people, and his care for the people's wellbeing. It is a veiled pointer to David's greater Son. He is the one who did what was right in God's sight and prospered, having gained the victory over the fundamental enemies of sin, Satan, death and hell. The Lord builds up the walls of the eternal city to provide safety for His people (Ps. 51:18; Isa. 26:1-4).

The Chronicler keeps on encouraging his readers to seek God. This means loving God freely and wholeheartedly, trusting Him and living in obedience to His word (see 2 Chron. 15:2, 4, 12). We are urged to live by God's word, and faithful preachers and teachers of God's revealed Word are given to keep us in the good way and to enable us to encourage one another (Ezra 8:15-21; 1 Cor. 10:11; Col. 3:16-17; 2 Tim. 3:14-4:5).

God's help (vv. 7, 15) often comes to His people through very mundane ways (v. 13), but there are occasions when He uses extraordinary means. But whichever way, we can praise God for His 'wonderful' works (Ps. 40:5). Above all, when we were all in a helpless and hopeless mess, God sent His Son to rescue poor sinners. Our despised and rejected Saviour was raised and exalted after accomplishing the redeeming work of the cross. This was the Lord's doing and 'it is marvellous in our eyes' (Ps. 118:22-23). No wonder on the day of Pentecost those filled with the Spirit proclaimed 'the wonderful works of God' (Acts 2:11)!

Infidelity and punishment (26:16-21)

2 Kings 15:5 briefly reports that Yahweh had struck the king with leprosy so that he was barred from the temple and kingly duties, but Chronicles provides the details of why this punishment fell upon the king.

> 26:16. But when he was strong his heart was lifted up, to his ruin, and he acted unfaithfully toward Yahweh his God and entered

the temple of Yahweh to burn incense on the altar of incense. 17. So Azariah the priest came after him, and with him were eighty priests of Yahweh, sons of valour. 18. And they stood by king Uzziah and said to him, 'It is not for you, Uzziah, to burn incense to Yahweh, but for the priests, the sons of Aaron, who are consecrated to burn incense. Get out from the sanctuary, for you have acted unfaithfully and you will have no honour from Yahweh God.' 19. Then Uzziah was furious and he had in his hand a censer to burn incense. And while he was furious with the priests, leprosy broke out on his forehead, before the priests in the house of Yahweh, beside the incense altar. 20. And Azariah the chief priest and all the priests turned to him, and there he was, leprous on his forehead; so they hurried him out from there, and he also hurried to get out, because Yahweh had struck him. 21. And Uzziah the king was leprous until the day of his death and he lived in a separate house, leprous, for he was cut off from the house of Yahweh. Then Jotham his son *was* over the king's house judging the people of the land.

As often in Chronicles, a king's reign is divided into two parts, one indicating a king's good points and the other his bad ones. The Chronicler introduces this second part to Uzziah's reign by repeating the verb 'strong' with which he closed the previous paragraph (vv. 15-16). Two of the Chronicler's key terms are found in verse 16 – 'strong' and 'unfaithful'. Instead of Uzziah using his strong position wisely and humbly, it made him arrogant. His heart became 'haughty (literally 'lifted up'; see 2 Chron. 25:19) and it led to his downfall. The form of the verb for 'downfall', 'ruin' or 'destroy' could be rendered 'act corruptly' (see 2 Chron. 27:2). The verb in its many Hebrew forms is another of the Chronicler's favourites (1 Chron. 20:1; 21:12, 15; 2 Chron. 12:12; 21:7; 24:23; 25:16; 34:11; 35:21; 36:19). Instead of his 'heart' delighting in the ways of Yahweh (2 Chron. 17:6), he acted 'unfaithfully (*mā'al*; see vv. 16, 18; 1 Chron. 10:13) toward Yahweh'. Like Rehoboam, it was when Uzziah was 'strong' that infidelity arose and expressed itself in rebelling against God's law (see 2 Chron. 12:1-2). The sin of pride led to further sin. The ceremonial law required the priests alone to enter the nave of the temple and burn incense on the golden incense altar (1 Chron. 28:18; 2 Chron. 13:10-22; Exod. 30:1-10; Num. 16:40; 18:1-7). Whether this occasion was during the daily ritual of offering incense morning and evening or on the annual Day of Atonement when the high priest alone entered the inner sanctum with animal blood amid plumes of incense smoke is not stated (Exod. 30:7-8; Lev. 16:12-14). Incidents recorded during the wilderness wanderings underlined God's holiness and the reason why entrance into the holiest parts of the temple and burning incense were reserved for the ordained priests. When Aaron's sons offered 'strange' fire they were killed (Lev. 10:1-3) and it was the exclusive right of the priests to offer incense that was at the heart of Korah's rebellion. As a result of that whole incident, extra precautions were taken to prevent people sinning with regard to the holiness of the sanctuary and thus provoking God's wrath (see Num. 16). The king was only allowed to go as far as the great bronze altar for burning sacrifices in the temple courtyard (2 Chron. 6:12-13; 7:7).

The high priest (see v. 20), Azariah, who is not listed among those mentioned in 1 Chronicles 6, accompanied by eighty other priests, followed the king to prevent him engaging in this highly provocative and dangerous action. The priests are described literally as 'sons of valour', a phrase that is used elsewhere of soldiers (v. 17; Deut. 3:18 and see above vv. 12-13 for 'valour,' *ḥāyil*). Priests were allowed to bear arms (1 Chron. 12:27-28; 2 Chron. 23:7). Clearly, they were prepared to use force if necessary to remove the royal trespasser. Azariah's brave reprimand (v. 18) reminded the king that the priests had been specially set apart and had the sole right to burn incense, so he was directed to leave immediately as he had acted 'unfaithfully' (*mā'al*). Unlike David, Solomon and Jehoshaphat, Uzziah would receive no honour from God if he continued in his illegal action (1 Chron. 29:28; 2 Chron. 1:12; 17:5; 18:1). God is slow to anger and He gave the king ample time to repent. But Uzziah's reaction was the same as that displayed by king Asa when he was rebuked (2 Chron. 16:10). Instead of repenting, as Rehoboam did when he was challenged (2 Chron. 12:6-7), Uzziah was furious with the priests and stood stubbornly before them by the incense altar with the censer in his hand (v. 19). This scene had some similarities to the Korah incident (Num. 16:6-7) and the divine judgment in both cases was swift and sudden.

The king was not killed but a nasty skin complaint broke out on his forehead (v. 19). As with Asa and Jehoram the punishment took the form of a disease (see 2 Chron. 16:12-13; 21:12-19). The verb 'to break out' is normally used of the sun 'coming out' or 'rising' or figuratively of the Lord arising (Judg. 9:33; Jonah 4:8; Isa. 60:1). Interestingly, the 'leprosy' appeared at the very spot where the high priest's golden rosette or medallion was displayed and on which was written 'Holy to Yahweh' (Exod. 28:36-38). The place that bore the sign of the priest's office and protection as he officiated on behalf of the nation's guilt, became, in the king's case, the area where the 'leprosy' appeared, indicating unholiness, pollution and rejection. 'Leprosy' is the traditional translation, but the meaning of the Hebrew is much broader than the modern conception of leprosy, known as Hanson's disease. It covered various kinds of scaly or disfiguring conditions that became obvious on human skin, on clothing and even on articles made of leather, as well as mildew or fungus that sometimes appeared on walls of houses (see Lev. 13–14). In humans it was tantamount to a living death. The wording 'turned towards him and there he was leprous' recalls the same phraseology in the case of Miriam when Aaron 'turned towards Miriam and there she was leprous' (Num. 12:10). Miriam was punished with this skin disease when she questioned Moses' authority, although she was later healed through Moses' intercession (Num. 12:1-15; see also Naaman and Gehazi in 2 Kings 5).

In the end, no force was required to hustle the king out of the temple; he himself rushed out when he realised that he had been 'struck' by God (v. 20). Verse 21 parallels the words of 2 Kings 15:5 and recounts how the king remained a 'leper' until the day of his death, living in 'a special house', literally 'a house of freedom', a unique expression which may mean either a house on his own, free from royal responsibilities, or that he lived in freedom at home, or a euphemism for an isolation house. But his disease also meant he was barred from the temple on account of his ritually unclean condition (see Lev. 13:46; Num. 5:1-4). The king who wished to carry out the same priestly duties as those set apart for that exclusive purpose was now dependent on those priests to inspect his skin disease and to ban him altogether even from areas

of the temple where his subjects were free to congregate
(Deut. 24:8-9). Jotham, his son, became co-regent and had
the responsibility of administering the royal household as
well as governing the country. The verb 'judge' is used in
the wider sense of 'ruling' but is a reminder of the early local
rulers in Israel (see Judg. 2:16-19). Jotham ruled 'the people
of the land', that is, the ordinary, common people (v. 21; see
2 Chron. 23:13, 20, 21).

Conclusion (26:22-23)

> 26:22. Now the rest of the acts of Uzziah, the first and the last,
> Isaiah the prophet the son of Amoz wrote. 23. And Uzziah
> rested with his fathers and they buried him with his fathers in
> the burial field that belonged to the kings, for they said, 'He is
> leprous'. Then Jotham his son reigned in his place.

The phrase 'the first and the last' occurs nine times in
Chronicles but never in Kings (see 1 Chron. 29:29). Whether
the canonical book of Isaiah is in mind is uncertain as it
is possible that the prophet's words were found as part of
the Chronicler's main source (see also 2 Chron. 32:32). It
was in the year that Uzziah died that Isaiah saw the Lord
(Isa. 6:1). The Chronicler adds that though he 'lay down' in
death 'with his fathers' and was 'buried with his fathers',
he was not actually buried among the royal tombs but near
them in the royal burial field. Though there is no legislation
requiring separate burial for 'lepers', the Chronicler makes
a point of emphasising that the king remained in a ritually
unclean condition through to his death. Those who buried
him acknowledged this: 'He is leprous.' They desired others
to appreciate this fact by keeping his remains at a distance
from the usual graves. In this way the Chronicler indicates
that Uzziah had no 'honour' in death (see v. 18).

Application

Uzziah becomes a warning to us, especially when God
providentially gives success and prosperity, not to become
proud and think that no position or office is barred to us.
God's Word stresses that the Lord resists the proud but gives
grace to the humble (Prov. 3:34; James 4:6; 1 Pet. 5:5b).

The mention of the Isaiah source, though not the same as our canonical book of Isaiah, does draw attention to the prophet's own confession of moral uncleanness and that of his people before the holy presence of God in the year that king Uzziah died (Isa. 6:1). From the earthly incense altar where Uzziah had received divine judgment, Isaiah received divine grace when burning coals from the heavenly incense altar touched his lips to bring forgiveness, acceptance and wholeness (Isa. 6:1-7). The condition of Isaiah's people is suggestive of a 'leper' with the depiction of their sin in terms of putrid sores (Isa. 1:6). Later, Isaiah shows how the Servant of Yahweh would become like a 'leper', using words like 'strike' or struck', which are often associated with 'leprosy' (Isa. 53:4, 8). The noun from this same word family, which is often translated 'plague' or 'disease', appears sixty-six times in Leviticus 13–14 and a better modern equivalent would be 'an attack' (see 2 Chron. 6:28-29). While priests could diagnose and monitor 'leprosy', they could not heal the condition. Our holy Saviour, Jesus, the best of priests, touched lepers, cleansed them and made them whole, thus pointing to His saving power to cleanse from sin and make us whole as a result of His atoning death.

Jotham's reign (27:1-9)

This short account of Jotham's reign is very similar to the parallel text of 2 Kings 15:32-38 but it omits any reference to the opposition of Rezin and Pekah (2 Kings 15:37) and adds items that reflect the concerns of the Chronicler. Unlike the previous three reigns which have each been divided into good and bad periods, nothing but good is said of Jotham himself while his son Ahaz in the following chapter exhibits all that is bad. Both the opening and the closing verses of Jotham's reign mention his age and the length of his reign (vv. 1, 7), thus forming an *inclusio* (see also 2 Chron. 21:5, 20a). The central paragraph (vv. 3-6) reveals how the king followed in the good ways of his father and the blessing that resulted.

Contrast with his father (27:1-2)

27:1. Jotham was twenty-five years old when he became king, and he reigned sixteen years in Jerusalem and his mother's name was Jerushah the daughter of Zadok. 2. And he did what was right in the sight of Yahweh, according to all that his father Uzziah had done, only he did not enter the temple of Yahweh, but the people were still acting corruptly.

Jotham's sixteen-year reign will have included a ten-year period when he shared power with his father who was prevented from governing on account of his ritually and morally unclean condition. The length of his reign clearly did not include a co-regency of at least three years with his son Ahaz (see (2 Kings 15:30; 16:1; 17:1). Some think that Jotham actually died before Uzziah and that Ahaz became co-regent at that point, but the chronological problems cannot all be solved on our present knowledge. Unusually, the home city of Jotham's mother, Jerushah, is not given (see 2 Chron. 13:2; 24:1; 25:1; 26:3). Perhaps she was from a distinguished family, especially if her father or ancestor, Zadok, was related to the priestly line. Zadok was a name associated with the priests, and marriages between royal and priestly families were not unknown (1 Chron. 6:12 [5:38]; 9:11; 15:11; 2 Chron. 22:11). If this is the case, then it presents an interesting detail in the light of Jotham's father who wilfully undermined the distinction between the office of priest and king whereas Jotham himself respected the unique position of the priests.

As in the case of Uzziah, Jotham did what was right before Yahweh, remaining true to God to the end of his life. There were no obvious exceptions, and, unlike his father, he did not allow success to go to his head by seeking God-given privileges that belonged to others. Comparing this account with Kings, the Chronicler is concerned more with the temple's desecration by Uzziah and then, by way of contrast, of Jotham's respect for the sanctuary. The Chronicler assumed his readers had read the earlier work where it is stated that 'the high places' were not removed (2 Kings 15:35), but, as in Kings, it is the people who are the ones criticised. While Kings notes that the people worshipped at these shrines, the Chronicler describes their activity as corrupt or destructive, using the same verbal form for Uzziah's 'destructive' or 'corrupting' behaviour (2 Chron. 26:16).

Jotham blessed by God (27:3-6)

> 27:3. He built the upper gate of the house of Yahweh and he built
> extensively on the wall of Ophel. 4. And he built cities in the
> hill country of Judah and in the forests he built fortresses and
> towers. 5. He also fought with the king of the sons of Ammon
> and prevailed against them. And the sons of Ammon gave to
> him in that year one hundred talents of silver and ten thousand
> kors of wheat, and barley ten thousand. This the sons of Ammon
> returned to him and in the second year and the third. 6. So
> Jotham became strong, because he established his ways before
> Yahweh his God.

Jotham continued all the positive activity of his father
Uzziah including his building projects for the security of
his realm and the continued military dominance over the
Ammonites that resulted in a colossal amount of tribute being
received over a period of three years. All these activities were
indications of divine blessing. Four times in verses 3 and 4 the
verb 'build' is found. While his father did extensive work on
the city wall after it had been destroyed by Joash the northern
king (2 Chron. 25:23; 26:9), no comment was made of any work
on the temple. But in Jotham's case, the first task mentioned
is the rebuilding of the upper gate which served as one of the
entrances to the temple precincts and was located between
the old court and the new court (see 2 Chron. 20:5; 23:20).
It is to be identified with the Upper Benjamin Gate on the
northern side of the temple facing the territory of Benjamin
and near to the northern gate of the city wall which also
had the name Benjamin (Jer. 20:2; 37:13; 38:7; Ezek. 8:14; 9:2).
The precise location of the 'wall of Ophel' is uncertain but
it is associated with the northern part of the original city
of David and to the south of the temple (2 Chron. 33:14;
Neh. 3:26; 11:21). The singular 'hill' or 'mountain' of Judah is
only found elsewhere in the Bible in Joshua 11:21; 20:7; 21:11
(see 2 Chron. 21:11 where the plural form is used), suggesting
some specific area in the hill country where cities were built.
Jehoshaphat had built 'fortresses' as well as 'store cities'
in Judah (2 Chron. 17:12), while both Asa and Uzziah had
constructed 'towers' (2 Chron. 14:7[6]; 26:9-10). But Jotham's
building was not in the wilderness but in the forest areas
probably along the Shephelah of the Judean foothills.

Only one incident is recorded of Jotham's military successes. Uzziah was engaged in a battle with the Ammonites (2 Chron. 26:8) and clearly a further encounter with the enemy was necessary before they were finally subdued. The tribute brought to Jerusalem for at least three years included typical items like silver, wheat and barley. One 'kor' was equivalent to a donkey load of grain. Solomon was prepared to pay king Hiram of Tyre twenty thousand kors each of wheat and barley for his help in building the temple (2 Chron. 2:10). One hundred talents of silver was the amount that Amaziah paid to hire troops from northern Israel (2 Chron. 25:6). Such wealth pouring into Jerusalem was a reminder of the David–Solomon era and Jotham became strong like Solomon (v. 6; 2 Chron. 1:1) and indeed as had his father Uzziah before his treacherous action (2 Chron. 26:8, 15, 16). The Chronicler presses home his theological message by commenting that the king's strength was as a result of living in obedience to God's will. The verb 'to establish' or 'prepare' (kûn in the hiphil) is another of the Chronicler's key terms. Sometimes he makes the point that it is Yahweh who establishes or directs people but here the responsibility of the individual is stressed. The phrase 'he established his ways' is not unlike 'set one's heart' on God (1 Chron. 29:18; 2 Chron. 20:33).

Conclusion (27:7-9)

27:7. Now the rest of the acts of Jotham and all his wars and his ways, there they are written in the book of the kings of Israel and Judah. 8. He was twenty-five years old when he became king, and he reigned sixteen years in Jerusalem. 9. And Jotham rested with his fathers and they buried him in the city of David and Ahaz his son reigned in his place.

There is no reference in Chronicles to any attack from the north by the Israelite–Aramean coalition during this period (2 Kings 15:37), for it was not relevant to Jotham and the divine blessing that rested on his reign. As the Chronicler introduces the source for his account of the king's reign, his own concluding summary speaks of 'all his wars and his ways', instead of 'and all that he did' found in the earlier history (2 Kings 15:36). The reference to Jotham's 'wars' will not only include those against Ammon but possibly the initial confrontation with the northern coalition (see 2 Chron. 28:5-8; Isa. 7:1-19), while 'his ways' may refer back to his piety (see v. 6).

The repetition of the king's age at his accession and the length of his reign (see vv. 1 and 8) should not be omitted as a marginal gloss as some scholars suggest but is a deliberate means of introducing an *inclusio,* similar to the one for Jehoram's reign (2 Chronicles 21:5, 20a). Compared with his father, who reigned fifty-two years, Jotham's kingship was short, but it ended well, with nothing negative said of him. He was buried in the 'city of David' and, as nothing further is said, he was presumably given an honoured place in the royal graveyard, unlike his father and so many of the previous kings since Jehoshaphat (2 Chron. 21:20; 22:9; 24:25; 26:23).

Application

Jotham's kingship provided a small but important reminder of the ideal Davidic king. The account also indicates the importance of not only beginning well but ending well. He who endures to the end will be saved (Mark 13:13). Like Enoch who walked with God and 'pleased God', he did not live as long as others, but he 'prepared his ways before Yahweh' and 'did what was right in God's sight' (Gen. 5:18-24; Heb. 11:5-6). Believers are urged not only to be inspired by the witnesses who have run the race before them, but to look to the best Davidic king of all, our Lord Jesus Christ, who for the joy set before Him endured the cross and despised the shame and is now seated at God's right hand (Heb. 12:1-2). Mentioning the defeat of the Ammonites would have been of special interest to those building the wall of Jerusalem under Nehemiah. The enemies who were conspiring together to attack Jerusalem and cause confusion included Arabs and Ammonites (Neh. 4:7-16).

Ahaz's reign (28:1-27)

Following the very positive depiction of Jotham, the contrast with the kingship of his son Ahaz could not be more glaring. Ahaz is the wicked son of a righteous father. The account follows the same basic shape found in 2 Kings 16:1-20, but by means of extra material, the apostasy of Ahaz is emphasised further and his complete powerlessness in the face of invasion highlighted. Overall, the chapter shows how Ahaz's infidelity led to enemy attack (vv. 1-15) and how enemy attack led to even greater infidelity (vv. 16-27). It also reveals that despite mercy being shown to Judah (vv. 9-15), the king looked for help in wrong directions resulting in the ruin of himself and his people (vv. 16-25).

Introduction (28:1-5)

> 28:1. Ahaz was twenty years old when he became king, and he reigned in Jerusalem sixteen years; and he did not do what was right in the sight of Yahweh like David his father. 2. But he walked in the ways of the kings of Israel and also made cast images for the Baals. 3. And he burned incense in the valley of the son of Hinnom and burned his sons in the fire according to the abomination of the nations whom Yahweh had driven out before the sons of Israel. 4. And he sacrificed and burnt incense on the high places, on the hills and under every green tree. 5. Therefore Yahweh his God gave him into the hand of the king of Aram and they defeated him and they took captive from him a great number of captives and brought *them* to Damascus. Then he was also given into the hand of the king of Israel who struck him with a great defeat.

Even though Pekah, the ruler of northern Israel, is mentioned later (v. 6), the Chronicler continues his usual practice of omitting any synchronism with that kingdom (v. 1; see 2 Kings 16:1). Both Ahaz and his father reigned for sixteen years, but while Jotham 'did what was right' in Yahweh's eyes, he 'did not do what was right' (v. 1). This evaluation using the same verb but with the negative adverb is unique in Chronicles, the nearest examples being the adverse assessment of the reigns of both Jehoram and Ahaziah who 'did evil' in Yahweh's eyes; and, like them, Ahaz is criticised for behaving or leading a life ('walked') like the northern kings (v. 2; 2 Chron. 21:6; 22:4). Interestingly, Ahaz's name ('he has grasped') is the same as that of Ahaziah ('Yahweh has grasped') if the divine name 'Yah' ('-iah') is added. Whereas his father and grandfather are compared with their immediate fathers (2 Chron. 26:4; 27:2), Ahaz is contrasted with 'his father' David, which makes him the only Judean king in Chronicles to be compared unfavourably with his illustrious ancestor (v. 1; see 2 Chron. 17:3; 29:2; 34:2). He is the very antithesis of the ideal king.

The information concerning the moulded images of the Baals, not found in Kings, is an example of how Ahaz was following in the steps of the northern kings like Jeroboam I and Ahab's family (1 Kings 14:9; 16:31-32; 2 Chron. 13:8-9; 23:17). But even worse, he became like the former Canaanite inhabitants of the land that Israel occupied, whom God had destroyed on account of their wickedness (v. 3). Already the Chronicler is hinting that Judah is heading for exile unless there is a change of course. The burning of the king's sons is an example of child sacrifice practised by the Canaanites and is described as a capital offence in the Mosaic law. Human sacrifice was offered to the god Molech by the king of Moab (Lev. 18:21; 20:2-5; Jer. 7:31; 19:5-6; 32:35; Ezek. 16:20-21; see 2 Chron. 33:6). The valley of Hinnom (*gê' hinnōm*) lay to the southwest of Jerusalem and was the place where this 'abomination' was carried out and it led to its name, Ge-hinnom or Gehenna, being used for the final place of torment after death (Matt. 5:22; Mark 9:43, 47; Luke 12:5; James 3:6). In addition, Ahaz encouraged idolatrous devotion at the high places, and such worship at sacred sites was one of the reasons for the downfall of the northern kingdom (1 Chron. 5:25-26; see 2 Kings 17:10-18).

God's judgment descended upon king and people on account of Ahaz's shameless apostasy. It took the form of enemy attack and defeat by the Arameans of Damascus and the northern kingdom of Israel. The Syro-Ephraimite coalition, as it is called, brought great distress to Judah at this time, and they overran most of the country but failed to take Jerusalem (2 Kings 16:5-7; Isa. 7:1-6). Through Isaiah's influence, Ahaz refused to join the coalition which had the aim of withstanding Assyrian aggression, but contrary to Isaiah's advice the king sought help from the Assyrians in order to prevent further northern aggression instead of relying on Yahweh. While the coalition was not able to achieve complete victory over Judah, as the book of Kings indicates, nevertheless, in separate but coordinated actions, it was able to invade, slaughter and take captive many of Judah's inhabitants and this is what Chronicles highlights. It was

Yahweh, his God, who was actively involved in delivering
Ahaz into enemy hands (v. 5).

Application

Around the time of the Babylonian exile a proverb had
been circulating which people were using to blame their
circumstances on the sins of their fathers. They were
taking the point made in the second commandment too
far. It was true to a certain extent that the sins of the fathers
did have repercussions for future generations (Exod. 20:5;
Matt. 23:35, 36). However, both Jeremiah and Ezekiel
challenged the false conclusions that were being made.
The sequence that we find in Ezekiel 18:5-18 concerning a
good father followed by a bad son is what the Chronicler
presents. Jotham is the righteous father whereas his son,
Ahaz, is the exact opposite. Each generation is responsible
before God for its attitude and behaviour.

While most people are horrified to read of such ancient
practices as child sacrifice and rage against similar abhorrent
acts carried out today in certain cultures and pagan cults, yet
every day with the approval of many western governments
thousands of unborn babies are killed in abortion clinics
mostly on the grounds that it is the human right of the
mothers who carry them.

Relations with Northern Israel (28:6-15)

28:6. For Pekah the son of Remaliah killed a hundred and twenty
thousand in Judah in one day, all sons of valour, because they
had forsaken Yahweh the God of their fathers. 7. And Zichri,
a valiant one of Ephraim, killed Maaseiah the king's son and
Azrikam the leader of the house and Elkanah who was second
to the king. 8. And the sons of Israel captured of their brothers
two hundred thousand women, sons and daughters; and they
also plundered much booty from them and they brought the
booty to Samaria.
9. But a prophet of Yahweh was there whose name was Oded
and he went out before the army that was coming to Samaria
and he said to them, 'Indeed because of the burning anger of
Yahweh the God of your fathers against Judah, he gave them into
your hand, but you have killed them in a rage that has reached

up to heaven. 10. And now it is the sons of Judah and Jerusalem you are intending to subjugate as your male and female slaves? Is there not except with you yourselves guilt towards Yahweh your God? 11. And now, listen to me, and return the captives whom you have taken captive from your brothers, for the fierce wrath of Yahweh is upon you.' 12. Then some men of the heads of the sons of Ephraim, Azariah the son of Johanan, Berechiah the son of Meshillemoth, and Jehizkiah the son of Shallum, and Amasa the son of Hadlai, stood up against those who were coming from the war, 13. and they said to them, 'You shall not bring the captives here, for you are intending *to bring* on us guilt against Yahweh to add to our sins and guilt, for our guilt is great for there is fierce wrath against Israel.' 14. So the armed men left the captives and the booty before the officials and all the assembly. 15. And the men who had been mentioned by name arose and seized the captives and with the booty they clothed all their nakedness. And they clothed them and gave them sandals, and fed them and gave them drink and anointed them and they led all the feeble of them on donkeys and brought them to Jericho, the city of palms near their brothers; then they returned to Samaria.

It is an encounter with northern Israel that is the Chronicler's chief concern, and his account assumes that the narrative in Kings has been read. After the end of the Jehu dynasty in the north, there was much instability but Pekah the son of Remaliah, an officer, assassinated Pekahiah, the Israelite king, and ruled in his place for twenty years before he was similarly assassinated. It was during his reign that Assyria had invaded the northern area of Israel and carried away many captives (2 Kings 15:25-31).

The Chronicler's version stresses yet again important theological points. In the days of Abijah, it was Yahweh who had delivered Israel into Judah's hand because they relied on God, and it was Israel who had 'forsaken' Yahweh (2 Chron. 13:16-18). On this occasion, it was Judah who had done the forsaking ('*zb*, verse 6; see 1 Chron. 28:9; 2 Chron. 7:22; 12:5; etc.). Furthermore, it was the God of their fathers they had abandoned (see 1 Chron. 5:25). Ahaz was behaving like the northern kingdom, and it was the northern kingdom that became God's means of punishing Judah. The colossal number of warriors killed in one day and of families taken captive indicates a massive defeat. To add force to the crisis situation, some influential men belonging to the king's household are named among the dead and the account even identifies the northern hero who killed the king's son (vv. 7-8). It is not entirely clear, but the reference to the women and children is probably indicating that the figure included them while the use of the word 'brothers' continues to emphasise the close relationship between the kingdoms of Israel and Judah and which becomes an important factor in what follows (v. 8; see 2 Chron. 11:4). All the captives and the booty plundered were brought to the capital city of Samaria.

Oded is the third prophet of Yahweh from the north mentioned in Chronicles, the other two being Micaiah and Elijah (2 Chron. 18:6-27; 21:12-15). He met the victorious army before it entered Samaria and the message he delivered introduces themes that the Chronicler wished once again to stress. The prophet first showed that the northerners had no right to boast of their success. They were being used by God to punish the southern kingdom. The true cause of Judah's defeat was the anger of Yahweh against His people. He reminded them that this God is 'the God of your fathers' (v. 9; 2 Chron. 13:12). Despite the schism and apostasy, the people of the northern kingdom were still considered to be Yahweh's people and Yahweh was not only the God of their fathers but 'your God' (vv. 9-10). In addition, the prophet made it clear that it was 'from your brothers' they had taken prisoners (v. 11). This same point is made by the prophet Shemaiah when he called on Rehoboam not to fight against their brothers in the north (2 Chron. 11:2-4).

The prophet then accused his people of excessive brutality. In Chronicles, the term 'rage' is used of uncontrolled, sinful anger (2 Chron. 16:10; 26:19). It is an outrage that had reached heaven, in the sense of its scale (see Ps. 57:10[11]; Ezra 9:6) and in that it had reached Yahweh's attention in His dwelling-place (2 Chron. 6:21, 30, 39). The prophets often denounced the nations for their violent actions even when they were instruments of God's judgment (Isa. 10:15-16; Hosea 1:4; Hab. 2:8, 17). By emphasising 'Judah and Jerusalem', Oded accused them of enslaving a people who had remained loyal to the Davidic king and to the city associated with David and the temple. For fellow Israelites to be forced into slavery was against the Mosaic law and contrary to the spirit of brotherly love (Lev. 25:42-43, 46; Jer. 34:8-17; Neh. 5:1-13). The prophet's final point was to indicate that in this whole event it was before God they had incurred serious guilt (another of the Chronicler's key terms and found only here in the plural to indicate its enormity).

After the prophet's accusations, there came an instruction and a warning (v. 11). Already the fierce wrath of God was upon them (see also v. 13), so they were urged to free their captives and return them home. It is quite striking the number of times the Chronicler uses words for captivity and slavery in this chapter. Verse 5 had already introduced the subject with reference to Judahites being carried away captive to Damascus and later they will be carried captive by the Edomites (v. 17). In this central passage, it is not other nations but fellow Israelites who are deporting them (vv. 8, 10, 11, 13, 14, 15).

The prophet's call to return the captives could well have been completely ignored by a jubilant army bent on enjoying the benefits of their campaign, but Oded had the support of four leading men from Ephraim, the dominant tribe of the north, who confronted the returning soldiers. Three out of the four have names that are compounded with God's personal name, Yahweh – Azariah, Berechiah and Jehizkiah (v. 12). No mention is made of king Pekah. He could have sent the delegation or, as some scholars have suggested, he may already have been assassinated. These Ephraimite leaders might well indicate that, as in the days of Elijah, there were still those in the north who had not bowed the knee to Baal (see 1 Kings 19:18). The Ephraimites first took up the prophet's final appeal and made it into a command not to bring the captives into Samaria. The reason they gave adds to the one already mentioned concerning incurring guilt. They confessed in words similar to the prophet that not only did they already stand under Yahweh's 'fierce wrath' (vv. 11, 13), but they would be increasing their guilt if they did not send the captives back. Are they admitting guilt over the kingdom's original split from the south (2 Chron. 10; 13:4-12) or because they had gone overboard in the slaughter of their brothers? Probably both are in mind.

Amazingly, those hardened warriors heeded the appeal, released their claim on the captives and the spoil, and handed all to the leaders and the assembly of Israel that had gathered (v. 14). Then the four principal officials set about hiding the shame of those taken prisoner by clothing the naked from the loot and preparing all of them with clothes, sandals, food and drink for a trek of over thirty miles (about fifty-one kilometres) to the border city of Jericho in the northern territory (Josh. 16:1; 18:12; see 1 Kings 16:34; 2 Kings 2:4, 15-18). Those whose wounds needed attention were anointed with healing oils and donkeys were provided for those too weak to walk. Jericho was traditionally known as 'the city of palms' (Deut. 34:3; Judg. 1:16; 3:13) and it was here that David's servants stayed after they were greatly humiliated by the Ammonites (1 Chron. 19:5). Its oasis and trees remain a pleasant spot to this day.

Application

Judah's captivity at this time anticipated both their own future captivity in Babylon and more immediately the northern kingdom's captivity by the Assyrians some ten years later. God in His grace provided ample opportunity by means of these various typological exiles to call the people to repent and turn back to Him. All the calamities and extreme difficulties that people face in this life are pointers to the great calamity to come. God warns through these temporal judgments before the final day of wrath arrives.

The prophet Oded's message gave no encouragement to the northerners to think they were any better than Judah. Moses had stated that it was not because of Israel's righteousness but on account of the wickedness of the Canaanites that God was giving them the land (Deut. 9:5). Matthew Henry remarks that there is no place for Gentile believers to boast, for as national Israel was broken off because of unbelief, God would not spare Gentiles if they remained high-minded (Rom. 11:18-21).

The Ephraimites expressed a humble, repentant spirit that showed itself in acts of kindness to the prisoners. Such actions follow Yahweh's own example which He desires His people to imitate (Ps. 146:7-8; Isa. 58:6-7).

The passage spoke strongly to the post-exilic people not to think of the northern tribes as beyond redemption. They were to have a concern for them. As there were Ephraimites who listened to a prophetic call, so God could work in what might have seemed like the most unlikely of settings in the Samarian region when the Chronicler was writing. In view of God's amazing love toward His unworthy people, Christians today are encouraged to have a humble and merciful attitude toward others who may at present be deeply depraved and far off from God's kingdom. It is also a reminder to evangelical churches that within generally apostate denominations there are individuals and groups who remain loyal to God and His people.

Jesus employed this passage, especially verse 15, to expound the question of who is one's neighbour in His parable of the Good Samaritan (Luke 10:25-37). He deliberately used a 'northerner', a Samaritan, and showed how he anointed the wounded man who had been on his way to Jericho, carried him on a donkey and provided for his immediate needs. Jesus' true disciples who love God will respond by loving their fellow human beings without questioning their race, gender, nationality or religious state.

Relations with the nations (28:16-21)

28:16. At that time, king Ahaz sent to the kings of Assyria for help. 17. For again the Edomites had come and attacked Judah and carried away captives. 18. And the Philistines had raided the cities of the Shephelah and the Negeb of Judah and had seized Beth-shemesh and Aijalon and Gederoth and Soco and its villages, and Timnah and its villages, and Gimzo and its villages, and they lived there. 19. For Yahweh humbled Judah on account of Ahaz king of Israel because he had allowed permissiveness in Judah and was completely unfaithful to Yahweh. 20. So Tilgath-Pilneser, king of Assyria, came against him and distressed him and did not strengthen him. 21. For Ahaz distributed *the contents of* the house of Yahweh and the house of the king and the officials and gave them to the king of Assyria but there was no help for him.

This paragraph opens and closes with reference to Assyria from where Ahaz was hoping to receive 'help', instead of finding it in Yahweh (vv. 16, 21; see 1 Chron. 5:20; 2 Chron. 14:11).

Judah was invaded not only from the north by Israel but from the south by the Edomites and from the west by the Philistines. In 2 Kings 16:6, the Edomites with the help of the Arameans took the opportunity to regain control of Elath; however the Chronicler probably has another occasion in mind when the Edomites invaded Judah and were able to take away captives (v. 17; see v. 5). As for the Philistines, when his grandfather was king, three cities had been seized from them, but under Ahaz six cities in the same area had been gained by the Philistines in periodic raids (v. 18; see 2 Chron. 26:6-7). Though the 'Negeb' or southern region of Judah is mentioned, all the cities named were in the 'Shephelah' or lowlands.

At this point, the Chronicler stops his account to press home his message that Judah's 'low' condition was the result of the infidelity of Ahaz. Under Abijah it was the northern kingdom that had been brought into subjection but under Ahaz it was Judah that had been humbled (v. 19; see 2 Chron. 13:18). Ahaz had given his people free rein. The gross unfaithfulness of Ahaz toward Yahweh (see 1 Chron. 10:13) encouraged the whole kingdom to behave in a promiscuous way. It was Pharaoh's complaint to Moses that he had caused the people to become lax in carrying out their burdensome tasks (Exod. 5:4). Another form of the same verb is used of Israel's lack of restraint in the golden calf incident (Exod. 32:25). Both king and people were guilty, and God had punished them severely. Surprisingly, Ahaz is referred to as the 'king of Israel' and the Chronicler continues to use the name 'Israel' rather than Judah through to the end of the chapter (vv. 23 and 27). It may be at this lowest of points in Judah's history and in the light of the humble repentant attitude of those northerners, together with the fact that the northern kingdom was about to fall to the Assyrians, the Chronicler could again speak of the one nation of Israel, albeit in a generally wretched position.[45]

Tiglath-Pileser III the king of Assyria (the form 'Tilgath-Pilneser' is unique to Chronicles; see 1 Chron. 5:6, 26), the one whom Ahaz had looked to for help against the Edomites and Philistines as well as against the Syro-Ephraimite coalition

---

45. Williamson, *1 and 2 Chronicles*, p. 348.

(v. 16; 2 Kings 16:7; Isa. 7), turned out in the end to bring him trouble rather than support. What help he did get from that quarter, as 2 Kings 16:8-9 shows, was bought at a price. It also meant that Assyria kept putting pressure on Judah for 'he came and distressed him' (v. 20) to continue paying tribute. Ahaz was thus forced to part with the wealth of the temple, the palace and even possessions belonging to his chief officers (v. 21). It was a foretaste of what was to come (Isa. 7:17; 2 Kings 18:14).

Ahaz's continued unfaithfulness (28:22-25)

> 28:22. And in the time of his distress, he continued to act unfaithfully toward Yahweh – that Ahaz the king! 23. For he sacrificed to the gods of Damascus that had defeated him and said, 'Because the gods of the kings of Aram helped them, I will sacrifice to them and they will help me.' But they became the stumbling of him and all Israel. 24. And Ahaz gathered the utensils of the house of God and cut in pieces the utensils of the house of God and he shut the doors of the house of Yahweh and he made himself altars in every corner in Jerusalem. 25. And in each city of Judah he made high places to burn incense to other gods, and he provoked Yahweh the God of his fathers.

Neither the kindness shown by the northerners (v. 15) nor the distress he was under (vv. 20, 22) brought Ahaz to his senses. Unlike Manasseh who humbled himself and repented when in 'distress' (2 Chron. 33:12), Ahaz dug his heels in and became even more 'unfaithful' (v. 22; see v. 19). The Chronicler emphasises the appalling attitude of the king by placing his name at the end of the sentence: 'that Ahaz the king!' Instead of crying out to Yahweh in his distress (see 2 Chron. 15:4) he turned to worshipping the gods of Damascus. He foolishly reasoned that the victory of the Arameans over him indicated that their gods were more powerful than Yahweh, whereas he should have realised that it was his own departure from Yahweh that was the issue. Again, one of the Chronicler's key terms 'help' is used twice in verse 23 (see vv. 16, 21) and he comments that such worship of foreign gods that Ahaz had encouraged had caused him and all his people to 'stumble' in the sense of to be ruined. This analysis is a reminder of what the prophet told king Amaziah, 'God has power to help and to cause stumbling' (2 Chron. 25:8), where exactly the same verb is used.

Not only did Ahaz encourage the worship of other gods but he discouraged the worship of Yahweh by destroying the temple utensils and closing the temple doors (v. 24). 2 Kings 16:10-16 relates how Ahaz had a pagan altar constructed on the lines of one seen in Damascus, but Chronicles prefers to mention how the king constructed altars on every street corner in Jerusalem and increased the number of high places throughout the kingdom for the purpose of worshipping other gods (vv. 24-25). No doubt those cities built by Jotham in the hill country of Judah which were lacking in such 'high places' were the ones chiefly in mind (2 Chron. 27:4). In this way Ahaz 'provoked' or 'vexed' (k's) Yahweh the God of his fathers. In the Hebrew Bible this verb is especially used of provoking Yahweh to anger by worshipping other gods (1 Kings 14:9, 15; etc.) but is used sparingly in Chronicles (see 2 Chron. 33:6; 34:25). Even the northerners had repented to prevent further wrath from God, but Ahaz only made his situation before God worse.

Conclusion (28:26-27)

> 28:26. Now the rest of his acts and all his ways, the first and the last, there they are written in the book of the kings of Judah and Israel. 27. And Ahaz rested with his fathers and they buried him in the city, in Jerusalem but they did not bring him to the graves of the kings of Israel. Then Hezekiah his son reigned in his stead.

The 'ways' of Ahaz were far different from those of his father (see v. 2; 2 Chron. 27:7). While 2 Kings 16:19 cites only the 'chronicles of the kings of Judah', the sources mentioned for Ahaz's reign in Chronicles refer to the book of the kings of 'Israel' as well as Judah (see 2 Chron. 16:11). Whether this is as significant as the reference to the Judean kings being described as 'the kings of Israel' (v. 27; see v. 19) is not certain. Now that the northern kingdom was on the point of being destroyed and with a king in the south no better than the kings of the north (v. 2), the way was open under a true Davidic king for 'all Israel' to be united at the central sanctuary in Jerusalem. The attitude of some of the northern leaders belonging to Ephraim, the dominant tribe, would have given encouragement to this possibility. Though Ahaz died a peaceful death in that he 'rested' or 'slept with his fathers', he was not given the honour afforded to worthy kings of the past. The Chronicler shows his displeasure by not referring to him being buried in the 'city of David' or 'with his fathers' (see 2 Kings 16:20) and adds that he was not brought to the royal cemetery (see also 2 Chron. 21:20; 24:25; 26:23). Though buried in the capital city of Jerusalem the Chronicler distances Ahaz, the worst of the Davidic kings, from king David.

Application

Other gods are no gods. The images that were supposed to represent these gods were in the likeness of humans or animals, but they were useless. Prophets like Isaiah and Jeremiah poked fun at the futility of such worship and the psalmists showed the folly of such practices. Paul indicates that though there are so-called gods they have no reality but behind such worship is the work of the devil and his evil spirits (1 Cor. 10:20). Foolish human hearts are darkened to worship the creature rather than the creator (Rom. 1:21-25).

The passage spoke powerfully to the Chronicler's contemporaries that northerners who trusted God and sought to live by God's word were to be accepted. With the coming of Jesus and His atoning work on the cross, those far off are brought near and the middle wall of division between Jew and Gentile has been broken down so that all from whatever background who put their faith in Christ are one (Eph. 2:11-16).

Hezekiah's reign (29:1–32:33)

For the account of Hezekiah's reign, Chronicles has four chapters to the three in 2 Kings 18–20 and contains a wealth of material not found in the earlier history. While one verse is allocated to Hezekiah's religious reforms in 2 Kings 18:4 and almost all the remaining material given over to recounting the king's relations with Assyria and Babylon, Chronicles devotes three chapters to the king's religious reforms and one to international relations and other matters. Apart from

David and Solomon, no other king receives so much attention in Chronicles and it becomes clear that Hezekiah is presented as a second David and Solomon rolled into one. The data in Chronicles covers the cleansing and restoration of the temple (29:1-36), the celebration of the Passover (30:1-27), arrangements for the continuation of the temple worship and the maintenance of its staff (31:1-21), deliverance from Assyrian aggression and the final years of the reign (32:1-33). Remarkably, the chapters are arranged in a similar way to the various grades of holiness found in Leviticus. In chapter 29, the temple, the holiest area of his kingdom, is the centre of attention, then the focus moves to the holy city of Jerusalem in chapter 30, followed by the rest of the country in chapter 31 and finally the unclean world at large in chapter 32.[46]

Refurbishing the temple and restoring its worship (29:1-36)
Apart from the first couple of verses of introduction to the reign which find a close parallel with 2 Kings 18:1-3, the rest of the chapter is unique to Chronicles. The king urges all the Levite families including the priests to sanctify themselves and the temple (vv. 3-19), then he takes the lead in restoring the temple worship (vv. 20-30), and the chapter concludes with the congregation participating with sacrifices and king and people rejoicing (vv. 31-36).

> 29:1. Hezekiah became king when he was twenty-five years old, and he reigned twenty-nine years in Jerusalem and the name of his mother was Abijah the daughter of Zechariah. 2. And he did what was right in the sight of Yahweh according to all that his father David had done.

Hezekiah's name appears in a number of biblical books including Jeremiah 26:18-19 and Proverbs 25:1. It was during his reign that Micah and Isaiah prophesied in the south and Hosea in the north (Isa. 1:1; 36-39; Hosea 1:1; Micah 1:1). His name is found spelled in four different ways in Hebrew. In the majority of cases in Chronicles it begins with 'Je-' ('Jehezekiah') whereas in Kings and Isaiah it is

---

46. Johnstone, *1 and 2 Chronicles*, Vol. 2, p. 188; Gordon J. Wenham, *The Book of Leviticus* (Grand Rapids: Eerdmans, 1979), pp. 18-25; Eveson, *The Beauty of Holiness*, pp. 146-60.

overwhelmingly spelt without the 'Je'. How the dates of all the eighth century kings fit together is still unclear at present but it seems fairly certain that Hezekiah was co-regent with his father Ahaz for some of his reign. Nothing more is known of Hezekiah's mother, whose name ends with 'Yah', the short form of God's covenant name 'Yahweh' (Isa. 12:2). 2 Kings 18:2 gives the abbreviated form of his mother's name: 'Abi'. Not only did Hezekiah 'do what was right' in the eyes of Yahweh (see 2 Chron. 14:2; 20:32; 24:2; etc.), he followed the example of David (v. 2). Comparing the various monarchs to king David is a common practice in the book of Kings but is employed very sparingly in Chronicles (2 Chron. 17:3; 34:2). The Chronicler makes this comparison because he will show how true this was in his portrayal of Hezekiah and in complete contrast to that of Ahaz his father (2 Chron. 28:1).

Hezekiah's speech (29:3-11)

> 29:3. He, in the first year of his reign in the first month, opened the doors of the house of Yahweh and repaired them. 4. And he brought in the priests and the Levites and gathered them in the east square. 5. And he said to them, 'Listen to me, Levites! Now sanctify yourselves and sanctify the house of Yahweh the God of your fathers and bring out the impurity from the holy place. 6. For our fathers acted unfaithfully and did what was evil in the sight of Yahweh our God and they forsook him; and they have turned away their faces from the dwelling place of Yahweh and have given their back. 7. Also they have shut the doors of the vestibule and put out the lamps. And they have not burnt incense or offered burnt offerings in the sanctuary to the God of Israel. 8. So the wrath of Yahweh was against Judah and Jerusalem and he has made them an object of trembling, of astonishment and of jeering, as you see with your eyes. 9. And indeed our fathers fell by the sword and our sons and our daughters and our wives were in captivity on account of this. 10. Now it is in my heart to make a covenant with Yahweh the God of Israel so that his fierce wrath may turn from us. 11. Now, my sons, do not be negligent for Yahweh has chosen you to stand before him to minister to him and to be his ministers and to make sacrifices smoke.'

As in verse 1 so in verse 3, the Chronicler wishes to draw the reader's attention to the importance of this particular king. In verse 1, Hezekiah's name appears first in the Hebrew sentence and in verse 3 the personal pronoun likewise occupies the emphatic opening position. The 'first month' probably refers to the first month of the new religious calendar year, Abib (Exod. 13:4; 23:15, and called Nisan after the exile in Neh. 2:1), rather than the first month after his father's death. This was the time when the Passover should be held (2 Chron. 30:1-3; Exod. 12; Lev. 23:4-8). From the very beginning Hezekiah, like Solomon, is seen to be concerned about the temple (2 Chron. 1-2). The doors to Yahweh's house, that is to the nave or holy place, which Ahaz had closed (2 Chron. 28:24), were opened and repaired. Then he assembled all the Levites, which included the priests, in the eastern square (v. 4). This was probably the one near the Water Gate of the city rather than the open square in front of the temple which had not yet been ritually purified (2 Chron. 32:6; Neh. 8:1, 3).

This royal speech to all the temple staff is introduced by the call for the Levites to 'hear' or 'listen' (v. 5; see 1 Chron. 28:2; 2 Chron. 13:4; 15:2; 20:20; 28:11) and it closes with encouraging words, addressing his audience using more intimate language: 'my sons' (v. 11). The king begins by urging them to purify themselves and Yahweh's house. Under both David and Solomon, when the ark was being moved, the Aaronic priests and Levites had been in a sanctified state (1 Chron. 15:12; 2 Chron. 5:11). Only a properly cleansed priesthood could offer acceptable worship (Lev. 8-9). The temple also needed to be ceremonially purified or cleansed because of the 'impurity' (niddāh) that was in the sanctuary. This term is used for a variety of ritually impure conditions including idolatry, immorality, touching a corpse and especially a woman's menstrual state (see Lev. 12:2, etc.; 15:19-20, 24-25; Num. 19:13, 20-21; Ezra 9:11; Ezek. 22:10; Zech. 13:1).

Hezekiah confesses the sin of his predecessors (v. 6; 'our fathers') which would have included his own father. Some of the Chronicler's key words are employed. The verb and noun from the m'l word family have been used throughout Chronicles to describe royal infidelity (1 Chron. 10:13; 2 Chron. 28:19, 22). Such unfaithfulness and evil in God's sight is more precisely defined as forsaking Yahweh, something that had been said of Judah generally (2 Chron. 28:6).

Abandoning their God had involved giving Yahweh's dwelling place 'their back' by turning to face the other way. Yahweh invited His people to 'seek his face' and David was one who had responded to that call (Ps. 27:4, 8). Giving someone your back instead of facing the person was highly disrespectful, but with regard to God, who had promised to hear prayer directed toward the place associated with His name (2 Chron. 7:12-15), it was also an indication of praying and worshipping something or someone other than God. Hezekiah is particularly thinking of his father's action in closing up the 'vestibule' which here stands for the temple itself (v. 7; 2 Chron. 28:24). In fact, besides 'vestibule', three other terms are used for the temple in verses 5-7: 'house of Yahweh', 'dwelling place of Yahweh' and 'sanctuary to the God of Israel'. Lamps that were never meant to go out, went out (Exod. 27:20-21; Lev. 24:1-4; 2 Chron. 4:20-21); there was no incense smell and the regular burnt sacrifices were not offered (v. 7). King Abijah had reminded Jeroboam and the northerners that in the Jerusalem temple the priests and Levites ministered daily, offering burnt offerings and incense and caring for the lamps (2 Chron. 13:11). Hezekiah's words concerning the results of God's wrath are reminiscent of Jeremiah's expressions regarding the tragedy of the exile (v. 8; see Jer. 29:18). Judah had experienced defeat and captivity during the reign of Ahaz at the hands of Pekah the northern king, the Arameans, the Edomites and the Philistines, as well as humiliation by the Assyrians (v. 9; see 2 Chron. 28:6-15, 17, 18, 20-21, 23).

After referring to the sin of the nation and God's punishment (vv. 6-9), Hezekiah sought to rectify the situation by expressing his intention (v. 10). That it was 'in his heart' or that it was an inner desire that he willed to perform, is a phrase that is used of David and Solomon concerning their plans for a temple (1 Chron. 17:2; 22:7; 28:2; 2 Chron. 6:7). His concern to make a covenant with Yahweh suggests a solemn commitment before God (see Ezra 10:3-5) to put right the wrongs of the past rather than any covenant renewal ceremony. Hezekiah's whole attitude was a sign of his repentant spirit as he looked expectantly for Yahweh to remove His fierce wrath that was hanging over the nation.

In view of all he had described, the king urged his audience, whom he addressed in the most intimate manner ('my sons', verse 11), not to be 'easy-going' with their responsibilities. He reminded the Levites as a whole, that they were specially chosen by Yahweh to minister at the sanctuary, and the priests in particular (Deut. 10:8; 18:5; 21:5; 1 Chron. 15:2), who were set apart literally 'to burn incense' but here used in the more general sense of making sacrifices smoke.

Application

After a period where conditions mirrored the great exile in Babylon, the Chronicler saw in Hezekiah a model of action for his own post-exilic community. They were to find encouragement and to give more attention to the worship of Yahweh in their newly-built temple and to seek God's presence there. The compiler of the Psalms gave added encouragement by including David's longing for the courts of Yahweh and also to see God's face (Deut. 4:29; Ps. 27).

The passage preaches to our own situations, encouraging leaders in our churches to engage in worship that is acceptable to God. Such worship includes offering our individual lives daily as living sacrifices, but it also involves our communal gatherings. Elders and deacons are set apart to lead and direct. We thank God there is a fountain open for all sin and 'uncleanness' (Zech. 13:1). The vileness of sin is likened to used sanitary towels (Isa. 64:6) but our Saviour's sacrificial blood cleanses from all such pollution (1 John 1:7-9).

29:12. Then the Levites arose: Mahath the son of Amasai and Joel the son of Azariah, from the sons of the Kohathites; and from the sons of Merari, Kish the son of Abdi and Azariah the son of Jehallelel; and from the Gershonites, Joah the son of Zimmah and Eden the son of Joah. 13. And from the sons of Elizaphan, Shimri and Jeiel; and from the sons of Asaph, Zechariah and Mattaniah. 14. And from the sons of Heman, Jehiel and Shimei; and from the sons of Jeduthun, Shemaiah and Uzziel. 15. And they gathered their brothers and sanctified themselves and came, according to the command of the king by the words of Yahweh, to cleanse the house of Yahweh. 16. And the priests came to the inner part of the house of Yahweh to cleanse *it* and they brought out all the uncleanness that they found in the temple of Yahweh to the court of the house of Yahweh, and the Levites received *it* and brought *it* out to the Kidron wadi. 17. And they began to sanctify on the first of the first month, and on the eighth day of the month they came to the vestibule of Yahweh. Then they sanctified the house of Yahweh for eight days, and on the sixteenth day of the first month they finished. 18. Then they came inside to Hezekiah the king and said, 'We have cleansed all the house of Yahweh, the altar of burnt offerings and all its utensils, and the table of the rows and all its utensils. 19. And all the utensils that king Ahaz during his reign had rejected in his unfaithfulness, we have prepared and sanctified; and there they are before the altar of Yahweh.'

There is an immediate response from the Levites but before describing their activity, the Chronicler names the ones who were put in charge (vv. 12-14). Two representatives from each of seven Levitical families are listed, first from the three original families: Kohath, Merari and Gershon (v. 12; 1 Chron. 6:16[1]), followed by Elizaphan who was the son of Uzziel whose family became an important group among the Kohathites (v. 13a; see Exod. 6:18, 22; Lev. 10:4; Num. 3:30; 1 Chron. 15:8). The final members were from each division of the singers: Asaph, Heman and Jeduthun (vv. 13b-14; 1 Chron. 25:1-31).[47] Before the ark was brought to Jerusalem in the proper way, David had commanded the Levites to sanctify themselves and the list of the family heads was cited, and this bears some similarity with the present arrangement (1 Chron. 15:5-10).

Hezekiah's instructions were in accordance with the overall spirit of God's word in the Mosaic law for the sanctification of those who ministered and for the purity of the sanctuary that had been defiled. It involved the removal and destruction of all the filth that was found in the holy place (v. 5; 2 Chron. 28:24). The leaders gathered the rest of the Levites, 'their brothers', and after sanctifying or consecrating themselves they set about purifying the temple (v. 15). It was the task of the priests to enter the temple itself, Yahweh's palace, as the Levites were not normally allowed to enter the sacred precincts. The 'inner part' probably refers to

47. In 13a the *Qere* reading is 'Jeiel' while the *Kethibh* is 'Jeuel', and in 14a the *Qere* is 'Jehiel' and the *Kethibh* is 'Jehuel'.

the holy rather than the most holy place (v. 16; 2 Chron. 5:7; 23:6). Everything unclean, which would have included the 'impurity' or 'filth' mentioned earlier (v. 5), was brought out by the priests into the courtyard for the Levites to dispose of in the Kidron valley. This area was considered unclean as it had become a public burial ground and dump as well as a site for the burning of foreign cultic objects (2 Chron. 15:16; 30:14; 2 Kings 23:4, 6, 12; Jer. 31:40).

The Chronicler carefully mentions that it took half a month to complete the work (v. 17). This not only indicates that the work was done thoroughly but it also prepares for the difficulty it presented over the celebration of the Passover in the first month, as the next chapter will show. When they had completed the work, the Levites reported back to the king explaining how both outside and inside the temple had been cleansed (v. 18). They had started the purification work with the outer courts of the temple where the altar of burnt offering was situated (see 2 Chron. 7:1-3) and by the beginning of the second week they had come to the 'vestibule' or temple porch (see 2 Chron. 8:12). It took them a further eight days to carefully clean the sanctuary itself. Only the table for 'the rows' of bread ('the showbread') is mentioned but the 'utensils' that Ahaz had discarded would have included ones associated with the golden lampstands and incense altar (v. 19). Ahaz was clearly the main ancestor Hezekiah had in mind on account of his 'unfaithfulness' (see v. 6). Particular mention is made of these utensils, for their recovery provided a preview of what happened as a result of the Babylonian exile (2 Chron. 36:18; Ezra 1 :7-11; Dan. 5:3).

Application

The temple vessels that had been taken to Babylon had been given back to those returning from exile (Ezra 1:7-11). They represented continuity with the best of the past. Their temple might not have been much to look at, but they were using in their worship the same golden implements appointed by David and made by Solomon for the original temple (1 Chron. 28:14-17; 2 Chron. 4:19-22). For Christians, the preaching of God's Word and the celebration of the two

ordinances of baptism and the Lord's Supper have provided
that same kind of continuity over two millennia.

Temple worship restored (29:20-30)

29:20. Then Hezekiah the king rose early and gathered the
officials of the city, and he went up to the house of Yahweh. 21.
And they brought seven bulls, seven rams, seven lambs and
seven male goats for a purification offering for the kingdom, for
the sanctuary and for Judah. Then he commanded the priests,
the sons of Aaron, to offer *them* on the altar of Yahweh. 22. So
they slaughtered the bulls, and the priests received the blood
and sprinkled it on the altar, and they slaughtered the rams and
sprinkled the blood on the altar, and they slaughtered the lambs
and sprinkled the blood on the altar. 23. Then they brought
near the male goats for the purification offering before the king
and the assembly and they laid their hands on them. 24. And
the priests slaughtered them and made a purification offering
with their blood on the altar to make atonement for all Israel,
for the king commanded the burnt offering and the purification
offering for all Israel.

25. Then he stationed the Levites at the house of Yahweh
with cymbals, with harps and with lyres, according to the
commandment of David and of Gad the king's visionary and of
Nathan the prophet; for the commandment was by the hand of
Yahweh by the hand of his prophets. 26. And the Levites stood
with the instruments of David and the priests with the trumpets.
27. Then Hezekiah commanded to offer the burnt offering on
the altar, and at the time the burnt offering began, the song
of Yahweh began and the trumpets, and accompanied by the
instruments of David the king of Israel. 28. So all the assembly
worshipped, and the song was sung, and the trumpeters *played*
the trumpets; all *continued* until the burnt offering was finished.
29. And when they had finished the burnt offerings, the king and
all who were present with him bowed down and worshipped.
30. And Hezekiah the king and the officials commanded the
Levites to give praise to Yahweh with the words of David and
Asaph the visionary. So they sang praises with gladness, and
they bowed head down and worshipped.

As Hezekiah had made it his prime business to purify the
temple (v. 3) so now he rose early to gather the leading members
of the Jerusalem community to witness the restoration of
the temple worship. David and Solomon had assembled all

the officials of Israel (1 Chron. 28:1; 2 Chron. 1:2-3) and for this important event Hezekiah did something similar but on a smaller scale (v. 20). The Chronicler uses another of his key terms, 'assembly' (*qāhāl*), later in the account to indicate that they were all united in the king's initiative (vv. 23, 28, 31-32; see 1 Chron. 28:8; 29:1, 10, 20; etc.). Throughout the ceremonies the king is seen to be directly involved, ordering what should be done and participating where appropriate (vv. 21, 25, 27, 29, 30). The whole event depicts Hezekiah as a second David and Solomon uniting the whole nation around the Jerusalem temple.

The sacrifices consisted of bulls, rams and lambs for the burnt offerings (vv. 21-22) and male goats for the purification offerings (traditionally translated 'sin' offering; verses 21, 23). Male goats were sacrificed as a purification offering for the people on the Day of Atonement and a ram for a burnt offering (Lev. 16:5, 15-22). During the consecration of Aaron and his sons, similar offerings and rituals were required (Lev. 9) and likewise at the consecration and cleansing of the altar, the sanctuary and the priests in Ezekiel's vision (Ezek. 43:18-27; 44:27; 45:18-20). The burnt offering which produced a 'sweet aroma to Yahweh' emphasised that God's wrath on account of sin was appeased through a propitiatory sacrifice (Gen. 8:20-21; Lev. 1:9). As for the purification offering, it spoke of cleansing from the defiling effects of human sin (Lev. 4). Though these sacrifices were to be made for specific groups (v. 21), the summary statement in verse 24 emphasises that on the king's orders they were for 'all Israel', that is, all the tribes of Israel (1 Chron. 11:1). The south had become as apostate as the north as a result of Ahaz's rule. The three groups specially mentioned included the 'kingdom' represented by the king, the 'sanctuary' meaning the temple represented by its ministers, and 'Judah' referring to the people and represented by the officials (v. 21). It is suggested by some that 'kingdom' (*mamlākāh*) in this context means 'royal household' because 'Judah' the kingdom, is mentioned later. But previous references to 'kingdom' (1 Chron. 29:11; 2 Chron. 13:8) may rather suggest the original Davidic kingdom that is equated with Yahweh's rule. That kingdom included north and south, and Hezekiah's rule is likened to the David–Solomon era and the king represented the whole Israelite nation as 'all Israel' (v. 24) implies.

King and leaders of the people would have been responsible for bringing the sacrificial animals, with the Levites perhaps helping in their slaughter (Lev. 1:5, 11; Ezek. 44:11), but it was the function of the priests alone to bring the sacrifices to the altar and to carry out the blood sprinkling rituals (see Lev. 17:6; Num. 18:17). While hands would have been laid on the heads of the animals selected for the burnt offerings (Lev. 1:4), attention is drawn to it in the case of the purification offering, for this was more specifically related to sin and guilt and the need for cleansing, whether in reference to the whole assembly of Israel, or its leaders or individuals (Lev. 4:3-5, 13, 22, 27). There are some similarities to the Day of Atonement rituals at the sanctuary, where it is shown that moral and ritual uncleanness affected the place of worship (Lev. 16:11, 15, 16, 20). Placing the hand on the victim's head would have involved confessing Israel's sins (Lev. 16:21-22) and was symbolic of the transfer and removal of the people's sin and guilt to the animal. The emphasis in the purification offering was on cleansing from sin's defiling effects, as the sprinkled blood suggests, whereas the burning of the sacrifice, as in the case of the burnt offering, pointed to the removal of God's wrath on account of the sin. It was both an expiatory and a propitiatory sacrifice 'to atone' for Israel's sin.

True to his general interest in temple music, the Chronicler does not forget to mention the place of the Levitical singers and instrumentalists. The reinstatement of temple music at the consecration ceremony, again presents Hezekiah as a new David as well as showing similarities with Solomon's activity at the dedication of the temple which included musical accompaniment (2 Chron. 7:6). Hezekiah is careful to make clear that all was done in accordance with the command of David and his prophets. The Mosaic law gave no instructions concerning music at the sanctuary. David himself was reckoned among the prophets and received special revelation, even in written form (1 Chron. 28:19; 2 Chron. 8:14), and no doubt the Chronicles of Nathan and Gad, cited among the Chronicler's sources, are also in mind (1 Chron. 29:29). While the priests were responsible for blowing trumpets (v. 26;

1 Chron. 15:24; 16:6; 2 Chron. 5:12-13; 13:12-14), the Levites used the instruments that David produced to praise God (vv. 26-27; 1 Chron. 23:5; 2 Chron. 7:6). Besides the earlier sacrifices, further burnt offerings were made to the accompaniment of music and singing (v. 27; see 1 Chron. 23:30-31; 2 Chron. 23:18) while the 'assembly' (see v. 23) prostrated themselves in worship. It is emphasised that king and all present bowed reverently in worship (vv. 29-30). Such a practice occurred when the glory of Yahweh appeared and fire came down to consume the first sacrifice at the temple's dedication (2 Chron. 7:3). Verse 30 is perhaps a summary statement, but it reveals that there was real heartfelt joy as the Levites praised God and all prostrated themselves with heads bowed to the ground. The psalms of David and Asaph were used in their songs of praise (see the Psalter especially Books One and Two for David: Pss. 1–72; Book Three for Asaph: Pss. 73–83).

The people worship and rejoice (29:31-36)

> 29:31. Then Hezekiah answered and said, 'Now that you have consecrated yourselves to Yahweh, come near, and bring sacrifices and thank offerings into the house of Yahweh.' So the assembly brought sacrifices and thank offerings, and all who were of willing heart *brought* burnt offerings. 32. And the number of the burnt offerings that the assembly brought was seventy bulls, one hundred rams and two hundred lambs; all these were for a burnt offering to Yahweh. 33. The consecrated things were six hundred bulls and three thousand sheep. 34. But the priests were too few and were not able to skin all the burnt offerings; therefore their brothers the Levites supported them until the work was finished and until the *other* priests had sanctified themselves, for the Levites were more upright of heart in sanctifying themselves than the priests. 35. And besides the many burnt offerings, there was the fat of the peace offerings, and the drink offerings for the burnt offerings. So the service of the house of Yahweh was established. 36. Then Hezekiah and all the people rejoiced over what God had re-established for the people, for the thing happened suddenly.

Unlike the original dedication of the temple, where Solomon alone is mentioned as offering sacrifices, Hezekiah encouraged the assembled representatives of the people to actively participate in bringing sacrifices. Such involvement by the people was noted in the enthronement of David and in response to his call to contribute gifts toward the building of the temple (1 Chron. 12:40; 29:5-9). The assembly had already been consecrated through the previous offerings that were made on their behalf (see vv. 21, 24). A Hebrew idiom 'fill the hand' that is normally found for the consecration of priests (Exod. 28:41; 29:9, 35; 32:29; Lev. 8:33; 16:32; 21:10; Num. 3:3) is used here in a wider sense (v. 31; see also 1 Chron. 29:5; 2 Chron. 13:9). The king encouraged the people to show their appreciation as a consecrated community by presenting sacrifices in which they had the right to participate. Two main types of sacrifice are mentioned: the peace offering and the burnt offering. There were three types of peace offering and the one appropriate to this occasion was the 'thank offering'. This type would be better translated 'praise' offering for it was presented to glorify God and was often intended as an expression of love and gratitude (see Ps. 56:12-13; Jer. 33:11).[48] The word 'sacrifice' when found on its own usually stands for the peace offering so that the words 'and thank offerings' should be regarded as an explanation (an epexegetical phrase) of the type of sacrifice it was, namely, a 'thanksgiving sacrifice'. Peace offerings were free-will sacrifices and were the only ones where the worshipper was allowed to eat part of the meat offered and share it with family and friends (Lev. 3:1-17; 7:11-34).

For this occasion, the people also freely brought burnt offerings (Lev. 1). This substitute propitiatory sacrifice was wholly set apart to Yahweh for destruction so that the people were to see themselves as preserved alive to be wholly dedicated to Yahweh. The exact phrase 'willing heart' is found elsewhere only in the case of the people's generous gifts for the tabernacle (Exod. 35:5, 22), but the verbal form from the same word family as 'willing' (nāḏîḇ, verse 31) is used a number of times for the whole-hearted, joyful, willing contributions to the work of building the temple (1 Chron. 29:5, 6, 9, 14, 17).

There is an interesting note in verse 34 that reveals again the Chronicler's special interest in the Levites generally. It placed the priests on this occasion in a bad light while it portrayed the

---

48. See Eveson *The Beauty of Holiness* for the various sacrifices in Leviticus 1-7.

Levites as more sincerely devoted in consecrating themselves. Hezekiah's religious reforms were his first concern when he became sole ruler and because they had been undertaken so quickly (vv. 3, 36), it meant that many of the priests had not consecrated themselves in time for the rededication ceremonies, even though the king had urged them to do so (v. 5). The Mosaic law required the offerer to flay the animals for sacrifice (Lev. 1:5-6) but on this occasion the priests were to do it and because there were not enough of them ritually prepared, the Levites came to the rescue. David had encouraged the Levites to assist the priests in their work (1 Chron. 23:28, 32) and in this emergency they were all ready for action.

Not only were the burnt offerings wholly offered up on the altar of burnt offering but so also was the fat of the peace offerings (v. 35a; see Lev. 3:3-4, 9-11, 14-17). Few details of the drink offering are provided in the Mosaic law, but it accompanied the burnt offering (Exod. 29:40; Num. 15:5, 7, 10). Like a second Solomon, Hezekiah had satisfactorily accomplished the work he had set out to do (v. 35b; 2 Chron. 8:16) and it resulted in the kind of joy that was witnessed after the dedication of the temple (v. 36; 2 Chron. 7:10). The reason for the rejoicing was on account of the speed with which the restoration work and the re-establishment of the worship had been accomplished. They also rejoiced because they saw that it was all due ultimately to God, which meant that instead of experiencing Yahweh's wrath they received His blessing.

Application

Again, the chapter's lessons spoke to those in the post-exilic period encouraging them to be zealous in their worship at the temple. It would have encouraged the Levites as well as the priests to be eager in carrying out the sanctuary rituals and for there to be no rivalry between them (Ezra 8:15-20). Jesus exercised zeal for God's house when He cleansed the temple and so fulfilled the words of the prophets (John 2:17; Pss. 69:9; 119:139; Zech. 14:21; Mal. 3:1-4). It was a symbolic declaration of the end-time judgment anticipating a purification that would involve the temple's complete destruction. The Lord Himself experienced that end-time judgment as He endured the wrath of God for sinners on the cross. At the same time, by his death and resurrection He fulfilled all that the temple and its sacrificial system symbolised and pointed to Himself as the new temple for all nations (Isa. 56:7; Mark 11:17; John 2:19-22).

The Passover kept (30:1-27)
The Chronicler proceeds to describe the first Passover celebration of Hezekiah's reign. There are some significant parallels with the previous chapter. A similar structure is evident where there is first a call to action (vv. 1-12; see 2 Chron. 29:4-11) followed by the need for purification and an account of the joyful worship (vv. 13-27; 2 Chron. 29:12-35). Hezekiah's letter to the people contains the same kind of earnest appeal and language that is found in his speech to the Levites (vv. 6-9; 2 Chron. 29:5-11). In addition, each report stresses a number of themes dear to the Chronicler, including the importance of the 'assembly' (*qāhāl*), purification before worship and joyful celebration.

Chapter 30, however, does reveal other concerns that relate to the unity of the north and south and the celebration of the Passover. While the focus in chapter 29 was on the temple, its purification and worship, with a variety of names being employed to describe the sanctuary, this chapter emphasises the importance of assembling in the city of Jerusalem (vv. 1-3, 5, 11, 13-14, 21, 26). This is in marked contrast to the previous chapter where there was no mention of the city apart from in the phrase 'Judah and Jerusalem'. The chapter again presents Hezekiah in the guise of a new David and Solomon. At present there is no satisfactory solution to the chronological problems surrounding Hezekiah's reign but allowing for a co-regency with Ahaz, it would appear that by the time he became sole ruler the northern kingdom had fallen to the Assyrians. However, with the Assyrians experiencing some political instability at home and coming under pressure from other parts of the empire, it enabled Hezekiah to make full use of this window of opportunity to contact the remaining Israelites in the north.

The chapter takes the following basic shape: the decision to hold a Passover and to invite all Israel (vv. 1-5); the invitations sent and the mixed response (vv. 6-12); the Passover and Festival of Unleavened Bread celebrated (vv. 13-27).

30:1. And Hezekiah sent to all Israel and Judah and also wrote letters to Ephraim and Manasseh, to come to the house of Yahweh in Jerusalem, to get done a Passover for Yahweh the God of Israel. 2. And the king and his officials and all the assembly in Jerusalem had taken counsel to get the Passover done in the second month. 3. For they were not able to do it at that time because the priests had not sanctified themselves in sufficient numbers and the people had not gathered together to Jerusalem. 4. And the thing was right in the sight of the king and in the sight of all the assembly. 5. So they set up a decree to be proclaimed in all Israel, from Beersheba to Dan, to come to get done a Passover to Yahweh the God of Israel in Jerusalem for they had not done *it* on such a scale according to what was written.

The first verse provides both an introduction to what follows and a summary of the whole chapter. It was not untypical for a royal oral proclamation to be supported by written letters (2 Chron. 36:22). The phrase 'all Israel' is used deliberately both to describe the northerners and as a comprehensive description of the whole land of Canaan and its people. 'Ephraim and Manasseh', being the leading tribes of the north, represent the whole of the former northern kingdom (Gen. 48; Num. 26:28-37; Josh. 16-17), and they along with 'Judah' indicated the king's desire to see 'all Israel' in Jerusalem at the temple for this festive occasion and to worship 'the God of Israel'. The Passover, which from the beginning was associated with the festival of Unleavened Bread (Exod. 12), was in its origins a family activity, but for life in Canaan it was to be a pilgrim festival at the central sanctuary to commemorate Israel's redemption and exodus from Egypt (Exod. 12-13; Lev. 23:4-8; Num. 28:16-25; Deut. 16:1-8).

Verses two to five explain the circumstances which led to this proclamation. It provides another example of democratisation, first noticed in Chronicles when David proposed to bring the ark to Jerusalem. Solomon also sought to consult the people and so did Jehoshaphat (1 Chron. 29:1, 10, 20; 2 Chron. 1:3-5; 6:3, 12, 13; 20:5, 21). Hezekiah obtained the approval of the ordinary people who made up the 'assembly' in addition to his officials (vv. 2, 4; see 1 Chron. 13:1-4). The 'assembly' (*qāhāl*) is mentioned six times in the previous chapter and nine times in this chapter and is one of the means the Chronicler uses to emphasise the unity of the people in this communal festival (vv. 2, 4, 13, 17, 23, 24, and twice in 25). A decision was made to hold the Passover 'in the second month' instead of the fourteenth day of the first month as the law stipulated (Exod. 12:2-6; Lev. 23:5). The Mosaic law did in fact allow for a delay of one month for anyone who was ritually unclean or was unavoidably absent on a journey (Num. 9:9-11). That provision is applied more generally on this occasion as the Chronicler explains (v. 3). Not all the priests had sanctified themselves (see 2 Chron. 29:34) and the people had not been able to gather together in time at Jerusalem.

So with the support of the people (v. 4), a decree was formulated and proclaimed throughout 'all Israel', with the additional descriptive phrase 'from Beersheba to Dan' making clear that the whole of the promised land was covered as in the days of king David (v. 5; see 1 Chron. 21:2). God's people from all the tribes were summoned. The normal order – 'from Dan to Beersheba' – is reversed, reflecting the Chronicler's way of thinking from south to north (see 1 Chron. 13:5; 2 Chron. 19:4). At the close of verse 5, 'on such a scale' translates 'with regard to abundance' and probably means that during the divided monarchy period the people from all over Israel had not gathered before in such large numbers for a Passover as the Mosaic law required (Deut. 16:1-8).

Application

Herman Bavinck reminds us that the 'foundations of the Christian church were laid in the days of the Old Testament'.[49] The numerous references to 'assembly' in Chronicles (*ekklēsia* in the LXX) are important for our understanding of the New Testament Church. Jesus expected His disciples to have this background in mind when He spoke about the church (Matt. 16:16-19; 18:15-20).

As Hezekiah, following the example of David and Solomon, took the people of God into his confidence and gained their support before proceeding with his plans, so we find the

---

49. Herman Bavinck, *Reformed Dogmatics*, Vol. 4 (Grand Rapids: Baker Academic, 2008), p. 277.

apostles acting in consultation with all the members of the church (Acts 1:15; 6:1-6; 15:22). Elders of churches are never to be seen as dictators. David's greater Son, the good shepherd, led by example when He encouraged His disciples to do as He had done for them in washing their feet (John 13:12-17). Ministers must instruct, guide and lead forward but never impose their wills and drive their flock (see 1 Pet. 5:3). It is a great blessing when leaders and people move together to advance Christ's kingdom and honour God's name.

> 30:6. And the runners went with the letters from the hand of the king and his officials through all Israel and Judah and according to the commandment of the king, saying, 'Sons of Israel, return to Yahweh, the God of Abraham, Isaac and Israel, that he may return to the escaped ones who are left to you from the palm of the kings of Assyria. 7. And do not be like your fathers and your brothers who were unfaithful to Yahweh the God of their fathers so that he gave them to desolation as you see. 8. Now do not be stiff-necked like your fathers, give your hand to Yahweh and come to his sanctuary which he has sanctified for ever, and serve Yahweh your God so that his fierce wrath may turn from you. 9. For when you return to Yahweh, your brothers and your sons *will find* mercy before their captors so that they may return to this land, for gracious and merciful is Yahweh your God and he will not turn away *his* face from you if you return to him.'
>
> 10. So the runners passed on from city to city in the land of Ephraim and Manasseh and as far as Zebulun, but they were laughing at them and mocking them. 11. Only men from Asher and Manasseh and Zebulun humbled themselves and came to Jerusalem. 12. Also in Judah, the hand of God gave them one heart to do the commandment of the king and the officials by the word of Yahweh.

As in verse 1, the emphasis is on 'all Israel', but the addition of 'Judah' (v. 6) makes it clear that the letters were sent to the southern kingdom of Judah as well as to the northern tribes (see vv. 10-12), even though in the first instance the appeal was to the remnant left in the north (v. 6b). Sermon-like messages addressed to various people are a common feature of Chronicles. Familiar topics appear and the 'sermon' has a structure where the positive call to 'return' to God provides the frame (vv. 6b, 9) around which negative commands are issued using such sound-bites as 'unfaithful', 'desolation',

'your fathers', Yahweh's 'sanctuary' and God's 'fierce wrath'
(vv. 7-8). The style of the sermonic letter is like Zechariah 1:1-6,
but this message is not from a prophet but from the king
himself. It is addressed to 'the sons of Israel', a familiar phrase
that reminded them of their origins (1 Chron. 2:1) and they are
urged to return to Yahweh. The verb used is 'to turn' (šûḇ) and
it is employed six times in this letter not only to express the
people's repentance (vv. 6, 9) but also God's turning toward
them (v. 6), the turning away of His wrath (v. 8) and the return
from exile (v. 9). The plea for the people to 'turn' or 'repent'
is coupled with the encouraging truth that God is ready to
'turn' or 'return' to them (v. 6).

Yahweh is identified as 'the God of Abraham, Isaac
and Israel' which reminded them of the exodus and their
redemption from Egyptian slavery (v. 6; see Exod. 3:6, 15,
16; 4:5). Again, 'Israel' is the Chronicler's preferred way of
referring to 'Jacob' (1 Chron. 29:18; see 1 Kings 18:36). It is
clear that king and kingdom had ceased to exist in the north
with the reference to those left by the Assyrians. The plural
'kings' (v. 6; see 2 Chron. 28:16) is a reminder that a number of
Assyrian kings contributed to the end of the north including
Tiglath-pileser III, Shalmaneser V and Sargon II (1 Chron. 5:6,
26; 2 Chron. 28:20; 2 Kings 17:3; 18:9; Isa. 20:1). Urging the people
not to be like their 'fathers' or 'brothers' stressed the guilt of
Judah under Ahaz as well as that of the northerners when the
kingdom first divided, while the call to 'return' to Yahweh
highlighted their own responsibility in breaking the cycle of
unfaithfulness (māʿal; see 1 Chron. 2:7; 10:13). The punishment
is 'desolation' or 'waste' but in the sense of being a sight of
'horror' or 'astonishment' (šammāh; see 2 Chron. 29:8; Jer. 18:16;
25:9, 11; etc.). It is a word that described both the land and the
people under the final covenant curse of exile (Deut. 28:37).

Again there is an appeal for the people not to be like their
'fathers' (v. 8, see v. 7) who were 'stiff-necked'. This idiomatic
expression occurs many times in the Hebrew Bible for Israel's
stubbornness, using either a verbal or adjectival form of the
root letters qšh for 'stiff' or 'hard'; (Exod. 32:9; 33:3, 5; 34:9;
Deut. 9:6, 13; 10:16; 31:27; etc.). The opposite of this obstinate
position toward Yahweh is one of submission to Him and this
attitude is also expressed figuratively as 'to give' or to 'reach

out' one's hand, an idiom that is often indicative of cementing some kind of promise or relationship, much like a modern handshake after a deal has been struck (see 2 Kings 10:15; 1 Chron. 29:24; Ezra 10:19; Lam. 5:6; Ezek. 17:18). In practice that meant, for the northerners, being prepared to humble themselves and come to Yahweh's sanctuary in Jerusalem which they had long deserted in favour of their own temples (2 Chron. 11:14-15; 13:8-9). For Judah, it meant worshipping once more at the central sanctuary that had been closed up during the reign of Ahaz. What Yahweh had pronounced holy from the start, Hezekiah had cleansed and made holy, and so all Israel was urged to serve Yahweh by worshipping at His sanctuary so that His 'fierce wrath' (v. 8; 2 Chron. 28:11, 13) might 'turn' from them.

As the king pressed home the call to repentance, he encouraged the people with the prospect of a return from exile for those already taken captive or from any future captivity. It recalls Solomon's prayer (2 Chron. 6:38-39), especially the words not included in the Chronicler's account (1 Kings 8:50). The 'mercy' that an enemy might show toward captives was what the northerners had shown toward their brothers in the south when they defeated and captured many of them during Ahaz's reign (2 Chron. 28:12-15). It was one of the basic beliefs in Israel that Yahweh was a 'gracious and merciful' God (Exod. 34:6; Neh. 9:17, 31; Pss. 103:8; 111:4; 112:4; 145:8; Joel 2:13; Jonah 4:2).

Those sent to deliver the king's decree received a mixed reaction, and the Chronicler concentrates first on the response in the north (vv. 10-11) and then in Judah (v. 12). The northern tribes named are a sample to indicate that the whole of Canaan was covered. Ephraim and Manasseh were the main tribes of the northern kingdom (see v. 1) while Zebulun lay in the Galilee region bordering Manasseh, with Asher in the far north by the sea. Issachar is included in verse 18. No mention is made of the Transjordan tribes probably because they had been deported earlier by Tiglath-pileser III with no remnants of Israel left (1 Chron. 5:26). From the majority in the north there was a general rejection, expressed by continuous jeering similar to that experienced in the time of Nehemiah and by the psalmist (Neh. 2:19; 4:1[3:33]; Ps. 22:7[8]).

But there were some from all over the north who were receptive and 'humbled themselves' in the manner required by Yahweh (2 Chron. 7:14; 12:6, 7, 12) and they showed their repentant spirit by 'coming to Jerusalem' (v. 11). As for those in Judah, they were much more united in their support of the king and his officials, similar to the occasion when 'the rest of Israel' was united in making David king (1 Chron. 12:38[39]). The Chronicler considers this to be due to the 'hand' or power of God. It was the kind of unity the prophets spoke of in relation to the new covenant when God would give the people 'a single heart' that would express itself in exclusive devotion to God (Jer. 32:39; Ezek. 11:19). As with the purification of the temple so the proposed Passover celebration was based on the authority of God's revealed word.

Application

The kind of unity expressed in the passage was experienced by the early believers (Acts 4:32). It takes a work of the Spirit to unite people of differing cultures and personalities. The lack of unity and unkindly attitudes that are sometimes displayed by professing Christians belonging to Bible-believing gospel churches are shocking. Often such critical judgments are founded on hearsay and are used to support their personal agendas rather than in a genuine desire to appreciate differences and work toward a better understanding of the views of fellow Christians.

We can differ over secondary issues such as the type of music sung, and expressions of worship displayed, without accusations of denying the faith or not being truly biblical. Using terms like 'charismatic' in a pejorative way only makes things worse. We do not learn. In the eighteenth century the people of the spiritual awakening were nicknamed 'Methodists' or 'enthusiasts', and in the Reformation period 'Anabaptist' became a term to tar all who did not toe the party line on baptism. Genuine differences of interpretation that do not deny Scripture or the gospel are no excuse for condemning believers and churches wholesale and denouncing them as being 'on a slippery slope' and so intimating that they are beginning to depart from the true faith. Christians and churches must be careful that by such reactions they are not themselves acting in an unbiblical manner and putting themselves in the way of judgment. Scripture warns that pointing out error and heresy without full knowledge and without that spirit of love and concern for God's people can rebound on those who criticise.

As part of the ultimate exile of desolation that Jesus endured, He was jeered and viewed as a figure of revulsion. The words of Isaiah's Suffering Servant express the sad attitude of people toward Him, from the time Jesus lived in Canaan to the present: He was 'despised and rejected' and there was 'no beauty' for people to desire Him (Isa. 53:2-3).

> 30:13. Then many people gathered at Jerusalem to celebrate the festival of Unleavened Bread in the second month, a very large assembly. 14. And they arose and removed the altars which were in Jerusalem and they removed all the ones for burning incense and threw *them* into the Kidron wadi. 15. Then they slaughtered the Passover on the fourteenth of the second month and the priests and the Levites were ashamed and sanctified themselves and brought the burnt offerings of the house of Yahweh. 16. And they stood in their place according to their custom, according to the law of Moses, the man of God, the priests sprinkling the blood from the hand of the Levites. 17. For *there were* many in the assembly who had not sanctified themselves, so the Levites had to slaughter the Passover for all who were not clean to sanctify *them* for Yahweh. 18. For a majority of the people, many from Ephraim and Manasseh, Issachar and Zebulun had not purified themselves, yet they ate the Passover not as it was written. But Hezekiah prayed for them, saying, 'May the good Yahweh provide atonement for 19. everyone who sets his heart to seek God, Yahweh the God of his fathers, though not according to the purification of the sanctuary.' 20. And Yahweh listened to Hezekiah and healed the people.

This is a most interesting and remarkable account of an irregular celebration. It not only describes for the first time in the Bible an actual pilgrimage to Jerusalem to celebrate the Passover and Unleavened Bread festival, but it stresses how it took place at an unusual time. The Mosaic law did allow the festival to take place in the second rather than the first month, but only in exceptional circumstances, and the first part of this chapter has shown why the exception could be applied on this occasion. But the narrative indicates that there was another problem that led to an even more amazing concession. It depicts participation in the event by ceremonially unclean people who according to the Mosaic law were explicitly prohibited under pain of being 'cut off' from God's people. Furthermore, the people decided to keep on celebrating for a further week. The whole event is quite extraordinary.

As a result of the account in the first part of the chapter, verse 13 provides a summary statement noting the great assembly that gathered together in Jerusalem and also that it occurred in 'the second month'. For the first time in the chapter, 'Unleavened Bread' is mentioned which in the law was closely associated with the Passover. It began the day after the slaughter of the Passover lambs and normally lasted seven days and is introduced at this point because of what follows. Often in the Bible, the festival of Unleavened Bread incorporates the celebration of the Passover. The verb 'to celebrate' translates the word that is earlier rendered 'to do' or 'to get done' ('āśāh; verses 1-3).

Not only did the temple need cleansing (2 Chron. 29), but Jerusalem also itself needed to be purified of all the evidences of false worship that Ahaz had introduced in every corner of the city (v. 14; 2 Chron. 28:24). Like the 'filth' taken from the temple, these defiling items were thrown into the Kidron valley (2 Chron. 29:16).

As the law required, the pilgrims slaughtered the Passover lambs on day fourteen (see Exod. 12:3-6, 21) but yet again it is emphasised that it happened during the second month (v. 15; see vv. 2, 13). The Levites here as well as the priests are seen to need ritual preparation in order to receive the people's sacrifices (see v. 3), especially in view of what is reported in verse 17. They were probably 'shamed' on account of the people's enthusiasm and zeal. The occasion demanded many more priests and Levites and therefore they needed to bring their own burnt sacrifices to the temple as part of the ritual for 'sanctifying themselves' or 'making themselves holy' (v. 15). For the first time, details are given of what happened to the blood of the Passover lambs (v. 16). In the original Passover the blood was sprinkled on the doorposts and lintels of Israel's houses, but with the lambs now being brought to the temple (Deut. 16:5-6), the blood was taken by the Levites from the family members sacrificing their animals and given to the priests who sprinkled the blood presumably on the altar of burnt offering, as was done with other sacrifices (Lev. 1:5; 3:2). It spoke of protection from God's judgment, purification from sin's defiling effects and consecration or separation to Yahweh (Exod. 12:13, 22-23; Ezra 6:19-22). The Levites acted as intermediaries between the people and the priests, for the Mosaic law stated that the Levites were to assist the priests (Num. 3:6). Moses is again referred to as 'the man of God' (v. 16; 1 Chron. 23:14; see 2 Chron. 24:6, 9 for 'servant of God/Yahweh').

A further difficulty arose which required the Levites to actually slaughter the Passover lambs as well as present the blood of the sacrificial victims to the priests. Because of the rush to make this festival happen even with the unusual postponement of a month, it still resulted in many people, especially those from the north, being in a ritually unclean state (vv. 17-18a). Preparations for the original Passover began four days before the lambs were slain and this would have helped reduce the numbers of the ceremonially unclean (Exod. 12:3). It was as a result of people becoming unclean through touching a corpse, that Yahweh's ruling through Moses had allowed people in that condition to celebrate on the same day in the following month (Num. 9:6-11). However, no exceptions were made in the Mosaic law for unclean persons to eat the Passover. In the case of the peace offerings where the people could eat part of the sacrificial meat with family and friends, it was forbidden on pain of being cut off from God's people for them to eat in an unclean state (Lev. 7:20-21). In some respects the Passover was similar to the peace offerings in that in each case it involved the people eating the sacrificial meat. Thus a further acute situation existed, for those unclean people from the north whose Passover lambs the Levites slaughtered on their behalf actually participated in the Passover meal contrary to the rules of the sanctuary (vv. 18, 19b; see Lev. 15:31).

Hezekiah understood the grave position they were in and interceded on their behalf. He pleaded on the basis that God is 'good' (v. 19). This is a characteristic of Yahweh that becomes something of a creed in Israel (1 Chron. 16:34; 2 Chron. 5:13; 7:3; Pss. 34:8[9]; 100:5; 107:1; 118:1; 135:3; 136:1). It is often used with the idea of divine kindness and that is close to the meaning in this context but even earlier the king had spoken in his letter of God's grace and mercy to such people. Hezekiah did not actually pray for pardon for the people, but that God would provide the 'atonement' necessary for the forgiveness of those who humbly sought Him. The king's request was in the spirit of God's promise to Solomon (2 Chron. 7:14). They are people who had already shown their repentant, humble spirit in turning from their apostate ways and responding to Hezekiah's call to come to the temple in Jerusalem (vv. 6-11). Where Yahweh speaks of 'those who seek (*bqš*) my face', Hezekiah employs a similar phrase: 'set their hearts on seeking (*drš*) Yahweh', and both these verbs are used synonymously and are central to the Chronicler's message (1 Chron. 10:13-14). In one brief sentence, which the Masoretic Text sets apart from the verses before and after, the goodness of God is revealed in that He 'listened' to Hezekiah's prayer and 'healed' (see 2 Chron. 7:14). When David sinned, Yahweh sent a pestilence that killed many people and even sent an angel with the intention of destroying Jerusalem (1 Chron. 21:14-15). The original Passover saved Israel from the final plague that had involved the destroyer bringing death to every Egyptian home (Exod. 11:1-12:30). The reality of both Yahweh's judgment and grace was brought home to king and people on this occasion.

> 30:21. So the sons of Israel who were present in Jerusalem celebrated the Festival of Unleavened Bread seven days with great joy; and the Levites and the priests praised Yahweh day by day, with powerful instruments of Yahweh. 22. And Hezekiah spoke encouragingly to all the Levites who taught good understanding for Yahweh, and they ate for the seven-day appointed time, sacrificing peace offerings and making confession to Yahweh God of their fathers. 23. Then the whole assembly took counsel to do another seven days, and they did seven days with joy. 24. For Hezekiah the king of Judah contributed to the assembly a thousand bulls and seven thousand sheep, and the officials contributed to the assembly a thousand bulls and ten thousand

sheep; and a great number of priests sanctified themselves. 25. The whole assembly of Judah and the priests and the Levites, and all the assembly that came from Israel, and the resident aliens who came from the land of Israel, and those who lived in Judah rejoiced. 26. So there was great joy in Jerusalem for since the days of Solomon the son of David, the king of Israel, there had been nothing like this in Jerusalem. 27. Then the Levitical priests arose and blessed the people, and their voice was heard; and their prayer came to heaven, to his holy habitation.

The day after the Passover was observed, the festival of Unleavened Bread commenced (v. 21; see v. 13). In the Bible the two events were closely associated and often the entire celebration could be referred to using either name. The lambs for the Passover meal were normally slaughtered in the temple during the afternoon of the fourteenth of Abib or Nisan (the pre- and post-exile names; Deut. 16:1; Neh. 2:1), the first month of the religious calendar, and the meat eaten after sunset which was then the fifteenth day (the Jewish day began at sunset) and which was then the first day of the seven-day festival of Unleavened Bread which ended on the twenty-first of the month (Exod. 23:15; Lev. 23:6-8; Num. 28:16-25; Deut. 16:8; see Mark 14:1-2). Joy marked the occasion (vv. 21, 23, 25, 26; see Ezra 6:22) and, as with the coronation of David (1 Chron. 12:40), it involved all the tribes of Israel ('the sons of Israel'; 1 Chron. 2:1). There is no justification, as in some versions, for emending the unique phrase 'with instruments of might' to read *'singing* with all their might'(verse 21). It refers to the loud or resounding musical instruments that had God's approval (1 Chron. 15:16; 16:42; 2 Chron. 29:27).

In view of their immense workload, the king, as a considerate leader, gave a special word of support to all the Levites including the priests (v. 22; 2 Chron. 29:5). The idiomatic phrase translated 'speak encouragingly' (literally 'speak to the heart of') is used of Joseph's tender words to his brothers and also of the call to speak 'comfortably' to Jerusalem (Gen. 50:21; Isa. 40:2). The function of the temple staff is described in an unusual way, employing a word sometimes found in psalm headings (*maskil*; see Ps. 32). It probably relates to their teaching role (see Deut. 33:10; Mal. 2:6-7), especially in this context, of assisting the people with the sacrifices. Peace or fellowship sacrifices enabled the people as well as the priests to continue to eat meat throughout the seven-day festival. The verb for 'to confess' in the form found here (the *hithpael* of *ydh*) means confessing sin but most other forms of the verb express the idea of confessing thanksgiving to God, thanksgiving being one of the peace offering types (1 Chron. 16:8, 34; Lev. 7:11-18).

Having eaten for the seven-day 'appointed time' (*mô'ēḏ*, v. 22), the exuberant assembly, of its own volition, agreed to continue the celebrations for a further seven days. Again, it makes this occasion a most extraordinary event and witnesses to the people's spontaneous joy and religious fervour, for there was no special reason in the religious calendar for spilling over into a second week. The celebrations bear some similarity to the festivities surrounding Solomon's dedication of the original temple which lasted two weeks, although in that instance the second week involved the keeping of the festival of Tabernacles (2 Chron. 7:8-9). Helping to support the people's enthusiasm, the king and his officials contributed liberally to the supply of sacrifices and meals needed for this further week of festivities, while the priests made up for former deficiencies and were present in adequate numbers (v. 24; see 2 Chron. 29:34).

The Chronicler makes a point of listing all who participated (v. 25). It included 'all the assembly' of Judah, including all the temple ministers, and 'all the assembly' that came from the north, which he refers to as 'Israel', together with 'sojourners' or 'resident aliens' from the north as well as those who lived in Judah. Interestingly, the phrase 'land of Israel' is often linked with 'resident aliens' in this book (v. 25; 1 Chron. 22:2; 2 Chron. 2:17[16]; 2 Chron. 34:7). Some have wondered if some of these resident aliens were from among those the Assyrians had resettled in the northern territory. In Chronicles, those not of Israelite stock are not viewed as foreigners but very much a part of Israel's life and worship. It assumes the sojourners or resident aliens had been circumcised and witnesses to their knowledge of the Mosaic law (Exod. 12:48-49; Num. 9:14). The theme of joy continues to be emphasised and the Chronicler adds what has been hinted at a number of times earlier, that Hezekiah is a second Solomon (v. 26). He had achieved a celebration and expression of joy in Jerusalem among representatives of all Israel that was without parallel since the time of Solomon. The comparison is heightened by giving to Solomon his full title: 'Solomon the son of David the king of Israel.'

The account is brought to a satisfactory close with a statement that the priests rose to pronounce a blessing on the people, probably one similar to the Aaronic blessing in Numbers 6:22-27. It was given to the priests, not the Levites in general, to bless God's people (see Lev. 9:22; Deut. 21:5; 1 Chron. 23:13). Contrary to some versions and translations, the traditional text does not say 'priests and Levites' but literally 'the priests, Levites' meaning the Levitical priests. Though the content of the blessing is not expressed, it is stressed that Yahweh heard it. The blessing is described as a 'prayer' that was received in God's holy, heavenly home. The same phrase 'holy habitation' is found in Deuteronomy 26:15 (see also Ps. 68:5[6], and the same term for 'habitation' is used of an animal's den or lair in Jer. 10:22). Again, there are echoes of Solomon's dedicatory prayer that God would hear in heaven the prayers made at or toward the temple (2 Chron. 6:21).

Application

The picture of the people of God assembled together as 'church' or 'assembly' under the rule of God's Davidic king in Jerusalem is a pointer to Jesus our King and those united to Him from all nations to form His Church, the new Jerusalem. In the Psalter this idea is taken further with Yahweh's words in Psalm 2:6 giving us the initial prompt: 'I have set my king on my holy hill of Zion.' Paul speaks of the spiritual city, 'the Jerusalem which is above' while Hebrews refers to the heavenly Jerusalem, the city of the living God, and Revelation draws our attention to the great and holy city, the new Jerusalem. This is the city, Mount Zion, where all God's people come and belong.

The Gospel of John connects very clearly Jesus' cleansing of the temple with the time of Passover and emphasises that Jesus is God's Passover lamb bringing freedom from sin, Satan and the judgment we deserve. He is the 'Lamb of God' who takes away the sin of the world through His death and resurrection.

The religious reforms (31:1-21)

Following the cleansing of the Jerusalem temple in the previous chapter, a brief account is given of the people's own willingness to see the whole land cleansed of false worship (v. 1). The king is then portrayed, once more, like a second David and Solomon, as he reorganises the priests and Levites (v. 2) and arranges for their proper material support (vv. 3-19), and the chapter concludes with a glowing assessment of his reforms (vv. 20-21). Though Hezekiah is prominent in the reforms, the Chronicler continues to emphasise the important part played by the people. There are only a few verses that parallel those found in the earlier history such as verse 1 (2 Kings 18:4) and verses 20-21 (2 Kings 18:5-7a).

> 31:1. Now when all this was finished, all Israel who were present went out to the cities of Judah and broke the standing-stones in pieces, cut down the Asherim, and tore down the high places and the altars, from all Judah and Benjamin, and in Ephraim and Manasseh, until all were destroyed. Then all the sons of Israel returned to their cities, everyone to his possession.

The religious enthusiasm of the people in the celebration of the Passover at Jerusalem, recounted in the preceding chapter, continued as 'all Israel', that ideal union of twelve tribes that is otherwise referred to as 'the sons of Israel', set about destroying the symbols of pagan worship and the illegitimate high places and altars throughout the land of Judah and the former northern kingdom, represented by Ephraim and Manasseh, before returning to their 'possessions' (1 Chron. 9:2). This same kind of reforming zeal was seen by king Asa (2 Chron. 14:3[2]), but in this instance the Chronicler emphasises the people's involvement, something that was lacking during Jehoshaphat's reign (2 Chron. 20:32-33). From first of all cleansing the temple, then the city, finally the whole land is cleansed.

> 31:2. And Hezekiah appointed the divisions of the priests and the Levites by their divisions, each in proportion to his service with reference to the priests and to the Levites, for burnt offerings and for peace offerings, to serve and to give thanks, and to praise in the gates of the camps of Yahweh.

For the worship of the temple to continue on a regular basis, Hezekiah first restored the divisions of the priests

and Levites initially set up by Solomon according to David's
instructions (2 Chron. 8:14) but which had probably lapsed
during the time of Ahaz. A clear division of service is shown
between the ministry of the priests in offering the sacrifices
of burnt offering and fellowship offerings (1 Chron. 16:39-40)
and the responsibility of the Levites which lay in giving
thanks and praising (1 Chron. 16:4, 41). The verb 'to serve'
or 'minister' could well apply to both the priests and the
Levites (1 Chron. 16:37; 2 Chron. 8:14). All this took place
within the gates of the temple, here referred to figuratively
as Yahweh's 'camps' (see 1 Chron. 9:19) and was a reminder
of the tabernacle in the wilderness (Num. 2:17).

> 31:3. Also the king's share from his possessions was for the burnt
> offerings: for the morning and the evening burnt offerings, and
> the burnt offerings for the sabbaths and for the new moons and
> for the appointed festivals, as it is written in the Law of Yahweh.
> 4. Also he said to the people, to those living in Jerusalem, to give
> the share due to the priests and the Levites, so that they might
> be strong in the Law of Yahweh. 5. And as soon as the word
> spread, the sons of Israel gave in abundance the first-fruits of
> grain, new wine and oil and honey and all the produce of the
> field, and they brought in abundance the tithe of everything.
> 6. And the sons of Israel and Judah, who were living in the
> cities of Judah, they also brought the tithe of oxen and sheep,
> and the tithe of holy things which were dedicated to Yahweh
> their God and put in heaps. 7. In the third month they began
> to establish the heaps, and they finished in the seventh month.
> 8. And Hezekiah and the officials came and saw the heaps and
> they blessed Yahweh and his people Israel. 9. Then Hezekiah
> inquired of the priests and the Levites concerning the heaps. 10.
> And Azariah the chief priest, from the house of Zadok, said to
> him, and he said, 'Since they began to bring the contributions
> into the house of Yahweh, we have had enough to eat and have
> plenty left, for Yahweh has blessed his people; and what is left
> is this abundance.'

For the temple staff to do their work properly, they and their
families needed to be adequately provided for in terms of
food. The account first mentions Hezekiah's 'portion' or 'share'
(v. 3), involving animals from his own possessions which he
gave for the regular daily sacrifices and the weekly Sabbath,
as well as for the special monthly and annual offerings in the

religious calendar (1 Chron. 23:31). Like David, Hezekiah set an example for the people to follow (1 Chron. 29:3-5). It is the list of offerings required in the Mosaic law (Num. 28-29) that the king freely provided. Two extra lambs were sacrificed as burnt offerings on the Sabbath day. Besides the additional sacrifices, the beginning of each month ('new moon') provided an opportunity for families and friends to eat together (1 Sam. 20:5-6; 2 Kings 4:23). The appointed festivals were the annual events of Passover and Unleavened Bread, Weeks and Tabernacles (see 2 Chron. 2:4[3]) when many more sacrifices were needed. Solomon offered the required sacrifices on all these occasions (2 Chron. 8:12-13).

While Hezekiah made sure the required sacrifices were offered, he directed the people of Jerusalem to set aside portions for the daily needs of the priests and Levites (v. 4). These 'portions' would have included tithes (Num. 18:21), first-fruits (Num. 18:12-13) and parts of such sacrifices as the grain, peace (fellowship), sin (purification) and guilt (compensation) offerings (see Lev. 6:14-7:21).[50] Again, as in verse 3, reference is made to 'the law of Yahweh', which the Chronicler associates with God's written word through Moses and authoritative for the nation's life and worship (1 Chron. 6:49; 16:40; 22:12; 2 Chron. 8:13; 12:1; 17:9). The reason given could be one of two things depending on who is the subject of the verb 'they may be strong'. If it is a reference to the priests and Levites, this would suggest that in having sufficient supplies they would be enabled to fulfil their God-given duties at the temple or in the study of the law without hindrance. If the people are the subject then it means that in fulfilling their obligations they would be indicating their zealous commitment to Yahweh's law.

Hezekiah's decree spread wider than he had originally intended, for the whole population of the 'sons of Israel' (v. 5; see v. 1) brought their portions to the temple as the law prescribed (Deut. 12:5-6). It included those 'sons of Israel' who lived with the Judeans in the cities of Judah (v. 6; see 2 Chron. 10:17). The first-fruits of grain, new wine, oil and

---

50. See Eveson, *The Beauty of Holiness*, for comments on the terms for the various sacrifices.

honey and the rest of the produce of the field were for the priests (Num. 18:12) while the tithes which included crops, fruit and livestock were for the Levites (Num. 18:21). Tithing the cattle and sheep is mentioned in Leviticus 27:32-33. Twice the giving is described as 'in abundance' (v. 5) and the repeated use of 'heaps' (vv. 6-9) indicates the people's generosity. Such enthusiastic giving was last mentioned in the time of Joash (2 Chron. 24:8-14). Tithing the 'holy things' (v. 6) refers to the tithing of the people's tithes that had been given to the Levites. The Levites themselves gave to the priests a tenth of the tithes they received from the people (see Neh. 10:38[39]; 12:47).

They began piling up the heaps in the third month around the time of the festival of Weeks or Harvest (Exod. 23:16; Lev. 23:15-22; Num. 28:26; Deut. 16:9-12) when the grain harvest was gathered in. The contributions kept arriving right through to the seventh month when the grapes and other fruit had been gathered in at the time when the great harvest celebrations took place at the Festival of Ingathering, otherwise known as Tabernacles (Exod. 23:16; 34:22; Lev. 23:34-36; Deut. 16:13-17). On seeing the generous response of the people, Hezekiah and the officials 'blessed' Yahweh in the sense of reverently worshipping Him and 'blessed' the people by either congratulating them on their efforts or more likely in this context offering a prayer-wish that God would be benevolent toward His people (v. 8). It was the duty of the priests to give Yahweh's special blessing (1 Chron. 23:13; Num. 6:22-27) but here Hezekiah follows David and Solomon in blessing the people (1 Chron. 16:2; 2 Chron. 6:3).

Hezekiah is intrigued by the heaps and is told that the priests and Levites had received from the people more than enough. It indicated two things: that God had given a bountiful harvest and that the people in turn had not been backward in bringing all their tithes and offerings for the support of the temple staff. It is acknowledged by the chief priest that it was all an indication that Yahweh had 'blessed' His people (vv. 9-10). This chief priest is called Azariah, a common name in the family, and a descendant of Zadok the high priest in the time of David and Solomon. He is not listed among the high priests in the introductory genealogies and that is not unusual as the lists are not complete (1 Chron. 6:9-14[5:35-40]). It is unlikely that he was the Azariah who rebuked Uzziah some forty years earlier (2 Chron. 26:17), but probably a grandson named after him as was a common custom in those days.

Application

God does reward faithfulness. The Chronicler's account would have supported Malachi at a time when the people were 'robbing' God by not paying their tithes and offerings. They are urged to bring 'the whole tithe into the storehouse' and to see whether God would 'not open for you the windows of heaven and pour out a blessing for you' (Mal. 3:8-10). The passage challenges Christians to give wholeheartedly to the work of the Lord (see 2 Cor. 8–9). What are we doing with our money? Are we adequately supporting the ministers and pastors of our churches? Is the work of evangelism and overseas missions suffering through lack of finance? Are we enthusiastic in giving of our time and effort to helping our local church?

31:11. Then Hezekiah commanded them to prepare chambers in the house of Yahweh, and they prepared them. 12. And they faithfully brought the contributions and the tithes and the dedicated things; and the leader over them *was* Cononiah, the Levite, and Shimei his brother *was* second. 13. And Jehiel and Azaziah and Nahath and Asahel and Jerimoth and Jozabad and Eliel and Ismachiah and Mahath and Benaiah *were* overseers under the hand of Cononiah and Shimei his brother, by the appointment of Hezekiah the king and Azariah the leader of the house of God.

14. And Kore the son of Imnah the Levite, the keeper of the east gate, was over the free-will offerings to God, to distribute the contributions of Yahweh and the most holy things. 15. And at his hand *were* Eden and Miniamin and Jeshua and Shemaiah, Amariah and Shecaniah, in the cities of the priests, to distribute faithfully to their brothers by divisions to great and small alike. 16. Besides those enrolled by genealogy, *they distributed* to males from three years old and up, to everyone who entered the house of Yahweh *to do* the daily duty of their service, by their offices according to their divisions. 17. And enrolled by genealogy, the priests according to their father's house, and the Levites from

twenty years old and upward by their offices by their divisions. 18. And to those enrolled by genealogy, with all their children, their wives and their sons and their daughters, the whole assembly, for in their faithfulness they kept themselves holy. 19. Also for the sons of Aaron, the priests, who were in the fields of the common lands of their cities, in every single city, there were men who were designated by name to distribute portions to every male among the priests and to everyone enrolled by genealogy among the Levites.

Verses 11-13 deal with the storing of the people's contributions and verses 14-19 are concerned with the distribution of the gifts.

The surplus supplies needed to be stored properly and not left in heaps, so the king arranged for the chambers in the temple to be made available and for temple staff to be put in charge (v. 11). David had made plans for such chambers in the temple and for the Levites to help the priests with regard to these and other parts of the temple (see 1 Chron. 23:28; 28:12; 1 Kings 6:5, 6). There were such chambers and Levitical staff in the second temple (1 Chron. 9:26, 33). The various types of gifts brought into the store chambers are identified (v. 12) and included the 'contributions' which probably refers to the first-fruits (v. 5), the tithes (vv. 5b-6) and the 'dedicated' or 'holy' offerings that represented the Levites' tithes for the priests (v. 6). It is noted by the Chronicler that there was swift fulfilment of Hezekiah's command (v. 11) and that the storing of all the supplies was carried out 'faithfully' (v. 12; see vv. 15, 18).

Those supervising the whole project were ten in number under the command of Conaniah and his brother Shimei who was second in command (vv. 12-13). Though Conaniah alone is referred to as a Levite, all twelve would have been of the same tribe. They were answerable to the king and to Azariah, the high priest, who is here given the title of 'leader of the house of God' (v. 13b; see v. 10 and 1 Chron. 9:11; 2 Chron. 35:8; Neh. 11:11).

More Levites were involved in the distribution of the offerings (vv. 14-15). The gatekeeper in charge of the east gate was put in charge with six others (see 1 Chron. 26:17) who 'faithfully' assisted him (see verse 12). Among the tithes and first-fruits and donations set apart for the priests, mention is also made of the 'free-will offerings', which were gifts freely given and not required in the Mosaic legislation. The task of these men included distributing the contributions in 'the cities of the priests' (v. 15). The priests had thirteen cities assigned to them (Josh. 21:19). As the following verses make clear, 'great and small' refer to all the priests from the youngest to the oldest, and the 'divisions' concern the allotted duties of the various Levitical families (see v. 2; 1 Chron. 23:6; 24:1; 2 Chron. 8:14).

The translation and meaning of verses 16-19 are uncertain but the general sense is clear. All the priests and Levites and their families received sufficient supplies from the people's gifts. They included those living in Jerusalem and working at the temple (vv. 16-18) as well as those living throughout the country (v. 19). The verses read as if the Chronicler is extracting material from a larger genealogical register ('enrolled by genealogy'; verses 16, 17, 18, 19). Verse 16 indicates that when a priest who came from outside Jerusalem with his family to serve in the temple, none of his young sons from the time they were weaned ('from three years old and upward') would miss out from the distribution. In verse 17 a distinction is made between the priests and Levites, with the priests being enrolled according to their ancestral houses to maintain the purity of their lineage (Lev. 21:7-15; Ezra 2:62-63), whereas the Levites were enrolled on the basis of their duties ('offices') and according to how they were organised ('their divisions'). The age at which they were enrolled was twenty, a ruling set by David (1 Chron. 23:24, 27; Ezra 3:8) but originally it was set at thirty and at twenty-five depending on the type of service involved (Num. 4:3; 8:24; 1 Chron. 23:3). Verse 18 may be continuing to deal with the Levites and to indicate that their entire households were provided for in the distribution. Although it is not stated in the Mosaic law, the Chronicler frequently refers to the holiness of the Levites as well as the priests (1 Chron. 15:14; 2 Chron. 29:5, 12-15, 34b). The final verse dealing with the allocation of gifts (v. 19) concerns priests and Levites living outside Jerusalem. While a distribution was made to those who lived in the cities of the priests (see v. 15), some of the men of those cities were 'designated by name' to hand out supplies to those living in the 'fields of common land' belonging to those cities (1 Chron. 6:54-81[39-66]).

> 31.20. Thus Hezekiah did throughout all Judah, and he did what was good and right and faithful before Yahweh his God. 21. And in every work that he began in the service of the house of God, and in the law and in the commandment, to seek his God, he did *it* with all his heart, and he prospered.

The account of Hezekiah's reforms, especially in his concern for the wellbeing of the priests and Levites throughout his kingdom (v. 20a), closes with a very positive evaluation. There are echoes of 2 Kings 18:5-7 and along with 2 Chronicles 29:2 it provides a frame within which this part of the king's reign is assessed. Hezekiah is the only king to receive the threefold description of doing 'what was good and right and faithful before Yahweh' (v. 20). David did 'what was right' in the sight of God (2 Chron. 29:2) and Asa 'did what was good and right' (2 Chron. 14:2). The term for 'faithful' (*'emet*) can refer to doing what is true as opposed to false or being unreliable. Here it means that the king was true to God in faithfully living out God's will (see 2 Chron. 32:1). Hezekiah, as a second Solomon, 'prospered' (1 Chron. 22:11, 13; 29:23; 2 Chron. 7:11; 32:30). Those who seek to oppose God cannot expect to prosper (2 Chron. 13:12; 24:20). This reward from God is because in all his work in the service of the temple, delineated in the previous chapters, in which he fulfilled God's commandment as set out in the Mosaic law, Hezekiah had done so 'with all his heart' (v. 21; see 2 Chron. 22:9) just as it is recorded of David in 1 Kings 14:8. All his activities indicated the ways in which he sought (*drš*) God, which is a customary summary expression in Chronicles for devotion and faithfulness to God (see 2 Chron. 14:4[3]), the very opposite of what was seen in the life of Saul (1 Chron. 10:13-14).

Application

There are numerous exhortations in the New Testament of the need to provide adequately for those whose employment is in the ministry of proclaiming and teaching the gospel and caring for those members of the Christian community who are in need (Phil. 2:25-30; 4:14-19; 2 Cor. 8-9; Acts 6:1-4; 20:32-35).

Everything should be done decently and in order (1 Cor. 16:1) with proper supervision of gifts received and distributed so that there is accountability with no one deserving of help left out.

God prospers those who are faithful to Him (Ps. 1:1-3). While the wicked are often allowed to prosper in this life their end is hopeless (Ps. 73). The emphasis in the Bible is not only on temporal prosperity but on a spiritual life that opens out into eternal blessing (Ps. 36:9; Matt. 5:3-12; 19:29). Our Lord presents the most obvious example. The true anointed one, as Yahweh's servant, enabled the Father's will to prosper through His death and resurrection (Isa. 53:10).

Victory, illness and honour (32:1-33)

Thus far the Chronicler's account of Hezekiah's reign has dealt with the temple and its purification (ch. 29), Jerusalem's purification (ch. 30) and the land's purification so that from the land's productivity the people were able to present their tithes, first-fruits and free-will offerings in abundance for the benefit of the temple staff (ch. 31). The narrative of Hezekiah's kingship widens its scope to report the attitude of the world powers toward Israel. It parallels in a greatly reduced form the account in 2 Kings 18–19 and Isaiah 36–39 and it is clear that the Chronicler expected his readers to be familiar with those biblical books. The chapter covers Hezekiah's defence against Sennacherib's invasion (vv. 1-8), Sennacherib's verbal attacks (vv. 9-19), Hezekiah and his people's deliverance (vv. 20-23), and closes with Hezekiah's failures and successes (vv. 24-33).

Sennacherib's invasion (vv. 1-8)

32:1. After these faithful things, Sennacherib king of Assyria came and invaded Judah; and he encamped against the fortified cities, and he thought to conquer them for himself. 2. And when Hezekiah saw that Sennacherib had come, and that his face was set for war against Jerusalem, 3. he took counsel with his officials and his warriors to stop the waters of the springs which were outside the city; and they helped him. 4. And many people gathered together, and they stopped all the springs and the stream that ran through the middle of the land, saying, 'Why should the kings of Assyria come and find much water?' 5. And he strengthened himself and built all the wall that was

broken, and it went up on the towers, and outside he built the
other wall; he also strengthened the Millo of the city of David,
and made weapons and shields in abundance. 6. And he set
military officials over the people and gathered them together
to him in the square at the city gate, and spoke encouragingly
to them, saying, 7. 'Be strong and courageous. Do not be afraid
or dismayed before the king of Assyria, and before all the
horde that is with him; for there are more with us than with
him. 8. With him is an arm of flesh but with us is Yahweh our
God, to help us and to fight our battles.' And the people braced
themselves by the words of Hezekiah king of Judah.

Literally, the chapter opens with 'After these things and
these faithful' which is translated as a hendiadys, where
the two words 'things' and 'faithful' are joined by 'and' to
express the single idea: 'faithful things'. The clause draws
attention again to Hezekiah's faithfulness in the reforms he
enacted (2 Chron. 31:20). Like Abraham's testing experience
by God (Gen. 22:1), the king's faithfulness is severely tested
by Sennacherib's invasion in 701bc and his determination to
conquer Judah. It is akin to Zerah's attack which is reported
after Asa had carried out religious reforms (2 Chron. 14:2-15).
In the Assyrian king's own inscriptions which have been
preserved, he claims to have captured forty-six Judean cities
(see also 2 Kings 18:13; Isa. 36:1). The climax of his military
activity was his plan to take Jerusalem. Hezekiah wisely
took advice, as David and Jehoshaphat had done in the past
(vv. 2-3; 1 Chron. 13:1; 2 Chron. 20:21). Taking what defensive
measures he could in the face of an enemy attack was sensible
and it is not seen by the Chronicler as evidence of relying
solely on his own ingenuity. Some have wrongly applied
Isaiah 22:1-14, over which there are differing opinions, in
support of an interpretation that portrays Hezekiah's actions
as a failure to trust God and his encouraging words are
seen as hypocritical (vv. 2-9).[51] The passage does not read in
that negative way. Along with his officials and valiant men,
Hezekiah first prepared for a possible siege by depriving the
Assyrians of clean drinking water. They had the support of

---

51. See Pratt, *1 and 2 Chronicles*, pp. 449-52. For a sober reflection on the
Isaiah text, see E. J. Young, *Isaiah*, Vol. 2 (Grand Rapids: Eerdmans, 1969), pp.
100-01.

many people in blocking up 'the springs', possibly the Gihon in the Kidron valley east of the city, and the 'stream' or *wadi* that flowed through the land, which may refer to the spring at Enrogel which lay two miles (about three kilometres) to the south (vv. 3-4).

Then the king 'strengthened himself,' which is used in a positive sense by the Chronicler (v. 5; 2 Chron. 1:1; 12:13; 13:21; 17:1; 21:4; 27:6), by building up the city defences that had probably fallen into disrepair under Ahaz. Both Uzziah and Jotham had undertaken to build up the city walls and Hezekiah went further so that the walls were raised to the height of the towers. The Hebrew is difficult, and some suppose that the towers were erected on the walls. He also constructed a new outer wall. It may well be that this is the massive twenty-three feet (seven metres) thick wall on the western hill that was discovered in the twentieth century. The 'Millo', which was probably the supporting terraces that connected the temple to the slopes of the old city of David, was 'strengthened'. The same verb is used at the beginning and end of verse 5 and, as many suggest, may be a pun on Hezekiah's name ('may Yahweh strengthen'). There is only one other occurrence of the name Millo in Chronicles, and it is in a reference to David's building project in that same area (1 Chron. 11:8; 1 Kings 11:27). Again, Hezekiah is likened to a second David and Solomon.

The king's final practical measure against the enemy was to equip and reorganise the army (vv. 5b-6a). But more to the point, he gathered them together at the city square, probably the one by the eastern gate (v. 6b; see 2 Chron. 29:4), and encouraged them with words that focused their minds not only on their own preparations but on Yahweh's power to help them in the emergency. The phrase 'spoke encouragingly to them' is literally 'he spoke to their heart,' which is similar to Isaiah's comforting words, 'speak to the heart of Jerusalem' (Isa. 40:1).

In Hezekiah's speech, the opening exhortation echoes Moses' words to Joshua as well as Joshua's own words to his officers and David's encouragement of Solomon (v. 7; Deut. 31:6-8; Josh. 1:9; 10:25; 1 Chron. 22:13; 28:20; see 2 Chron. 20:15, 17). The reason why the people were urged to be fearless was not to be on account of their trust in the practical measures they had taken but because Yahweh was their God (v. 8). Elisha had reassured his fearful servant with similar words to those of Hezekiah: 'Do not be afraid, for those with us are more than those with them' (v. 7b; 2 Kings 6:16). Hezekiah continued in verse 8 to press home the reason for not fearing. All the human resources including the gods ('arm of flesh'; see Jer. 17:5) in which the Assyrians trusted were worthless whereas Israel had Yahweh their God with them to help them and to fight their battles. Five times within the space of two verses the preposition 'with' is used. The king's language is a reminder of Isaiah's words to Ahaz concerning Immanuel and Jahaziel's prophecy to Jehoshaphat (Isa. 7:14; 8:8; 2 Chron. 20:15, 17). Such was the power of Hezekiah's words that those who heard were able to 'brace themselves' or 'prop themselves up' on the basis of them.

Application

In the face of impending trouble it is right to take what precautions we can but at the same time we are warned not to put our ultimate trust in them but in the Lord, for as Hezekiah states, the arm of flesh will fail. The Christian's war is not against flesh and blood, and only with the spiritual armour that God supplies through His eternal Son, Immanuel, can victories be won, and the strongholds of Satan destroyed (2 Cor. 10:3-5). 'Immanuel' which means 'God with us' was the sign given to Ahaz, Hezekiah's father, and it formed a message of good news as well as judgment to king and people (Isa. 7:14; 8:8b, 10b). It is this Immanuel who came to save His people from their sins and has promised to be with His people locally as well as in spreading the gospel worldwide (Matt. 1:21-23; 18:20; 28:20). It is also vital to remember that although the Chronicler can show that God does reward faithfulness, and disciplines and punishes unfaithfulness, not all trouble that comes to the believer is directly the result of particular sin. To those who are trusting God, He will send testing experiences that are aimed to draw His people closer to Him.

Sennacherib's verbal attacks (vv. 9-19)

32:9. After this, Sennacherib king of Assyria sent his servants to Jerusalem (but he himself was at Lachish and all his military forces with him), to Hezekiah king of Judah and to all Judah who were in Jerusalem, saying, 10. 'Thus says Sennacherib king of Assyria: On what are you trusting, while living under siege in Jerusalem? 11. Is not Hezekiah enticing you to give you over to die by famine and by thirst, saying "Yahweh our God will deliver us from the hand of the king of Assyria?" 12. Did not this same Hezekiah take away his high places and his altars, and command Judah and Jerusalem, saying, "Before one altar you shall worship and on it burn sacrifices?" 13. Do you not know what I and my fathers have done to all the peoples of the lands? Were the gods of the nations of the lands at all able to deliver their land from my hand? 14. Who among all the gods of these nations that my fathers devoted to destruction was able to deliver his people from my hand, that your God should be able to deliver you from my hand? 15. Now, therefore, do not let Hezekiah deceive you or entice you like this, and do not believe him; for no god of any nation or kingdom is able to deliver his people from my hand or the hand of my fathers. How much less will your gods deliver you from my hand?' 16. And his servants spoke even more against Yahweh God and against Hezekiah his servant. 17. He also wrote letters to insult Yahweh the God of Israel, and to speak against him, saying, 'As the gods of the nations of the lands did not deliver their people from my hand, so the God of Hezekiah will not deliver his people from my hand.' 18. Then they called out with a loud voice in Jewish to the people of Jerusalem who were on the wall, to frighten them and terrify them, in order that they might capture the city. 19. And they spoke concerning the God of Jerusalem as if he were like the gods of the peoples of the earth, a product of human hands.

The fifty-five verses of 2 Kings 18:17–19:34 are here reduced to twelve verses and the Chronicler again takes it for granted that his readers will have read the fuller version of events. Chronicles presents in summary form the long communication that Sennacherib sent to Jerusalem while he lay siege to Lachish some twenty-eight miles (forty-five kilometres) southwest of Jerusalem (v. 9; for Lachish, see 2 Chron. 11:9). The whole Assyrian campaign in Judah was commemorated by Sennacherib with a large mural carved in stone in one of his palaces. Sennacherib's servants or emissaries introduced their verbal attack with the typical messenger formula familiar in the prophetic writings: 'Thus says Sennacherib' (v. 10; 1 Chron. 17:4; Isa. 10:24; etc.). They sowed doubts in the minds of the people of Jerusalem concerning Hezekiah's motives and words and thus hoped to break their morale and bring about an early surrender. The question was whether the people could trust Hezekiah's words concerning Yahweh's ability to deliver them from the Assyrians (vv. 10-11).

The Chronicler does not restate the earlier history which mentions the tribute that Hezekiah paid the Assyrians or the Assyrian charge that Hezekiah had made an alliance with Egypt (2 Kings 18:14-21). He concentrates on the chief point in the psychological warfare which had the aim of undermining Hezekiah's authority. The people were being deceived and could only expect to die of hunger and thirst if they held out against Assyria (v. 11). They went on to argue that it was Hezekiah's religious centralisation reforms that had brought about the situation in which Israel found itself (v. 12). A further argument was an appeal to the Assyrian successes in the past against people groups in other lands (v. 13). The gods of those nations were not able to deliver them and so, despite what Hezekiah believed and said, Israel's deities were no match for Sennacherib. It is interesting that the Chronicler keeps to the language of the Assyrians by referring to Israel's 'gods' as if their religious position was polytheistic (v. 15). The Assyrians acknowledged that their victories brought honour to their own pagan gods because they placed conquered peoples 'under the ban' in the same way that Israel devoted Jericho to Yahweh for destruction (v. 14; Josh. 6:17, 21; Achan's sin in not devoting all to Yahweh is mentioned in 1 Chronicles 2:7).

Verse 15 presents concluding advice to Israel. They are urged not to let Hezekiah deceive and seduce them. Trusting what he had said would be useless because no god had been able to save a nation from Sennacherib or his predecessors and in view of what had been argued concerning Hezekiah's treatment of Israel's god there was no prospect of deliverance from that quarter. The message was very powerful, and Sennacherib's envoys uttered further blasphemies and insults against Yahweh and Hezekiah His servant as the Chronicler indicates (v. 16). It provided an example of the way the kings of the earth set themselves 'against Yahweh and His anointed' (Ps. 2:2). Two expressions that continually appear throughout the message are the verb 'to deliver' and the noun 'hand'

(vv. 11, 13, 14, 15), the first used in doubting God's power to deliver His people and the second to emphasise Sennacherib's ability to be victorious.

Two further methods were used by the Assyrians to weaken the spirits of God's people. First, letters were sent which underlined what the messengers had expressed, with 'deliver' and 'hand' used in combination once more. They revealed Sennacherib's boast that as the gods of other nations had not been able to save their people from his power so Hezekiah's God would be impotent to deliver Israel from the Assyrian king's power (v. 17).

Second, a megaphone approach was used with the idea of so frightening the people that they would quickly surrender. The Assyrian envoys craftily shouted to the people on the city walls in Hebrew rather than using the international Aramaic language of diplomacy found in Assyrian court documents of the time (v. 18). Much space is given over to this new threat in Kings, but the Chronicler summarises what was said showing how they blasphemed Israel's God, here referred to as 'the God of Jerusalem' (v. 19; see Ezra 7:19 for the only other occurrence of this title). In verse 17, Yahweh was described as 'the God of Hezekiah'. The Chronicler indicates for the benefit of his readers that, in fact, as Hezekiah had made clear in his prayer (2 Kings 19:18; Isa. 37:19), Israel's God cannot be compared to gods of nations whose idols are all human productions (v. 19).

Application

Pluralistic ideas have long been around concerning religion. It is supposed that all deities are basically the same. But the Bible emphasises that there is only one true and living God (Jer. 10:10) and that humans are ultimately accountable to Him alone. The temptation to distrust God can take many forms but they are all a consequence of Satan's initial lying insinuations to doubt God: 'Has God said?' (Gen. 3:1).

Yahweh's deliverance (vv. 20-23)

32:20. Then Hezekiah the king and Isaiah the son of Amoz the prophet prayed because of this, and they cried out to heaven. 21. And Yahweh sent an angel who annihilated every valiant warrior and commander and officer in the camp of the king of Assyria. So he returned shame-faced to his land. And when he went into the house of his god, some of those who came out from his own innards felled him there with the sword. 22. Thus Yahweh saved Hezekiah and the inhabitants of Jerusalem from the hand of Sennacherib the king of Assyria, and from the hand of all, and he provided for them on every side. 23. And many brought gifts to Yahweh to Jerusalem, and precious things to Hezekiah king of Judah, so that he was exalted in the sight of all nations from that time on.

To the taunts and pressure from the Assyrian king all geared toward undermining the confidence of Judah's leaders and people in Yahweh and His anointed king, Hezekiah displays trust in God by praying 'to heaven', which recalls Solomon's dedication prayer to God whose home is in heaven (2 Chron. 6:21). In this he had the supporting prayers of the prophet Isaiah (v. 20). Again, the details are given in the earlier history where the king's own prayer is recorded as well as the request for the prayers of Isaiah (2 Kings 19:2-5, 15-19). It is the kind of humble response in a desperate situation that would lead Yahweh to hear and act (2 Chron. 7:14). The Chronicler dispenses with much of the details related in Kings in order to call attention to one of his main messages which is that God does answer the humble cries of His people (see 1 Chron. 4:10). Two results followed. Firstly, Sennacherib was forced to retreat to his country in disgrace because his army had vanished through angelic activity (v. 21). The word translated 'annihilated' literally means 'to hide' (the *hiphil* of *khd*). Yahweh's 'angel' had acted to wipe out or obliterate the enemy in the same way that Jeroboam's dynasty was wiped out and the Canaanites cut off (Exod. 23:23; 1 Kings 13:34). By so doing the angel had brought about Israel's deliverance (see Ps. 34:7[8]). The second result was the assassination of Sennacherib by those of his own offspring (v. 21b), which happened some twenty years later. Ancient Near Eastern inscriptions also mention that he was murdered by his own family.

The Chronicler, in his summary statement, is eager to show that Yahweh did save king and people from 'the hand' of this seemingly all-powerful pagan ruler (v. 22; see vv. 13-15,

17). In fact, God saved from 'all' others just as David had been saved from all his enemies (1 Chron. 11:14; 18:6, 13). In addition, Yahweh led His people like a shepherd guiding His flock to water ('he provided for them', v. 22b; see Isa. 40:11; 49:10; Pss. 23:2; 31:3[4]). It is similar to the theme of 'rest' that the Chronicler presents as a reward for faithfulness (1 Chron. 22:9, 18; 2 Chron. 14:5-7; 15:15; 20:30). Hezekiah also received world recognition like David and Solomon did, with many bringing gifts or tribute as had happened during the heyday of the united monarchy period (1 Chron. 14:17; 2 Chron. 9:23-24).

Hezekiah's failures and successes (vv. 24-33)

32:24. In those days Hezekiah became mortally ill, and he prayed to Yahweh; and he spoke to him and gave him a sign. 25. But Hezekiah did not respond according to the benefit done to him, for his heart was lifted up; therefore wrath came upon him and upon Judah and Jerusalem. 26. Then Hezekiah humbled himself for the pride of his heart, he and the inhabitants of Jerusalem, and the wrath of Yahweh did not come upon them in the days of Hezekiah.

These two verses contain further examples of answers to prayer but the circumstances in each case are very different. The first is a very brief note stating that when Hezekiah became dangerously ill and prayed to Yahweh, the king was heard, and a 'sign' or 'wonder' was given him. Clearly the reader is expected to have read the details of the incident recorded in 2 Kings 20:1-11 (see also Isa. 38:1-22) which indicates that God did promise to heal the king after first telling him that he would die. The text of Kings also explains the meaning of the sign and reveals that God communicated with Hezekiah through the prophet Isaiah. It is because of what is said later (v. 31) that the Chronicler specifically mentioned the miraculous 'sign', using the same term for 'wonder' that God did in Egypt (môp̄ēṯ; see Exod. 4:21;11:9-10; 1 Chron. 16:12).

The second example expresses the truth of Yahweh's promise to Solomon (2 Chron. 7:14). It describes the king's repentant attitude which led to the removal of God's wrath that was hanging over him and his people because of his sin (vv. 25-26). That 'wrath' came as a result of Hezekiah's pride.

Instead of 'making a return' or responding with gratitude for his healing, the king displayed an arrogant spirit. It is possible that this is the reason for Isaiah's condemnation (Isa. 22:1-14). There may have been great celebrations at the king's recovery and, coupled with this, Hezekiah and his officials were keen to brag about their resources to the Babylonian envoys (v. 31; 2 Kings 20:12-13). But God always provides opportunity for repentance. Unlike Uzziah who failed to heed warnings about his sinful activity when his 'heart was lifted up' (2 Chron. 26:16-19), Hezekiah 'humbled himself,' and so did the people of Jerusalem, resulting in the wrath being averted or rather delayed (v. 26b; see 2 Kings 20:17-19; Isa. 39:5-8).

> 32:27. And Hezekiah had very great riches and honour and he made for himself treasuries for silver and for gold, and for precious stones and for spices, and for shields and for all kinds of desirable utensils. 28. Also storehouses for the produce of grain and wine and oil; and stalls for all kinds of cattle, and flocks for the stalls. 29. And he provided cities for himself and flocks of sheep and cattle in abundance; for God had given him very many possessions. 30. This same Hezekiah closed the upper outlet of the waters of Gihon and directed them along to the west side of the city of David. And Hezekiah prospered in all his works. 31. And so when the envoys of the officials of Babylon, whom they sent to him to inquire about the wonder that was on the land, God forsook him, in order to test him, to know all that was in his heart. 32. Now the rest of the acts of Hezekiah and his loyal acts, there they are written in the vision of Isaiah the son of Amoz the prophet on the book of the kings of Judah and Israel. 33. So Hezekiah rested with his fathers, and they buried him in the ascent to the tombs of the sons of David; and all Judah and the inhabitants of Jerusalem did him honour at his death. Then Manasseh his son reigned in his place.

Before mentioning the visit of the envoys from Babylon, the Chronicler describes Hezekiah's wealth, honour and construction work in Jerusalem. Again, the king is like a new David and Solomon (1 Chron. 29:28; 2 Chron. 1:11-12; 2 Chron. 9:9, 15-16, 22, 24; see also Jehoshaphat in 2 Chron. 17:5; 18:1) and as David acknowledged, it is made clear that the king's possessions and reputation came from God (v. 29;

1 Chron. 29:12). The building work mentioned will have included what is known to archaeologists as the Siloam tunnel. It was a massive feat of engineering which involved cutting through rock for a distance of 1,777 feet (542 metres), in order to bring water from the spring of Gihon in the Kidron valley to a pool in the city of David (see also 2 Kings 20:20). A contemporary inscription in cursive Hebrew script gives details of this construction and includes the word 'outlet' (*môṣā'*, v. 30). Whether Isaiah 22:9 is referring to this or some other project cannot at present be determined.

The Chronicler stresses once more that Hezekiah 'prospered' (v. 30b) which again associates him with all that was best concerning Solomon (see 1 Chron. 29:23; 2 Chron. 31:21). This 'success' was true even in the report concerning the foreign emissaries. The opening words of verse 31 ('And so when ...') suggest that this was another example of prospering. In this one verse Chronicles not only summarises what takes eight verses to relate in 2 Kings 20:12-19 (Isa. 39:1-8), but it also provides some extra information. The Babylonian envoys were particularly interested in the 'wonder' that Yahweh gave to Hezekiah (see v. 24), which is understandable given the nation's special interest in astrology. More importantly, the Chronicler also reveals the divine intention behind the foreign visit. In judgment and grace God left Hezekiah to his own devices to test him. It was the king's pride that made him grovel to the Babylonians and it exposed the true state of his heart (v. 25), but after this severe lapse he did repent and trust God (v. 26). The Chronicler could thus record that Hezekiah prospered or succeeded in his behaviour before God as well as in all his works (v. 30b) and religious reforms (2 Chron. 31:21b).

In the concluding summary of Hezekiah's reign, the Chronicler directs the reader to 'the vision of Isaiah ...' which is to be found in his main source, 'the book of the kings of Judah and Israel' (see 2 Chron. 16:11). Interestingly, the book of Isaiah begins with the title 'The vision of Isaiah the son of Amoz' (Isa. 1:1) but, as the Chronicler has stated, his source is not that canonical book. His source is said to provide further information relating to Hezekiah's actions and 'loyal' or 'pious acts' (literally 'his loyalties', *ḥªsāḏāw* from the word *ḥeseḏ* often translated 'steadfast love' or 'kindness'). The expression refers to the king's loving commitment to God and is applied also to Josiah (2 Chron. 35:26; see Neh. 13:14).

This positive assessment of Hezekiah's reign (see also 2 Chron. 29:2) ends with a fulsome description of his burial that is not found in Kings. The 'tombs of David' are mentioned in the account of rebuilding the walls of Jerusalem (Neh. 3:16). What the term 'ascent' means in this context is not certain, but it suggests it was in a prominent and important spot among David's royal descendants. Only of Hezekiah does the Chronicler record that the inhabitants of Jerusalem accorded him special respect on his death. Probably he received the kind of burial described in 2 Chronicles 16:14 (see Jer. 34:5). Despite his failures, he is depicted as the greatest of the Davidic kings since David and Solomon.

Application

The Chronicler's presentation of Hezekiah, following the kind of desperate situation under his father Ahaz, would have been an encouragement to his first readers not to give up hope concerning a new Davidic ruler. That hope proclaimed by prophet and Chronicler has been realised in the one who is greater than even David and Solomon (Matt. 12:42; Mark 12:35-37).

Unlike Satan and the lying spirits whose aims, in the varying testing experiences God gives, are to trap and destroy (1 Chron. 21:1; 2 Chron. 18:19-24; Matt. 4:1-10; 1 Pet. 5:8), God intends them to bring His people closer to Himself by humbling them and deepening their faith (Job 1-2; 40:3-5; 42:1-6; 2 Cor. 12:7-10). When the text states that God tested the king to know what was in his heart, it does not mean that God was ignorant. God knows us through and through. God looks on the heart. Nothing is hidden from Him. The Hebrew idiom 'to know all that was in his heart' means to bring it to the surface so that the person can be brought to repentance.

God does not, like Satan, entice us to do wrong. He tests so that we might be aware of our weaknesses and the sinfulness of our hearts. Jesus speaks of the testing that would come to Peter and the other disciples. But he does not give us more than we can deal with and also shows a way of escape (Luke 22:31-32; 1 Cor. 10:13).

Manasseh's reign (33:1-20)

Hezekiah's son Manasseh has the distinction of being the longest reigning monarch of all the kings of Israel. The first half of the Chronicles' account (vv. 1-9) follows closely the parallel text in 2 Kings 21:1-9. But then in place of the long prophetic denunciation of Manasseh's rule and the statement concerning his violent actions that present him as the most wicked of the Judean kings (2 Kings 21:10-16), Chronicles presents unique material to show that no one is beyond redemption (vv. 11-17). The Chronicler's presentation does not contradict Kings but supplements it, showing why Judah's exile did not occur in Manasseh's reign. In the accounts of previous kings, the Chronicler has highlighted how some started acceptably and then failed to humble themselves later. With Manasseh the opposite occurs: he starts as the worst of kings but ends well. The record of his reign opens with an introduction and evidence of Manasseh's apostasy (vv. 1-9), then recounts his punishment and restoration (vv. 10-13), the evidences of his conversion (vv. 14-17), and concludes with his death and burial (vv. 18-20).

Manasseh's apostasy (33:1-9)

After the introduction (v. 1), the first part of Manasseh's reign is framed by reference to his evils and by a comparison with the nations Israel destroyed (vv. 2, 9). A further division marker occurs with the repetition of the phrase 'evil in the sight of Yahweh' (vv. 2, 6). There are some significant variations from the account in 2 Kings 21:1-9.

> 33:1. Manasseh was twelve years old when he became king, and he reigned fifty-five years in Jerusalem. 2. And he did evil in the sight of Yahweh according to the abominations of the nations whom Yahweh had dispossessed before the sons of Israel. 3. And he rebuilt the high places which Hezekiah his father had torn down; and he raised up altars for the Baals, and made Asherahs, and he bowed down to all the host of heaven and served them. 4. He also built altars in the house of Yahweh of which Yahweh had said, 'In Jerusalem shall my name be for ever.' 5. And he built

altars for all the host of heaven in the two courts of the house of Yahweh. 6. Also he made his sons pass through the fire in the valley of the son of Hinnom; and he practised soothsaying and divination and sorcery and consulted mediums and spiritists. He did much evil in the sight of Yahweh to provoke him. 7. And he put a carved image of the idol which he had made in the house of God, of which God had said to David and to Solomon his son, 'In this house and in Jerusalem, which I have chosen out of all the tribes of Israel, I shall put my name for ever. 8. And I will not again remove the foot of Israel from the land which I have appointed for your fathers, if only they will be careful to do all that I have commanded them: all the law and the statutes and the rules by the hand of Moses.' 9. So Manasseh misled Judah and the inhabitants of Jerusalem to do more evil than the nations whom Yahweh had destroyed before the sons of Israel.

In order to fit Manasseh's dates with other chronological notices, scholars often assume a co-regency with Hezekiah of about ten years but there can be no certainty. Up to this point, Uzziah had been the longest reigning monarch in Israel (2 Chron. 26:3), but now Manasseh enjoyed that position with his reign of fifty-five years. While health, wealth and long life are often presented by the Chronicler as indications of God's blessing for obedience and faithfulness (1 Chron. 29:28), this is not always the case. There are many anomalies and hidden circumstances to consider. The Old Testament recognises that evil people can prosper in this life while those committed to God can suffer much, and it is only by taking account of their end that God's people can gain a proper perspective (see Ps. 73). While Kings leaves the reader with the mystery of God's providence in granting long life to such a depraved king, the Chronicler provides a glimmer of light. The temporal blessings and curses associated with the Sinai covenant were pointers to eternal realities and the Chronicler preaches to his readers concerning personal responsibility, however long or short a life may be, while not forgetting the effects of rebellious activity that would lead to the curse of exile.

Unlike his previous policy, from here until the end of the monarchy in Judah, the Chronicler omits any reference to the mothers of the various kings. Similarly, at the close of each reign there are no more references to the phrase 'rested with his fathers'. There seems to be no obvious reason for these omissions other than the Chronicler decided on a change.

Verse 2 introduces the list of 'abominable' practices mentioned in verses 3-6 and for which evils the Canaanites were condemned and dispossessed by Israel. The Chronicler expects his readers to remember from 2 Kings that Manasseh's rebellious actions were the final straw that led to Israel's exile (2 Kings 21:12-15; 23:26; 24:2-3) and he himself does not contradict that verdict. While Kings has this bigger picture in view, Chronicles concentrates more narrowly on Manasseh himself and the effects that the whole of his reign had on Judah during his lifetime. The 'abominations' associated with the former occupants of the land are those described in Deuteronomy 18:9-14. Apparently, it was not Assyrian practice to compel vassal states to worship the gods of Assyria. Thus Manasseh's apostasy was not politically motivated but the result of innate rebellion against the true and living God. He undid all the religious reforms of his father and followed in the footsteps of his grandfather, who had, until Manasseh's reign, been the worst king of Judah (see 2 Chron. 28:1-4, 22-25). What had been 'torn down' in Hezekiah's day (2 Chron. 31:1) was rebuilt. These 'high places' were not used as locations for worshipping Yahweh but erected for pagan worship.

'Baals' and 'Asherahs' (v. 3) are probably plurals of intensification, to express the enormity of the sin. The 'Asherahs', sometimes translated as 'sacred poles', were most likely images of the Canaanite goddess of fertility, while Baal was the male deity of weather and fertility. Bowing down to worship 'the whole host of heaven' refers to the sun, moon and stars which were regarded as personifications of powerful Ancient Near Eastern deities (Deut. 4:19; 17:3). For Israel, 'Yahweh of hosts' was their God, and the heavens declared His glory (1 Chron. 11:9; see Ps. 19:1-6), but altars were built in the temple courts to astral deities as well as to other gods (vv. 4-5). God's name refers to His revealed character and was associated with the ark of the covenant which lay in the inner sanctum or 'holy of holies' (1 Chron. 13:6). It was in the temple in Jerusalem that God chose to place His name 'for ever' (2 Chron. 6:5-6; 7:16) in fulfilment of God's word through Moses (Deut. 12:4-5).

Yet Manasseh was involved in the same despicable practice of child sacrifice as Ahaz (v. 6; 2 Chron. 28:3; Deut. 12:31), with the plural 'sons' again being used to magnify the atrocity (v. 6; see v. 3; 2 Kings 21:6). Among the Canaanites it was hoped that through this means they might gain the favourable intervention of the gods. The context suggests this practice may have also been used for divination purposes (see also Deut. 18:10-11). Further illicit means of gaining insights into the future follow: 'practising soothsaying' (ʿônēn) which may have involved magical incantations or making predictions through the formation of the clouds; 'practising divination' (niḥēš) involved interpreting omens or signs in natural phenomena as Joseph is said to have done using a cup (Gen. 44:5, 15); 'practise sorcery' (ciššēp) which may suggest cutting up herbs to make a magic brew; a 'medium' (ʾôḇ) was one who communicated with the dead and it was such a person whom Saul consulted (1 Chron. 10:13; see Isa. 29:4); 'spiritist' or 'wizard' (yidʿônî) is little different from a medium and the terms are often found together (Lev. 19:31; 20:6, 27; Isa. 8:19; 19:3), but perhaps it referred to a person who had a more precise knowledge of the deceased. In engaging in all this 'evil', which was so contrary to Yahweh's will for His people, Manasseh 'provoked' God to anger (see 2 Chron. 28:25).

The second part of the section beginning with verse 7 is devoted to one main item, the placing in the temple of a 'carved image' of a 'figure' or 'statue', most possibly of the goddess 'Asherah' (see 2 Kings 21:7). The term 'statue' (semel, a rare word only found elsewhere in the Bible in Deuteronomy 4:16 and Ezekiel 8:3, 5), is used in a fourth-century B.C. Phoenician inscription to describe a statue of the goddess Astarte. For the Chronicler, this pagan symbol that Manasseh 'put' in the earthly house where Yahweh had 'put' His name, expressed the depth of Manasseh's depravity. Though the words that God said to David and Solomon find no exact parallel elsewhere, they do convey the point made in many passages concerning the election of Jerusalem and the temple where Yahweh revealed Himself (v. 7; see v. 4; 2 Chron. 6:5-6, 10-11; 7:16). The permanent presence of Yahweh among His people was the assurance that they would be settled in the land promised to their forefathers. But it was conditional on Israel keeping the commandments of Yahweh given to Moses (v. 8). This was all set out in the Sinai covenant which promised blessings in the land for obedience to God's law and various curses culminating in exile for disobedience (Lev. 26; Deut. 28).

Chronicles indicates that it was the king himself who caused Judah and Jerusalem to err. Manasseh had so misled them that they were more at fault than the Canaanites whom Yahweh destroyed (v. 9; see v. 2). The clear message is that they deserved the same judgment. God used Israel to punish the Canaanites; he used the Philistines to kill Saul; and the Assyrians were used to punish the northern kingdom of Israel (1 Chron. 5:26; 10:1-14).

Application

The old 'abominations' are still with us and people blinded by Satan still consider the physical world and objects within it as worthy of worship. Paul preached to such people in Lystra and Thessalonica and had the privilege of seeing them turn from idols to serve the living and true God and to wait for His Son who delivers us from the coming wrath of God (Acts 14:11-18; 1 Thess. 1:9-10). Isaiah warned those living in darkness against seeking mediums instead of seeking God through His revealed word (Isa. 8:19-22). More subtle are games such as the Ouija board which fall within the category of divination and continue to both fascinate and destroy lives in the western world today. Light has shone into the darkness in the person of God's Son, and we are urged to repent and believe the good news (Isa. 9:1-7; Matt. 4:12-17).

Manasseh's punishment and restoration (33:10-13)

> 33:10. And Yahweh spoke to Manasseh and to his people, but they did not listen. 11. Therefore Yahweh brought against them the commanders of the army of the king of Assyria who took Manasseh captive with hooks, bound him with bronze *shackles* and brought him to Babylon. 12. Now when he was in distress, he entreated the favour of Yahweh his God and humbled himself greatly before the God of his fathers. 13. And he prayed to him; and he accepted his entreaty, and he heard his plea for favour and returned him to Jerusalem to his kingdom. Then Manasseh knew that Yahweh is God.

In verse 10, the Chronicler summarises what is found in 2 Kings 21:10-16 and though he does not mention the prophets whom Yahweh used to speak to Manasseh and the people, he does refer to them later in verse 18. The substance of the prophetic message concerning the coming judgment on Judah that king and people ignored is deliberately omitted by the Chronicler in order to focus on the immediate judgment that fell on Manasseh. It served as a preview of what would eventually happen to the kingdom, and the Chronicler makes it clear that this was Yahweh's doing (v. 11). The Assyrian army officers took Manasseh and led him like an animal to exile in Babylon. An Assyrian painting shows captives being led by ropes attached to their noses or faces with hooks or rings. The term 'hooks' (*ḥōḥîm*) can mean briers or brambles (2 Chron. 25:18) and suggests something spiky like a hook. It is used for a hook in the jaw of Leviathan (Job 41:2[40:26]). A similar word (*ḥaḥ*) and translated as 'hook' or 'ring' is employed to describe those carried away captive (2 Kings 19:28; Ezek. 19:4, 9). Manasseh was also bound with bronze chains, as happened later to Jehoiakim (2 Chron. 36:6). Instead of the Assyrian capital Nineveh, the king was taken to Babylon which at this time was under the control of Assyria, a fate that Jehoiachin was to experience (2 Chron. 36:10).

The report of Manasseh's conversion is expressed in language typical of the Chronicler. Both Ahaz and Manasseh suffered 'distress', but unlike his grandfather (2 Chron. 28:22), Manasseh 'humbled himself' (v. 12) which means he was repentant (see 2 Chron. 12:6, 12; 32:26). It is another reminder of God's response to Solomon's dedicatory prayer (2 Chron. 7:14). As his rebellion against God had been enormous ('much evil,' v. 6), so the addition of the adverb 'very' or 'greatly' (*mᵉʾōd*) expresses his deep repentant spirit before 'the God of his fathers' (v. 12; 2 Chron. 21:10; 28:25). This was the God who had made a covenant with Abraham and who had heard the groans of the sons of Israel in Egypt and acted to deliver them (Exod. 2:23-25). The phrase, 'to entreat the favour of,' is literally 'to make the face pleasant,' and is used a number of times with reference to appeasing the face of Yahweh (Exod. 32:11; 1 Kings 13:6; Dan. 9:13; Mal. 1:9). It was this God who had brought Manasseh low who graciously restored him to his kingdom having heard his plea for favour and accepted his prayer, even as Solomon had pleaded, and Yahweh had promised (v. 13; 2 Chron. 6:36-39; 7:14). The statement that Manasseh now 'knew that Yahweh is God' (v. 13b) expressed that he was personally convinced that Yahweh was the real and living God, especially in the light of his earlier belief in the worship of pagan gods. Now he knew that there was no other god but Yahweh (Deut. 4:35, 39; Jer. 10:1-10). This knowledge of God was not merely intellectual and factual but relational. The exodus event brought Pharaoh to appreciate personally the power and supremacy of God, but for Israel it meant more in that it involved a covenant relationship where God promised to be their God and to live among them and for them to be His special people (Exod. 5:2; 6:7; 7:5, 10:2; 14:4, 18; 29:45-46; Lev. 26:11-12). In Ezekiel, the phrase occurs numerous times to emphasise God's power, especially to punish (Ezek. 6:10, 13; etc.).

Evidences of Manasseh's conversion (33:14-17)

33:14. Afterwards he built an outer wall for the city of David from the west of Gihon, in the valley, to the entrance of the Fish Gate; and it enclosed Ophel, and he raised it to a very great height. Then he put commanders of the army in all the fortified cities of Judah. 15. And he took away the foreign gods and the idol from the house of Yahweh, and all the altars that he had built on the mountain of the house of Yahweh and in Jerusalem; and he threw them out of the city. 16. He also built the altar of Yahweh and sacrificed peace offerings and thank offerings on it, and commanded Judah to serve Yahweh the God of Israel. 17. Nevertheless, the people were still sacrificing on the high places, but only to Yahweh their God.

The evidences of Manasseh's conversion are now set out, introduced with the words 'after thus' or 'afterwards'. They include his building programme (v. 14) and religious reforms (vv. 15-17). Such activity is often shown by the Chronicler to be expressive of faithfulness to God and of following in the steps of David. Manasseh was concerned to protect God's people by strengthening the defences of Jerusalem (see 1 Chron. 11:8; 2 Chron. 26:9; 27:3-4; 32:5, 30) and placing military personnel in the fortified cities of Judah (see 2 Chron. 11:5-12; 14:6; 17:12-19). The 'Fish Gate' was probably the one on the northwest of the city (Neh. 3:3; 12:39; Zeph. 1:10), while the 'Ophel' refers to the area between the old city of David and the temple mount (2 Chron. 27:3).

Manasseh's religious reforms began by removing all the evidences of pagan worship, similar to the way Asa had begun his reign (v. 15; 2 Chron. 14:3). Having acknowledged and experienced that Yahweh was the one true God, he first threw out of the city the representations of those gods he had set up in the temple area including the obnoxious pagan statue, as well as the altars that he had erected all over the city (see vv. 3, 5, 7). Interestingly, the Chronicler refers to the temple area as 'the mountain of the house of Yahweh'. In Canaanite thought the mountain was where the gods lived and certainly Manasseh had introduced such Canaanite deities in the temple (vv. 4-5, 7). But such pagan thinking was a distortion of the truth. At the Red Sea, Israel sang of Yahweh bringing them to the mountain of God's inheritance where God ordained to dwell in His sanctuary (Exod. 15:17) and where Abraham was given a glimpse of the promised Saviour (Gen. 22; 2 Chron. 3:1). Prophets and psalmists sing of this glorious mountain of Zion (Isa. 2:2-4; 66:20; Micah 4:1-2; Pss. 15; 24:3; 48:1-2; 68:15-16; 87:1-3). Reformation included not only removing false forms of worship but reinstating true religion (vv. 16). Manasseh 'built' or 'rebuilt'[52] the bronze altar and began burning the peace or fellowship sacrifices together with thank offerings on it (see 2 Chron. 29:31; 30:22). He also urged the people to serve Yahweh their God in the sense of worshipping Him alone and living in a way that pleased Him. Unlike Hezekiah (2 Chron. 31:1; 32:12), Manasseh was not able to close down all the high places that he had rebuilt (v. 3), but he did manage to ensure that those local sanctuaries were free from pagan practices (v. 17).

Manasseh's death and burial (33:18-20)

33:18. Now the rest of the acts of Manasseh and his prayer to his God and the words of the seers who spoke to him in the name of Yahweh the God of Israel, there they are in the words

---

52. 'Build' (*bnh*) is the *Qere* reading, while 'established' or 'restored' (*kwn*) is the *Kethibh*.

of the kings of Israel. 19. Also his prayer and the acceptance of his entreaty, and all his sin and his unfaithfulness, and the places on which he built high places and set up the Asherim and the carved images, before he humbled himself, there they are written in the words of Hozai. 20. So Manasseh rested with his fathers, and they buried him in his house, and Amon his son reigned in his place.

The final paragraph, like the opening one, more closely parallels the text of 2 Kings 21:17-18. In this summary of his life, emphasis is placed on the earnest prayer that he had made to Yahweh (vv. 12-13). The Apocryphal work 'The Prayer of Manasseh,' which is considered canonical by the Eastern Orthodox Church and only survives in Christian circles, is a later pseudonymous work that was probably inspired by verses 18 and 19, but is certainly not a divinely inspired work. Prayer is one of the Chronicler's main themes which he has emphasised from the beginning of his work (see 1 Chron. 4:10; 5:20). In no way does the Chronicler dismiss or ignore Manasseh's sin, pointing out again the enormity of his apostasy and he even uses one of his key terms, 'unfaithfulness' (*m'l*, verse 19), to stress the seriousness of his behaviour and the reason for Judah's final exile (see 1 Chron. 9:1; 10:13). Yet, it is stressed again that all these rebellious actions were before he humbled himself and that God received his contrite pleas (v. 19).

No mention has been made in Chronicles of the prophets who had bravely spoken out in the name of Yahweh against Manasseh (2 Kings 21:10-16) except by implication (see v. 10), but in this section they are referred to and it is noted that their words were recorded in the main source, namely, the 'words' or 'records' of the kings of Israel (v. 18; see 2 Chron. 20:34; 24:27). A special source is cited for the Chronicler's unique material concerning Manasseh's repentance and the evidences of his changed life. The text speaks of an otherwise unknown prophet 'Hozai' (meaning 'my visionaries', v. 19b). Most scholars regard this as a scribal error and that the text should read 'his visionaries' or simply 'visionaries' with the LXX, and that it refers not to a prophet's name but most probably to the same prophetic source referred to in verse 18. Manasseh, like Ahaz, was not buried in the royal mausoleum but in his own 'house', meaning the grounds of the palace. In 2 Kings 21:18 it specifies that his body was buried in the garden of his house. It is possible that burial practices had changed due to lack of space in the royal tombs.

Application

Manasseh is presented as an example for the post-exilic people of one who became an exile and yet returned to his land, humbled and repentant, with new desires to please God and serve His people. It continues to encourage us all to humble ourselves and repent. No one is too far gone in sin for God to show mercy. The thief on the cross and Saul of Tarsus are obvious examples. If there was hope for these notorious people, there is hope for all who repent and believe.

The evidence of a changed life is a willingness to do God's will, showing concern for God's people and a desire to worship God aright. This does not remove in this life the effects of a person's rebellious ways. Manasseh's sins were the last straw that led to the judgment of exile. Some things cannot be undone and the effects of sinful behaviour, though forgiven by God, often have tragic results. Even while we are saved from the wrath to come, Christians still suffer the effects in this life of Adam's initial transgression in terms of illness and death. But whatever consequences from a previous sinful lifestyle and behaviour we may have to endure in this life, those effects do not last for ever. Praise God! Christ has won the victory so that there will be a new creation and Christians will have glorified bodies and will no longer experience sorrow, sickness and death.

The king's own exile on account of sin not only previewed Judah's exile to Babylon but typified Manasseh's descendant who experienced the ultimate exile, the curse of God-forsakenness on account of the sins of His people but who returned from the dead with a glorified body bringing the assurance of eternal felicity to all those who belong to His kingdom.

Amon's reign (33:21-25)

The Chronicler's account of Amon's brief reign is even shorter than that found in 2 Kings 21:19-26, but there are a couple of significant differences that press home the Chronicler's overall message.

33:21. Amon was twenty-two years old when he became king, and he reigned two years in Jerusalem. 22. And he did evil in the sight of Yahweh as Manasseh his father had done, for Amon also sacrificed to all the carved images that Manasseh his father had made and served them. 23. But he did not humble himself before Yahweh as Manasseh his father had humbled himself, but this Amon became more guilty. 24. Then his servants conspired against him and killed him in his house. 25. But the people of the land struck down all those who had conspired against king Amon, and the people of the land made Josiah his son king in his place.

As with the introduction to Manasseh's reign, there is no reference to the queen mother (v. 21; see 2 Kings 21:19). The account of Amon's life confines itself to recording his sins. He is first likened to his father in doing 'evil' with the main focus being on the carved images that his father had made, and he revived the pagan worship that existed during the period of Manasseh's apostasy (v. 22; see vv. 7, 15, 19).

It is verse 23 that contains two of the Chronicler's key themes and that clearly differentiates the son from the father, matters not indicated in Kings. While Manasseh 'humbled himself' before Yahweh, Amon remained unrepentant despite the example set by his father. Because he did not humble himself, Amon increased his guilt (or 'trespass') and this meant that he was ripe for God's judgment (1 Chron. 21:3; 2 Chron. 19:10; 24:18; 28:10, 13). No reason is given why the king's servants assassinated him, but for the Chronicler it was another example of God's wrath falling on the stubbornly rebellious (v. 24; see 2 Chron. 24:25; 25:27). The assassins were themselves assassinated by local people (v. 25, 'the people of the land'; see 2 Chron. 23:13, 20-21; 26:1; 36:1). The final ignominy is the Chronicler's omission of any reference to sources or to the king's burial. In this, his end is seen in terms similar to that of Athaliah of whom nothing else is reported after her judicial killing (2 Chron. 23:15).

Application

Like Ezekiel, the Chronicler taught through his account of the kings that each is responsible before God for the life that is lived. Though Amon had mixed messages from his father, he had the opportunity to humble himself. Though we are all sinners and deserve the wrath that hangs over all human ungodliness and unrighteousness, mercy and forgiveness are held out to those who repent and believe the gospel (Acts 17:30-31; Rom. 1:18; 2:12-16; 3:21-26).

Josiah's reign (34:1–35:27)

This is the last of the Davidic kings to receive considerable attention. In this Josiah follows Asa, Jehoshaphat and Hezekiah. The text parallels to a large extent the account in 2 Kings 22–23 but the Chronicler indicates that many of Josiah's reforms took place at an early stage in his kingship. He also gives more detail concerning the discovery of the Law Book, the covenant renewal and the circumstances surrounding Josiah's death. However, for the Chronicler, it is the celebration of the Passover that is the high point of the reign, and for this reason he gives a much more elaborate description of it than is found in Kings. Other concerns of the Chronicler include the theme of humility, seeking God and also his interest in the Levites. The record of Josiah's reign divides into three main sections: his faithfulness in following Yahweh (34:1-33), his Passover celebration (35:1-19), and the circumstances of his death and the lamentation that followed (35:20-27).

Josiah's faithfulness to Yahweh (34:1-33)

Under this heading we are introduced to Josiah's reign (34:1-2) and are informed of his initial reforms (34:3-7), his repairs to the temple (34:8-13), his discovery of the Law Book (34:14-21), the prophecy concerning the Book (34:22-28) and his renewal of the covenant (34:29-33).

> 34:1. Josiah was eight years old when he became king, and he reigned thirty-one years in Jerusalem. 2. And he did right in the sight of Yahweh, and walked in the ways of his father David and he did not turn aside to the right or to the left.

Judging by the age of his father, Josiah was born when Amon was sixteen (2 Chron. 33:21), and though the Bible is silent on the issue, he would have ruled through a regent possibly until the age of sixteen (see v. 3). In the case of Joash, he came to the throne aged seven and clearly Jehoiada the priest was the influential figure during the king's early years (2 Chron. 24:1-3). Again, as has become customary in Chronicles since the time of Hezekiah, the name of Josiah's mother is omitted (see 2 Kings 22:1). Like Asa, Jehoshaphat, Joash, Amaziah, Uzziah, Jotham and Hezekiah, Josiah did 'the right' in Yahweh's eyes (2 Chron. 14:2; 20:32; 24:2; 25:2; 26:4; 27:2; 29:2). This was in contrast to his father who did 'the evil' in Yahweh's sight (2 Chron. 33:22). As far as the Chronicler is concerned, only Jehoshaphat and Hezekiah shared with Josiah the distinction of following 'in the ways' of David (1 Kings 15:11 states that this was true also of Asa). However, of Josiah alone does the Chronicler state that 'he did not turn aside to the right or to the left' (but similar sentiments are expressed of Hezekiah in 2 Kings 18:6). The Chronicler's language echoes the words of Deuteronomy 5:32; 17:11, 20 and Joshua 1:7 which indicate that the phrase means faithful obedience to God's commandments.

Josiah's early reforms (34:3-7)

> 34:3. For in the eighth year of his reign, while he was still young, he began to seek the God of David his father; and in the twelfth year he began to purge Judah and Jerusalem of the high places, and the Asherim and the carved images and the cast images. 4. And they tore down the altars of the Baals in his presence, and he demolished the incense altars which were above them; and he shattered the Asherim and the carved images and the cast images and made dust of them and scattered *it* on the graves of those who had sacrificed to them. 5. He also burned the bones of the priests on their altars and cleansed Judah and Jerusalem, 6. and *likewise* in the cities of Manasseh and Ephraim and Simeon and as far as Naphtali with their swords all around. 7. And he broke down the altars and he beat the Asherim and the carved images into powder, and cut down all the incense altars throughout all the land of Israel. Then he returned to Jerusalem.

While Kings has deliberately collected all of Josiah's reforms and placed them in the context of the eighteenth year of his reign, it is clear that reforms were already in operation which led to the discovery of the Book. Chronicles however gives more precise details as to when the various reforms took place using chronological markers as was done during Asa's reign (vv. 3, 8; see 2 Chron. 15:10, 19; 16:1, 12). It was

when he was aged sixteen and 'still young' (v. 3) that Josiah
showed evidence of a heart for God. Solomon is described
as being only a 'youth' (*na'ar;* 1 Chron. 22:5; 29:1; see also
2 Chron. 13:7). To 'seek' (*drs*) God is one of the Chronicler's
favourite expressions for humble devotion to God (see
1 Chron. 10:13-14; 22:19; 2 Chron. 1:5; 7:14; 30:19; 31:21) and
an example of what that included is given later in verses
21 and 26. This Godward attitude of Josiah found practical
expression in the reforms he began to undertake when he
was twenty, the age when he probably took full responsibility
for his kingdom. This was the age when the Levites were
counted for service and young men were enrolled for army
duty (see 1 Chron. 23:24, 27; 27:23; 2 Chron. 25:5; 31:17; see
Num. 1:3, 18, 20; 26:2).

A brief report of his religious reforms is recorded in verses
3b to 7 (see 2 Kings 23:4-20 for a fuller description). Josiah began
in Judah and Jerusalem with the verb 'to cleanse' or 'purge'
framing this part of his rule (vv. 3b-5). He then extended his
reforming activity further afield into the former northern
kingdom (vv. 6-7). The Chronicler says nothing specific about
the cleansing of the temple (see 2 Kings 23:4-7) but assumes it
in his reference to Jerusalem and in his summary statement in
verse 8. He had already given a full description of what such
temple cleansing involved in his treatment of Manasseh's
restoration programme (2 Chron. 33:15-16). The 'high places'
will have included the ones Manasseh had built and then later
failed to remove (2 Chron. 33:3, 17). Even though people may
have used these local sanctuaries to worship Yahweh, they
had the tendency to become idolatrous as appeared to be the
case after Amon's brief reign, for they are associated in this
context with items that are clearly idolatrous. These included
the sacred poles for the goddess Asherah and carved and cast
images (v. 3b). Amon had sacrificed to the carved images that
Manasseh had made (2 Chron. 33:22). Cast images were made
by Ahaz for the Baals (2 Chron. 28:2). Asa's reforming zeal
was of a similar nature (2 Chron. 14:3-5).

It is especially noted that 'the altars of the Baals' were
torn down in Josiah's presence and that he cut down the
incense burners that perhaps hung above the altars. All the
representations of pagan gods were pulverised. Moses did

something similar with the golden calf that had been made to represent Yahweh (Exod. 32:20). The dust from these images was then thrown over the graves of those who had worshipped these gods. Although the Chronicler does not mention Josiah's slaughter of the priests, it is implied in the comment that their bones were burnt on their altars (see 2 Kings 23:20). Scattering the remains of the idolatrous objects over the graves and burning dead bodies on pagan altars was an act of desecration and would have expressed the total defilement of what had been considered most sacred by the pagan worshippers. But as far as Josiah was concerned the action had the opposite effect of purifying the land of all its idolatrous practices.

Josiah's reforming zeal extended to all the tribal areas of Israel (v. 6). Manasseh and Ephraim represented the main part of the former northern kingdom with Simeon in the deep south and Naphtali in the far north being equivalent to the Chronicler's usual way of describing the limits of Israel from 'Beersheba to Dan', which is the reverse order to that found in the earlier history (1 Chron. 21:2; 2 Chron. 30:5; see Judg. 20:1; 1 Sam. 3:20; 2 Sam. 24:2; 1 Kings 4:25). The latter part of verse 6 is difficult and the Masoretes themselves give various readings.[53] What is clear is that the idolatrous practices that Josiah destroyed in his own kingdom he succeeded in doing all over Israel ('the land of Israel'; see 1 Chron. 22:2; 2 Chron. 2:17[16]; 30:25) before returning to Jerusalem (v. 7; see vv. 3b-4). The text indicates that the king was directly involved in the whole reforming enterprise.

Josiah repairs the temple (34:8-13)

34:8. Now in the eighteenth year of his reign, to cleanse the land and the house, he sent Shaphan the son of Azaliah, and Maaseiah the chief of the city, and Joah the son of Joahaz the recorder, to repair the house of Yahweh his God. 9. And they

---

53. The traditional MT represented by the Leningrad MS reveals a problem at the close of verse 6 with the actual written text (*Kethibh*) suggesting 'the mountain of their houses' (*bəhar btyhm*) which could be a reference to mountain temples (see 2 Kings 23:19), but it must be supposed that a verb is missing or that some such verb as 'destroyed' is inferred from the previous verses. Other Masoretic MSS read 'chose their houses/temples' (*bāḥar btyhim*) which makes little sense. The Masoretic pointing (*Qere*) treats the phrase as one word meaning 'with their swords' (*bəḥarbōṯêhem*) but again the sentence is elliptical. A clever suggestion is that instead of *bahar* ('to choose'), *bi'ēr* ('he burned') should be read (see 2 Kings 23:16, 19).

came to Hilkiah the high priest, and they gave him the money that was brought into the house of God, which the Levites, the keepers of the threshold, had collected from the hand of Manasseh and Ephraim and from all the remnant of Israel, and from all Judah and Benjamin, and they returned to Jerusalem. 10. Then they put *it* in the hand of the workmen who had the oversight in the house of Yahweh; and the workmen who were working in the house of Yahweh gave it to repair and restore the house. 11.And they gave *it* to the craftsmen and builders to buy quarried stone and timber for joints, and to furnish the houses with beams which the kings of Judah had let go to ruin. 12. And the men did the work faithfully. And over them were Jahath and Obadiah the Levites of the sons of Merari, and Zechariah and Meshullam of the sons of the Kohathites to supervise. And *some* Levites, all who were skilful with instruments of music, 13. and were over the burden bearers and were supervising all who did work in any kind of service. And *others* from the Levites were scribes and officers and gate-keepers.

Another chronological note introduces the restoration work on the temple which is seen as part of the continuing work of purging the temple and land (v. 8a). On the other hand, it could be translated 'when he had purged the land and the temple' suggesting that the initial cleansing work had already been completed. The eighteenth year of Josiah's reign, when he was aged twenty-six, is mentioned again in the next chapter (2 Chron. 35:19), thus framing the three significant moments, that of finding the book of the Law, the covenant renewal and the Passover celebrations. While Kings emphasises the reforms that took place after finding the Law book, Chronicles shows that Josiah's reform work also led to finding the book. Both Joash and Hezekiah had engaged in repairing the temple (2 Chron. 24:4-14; 29:3-19) and Josiah's involvement indicated yet again the Chronicler's concern to show the significance of the temple for a true Davidic king, following the example of the ideal reigns of David and Solomon.

Only Shaphan is mentioned in the text of Kings, but the Chronicler names two other officials (v. 8), one the chief of the city (see 2 Chron. 18:25) and the other the recorder (see 1 Chron. 18:15). These royal representatives are seen as working together with the temple staff in repairing and restoring the temple. Hilkiah the high priest appears in the genealogical list of high priests in 1 Chronicles 6:13[5:39]. The Chronicler's interest in the Levites is again seen (see 2 Chron. 24:6). As doorkeepers they received money at the temple gates, but they also seem to have travelled throughout the former northern kingdom as well as in Judah to collect the money for the temple. They also had the oversight of the work (vv. 9, 12-13). The phrase 'remnant of Israel' (v. 9) is used to describe the survivors of the northern kingdom after the Assyrians had exiled many to other parts of their empire (see v. 21). For the Chronicler, it is another indication, as in the time of Hezekiah, of a return to a unity that focused on the temple, such as existed in the David–Solomon period. At the end of verse 9, the *Kethibh* text 'and the inhabitants of Jerusalem' is considered more appropriate by many scholars than the suggested *Qere* reading 'and they returned to Jerusalem'.

Despite some difficulties with the text, it appears that there were Levitical supervisors, who are named in verse 12 as coming from the Merari and Kohathite families, and there were workers who were joiners and stone masons together with their labourers who actually did the restoration work (vv. 10-11). The 'houses' that had been left by previous monarchs to fall into ruin (v. 11b), are probably the storerooms and other chambers in the temple complex (1 Chron. 26:20; 2 Chron. 5:1; 16:2). While in 2 Kings 22:7 the workmen handled the money 'faithfully', here it is used to indicate that the whole enterprise was done honestly and well (v. 12a). From other extant sources, it is clear that in the Ancient Near East, music was employed while construction work was in progress, so it is quite possible the Levitical musicians actually played music as well as acted as overseers of the workers (vv. 12b-13). The mention of the Levites who were scribes, officers and gatekeepers calls to mind the different functions they were assigned by David (1 Chron. 26:19, 29). The 'gatekeepers' would have had the task of making sure no one entered the special holy areas.

Application

After the exile, Zerubbabel, the governor appointed by Persia, was involved in rebuilding the temple (Zech. 4:8-10) and the Chronicler's account would have been yet further encouragement to the people to see that the work was done well (Ezra 3:8-9). Zerubbabel was himself a descendant of the royal Davidic line; like Josiah he was concerned for the house of God, and he would have been a tangible pointer to the future Messiah and the realisation of all that the old temple symbolised (see Hag. 1–2).

The discovery of the Law book (34:14-21)

34:14. Now when they were bringing out the money that had been brought to the house of Yahweh, Hilkiah the priest found the book of the law of Yahweh given by Moses. 15. Then Hilkiah answered and said to Shaphan the scribe, 'I have found the book of the law in the house of Yahweh.' And Hilkiah gave the book to Shaphan. 16. So Shaphan came with the book to the king, and brought back a further word to the king, saying, 'All that was committed into the hand of your servants they are doing. 17. And they have poured out the money that was found in the house of Yahweh, and have delivered it into the hand of the overseers and into the hand of the workmen.' 18. Then Shaphan the scribe told the king, saying, 'Hilkiah the priest has given me a book.' Then Shaphan read in it before the king. 19. Now it happened, when the king heard the words of the law, that he tore his clothes. 20. Then the king commanded Hilkiah, and Ahikam the son of Shaphan, and Abdon the son of Micah, and Shaphan the scribe, and Asaiah the king's servant, saying, 21. 'Go, inquire of Yahweh for me, and for those who are left in Israel and in Judah, concerning the words of the book that has been found; for the wrath of Yahweh that is poured out on us is great, because our fathers did not keep the word of Yahweh, to do according to all that is written in this book.'

This section parallels more closely the text of 2 Kings 22:8–23:3 but with a few details highlighting the Chronicler's concerns. Many scholars believe that in Chronicles the finding of the Law book is to be viewed as divine approval and a reward for Josiah's reforms. But although there are indications throughout Chronicles that the compiler was seeking to emphasise that reward or punishment follows faithful or sinful activity, it may be too subtle an idea in the present context. This is not so much a reward as an indication of the gravity of the king's position and that of his people, which then acted as a spur to further reform. As the Mosaic law indicated, the king was to possess a copy of God's law for himself and to read it continually (Deut. 17:18-20). Josiah's reaction on hearing it read out loud brought deep conviction of sin.

It was while the Levites were still bringing out the money collected from the people to support the workers, that the high priest Hilkiah found the book, an event that is emphasised by repetition in verses 14 and 15. The high priest then gave it to Shaphan the scribe, one of the king's representatives (see vv. 8-9), who subsequently took it to the king and read it in his presence (vv. 15-16, 18).

There are a number of reasons for it being the canonical book of Deuteronomy that was discovered. The word 'book' or more accurately 'a written scroll' (see Jer. 36:2; Ezek. 2:9) refers not to the five books of Moses but to one book. This 'book of the law' is a phrase that is repeated many times in Deuteronomy (see 28:61; 29:21; 30:10; 31:26; see also 17:18-19). It is described as the 'book of the covenant' (v. 30) which is especially appropriate for Deuteronomy with its list of blessings for obedience and curses for disobedience, a point that the Chronicler alone mentions (v. 24; see 2 Kings 22:16). In fact, the phrase 'all the curses written in the book' echo such words in Deuteronomy 29:20, 27. It is described as Yahweh's law, His 'torah' or 'instruction', meaning that it is of divine origin, but it was mediated through Moses (v. 14; literally 'by the hand of Moses').

Shaphan tactfully reported first on the splendid work carried out by all in connection with the temple restoration (vv. 16b-17). He then informed the king what the high priest had given him and proceeded to read the book's contents (v. 18). The preposition 'in' (b^e) need not have a sense different from 2 Kings 22:10 which states simply that 'he read it'. The verb translated 'poured out' (v. 17) could either refer to emptying the offerings placed in the treasury chest or to melting the offertory money to make a finer metal.

Many scholars have considered that while the response of Josiah in Kings is understandable given that there had been no mention of any reforms prior to finding the book, in Chronicles, where there have already been reforms, the king's reaction seems over dramatic. However, Josiah had listened to God's written word which had included references to the

king's responsibility to have a copy of it at hand as well as
to read from it continually and he would have heard all the
curses for disobedience. Tearing his clothes was a mark of
distress and dismay (v. 19; see 2 Chron. 23:13; Gen. 37:34;
Job 1:20) especially after hearing of the covenant curses,
which were expressions of divine wrath for not keeping
God's law (see v. 21).

Five of the king's top officials including Shaphan the scribe
and Hilkiah the high priest were commissioned to consult
Yahweh (v. 20). The verb 'consult' or 'inquire' is the one often
rendered 'to seek' (*drs*), and one of the Chronicler's key terms
(v. 21; see 1 Chron. 10:13-14). Josiah included the remnant of
the northern kingdom of Israel as well as Judah and himself
in the desire for divine guidance (see v. 9). The king perceived
that his people were under God's wrath on account of a failure
by their fathers to abide by Yahweh's word written in the Law
book. There had been an accumulation of infidelity built up
over a considerable time so that Josiah probably realised that
the final covenant curse was due, and the destruction of the
northern kingdom was clear evidence that God's word was no
empty threat. Josiah's response to hearing the divine words
was unlike that of Joash (2 Chron. 24:18-21).

The prophecy concerning the Law book (34:22-28)

34:22. So Hilkiah and *those* whom the king *appointed* went to
Huldah the prophetess, the wife of Shallum the son of Tokhath,
the son of Hasrah, keeper of the wardrobe. She lived in Jerusalem
in the Second Quarter. And they spoke to her concerning this.
23. Then she said to them, 'Thus says Yahweh the God of Israel,
Tell the man who sent you to me, 24. thus says Yahweh, I am
indeed bringing disaster on this place and on its inhabitants
all the curses that are written in the book that they read before
the king of Judah. 25. Because they have forsaken me and made
sacrifices smoke to other gods, so that they might provoke me to
anger with all the works of their hands, therefore my wrath will
be poured out on this place, and will not be quenched. 26. And to
the king of Judah, who sent you to seek Yahweh, thus you shall
say to him, Thus says Yahweh the God of Israel: Concerning
the words which you have heard, 27. because your heart was
tender, and you humbled yourself before God when you heard
his words against this place and against its inhabitants, and

you have humbled yourself before me, and you have torn your clothes and wept before me, I also have heard, oracle of Yahweh. 28. I will indeed gather you to your fathers, and you will be gathered to your graves in peace; and your eyes will not see all the disaster which I am bringing on this place and upon its inhabitants.' So they brought back word to the king.

This section of Chronicles continues to follow closely the parallel account in 2 Kings 22:14-20. The first part of the opening sentence is elliptical, which is a recognised literary form in Hebrew and the phrase indicates that Hilkiah the high priest was the leader of the delegation. In this particular emergency, seeking God meant seeking one of God's spokespersons and doing so quickly. The prophet living nearest to the temple and royal palace happened to be a woman. Only a few female prophets are mentioned in the Old Testament; they included Miriam, Deborah, the wife of Isaiah, and Noadiah (Exod. 15:20; Judg. 4:4; Isa. 8:3; Neh. 6:14). This prophetess resided within the capital city, the Second Quarter perhaps being either the northern extension of the old city or the area recently extended in the southwest and walled by Hezekiah (2 Chron. 32:5; Zeph. 1:10). Huldah is identified by her husband Shallum who was a descendant of 'the keeper of the wardrobe', a responsible position overseeing the royal robes. It is less likely he had charge of the temple wardrobe unless the family had Levitical or priestly links, which would be the case if Shallum is identified with Jeremiah's uncle (Jer. 32:7).

Huldah had a word from God for the king's representatives and it consisted of two oracles both introduced by the messenger formula, 'Thus says Yahweh' (vv. 23, 26). The first oracle (vv. 23-25) has a double introduction. It is made very clear that her words are Yahweh's words which the officials are commanded to tell the king, and in this context even a king is seen as an ordinary individual ('tell the man ...' v. 23). The message is aimed at the people as a whole and is one of judgment for Jerusalem and its inhabitants. It confirmed the words that the king had heard in the Law book concerning the covenant 'curses' (v. 24; see v. 21). The accusations follow with a further indication of judgment in verse 25. Using a term significant to the Chronicler, the prophetess charges the nation with having 'forsaken' ('zb) God. They had rejected

Yahweh in favour of making sacrifices to other gods (see
1 Chron. 28:9). The 'work of their hands' (v. 25) will include
the idols they had made as well as their general bad behaviour
(Isa. 2:8; 17:8; Jer. 25:14; 32:30). Successive generations in the
past had incurred God's wrath, especially during the reigns
of Ahaz, Manasseh and Amon, and Huldah's prophecy also
has reference to the state of the nation during the reigns of
the final four Davidic kings.

The second oracle (vv. 26-28) again begins with the
messenger formula and is for Josiah and consists of a message
of hope and blessing. This time the king's position as ruler of
Judah is acknowledged and Huldah's words directly concern
the words that the king had heard read in the Law book and
his response to them (vv. 26-27). Before the personal assurances
are given (v. 28), the reasons are spelled out (v. 27). They relate
to the king's contrite attitude which included a heart that was
'tender' or 'responsive' (sometimes translated 'inexperienced';
see 1 Chron. 22:5; 29:1; 2 Chron. 13:7), a humble attitude with
expressions of sorrow. These are the signs that Yahweh looked
for in a repentant person or nation and that would move God
to hear and act graciously (2 Chron. 7:14). The divine oracle
formula 'oracle of Yahweh' or 'utterance of Yahweh' (*n⁾'um-yhwh*)
is used twenty-one times by Amos often at the conclusion of an
oracle or as part of an introduction to a message but sometimes,
as in this case, in a medial position. Like the messenger
formula, which is also common in Amos, this phrase added
extra weight to the divine message. It is used numerous times
in Haggai's short prophecy. God's favourable response is the
promise that Josiah will have a peaceful burial and will not
experience the fall of Jerusalem and deportation to Babylon
(v. 28; see 2 Chron. 36:18-20). The same kind of message was
given to Hezekiah through the prophet Isaiah (2 Chron. 32:26).

Josiah's renewal of the covenant (34:29-33)

34:29. Then the king sent and gathered all the elders of Judah and
Jerusalem. 30. And the king went up to the house of Yahweh,
with all the men of Judah and the inhabitants of Jerusalem,
and the priests and the Levites, and all the people, from the
greatest to the smallest, and he read in their hearing all the
words of the book of the covenant which had been found in

the house of Yahweh. 31. Then the king stood in his place and made a covenant before Yahweh to follow Yahweh and to keep his commandments and his testimonies and his statutes with all his heart and with all his soul, to perform the words of the covenant that were written in this book. 32. Then he made all who were present in Jerusalem and Benjamin take their stand. So the inhabitants of Jerusalem acted according to the covenant of God, the God of their fathers. 33. Thus Josiah removed all the abominations from all the lands that belonged to the sons of Israel, and made all who were present in Israel serve Yahweh their God. All his days they did not turn away from following Yahweh the God of their fathers.

This paragraph parallels 2 Kings 23:1-3 but with added material. Following the report that the king received from the delegation concerning Yahweh's message through Huldah (v. 28b), Josiah did what he considered appropriate. As the fire of God's wrath would not be poured out on the nation during his lifetime, he made sure that for the rest of his reign he and his people would be bound to the terms of the covenant revealed in the Law book. Covenants are mentioned during the reigns of Asa and Hezekiah (2 Chron. 15:10-15; 29:10), but this one is in the context of the recently discovered Law book which is now called the 'book of the covenant' (v. 30; see Exod. 24:7 for a similar book), an appropriate name for the book of Deuteronomy. Like David and other Davidic kings, Josiah collected people together as an expression of unity and support (1 Chron. 11:1-3; 13:5; 28:1; 2 Chron. 5:2; 15:9; 23:2-3). The verb used here for 'gathered' is 'sp rather than the Chronicler's more usual term qbṣ. The 'elders' represented the people as a whole 'from Judah and Jerusalem' and the use of the word 'all' (three times in vv. 29-30) together with the phrase 'great and small' emphasises the unity and all-inclusiveness of the gathering. Also among the assembled were 'priests and Levites' (v. 30). Many scholars think that the Chronicler had in mind those Levites who had a prophetic ministry, particularly in song and music, especially as the parallel text in 2 Kings 23:2 refers to 'the priests and the prophets' (see 1 Chron. 25:1-5; 2 Chron. 20:14; 29:25, 30; 35:15). However, too much should not be made of this, as the phrase is used many times in Chronicles for all the Levites in general who were not priests (2 Chron. 35:18; see also 30:15, 25, 27; 31:2, 4, 9).

The renewal of the covenant began with the reading of the Law book which set out Yahweh's terms together with its lists of blessings and curses (see especially Deut. 27–29). It was Yahweh who had originally entered into covenant with His people at Sinai and now Josiah, standing 'in his place' in the temple court (see 2 Chron. 23:13; 2 Kings 23:3), committed himself wholeheartedly 'before Yahweh' to 'follow' (literally 'to walk after') Yahweh and to keep those instructions of Yahweh that were written in the book of Deuteronomy. In addition to 'commandments' and 'statutes' or 'decrees', mention is made of Yahweh's 'testimonies' or 'solemn declarations' (see 1 Chron. 29:19 and Deut. 6:17). The word 'testimony' (*'dh*) has been used for God's law in 2 Chronicles 23:11, and in 2 Chronicles 24:6 the temple is called 'the tabernacle of testimony'.

While the king's commitment was genuine (v. 31, 'with all his heart and soul'), it is possible, as distinct from 2 Kings 23:3b, that the Chronicler's way of expressing the people's response indicated that they were not so sincere (v. 32). There is no mention of the people's enthusiastic willingness to commit themselves as happened on previous national occasions (1 Chron. 29:9; 2 Chron. 15:15). It was Josiah who 'made' the people of Jerusalem and Benjamin pledge themselves ('made to take their stand') to that original 'covenant of God' that He had made with Israel. This is suggested again when the Chronicler states that the king 'made all who were present … serve Yahweh' (v. 33). It was by the king's authority and standing in the nation that the covenant was enforced, and the people remained true to Yahweh all the time he was in power. This was shown in the way he was able to keep all the 'lands', that is all the Israelite tribal territories, free from pagan and idolatrous practices ('abominations'). Jeremiah confirms these hints from the Chronicler of the people's general disinterest when he castigates Judah for not returning to Yahweh 'with her whole heart but in pretence' (Jer. 3:10).

Application

Though the future was bleak, Josiah still did what was right and encouraged the nation to follow in God's ways. This was important for the post-exilic community to hear as well as for Christians today. We are to be faithful even when there is no immediate prospect of blessing. Habakkuk trusted God and continued to live obediently despite the dismal situation in which he found himself (Hab. 3).

Reformation imposed from the top down might result in outward conformity yet without a general change of heart it will have little success long term. Hugh Puleston, the vicar of Wrexham parish church, who held the living from 1520 to 1566, conformed to the various significant changes in doctrine and worship that took place during the reigns of Henry VIII, Edward VI, Mary and Elizabeth! However, thankfully, through the ministry of God's word and the work of the Holy Spirit true reformation did take place in Britain (including Wrexham!) and many parts of Europe.

The Chronicler encourages believers not only to persevere in prayer but to be eager to hear God's written word and to respond to its contents with a humble, believing heart ready to live in obedience to it.

Josiah keeps the Passover (35:1-19)

In place of the three-verse account in 2 Kings 23:21-23, Chronicles gives this detailed description of Josiah's Passover that includes items related to the ceremony at the temple, the part played by the priests and Levites, and the emphasis on the instructions given by David and Solomon, all matters of particular interest to the Chronicler. Only the introduction (v. 1a) and the conclusion (vv. 18-19) show any close relationship to the narrative in Kings, but those references do provide the frame for this whole section in Chronicles (vv. 1a, 19b). The passage can be divided into two main parts: the preparations for the Passover (vv. 1-9) and the celebration of the Passover (vv. 10-19). In contrast to the account in Kings, the Passover is seen by the Chronicler as the climax of Josiah's reform movement. As it happened, the Passover was the first great festival mentioned that Israel kept when they initially entered the land under Joshua (Josh. 5:10-11) and the Chronicler presents Josiah's Passover as the last great festival prior to Israel's departure from the land.

Preparations for the Passover (35:1-9)

35:1. Now Josiah kept a Passover to Yahweh in Jerusalem, and they slaughtered the Passover on the fourteenth of the first month. 2. And he appointed the priests to their duties and encouraged them for the service of the house of Yahweh. 3. Then he said to the Levites who taught all Israel, who were holy to Yahweh, 'Put the holy ark in the house Solomon the son of David, king of Israel, built; there is no need to carry it on your shoulders. Now serve Yahweh your God and his people Israel. 4. Prepare yourselves according to your fathers' houses, according to your divisions, in the writing of David the king of Israel and the written document of Solomon his son. 5. And stand in the holy place according to the divisions of the house of your fathers belonging to your brothers the sons of the people, and the division of the father's house belonging to the Levites. 6. And slaughter the Passover, sanctify yourselves, and prepare for your brothers, to act according to the word of Yahweh by the hand of Moses.

7. Then Josiah contributed to the sons of the people flocks, both lambs and young goats, all for Passover offerings for all who were present, to the number of thirty thousand, and three thousand cattle; these were the king's possession. 8. And his officials contributed willingly to the people, to the priests and to the Levites. Hilkiah, Zechariah and Jehiel, the rulers of the house of God, gave to the priests for the Passover offerings two thousand six hundred *flock*, and three hundred cattle. 9. Also Conaniah and Shemaiah and Nethanel, his brothers, and Hashabiah and Jeiel and Jozabad, the chiefs of the Levites, contributed to the Levites for Passover offerings five thousand *flock* and five hundred cattle.

As with Hezekiah's Passover, all the focus is on the centralised worship 'in Jerusalem' at the temple (v. 1) and the presence of 'the sons of Israel' (vv. 17-18) with the inhabitants of Jerusalem for this special occasion. Unlike Hezekiah's celebration (2 Chron. 30:15), this Passover was according to the regular pattern set out in the law of Moses (v. 6). The Passover commemorated Israel's deliverance from the tenth plague and their redemption from Egyptian slavery. It was to be the first of months to them and the victim was to be slaughtered on the fourteenth day of that month (Exod. 12:2-6, 12, 21, 27; Lev. 23:5; Num. 9:1-5; Ezra 6:19-20).

In true Davidic style, Josiah first arranged the priestly duties (v. 2) and Levitical duties (vv. 3-6). The need for the priests to be 'encouraged' may suggest a certain reluctance on their part whereas the Levites were more conscientious (see 2 Chron. 29:34; 30:3). Though the priests were the main instructors of the people in God's law (2 Chron. 15:3; Jer. 5:31; 18:18; Hosea 4:6; Hag. 2:11; Mal. 2:7), Levites were also involved (Deut. 33:10; 2 Chron. 17:7-9; Neh. 8:7-9). There were various degrees of holiness in the Mosaic law, as there were of uncleanness, and the priest was to be more holy than others because of his work within the holy temple. The Levites were also set apart from the rest of Israel and therefore in that sense holy because they had had the duty of carrying the ark of the covenant (Deut. 10:8; 1 Chron. 15:2) as well as other work related to the tabernacle (Num. 3:5-39; 4:15; 8:19). When the ark came to rest in Jerusalem, first in the special place David had prepared for it and then later in the holy of holies of the temple that Solomon built, there was no longer need for the Levites to engage in this service (1 Chron. 23:25-26). It is possible that the ark needed to be removed while the renovation work was done and the placing of the ark back in its resting place 'in the house' that Solomon built was a re-enactment of that original ceremony (1 Chron. 28:2; 2 Chron. 5:4-7) and provided an opportunity for Josiah to underline David's instructions (1 Chron. 23-26; 2 Chron. 8:14). The full title given to Solomon suggests that Josiah is being presented as a second Solomon, who carries out David's will (see vv. 3-4, 15; see 2 Chron. 30:26). This is the last reference to the 'ark' in Chronicles and it is here described uniquely as 'the holy ark' (v. 3). Along with the temple, it was probably destroyed by the Babylonians.

Using a series of imperatives, Josiah urged the Levites to prepare for the Passover (vv. 3b-6). They are first reminded that they have this special privilege of acting for ('serve') both Yahweh and His people. Josiah then commanded them to 'prepare' (v. 4), first by organising themselves according to the family rosters, first drawn up by David and written in a document by Solomon which is no longer extant (see 1 Chron. 23-27; 2 Chron. 8:14). The same verb is used again at the end of the series of commands (v. 6) to emphasise the importance of getting everything ready for their brothers so that they might keep the Passover laws as commanded by God through Moses (Exod. 12:1-13; Deut. 16:1-8). In fact, the very term 'prepare' (*kûn*) becomes an important verb throughout the section (see vv. 4, 6, 10, twice in 14, 15, 16). The Levites were to 'stand' (v. 5) in the 'holy place' in the temple courtyard between the people and the priests who carried out the rituals at the bronze altar. Each family grouping within Israel, here called 'the sons of the people', meaning the ordinary people who were not priests or Levites (see also v. 7), had a corresponding Levitical family to serve them and in this way no household was neglected. In order to be in a position to 'slaughter' the animals, the Levites needed to be in a ritually clean state (v. 6). For Hezekiah's Passover, when many of the people were ceremonially unclean and unable to slaughter their own animals as required by the Mosaic law (Deut. 16:5-6), the Levites had acted on their behalf. Whether that is the situation here or because of the sheer number of worshippers, it is not clear where the slaughter was carried out by the Levites. On the other hand, it is possible that the call to slaughter the Passover is a reference to the Levites' own animals which had been given them by the officials (see vv. 8-9). The word 'brothers' expressed the unity of God's people, whatever their status in society.

As they did in the time of David and Hezekiah (see 1 Chron. 29:2-7; 2 Chron. 30:24), Josiah donated the Passover animals for the ordinary people to present and this was likewise followed by his officials who contributed freely for the benefit of all – 'to the people, to the priests and to the Levites' (vv. 7-8). Again, the unusual phrase 'the sons of the people' is employed to describe the ordinary 'lay' people (v. 7; see vv. 5, 12, 13; 2 Kings 23:6; Jer. 26:23) which suggests that even the poorest and least respected members of the community were not forgotten. The 'cattle' were given for the burnt offerings and fellowship (peace) offerings associated with the accompanying festival of Unleavened Bread (see vv. 12, 14, 17). The gifts were nearly twice the offerings presented at Hezekiah's Passover (2 Chron. 30:24). It is clear that beside the high priest Hilkiah (2 Chron. 34:9), there were two other senior priests who had a high position and they

contributed to their fellow priests (v. 8). Likewise, six chiefs
from among the Levites supplied Passover sacrifices for their
fellow Levites. The first three named are brothers, leaving the
other three as a possible separate group. Various orders of
Levites are mentioned in 1 Chronicles 15:17-18; 16:37-39. Some
of the names are identical with those from Hezekiah's reign
(v. 9; 2 Chron. 31:12-13) and may be due to the same name
being given to the grandchildren which seems to have been
a common practice during the monarchy period.

Celebration of the Passover (35:10-19)

> 35:10. So the service was prepared, and the priests stood in their
> places, and the Levites in their divisions, according to the king's
> command. 11. And they slaughtered the Passover and the priests
> sprinkled from their hands, and the Levites skinned. 12. Then
> they set aside the burnt offering to give them to the divisions of
> the fathers' house belonging to the sons of the people, to offer to
> Yahweh, as it is written in the book of Moses. So also *they did* to
> the cattle. 13. And they cooked the Passover with fire according
> to the ordinance; and they cooked the holy offerings in pots, in
> cauldrons and in pans, and brought them quickly to all the sons
> of the people. 14. Then afterwards they prepared for themselves
> and for the priests, because the priests, the sons of Aaron, were
> offering the burnt offering and the fat until night; so the Levites
> prepared for themselves and for the priests, the sons of Aaron.
> 15. And the musicians, the sons of Asaph, were in their places,
> according to the command of David, and Asaph, and Heman
> and Jeduthun, the king's visionary. And the gatekeepers were at
> each gate; they did not need to leave their service because their
> brothers the Levites prepared for them. 16. So all the service
> of Yahweh was prepared on that day, to keep the Passover and
> to offer burnt offerings on the altar of Yahweh, according to
> the command of king Josiah. 17. And the sons of Israel who
> were present kept the Passover at that time, and the festival of
> Unleavened Bread seven days. 18. No Passover like it had been
> kept in Israel since the days of Samuel the prophet; and none of
> the kings of Israel had kept such a Passover as Josiah kept, and
> the priests and the Levites, and all Judah and Israel who were
> present, and the inhabitants of Jerusalem. 19. In the eighteenth
> year of the reign of Josiah this Passover was kept.

The actual celebration of the Passover is framed by the same
phrase occurring in verses 10 and 16, using the passive form

of the now familiar verb 'to prepare' (see vv. 4, 6; 2 Chron. 8:16;
29:35) and emphasising that it was by the king's command.
Those officiating at the temple were the priests who 'stood in
their places' ready to engage in the rituals connected with the
altar of burnt offering and the Levites who stood prepared as
mentioned earlier (v. 5).

Two parts to the Passover ceremony are highlighted: the
sacrificing of the victims (vv. 11-12) and the eating of the meal
(vv. 13-15). Concerning the first part, it is not entirely clear
who slaughtered the animals (v. 11). It could have been the
people, as the law of Moses originally indicated for 'peace'
or 'fellowship' offerings, of which the Passover was a special
type (see v. 6; Lev. 3:2, 8, 12-13). On the other hand, it could
refer to the Levites, who were the last people to be mentioned
in verse 10, acting on behalf of the people as they did during
Hezekiah's Passover (2 Chron. 30:17). In the original Passover,
the blood of the animal was collected by each household,
and it was sprinkled on their doorposts and lintels, so that
the plague of death did not strike them (Exod. 12:7, 13, 22-23).
The commemoration of that event was now re-enacted at the
temple by the priests. There is no object to the verb 'sprinkle'
(v. 11), but it is clear that as on previous occasions it was
the blood of the slaughtered animals that was splashed on
the sides of the altar (see 2 Chron. 29:22; 30:16). The priests
would have received the blood from the Levites who were
also responsible for flaying the animals and setting aside
the portion that was to be burnt on the altar. It is important
to appreciate that the reference to burning the offering
(vv. 12, 14), which employs the term that normally has the
sense of 'whole burnt offering (ʿōlāh), denotes that part of the
Passover animal's innards including the fat that was burnt
on the altar to produce a 'sweet aroma' to Yahweh (Lev. 3:3-5,
9-11, 14-16). The reference to 'the book of Moses' (v. 12b) again
indicates that the Passover sacrifices at the temple were similar
to the fellowship or peace offerings set out in Leviticus 3. It
is possible, however, that the term 'burnt offering' may not
only refer to those fatty parts of the Passover flocks to be
burnt on the altar but to the separate whole burnt offerings
associated with the festival of Unleavened Bread where the
whole of the skinned animal was burnt up as Leviticus 1

required (see v. 17; 2 Chron. 30:13-15). The 'cattle' (v. 12b) will also refer to these whole burnt offerings connected to the Unleavened Bread festival rather than to the Passover animals (see Num. 28:17-25).

The Passover celebration also involved a fellowship meal where that part of the offering given back to the people was cooked and shared with family members, as the Mosaic law required (v. 13; Exod. 12:8-9; Deut. 16:7). Though the verb 'cook' is often translated 'boil' it can be used in a more general sense for roasting the meat in pots with fire and without water. The Levites kept up the tradition of the initial Passover when they ate 'in haste', by 'quickly' serving all the ordinary people (v. 13b). Only after they had provided for the common people did they make preparations for themselves and the other temple staff who had special duties. These included the priests (v. 14; see v. 6), who are clearly distinguished from the rest of the Levite tribe through their descent from Aaron (see 1 Chron. 15:4; etc.). Similarly, the musicians are singled out as Asaphites, a general term for the three Levitical musical families (Ezra 2:41; 3:10), and they were in their places as directed by David and his three original musical leaders, Asaph, Heman and Jeduthun, with Jeduthun described as the king's 'visionary' (v. 15; 1 Chron. 25:1-6). The gatekeepers were also able to remain at their posts through the goodwill of the other Levites who prepared the Passover meals for them (v. 15b).

Verse 16 not only helps frame the contents of verses 10-15 (see v. 10), but it also balances verse 1 with the reference to 'that day', which is a reminder of that important day of 'the fourteenth of the first month'. The verse also prepares for the fuller summary in verses 17-19. The 'burnt offerings' probably refer to the normal fire offerings that are associated with the festival of Unleavened Bread (see vv. 12, 14, 17). All the arrangements took place exactly as Josiah had ordered. It is now made clear that the Passover belonged together with the seven-day festival of Unleavened Bread (v. 17; see Exod. 12:1-20; Num. 28:16-25; Deut. 16:1-8; 2 Chron. 30:13, 21). It was a pilgrim festival in which the 'sons of Israel' (v. 17a) were 'present' from both north and south (v. 18, 'all Judah and Israel'). This was a unique occasion, surpassing even the one during Hezekiah's reign (see 2 Chron. 30:26). Unlike Hezekiah's, this Passover was completely regular, held on the right day and in the right way with the priests and Levites carrying out their duties to the letter as Josiah had directed. The number of offerings also exceeded those of Hezekiah. It expressed the unity of God's people which the Chronicler emphasises by simply using the name 'Israel' for the whole covenant community (see 'all Israel,' v. 3; 'king of Israel,' v. 4; 'sons of Israel,' v. 17; and 'kings of Israel,' v. 18 where 2 Kings 23:22 has 'the kings of Israel or of the kings of Judah'). The community which was united in keeping the Passover included the priests, the Levites and people from 'all Judah' and the former northern kingdom of Israel together with 'the inhabitants of Jerusalem'. The reference to Samuel, the last of the judges and the one associated with the beginning of the prophetic movement, represented the whole period from the settlement in Canaan to the rise of the monarchy in Israel. In this way, the Chronicler may well be calling to mind the first Passover event that Joshua held when they set foot in Canaan and began eating the produce of the land (Josh. 5:10-11). Samuel's name appears often in Chronicles (1 Chron. 6:28 [13]; 9:22; 11:3; 26:28; 29:29). The final verse of the section forms an inclusio with 2 Chronicles 34:8.

Application

This celebration served as the ideal model for the post-exilic community. The early chapters of Luke's Gospel focus on the temple in Jerusalem. Here Jesus was brought as a baby and again when at the age of twelve He made the pilgrimage with His parents for the annual Passover celebrations. Mary and Joseph were amazed to find their son in the temple and to be told by Him that He 'must' be about His heavenly Father's work (Luke 2:41-49). This 'necessity' meant setting His face to go to Jerusalem to die and rise again. He saw Himself as the true Passover lamb and it was from this celebratory meal, on the night in which He was betrayed, that Jesus instituted the Lord's Supper that spoke of His 'exodus' to establish the new covenant for the forgiveness of His people's sins (Luke 9:31, 51; 22:1-23, 37; 24:44-47; 1 Cor. 5:7). He received

God's sentence of death that all in Christ might not perish but be free to serve God.

The way the Levites served others before themselves provides a striking contrast to the attitude of some of the Corinthians at the celebration of the fellowship Supper (1 Cor. 11:17-34). Their example has also set the good tradition for the people to be served the bread and wine before those appointed to administer the elements.

The lament over Josiah's untimely death (35:20-27)

35:20. After all this, when Josiah had prepared the house, Necho the king of Egypt came up to fight at Carchemish on the Euphrates, and Josiah went out to meet him. 21. And he sent messengers to him saying, 'What have I to do with you, king of Judah? Not against you I *have come* today but against the house with which I am at war and God commanded me to hurry; restrain yourself from opposing God who is with me so he will not destroy you. 22. But Josiah would not turn his face from him but disguised himself in order to do battle with him and did not listen to the words of Necho from the mouth of God. So he came to fight in the plain of Megiddo. 23. And the archers shot at king Josiah and the king said to his servants, 'Take me away for I am badly wounded.' 24. So his servants took him out of the chariot and caused him to ride in his second chariot, and they brought him to Jerusalem. So he died and was buried in the graves of his fathers. And all Judah and Jerusalem mourned for Josiah. 25. And Jeremiah lamented for Josiah and all the male and female singers spoke about Josiah in their laments until today. And they made them a decree in Israel and there they are written in the Laments. 26. And the rest of the acts of Josiah and his loyalty, according to what is written in the law of Yahweh, 27. and his acts, the first and the last, there they are written in the book of the kings of Israel and Judah.

In place of the brief notice in 2 Kings 23:29-30 of Josiah's encounter with the Egyptian Pharaoh and its aftermath, the Chronicler provides a more detailed account of the incident that resulted in Josiah's tragic death and the deep mourning for him that followed.

The phrase 'after all this' (v. 20) opens the new section, and acts as a bridge moving the narrative on from the momentous eighteenth year of Josiah's reign dated 622/1 B.C., when he 'prepared' or 'restored' (*kûn*; see v. 4) Yahweh's house, to the final event that led to his death thirteen years later in 609 B.C. Extra-biblical sources also describe the activities of Necho II, a Pharaoh of the twenty-sixth dynasty, who ruled from 610 to 595 B.C. He was on his way to support, not to fight 'against' Assyria (see 2 Kings 23:29 where the preposition *'al* often translated 'against' can be a synonym for *'el* 'to'). For both Egypt and Assyria, the common enemy was the rising power of Babylon who had destroyed Nineveh, the capital of Assyria in 612 B.C. Necho was on his way to assist the Assyrians in their attempt to regain territory from the Babylonians. The Assyrian king had been forced to move his capital first to Harran and then to Carchemish, an important crossing-point on the Euphrates, about sixty-two miles (one hundred kilometres) northeast of Aleppo. It was to Carchemish the Egyptian king was heading. No information is given why Josiah wished to engage Necho in battle, but it is possible that since Hezekiah's day (2 Chron. 32:31), Judah had more interest in supporting Babylon than Assyria and so sought to frustrate Necho's attempt to help Assyria.

When Necho heard that Josiah had mobilised troops to meet him, he sent messengers to inquire why the Judean king was coming with hostile intent. The Pharaoh tried to dissuade Josiah from engaging in military action. First, using a common Semitic idiom, 'what to me and to you' that questioned what Josiah's intentions were (v. 21; Judg. 11:12; 2 Sam. 16:10; 1 Kings 17:18; 2 Kings 3:13; Matt. 8:29; etc.), Necho mildly rebuked the Judean king for interfering in an issue that did not concern him. He then went on to explain that his purpose was not to engage in a conflict with Judah but to continue the Egyptian policy of waging war on 'the house', which in this context meant the Babylonian king. Finally, Necho's argument became theological, urging Josiah not to oppose the God whom he believed was with him, the Egyptian king, and who had commanded him to hurry. The Pharaoh concluded his speech with the warning that the Judean king should stop opposing God otherwise God would destroy Josiah. This echoes the words of Abijah to Jeroboam (2 Chron. 13:12). If God was with the Egyptians then Judah would be fighting against God and would not prosper.

Whatever Necho understood about what he said, the Chronicler makes it clear that Pharaoh's words were from 'the mouth of God', just as Jeremiah's words were from 'the mouth of Yahweh' (v. 22; 2 Chron. 36:12). In adding this explanation, unlike Kings, Chronicles presents the reason why good king Josiah died so tragically. It underlines one of the Chronicler's key themes that to oppose God brings trouble. How was Josiah to know that Necho's words were from Yahweh? Though there is no certainty that the apocryphal work of 1 Esdras 1:26 is authentic in stating that Jeremiah endorsed Necho's words, it is very possible that Jeremiah had confronted Josiah with a message from Yahweh which informants were able to communicate to the Egyptian king before the messengers were sent to Josiah. Sennacherib was well aware of Hezekiah's words during the siege of Jerusalem (2 Chron. 32:10-12). The Chronicler makes Josiah's disobedience to God's word through Necho all the more outrageous by showing how like Ahab he had become, in seeking to frustrate the divine purpose by disguising himself (v. 22; 2 Chron. 18:29).

It was in the strategic plain of Megiddo that the battle took place (v. 22b) and, again, there are similarities to Ahab's end with both kings mortally wounded as a result of an archer's arrow and then being carried back home (vv. 23-24). Saul was likewise severely wounded by archers (1 Chron. 10:3). Chronicles gives more detail concerning the actual death of Josiah than is found in Kings. The fatally injured king was moved from his own battle chariot to a second chariot, similar to the one the Pharaoh gave Joseph (Gen. 41:43), and brought back to Jerusalem where he died. Though he received the deadly wound at Megiddo, he was not taken into exile but actually died in the safety of Jerusalem and was honoured by being buried peacefully 'in the graves of his fathers' with great lamentation by 'all Judah and Jerusalem' (v. 24b; see 2 Chron. 34:28). Jeremiah the prophet had held Josiah in high esteem (Jer. 22:15-16), and he too uttered a lament that has not been preserved. The canonical book of Lamentations has a different Hebrew title to the written 'Laments' referred to here (v. 25) and the content is quite different too. It became a 'decree' (ḥōq) or, in this context, 'custom', through to the time of the Chronicler ('to this day' see 1 Chron. 4:41) for male and female singers to remember Josiah in their laments, much like the ones in memory of Jephthah's daughter (Judg. 11:39-40).

Despite the sad end to Josiah's life as a result of his wilful disobedience to God's will, the Chronicler concludes by emphasising that overall his reign was marked by 'piety' or 'loyal deeds' that indicated his fidelity to Yahweh's law (v. 26; see 2 Chron. 32:32).

Application

Those who spoke prophetically did not always appreciate what they said, as was the case with Caiaphas concerning the death of Jesus (John 11:49-53). Nothing is hidden from God and no attempt at seeking to deceive or frustrate God's purposes through one's own sinful responses will succeed. Even good kings like Josiah and Hezekiah all fell short of the ideal presented by the David–Solomon era. The yearning was for a Davidic king who would more than realise the ideal. With Jesus we have the one greater than Solomon.

The post-exilic community needed to have examples of devotion to God's law to inspire them to action and that was witnessed in Josiah's obedience to what was written in the Law book. It was the reading and meditating on the law of Moses along with prayer that became the essential ingredients of spiritual life among the Jews through to the New Testament period both in the homeland and the Diaspora (Luke 1:5-6; 2:25, 36-37, 39; Acts 16:1, 13; 2 Tim. 1:5; 3:14-15). For Christians we now have the complete revelation of God's will for our lives in the books of the New as well as the Old Testament (2 Tim. 3:16-17).

8

Exile

(2 Chron. 36:1-21)

The end of the Judean kingdom and temple (36:1-21)

The record of events leading up to the exile is strikingly brief when compared with Kings. What is covered in twenty-three verses by the Chronicler takes fifty-seven verses in 2 Kings 23:31–25:30. Besides the continuing omission of the names of the queen mothers (see 2 Chron. 33:1-2), Chronicles omits the record of the various kings' deaths as well as a comparison with the kings before them. Also omitted are the theological reflections found in Kings, the details of invasions and destructions when compared with Kings, together with the omission of Gedaliah's governorship and the release of Jehoiachin from prison. The Chronicler presents, instead, his own theological evaluation.

In quick succession the last four Davidic kings are mentioned and from the way they are presented by the Chronicler, their reigns are herded together and thought of as one short era. Each of the four kings is introduced in the same way with the monarch's age (vv. 2, 5, 9, 11) and, more significantly, each is associated with exile: Jehoahaz to Egypt; Jehoiakim to Babylon; Jehoiachin to Babylon; and it is taken as read that Zedekiah was exiled to Babylon but at that point it is the people's destiny that interests the Chronicler more (vv. 4, 6, 10, 20). As if to provide a frame around the four kings and their exiles, the Chronicler highlights the prophet Jeremiah.

His name first appears after the death of the last good Davidic king Josiah (2 Chron. 35:25) and besides the significant reference to Jeremiah during Zedekiah's reign (v. 12), the account of the exile closes by mentioning the fulfilment of Jeremiah's prophecy concerning a seventy-year exile which ended with Cyrus' proclamation (vv. 21-22). It would appear, from the Chronicler's perspective, that the exile began after Josiah's death in 609 B.C. and finished with the Persian king's decree in 539/8 B.C. which is exactly seventy years.

Jehoahaz (36:1-4)

> 1. And the people of the land took Jehoahaz the son of Josiah and made him king in place of his father in Jerusalem. 2. Joahaz was twenty-three years old when he became king, and he reigned three months in Jerusalem. 3. Now the king of Egypt deposed him at Jerusalem; and he fined the land one hundred talents of silver and a talent of gold. 4. Then the king of Egypt made his brother Eliakim king over Judah and Jerusalem and changed his name to Jehoiakim. And Necho took Joahaz his brother and brought him to Egypt.

The first verse is better suited as the closing part of the previous paragraph that began with Jeremiah's lament at the tragic death of Josiah (2 Chron. 35:25-27). As they had done after the assassination of Josiah's father, 'the people of the land', that is the ordinary local people, acted to appoint a new king (2 Chron. 23:13, 20-21; 26:1; 33:25). On this occasion politics were clearly in evidence as the following verses suggest, for the people opted to anoint not the oldest son of Josiah but Jehoahaz (also spelt Joahaz in verses 2 and 4 and also known as Shallum in 1 Chron. 3:15; Jer. 22:11), who probably followed his father's distrust of Egypt's intentions. Following Necho's victory over Josiah, Judah was no longer in an independent position and the Pharaoh took advantage of his power by removing the popular choice and setting the pro-Egyptian older brother on the throne. Actually, Josiah's eldest son was Johanan, but nothing is known of his fate (1 Chron. 3:15). To cement his authority over the Judean king, he changed his name from Eliakim (God will establish) to Jehoiakim (Yahweh will establish).

At the same time he demanded tribute from Judah, and although crippling, it was a modest amount in comparison to that exacted by Sennacherib from Hezekiah (v. 3; 2 Kings 18:14). Thus after only three months on the throne in Jerusalem, Jehoahaz was carried off to Egypt. No report of his death is given (as in 2 Kings 23:34b), for the Chronicler wished to leave his readers with the exile theme. Jeremiah 22:11-17 presents the prophet's judgment on his reign.

Jehoiakim (36:5-8)

> 5. Jehoiakim was twenty-five years old when he became king, and he reigned eleven years in Jerusalem. And he did evil in the sight of Yahweh his God. 6. Nebuchadnezzar king of Babylon came up against him and bound him in bronze *shackles* to take him to Babylon. 7. Nebuchadnezzar also brought some of the vessels of the house of Yahweh to Babylon and put them in his temple in Babylon. 8. Now the rest of the acts of Jehoiakim and his abominations which he did, and what was found against him, there they are written in the book of the kings of Israel and Judah. Then Jehoiachin his son reigned in his place.

Much more detail of Jehoiakim is found in 2 Kings 23:36–24:7 and Jeremiah 22:18-23; 25:1; 26:20-24; 36:1-32. He was Josiah's son and a half-brother to Jehoahaz as they had different mothers. The Chronicler's only interest in this puppet king who owed his throne to Egypt (vv. 3-4) is to emphasise his evil and to indicate the parallel between the circumstances leading to the end of the monarchy and that of the temple. No details of his sinful rule are mentioned by the Chronicler such as is found in Kings and Jeremiah's prophecy. The term 'abominations', reminiscent of the rule of Ahaz and Manasseh and calling to mind the atrocities and evils of the Canaanites, sums up Jehoiakim's degenerate regime (see 2 Chron. 28:3; 33:2; 34:33).

Like Jehoahaz, Jehoiakim is associated with exile. It is questioned whether he was actually brought to Babylon as it may be that the intention to bring him to Babylon did not in the end materialise for some reason. This idea is based on comparing the text concerning Manasseh's exile where it reads that they 'bound him ... and brought him ...' while for Jehoiakim it merely states that Nebuchadnezzar 'bound him ... to take him.' (2 Chron. 33:11), but this might be over subtle. The whole area from the border of Egypt to the Euphrates had come under Babylonian control following

Nebuchadnezzar's victory at Carchemish in 605 B.C. (see Jer. 46:2) and the event is recorded in the Babylonian Chronicle. It was following that victory that Nebuchadnezzar besieged Jerusalem. Daniel 1:1 and Jeremiah 25:1 provide the date, the former, using the Babylonian system of reckoning, states it was Jehoiakim's third year while the latter, using the Palestinian system, gives the fourth year of the king's reign. If Jehoiakim was taken to Babylon it was at the same time that Daniel and his three friends were exiled and when some of the temple vessels were taken and housed in a pagan treasury (Dan. 1:1-3). As in the case of Manasseh, the king's exile was not permanent, judging by the account in Kings, but the lack of any reference to his burial may imply, as Jeremiah's prophecy seems to suggest, that Jehoiakim did not die a peaceful death.

The Chronicler makes a special note of the temple vessels (v. 7). Some of them were brought to Babylon. The word for temple (*hêḵāl*) can also mean palace, but in view of other references it seems that Nebuchadnezzar brought the holy vessels to his private pagan temple (see Ezra 1:7; Dan. 1:2). Mention will again be made concerning them in the case of Jehoiachin's deportation (v. 10) and when the temple was finally destroyed during Zedekiah's reign (vv. 18-19). Plans relating to the vessels and the construction of the whole temple were given to Solomon by David (1 Chron. 28:11-14; see 2 Chron. 4:16, 18-19; 5:1, 5). Further temple vessels were made during Joash's reign (2 Chron. 24:14). A preview of the exile took place when the northern kingdom defeated Judah and took away the vessels found in God's house (2 Chron. 25:24). The close connection between the Davidic king and the temple that the Chronicler has emphasised, continues to the end, only now he shows that the plundering of the temple vessels and the final ruin of the temple itself run parallel with the exile of the Davidic kings and the demise of the Judean monarchy.

Jehoiachin (36:9-10)

36:9. Jehoiachin was eight years old when he became king, and he reigned three months and ten days in Jerusalem. And he did evil in the sight of Yahweh. 10. At the turn of the year, king Nebuchadnezzar sent and brought him to Babylon with the costly vessels of the house of Yahweh and he made Zedekiah, his brother, king over Judah and Jerusalem.

Jehoiachin was Jehoiakim's son, and his reign receives even less space than his father's. He was also known as Jeconiah or Coniah (1 Chron. 3:16; Jer. 22:24; 24:1). A much fuller account of his kingship and what happened to him in exile is given in 2 Kings 24:8-17; 25:27-30 (see also Jer. 22:24-30). It is clear that the traditional text which puts the king's age on accession as eight years old has lost the word for 'ten' which when added would make 'eighteen', the number found in Kings, where we are also told that Jehoiachin's wives were carried into exile (2 Kings 24:8, 15). While the final paragraph of 2 Kings closes with Jehoiachin's release and favourable treatment by the Babylonians, suggesting a ray of hope for the Davidic dynasty, Chronicles views Jehoiachin as just another example of all that is contrary to the Davidic ideal resulting in the divine curse of exile. His brief reign of just over three months before being carted off to Babylon still continued the evil activity of his father's kingship and indicated even more starkly the God-forsaken position of king and nation.

It was at the turn of the year or spring time (v. 10; see 1 Chron. 20:1) that the Jerusalem siege took place and again the Babylonian Chronicle confirms the biblical record of how the city was taken and the king captured and how Nebuchadnezzar appointed a king of his own choice. This took place in 598/7 B.C. Zedekiah is the person the Babylonian king placed on the throne instead of Jehoiachin. He is referred to as the 'brother' of Jehoiachin but here used in the sense of 'relative' because Zedekiah was actually the son of Josiah and therefore Jehoiachin's uncle (1 Chron. 3:15; 2 Kings 24:17; Jer. 37:1).

Again, the Chronicler couples Jehoiachin's deportation with the transportation of more vessels from the Jerusalem temple (see vv. 7, 18). The vessels are described as 'costly' or 'desirable' (v. 10) and this description was used previously of the different kinds of costly items that Hezekiah collected for himself as well as of people's attitude to Jehoram who died 'without being desired' (2 Chron. 21:20; 32:27; see also Hag. 2:7; Dan. 11:8; etc.). These were the temple vessels that the false prophets believed would soon be returned to Jerusalem, whereas Jeremiah dashed any such hopes by prophesying that the remaining vessels in Yahweh's house would be carried away to Babylon until God's timing for their return (Jer. 27:16-22).

Zedekiah (36:11-21)

36:11. Zedekiah was twenty-one-years-old when he became king, and he reigned eleven years in Jerusalem. 12. And he did evil in the sight of Yahweh his God; he did not humble himself before Jeremiah the prophet from the mouth of Yahweh. 13. And he also rebelled against king Nebuchadnezzar who had made him swear by God; but he stiffened his neck and hardened his heart from returning to Yahweh the God of Israel. 14. Also all the officials of the priests and the people were extremely unfaithful, according to all the abominations of the nations; and they defiled the house of Yahweh which he had consecrated in Jerusalem. 15. And Yahweh the God of their fathers sent to them rising up early and sending by the hand of his messengers, because he had compassion on his people and on his dwelling-place. 16. But they kept mocking the messengers of God, despising his words, and scoffing at his prophets, until the wrath of Yahweh arose against his people, until there was no healing. 17. Therefore he brought against them the king of the Chaldeans, who killed their young men with the sword in the house of their sanctuary, and had no compassion on young man or young woman, old or decrepit; he gave them all into his hand. 18. And all the vessels of the house of God, the great and the small, and the treasures of the house of Yahweh and the treasures of the king and of his leaders, he brought all to Babylon. 19. And they burned the house of God, and tore down the wall of Jerusalem, and all its citadels they burned with fire, and destroyed all its desirable vessels. 20. And the remnant from the sword he carried into exile to Babylon, where they became slaves to him and to his sons until the reign of the kingdom of Persia, 21. to fulfil the word of Yahweh by the mouth of Jeremiah, until the land had satisfied her sabbaths. All the days that it lay desolate it kept sabbath, to fulfil seventy years.

From the material in Kings and Jeremiah, Zedekiah was another son of Josiah and had the same mother as Jehoahaz (2 Kings 23:31; 24:18; Jer. 52:1). Further information concerning Zedekiah is found in 2 Kings 24:17-25:7 and Jeremiah 37:1-21; 39:1-7; 52:1-11. The Chronicler, as with his treatment of the previous three kings, is concerned with exile, with the desecration of the temple and the plundering of its vessels, but in addition, he also stresses the sins of the king and the people that had brought about the destruction of Jerusalem and the temple and the deportation of the people. He also draws attention to Jeremiah the prophet, the final example of a long line of faithful messengers sent by a compassionate God, whose word was rejected by the king. The preaching of the Chronicler himself is heard in this passage with many of his key words being used.

Verse 11 is the only one that is paralleled in the text of 2 Kings 24:18a and 19a. The 'evil' that the king did in the sight of Yahweh is defined in terms of his not humbling himself to accept Yahweh's word to him through His prophet Jeremiah. To 'humble' oneself involves repentance for disobedience and a willingness to listen to Yahweh (see 2 Chron. 7:14). Zedekiah's own refusal to obey God's word through Jeremiah is documented a number of times by the prophet (see Jer. 27:1-28:17; 34:1-22; 37:1–38:28). In addition, Jeremiah had to contend with many false prophets who spoke of visions that came from their own hearts and not 'from the mouth of Yahweh' (v. 12b; Jer. 23:16). The reference to Zedekiah's revolt against Nebuchadnezzar (v. 13) in which the Judean king looked to Egypt for help was not only political suicide but went against all that Jeremiah was saying in the name of Yahweh. Ezekiel 17:11-21 speaks of this treaty oath that Zedekiah, who was now the Babylonian king's vassal, had sworn in the name of God. Unlike former Davidic kings like Jehoram, Ahaz and Manasseh who practised idolatrous pagan worship, Zedekiah's sins all involved disobedience to Yahweh's will through His prophets. He 'stiffened his neck' (2 Chron. 30:8; Deut. 10:16; Jer. 7:26; 17:23; 19:15; Neh. 9:16-17; Prov. 29:1) and 'hardened his heart' (Deut. 15:7). His hardened heart prevented him from 'turning back' or 'returning' to Yahweh (v. 13), which meant he did not repent and humbly trust Yahweh and His word through such prophets as Jeremiah. Repentance involves turning 'from' wicked ways (2 Chron. 7:14) and turning 'to' Yahweh (2 Chron. 15:4).

What was true of the king was even more evident in his subjects. Again, the books of Jeremiah and Ezekiel provide ample evidence of the attitude of all parts of the community toward Yahweh and His prophets. The leadership among the priests and people displayed increasing evidence of 'unfaithfulness' (*ma'al*, v. 14; see 1 Chron. 10:13), a term that speaks of treachery and infidelity. With regard to God, it involved giving to others what rightfully belongs to God alone. Toward the end of the introduction to Chronicles, it is recorded that Judah's deportation to Babylon was on account of 'unfaithfulness' (1 Chron. 9:1) and throughout the more detailed history the extent of that infidelity is made abundantly clear (2 Chron. 12:2; 26:16, 18; 28:19, 22; 29:6, 19; 30:7; 33:19). It included engaging in the abominable practices of the pagan nations around them, as had happened earlier in the time of Ahaz and Manasseh (2 Chron. 28:3; 33:2). The temple that had been set apart for Yahweh was defiled by the kind of atrocious activities described in Ezekiel 5:11; 8:5-18 (see Jer. 7:30; 16:18; 32:34).

Before the divine punishment struck, warnings were given through Yahweh's prophets who are described as His 'messengers' (v. 15). The Hebrew idiom 'rising early and sending' is often used by Jeremiah with the idea of 'sending early and often' or 'persistently sending' (Jer. 7:25; 25:4; 26:5; 29:19; 44:4). Throughout Israel's history, the Chronicler has been at pains to indicate that God uses various means to warn His people. David was warned by Joab (1 Chron. 21:3), Abijah warned Jeroboam (2 Chron. 13:4-12), Joash and his people were warned by prophets (2 Chron. 24:19), the priests warned Uzziah (2 Chron. 26:18), Hezekiah's runners were sent to the northern tribes to warn them (2 Chron. 30:6-11), and Josiah was warned by the Egyptian king Necho (2 Chron. 35:20-22). All God's warnings were evidence of His 'having compassion' on them; it is a verb that has the idea of 'sparing' them (*ḥāmal*, v. 15; see Mal. 3:17). This is the Yahweh who is slow to anger (Exod. 34:6) whom the Chronicler often describes as 'the God of their fathers' (1 Chron. 5:25), a phrase that indicates His commitment to them from the beginning of their history. He is also committed to the temple because it represents His heavenly dwelling-place on earth (2 Chron. 30:27; see 2 Chron. 6:18-21).

The participles with the verb 'to be', namely, 'they were mocking ... despising ... and scoffing', express the continuous nature of the people's rejection of God's word through His prophetic messengers and the build-up of terms conveys their increasing guilt (v. 16). Israel's sin had reached a point where Yahweh's wrath was so provoked that no 'healing' was possible. There could be no healing where there was no repentance (2 Chron. 7:14; 30:20). Their persistent rebellious attitude now tipped the scales for the final curse of God's wrath to fall upon them. The thought is similar to what was said of the Canaanites in Abraham's day, that 'the iniquity of the Amorites is not yet complete' (Gen. 15:16). When Israel entered the land under Joshua, the Canaanites finally experienced the punishment which their accumulated sins deserved. As God's people, Israel's punishment, though rightly deserved, is seen by the Chronicler as primarily a failure to respond to God's gracious warnings and pleadings (see Ezek. 18:30-32).

The remaining paragraph (vv. 17-21) concerning Zedekiah's rule describes in summary form the tragic events that led to the final exile from Judah including the indiscriminate slaughter of the people, the removal of the rest of the temple vessels and other treasures to Babylon, the burning of the temple and the destruction of Jerusalem's city walls. A fuller account is found in 2 Kings 25:1-21 and Jeremiah 39:1-10; 52:4-30.

In his wrath, Yahweh is the one who brought about the downfall of the nation, using Nebuchadnezzar as His agent. The Babylonian king is called 'the king of the Chaldeans' which is his proper title as he was the son of the founder of the Chaldean dynasty that ruled over the Babylonian empire from 605 B.C. Originally from southern Babylonia (Gen. 11:28), the Chaldeans came to prominence in Babylon during the eighth century so that Chaldea came to denote the whole of Babylonia and the name 'Chaldean' was used as a synonym for Babylon (Isa. 13:19; 47:1; 48:14). The enemy was ruthless with killings taking place in the nave of the temple, called 'the house of their sanctuary' (v. 17), which had already become polluted by the people's atrocious practices (v. 14). It was God's purpose to hand His people over to Nebuchadnezzar. Having spurned Yahweh's pity (v. 15), God's people, whether old or young, frail or disabled, male or female, received no pity from the Babylonians (v. 17; see Lam. 2:20-21; Ezek. 9:5-7).

All the treasures that former Davidic kings had acquired as blessings from God, ones that Hezekiah had shown the Babylonian ambassadors, were all taken to Babylon (v. 18; 2 Kings 20:12-17; Isa. 39:1-6). Special mention is again made of the despoiling of 'the vessels' from the temple and its treasures (see vv. 7, 10; see Jer. 27:21-22). God's blessing had also been seen in the building projects of faithful kings but now all was destroyed as a sign of God's curse (v. 19). These included the pulling down of the city walls and burning the 'citadels', a term used of prominent attractive buildings or royal fortifications ('armôn; see Lam. 2:5, 7; Amos 1:4; 2:5; 3:9-11; Ps. 48:3, 13[4, 14]). Fire consumed all the attractive, precious objects found in the citadels that brought pleasure to the eye (see Lam. 1:10-11; 2:4; Isa. 64:11[10]). Also burnt was God's house, the temple, an appropriate end to a place that had become so polluted by pagan objects of worship and the recent killings (v. 17). The 'exalted house' that Solomon had built for Yahweh to dwell in for ever was no more, thus fulfilling God's warning to Solomon and the Davidic descendants if they embraced other gods (see 2 Chron. 6:2; 7:21-22).

The remnant of those who escaped the sword were taken into exile (v. 20; 2 Chron. 7:19-20). As the treasures of the king and officials and the vessels and treasures of God's house were moved to Babylon so were the people and they became subject to Nebuchadnezzar and his successors. Nothing is said about the fate of Zedekiah or of the people who were left in Judah or of the governorship of Gedaliah. The Chronicler had no interest in those who were left in Judah or of Zedekiah for there was no future for his family line (2 Kings 25:6-7). As far as the Chronicler was concerned, the future lay with the descendants of those who had been taken out of their land to become 'slaves' to the Babylonians. God's people were back in an Egyptian-like situation as described in the covenant curses (Deut. 28:68). The word 'until' (v. 20) however gives the first ray of hope suggesting there will be an end to their servitude when a new regime takes over, namely, 'the kingdom of Persia.'

Verse 21 introduces another 'until' that encourages a further reason for hope based on the Mosaic scriptures and the prophetic message of Jeremiah. Yahweh's word through the mouth of Jeremiah indicated as early as Jehoiakim's reign in 605 B.C. that Nebuchadnezzar would be Yahweh's 'servant' to punish God's people. The land would be desolate, and the people would serve the Babylonians for seventy years (Jer. 25:8-13). Then later, during Zedekiah's reign, Jeremiah wrote a letter to the exiles following the events of 597 B.C. when Jehoiachin was taken to Babylon and again he offered them a future and the hope of a return after seventy years (Jer. 29:10-11). Jeremiah also intimated that the temple vessels would eventually ('until') be returned to their place (Jer. 27:22). This prophetic message of hope is fused by the Chronicler with the Mosaic law that refers to the land lying desolate and at rest during the covenant curse of exile (Lev. 26:33-35, 43). It would be a time for the land to enjoy its sabbaths, something that it did not experience when God's people lived in it. In other words, the land at rest would compensate for all the lost weekly Sabbaths and sabbatical years that the people had not observed (Lev. 23:3, 8, 21, 25, 31-32, 35, 39; 25:1-17). The second 'until' suggests an end to that sabbatical rest for the land and the Chronicler makes that clear by introducing the seventy-year period of Jeremiah's prophecy. This interpretation is completely in tune with the Mosaic law which promised a new beginning for God's covenant people (Lev. 26:40-45; Deut. 30).

What Jeremiah meant by the seventy years is hotly debated, some thinking it meant the normal life-span of a person (see Ps. 90:10[11]) so that the prophet is indicating that there would be no return for the generation that had gone into exile. Those living toward the end of the exile and into the post-exilic period were much exercised by Jeremiah's words. When Daniel read it he reckoned that the exilic period was coming to an end, and it led him to pray earnestly (Dan. 9), while Zechariah seems to have had in mind the period between the destruction of the temple in 587 B.C. and its rebuilding in 520-515 B.C. which is approximately seventy years (Zech. 1:12). Others suggest that the round figure could stand for the seventy-three years between the fall of Nineveh in 612 B.C. to the Babylonians and the fall of Babylon in 539 B.C. or to the sixty-six years from the accession of Nebuchadnezzar in 605 B.C. to the fall of Babylon. For the Chronicler, the exile began after the death of Josiah in 609 B.C. with the four final kings all experiencing deportation. Exactly seventy years later in 539 B.C. the Persian king uttered his announcement to 'go up'.

Application

Jesus castigated Jerusalem for killing the prophets and stoning the messengers that were sent to the people (Matt. 23:34-37). At the time when the disciples called attention to the grand, gleaming buildings of the temple that the Herods had beautified, Jesus prophesied the fall of Jerusalem and its temple, seeing it as proleptic of the final judgment at the end of the age (Mark 13; Luke 21:5-36). Jesus' words came to fulfilment in A.D. 70 when the Romans destroyed the whole city and to this day the temple has never been rebuilt. We are to take note of God's warnings, for though everything seems to continue as normal there is a day of reckoning. Though we might think God's judgment day is slow in coming, He is patient and not willing that any should perish but that all should come to repentance (2 Pet. 3:1-13).

9

Hope
(2 Chron. 36:22-23)

The proclamation of Cyrus (36:22-23)

36:22. And in the first year of Cyrus king of Persia, to fulfil the word of Yahweh by the mouth of Jeremiah, Yahweh stirred up the spirit of Cyrus king of Persia, so that he made a proclamation in all his kingdom, and also in writing, saying, 23. 'Thus says Cyrus, king of Persia: All the kingdoms of the earth Yahweh the God of heaven has given to me. And he has appointed me to build for him a house in Jerusalem which is in Judah. Whoever is among you from all his people, may Yahweh his God be with him and let him go up.'

Many scholars are of the view that the Chronicler completed his work with verse 21 and that the final two verses were added later from Ezra 1:1-3. Whereas verse 21 has an appropriately satisfying ending, it is argued that verse 23 is an abrupt unnatural conclusion that suggests it has been extracted from the beginning of the book of Ezra to give Chronicles a more hopeful and positive conclusion. But we have noted that verses 20-21 are not entirely pessimistic and the final verses develop the whisper of hope hinted at in those previous verses.

Having already mentioned the 'kingdom of Persia' in verse 20, the Chronicler sees Jeremiah's prophecy concerning the seventy-year exile fulfilled with Cyrus's proclamation encouraging God's people to go up and build God's house in

Jerusalem. Cyrus II, also known as Cyrus the Great, began by succeeding his father as king of Anshan (Elam) in 559 B.C. He eventually conquered a vast area of the Ancient Near Eastern world that stretched from the Mediterranean in the west to the Indus river in the east. The 'first year of Cyrus king of Persia' refers to the year he conquered Babylon in 539 B.C. and became the king of Mesopotamia. Cyrus calls himself by his first and original title, 'king of Persia,' on this occasion. He was also known as 'king of Babylon' and by more exalted titles such as 'king of the world'.

As Yahweh sovereignly used Nebuchadnezzar as his agent in bringing about the destruction of Jerusalem and its temple (2 Chron. 36:17), so he used Cyrus 'to fulfil' or 'complete' his purposes as prophesied by Jeremiah 29:10 for example. To stress God's active involvement, the Chronicler states that Yahweh 'stirred up' (literally 'awakened') the spirit of Cyrus to bring to an end the captivity of God's people. In the same way he had 'stirred up' Pul, the Assyrian king, to carry the Transjordanian tribes into captivity and had 'stirred up' the Philistines and Arabians against Jehoram (1 Chron. 5:26; 2 Chron. 21:16). This verb is actually used by Isaiah in his prophecies concerning Cyrus (Isa. 41:2, 25; 45:13), whom he describes in messianic terms as Yahweh's 'shepherd' and 'anointed' and active in bringing about the rebuilding of Jerusalem and the temple and the return of the exiles (Isa. 44:28; 45:1-3). Yahweh is not only Israel's God, but He is also Lord over the entire world including the all-conquering Cyrus, and it is Yahweh who had aroused Cyrus to make this benevolent proclamation.

The Hebrew literally states that God 'caused a voice to pass through all his kingdom' (v. 22). This proclamation was like the horn blast on the Day of Atonement that sounded the Jubilee year that brought liberty and a return of people to their possessions. The Hebrew literally states 'you shall cause the ram's horn blast to pass through on the tenth day ... on the day of atonement you shall cause the ram's horn blast to pass through your land' (Lev. 25:9). In both cases the same verb 'to cause to pass through' ('br) is employed. The edict was not only proclaimed orally but was also put in writing (see 2 Kings 19:9-14; 2 Chron. 30:1). It is more fully presented in

Ezra 1:2-4 with an original Aramaic text in Ezra 6:3-5, which was probably part of a much larger decree that covered the rebuilding of other temples in the various countries where Cyrus ruled. The Cyrus cylinder indicates that this liberal spirit expressed a general religious policy by the Persian kings toward those nations under their control.[1]

The proclamation is introduced with the 'messenger formula', 'Thus says Cyrus ...' (see 2 Chron. 32:10; 34:23) and in the context of speaking to the Jews, the king immediately acknowledged that Yahweh was responsible for his kingship over the nations he had conquered, and he believed that Yahweh had 'appointed' or 'commanded' him to build God's house in Jerusalem. The phrase 'all the kingdoms of the land/earth' (*kol-maml°ḵôṯ hā'āreṣ*, v. 23) echoes what is said concerning David's rule over 'all the kingdoms of the lands' (*kol-maml°ḵoṯ hā'ªrāṣôṯ*, 1 Chron. 29:30; see 2 Chron. 9:23). His statement did not mean that he had become a Yahweh worshipper for he actually confessed with gratitude his good fortune to all the high gods of his realm. The Cyrus cylinder also reveals that Cyrus saw himself as conqueror of the world and could call himself 'king of the four corners (of the earth)'. The addition of the explanatory phrase, 'which is in Judah', is the kind of precise terminology used in official documents.

Whereas the book of Kings ends with the release of the Davidic king Jehoiachin from prison, Chronicles closes with a prayer-wish by a foreign king for Yahweh to be with His people and an encouragement by this same emperor for them to 'go up' (*'lh*). At the end of Genesis, the Pharaoh had likewise urged Joseph to 'go up' (*'lh*) in order to bury his father in Canaan and had given him all the support he needed (Gen. 50:6-9). Where Chronicles ends, the book of Ezra begins and makes clear that it is to Jerusalem they must go to build God's house. By ending more abruptly with 'let him go up', the Chronicler leaves all his readers, wherever they are, with the prospect of a new exodus and encourages them to come together to a new city and a new temple. It takes

---

1. See D. Winton Thomas (ed.), *Documents from Old Testament Times* (New York: Harper Torchbook, 1961), pp. 92-94.

the reader back to the end of the introduction (1 Chron. 9) where we find God's people returning to Jerusalem.

Psalm 132 encouraged the exiles and post-exilic people to see the importance of the temple but not at the expense of David. Though Chronicles does not mention at the close the prospect of a new David, the reference to Cyrus provides a preview or type of the future messianic world ruler who would be involved in the building of the future temple.

Application

It was important that the post-exilic community and the Jews of the intertestamental period remained loyal to the Jerusalem temple and carried out the rituals as ordained in the Mosaic law. Not any temple would do, not the one built in Elephantine or on Mount Gerizim, only the Jerusalem one was God-ordained to prepare for and point to all that Messiah would accomplish through His atoning death and resurrection. Both the Psalms and Chronicles encouraged the Jews to love this temple until the realisation of all that it represented. It was when Jesus had gone through that blackest of nights and cried 'it is finished' that the veil of the temple was supernaturally torn from top to bottom to indicate that the earthly replica of the heavenly reality had become obsolete.

The Chronicler's work began like Genesis with Adam and showed how Israel was chosen from a whole host of nations and people groups. At the close of his work he shows how a representative of those nations was used to fulfil God's purposes for the future. Both Genesis and Chronicles end with Israel in an exile situation but with the promise and prospect of a return to the land of promise (Gen. 50:24-26; 2 Chron. 36:21-23).[2] Pharaoh's assistance in bringing Jacob's remains back to the land (Gen. 50:6-9) parallels the king of Persia's encouragement to the exiles to return. This all leads eventually to the fulfilment of the prophetic words concerning the nations and people groups of the world desiring to 'go up' to Jerusalem and to the house of God

---

2. See William J. Dumbrell, *The Faith of Israel* (Leicester: Apollos, 1989), p. 273.

(Isa. 2:1-5; Micah 4:1-5). Furthermore, just as Joseph is presented in Genesis as a type of the lion of the tribe of Judah bringing blessing to all nations (Gen. 41:57; 42:6), so Cyrus is depicted as a type of the promised messiah. In his concern for Yahweh's temple in Jerusalem, he is likened to a second David and to the messianic-like figure who is associated with the new exodus of Isaiah's prophecies. This messianic type whose proclamation announced a 'jubilee' of liberty and return for the Jewish captives, points us to the true Liberator of God's people. It was Jesus who read from Isaiah 61:1-2 about the one anointed to proclaim good news to the poor, liberty to the captives and the acceptable or jubilee year of the Lord. When He had finished, Jesus stated that the scripture was fulfilled in the hearing of the people (Luke 4:16-21).

Focusing at the close on Cyrus the world ruler rather than any Davidic ruler of the type that had been deposed, enabled the Chronicler to indicate like Isaiah and the Genesis account of Joseph, that Yahweh is the ultimate sovereign who has everything under control and will use the great potentates of this world to fulfil the worldwide promises He made both to Abraham and David. At the same time, it made clear that the future Davidic figure would be a world ruler unlike even the best of Israel's past glories. In God's purposes, Cyrus was a significant universal figure who, like the David–Solomon duo, pre-figured God's true Messiah and Shepherd who would gain the kingdoms of this world not by the devil's methods but through costly sacrifice (Matt. 4:8-11; John 12:31-33; 18:36). Jesus who was born in Bethlehem and lived in Nazareth came to Jerusalem to gain the victory over all the forces of evil through His atoning death and resurrection in order to draw people of all nations to Himself. It was in Jerusalem that the New Testament Church first gathered and from Jerusalem that the good news spread to the whole world. All are now encouraged to trust Jesus of David's royal line before the judgment day, for He is the King of kings and Lord of lords who has been given the name above every name and to whom on that final day every knee shall bow (Ps. 2; Isa. 45:22-23; Phil. 2:5-11).

Group Study Questions

Part Two: The David–Solomon Kingdom
(1 Chronicles 9:35–2 Chronicles 9:28)

1. Indicate why a person's bodily remains should be treated with dignity.

2. How is the description of Israel's defeat under Saul a preview of the events surrounding Israel's Babylonian exile?

3. Consider how the Chronicler's presentation of David would have encouraged the post-exilic community.

4. What early evidences of the Holy Spirit's power do we find in 1 Chronicles?

5. 'God's time is always the right time' – Have you found this to be true in your own experience?

6. Why are God's people on earth in a war situation? When and how will it end?

7. How does 1 Chronicles 13 help us understand Hebrews 12:28-29?

8. Consider how expressions of joy in worship can co-exist with respect for God.

9. What did the ark of God signify?

10. What does the Old Testament tabernacle typify?

11. How was the kingdom of God seen on earth in Old Testament times and how does it prepare for the preaching of John the Baptist and Jesus?

12. Why was David's census wrong and why is the Chronicler's account different from the parallel passage in Samuel?

13. Indicate the differences between pagan and biblical sacrifices.

14. Do the instructions given to the Levites have anything to say about the running of our churches today?

15. Is there any place for Christians to engage in 'casting lots'?

16. Consider the place of music in the life of the church and the individual believer.

17. Do you agree that we cannot properly understand what the New Testament means by church without considering the Old Testament background?

18. What are the benefits and dangers of tradition?

19. Under the new covenant, are there obligatory as well as free-will offerings?

20. Does worshipping God in the whole of life every day mean there is no place for special communal worship on the Lord's Day?

21. Why does the Chronicler idealise and stress the united rule of David and Solomon?

22. Consider the continuity and discontinutiy between Solomon's temple and the post-exilic temple. How does the reality far surpass those shadowy pictures and types?

23. What do we mean by God's transcendence and immanence? In what ways can both be true of God?

Part Three: The Judean Kingdom and its failure
(2 Chronicles 10–36)

1. Are there indications that the link between the northern tribes and the Davidic monarchy centred on Jerusalem was tenuous even before the schism?

2. Consider how King Jesus heals divisions and unites opposing parties.

3. In what ways does the situation of true believers in Rehoboam's time encourage and help Christians today?

4. What did 'walking in the way of David and Solomon' mean and what descriptive shorthand language would we use today?

5. Why was worship at Jerusalem so important until the coming of Christ?

6. What does seeking God mean? Do Christians need to seek God?

7. What is the difference between backsliding and apostasy?

8. Why is God's Word so important for individual Christians, as well as for the life of the church?

9. Can you give modern examples of how some current churches are encouraging Christians to accept the thinking and practices of the world?

10. The cry for justice is often heard in our countries. How can this be used evangelistically?

11. Give examples of importunate prayer in Chronicles and think of situations today where such prayer is needed.

12. Why should we trust what is proclaimed from God's Word?

13. What are the important factors to be considered in any efforts towards denominational church unity?

14. All the promises of God find their affirmative and certainty in Jesus. Use Chronicles to show the truth of this statement.

15. Why are close relationships with unbelievers dangerous for Christians?

16. Give modern examples to explain the adage 'what people sow they reap'.

17. Consider the exile theme throughout Scripture and ponder what it meant for Jesus.

18. Give examples from Chronicles to encourage Christians to trust God even when all His promises seem to have failed.

19. Why is the close connection between the Davidic king and the Jerusalem temple so important?

20. Why is commitment to the local church so important for Christians?

21. God is as just in killing people as in bringing them to life. Show how this is gospel truth.

22. Can you think of New Testament examples of people who seemed not to continue in the faith?

23. Why is the Old Testament condition translated 'leprosy' so appropriate in describing sin?

24. From Chronicles, give examples of Davidic kings who point us to Jesus the Messiah.

25. Where can we go to see the closest example of hell in this world?

26. What is to be the Christian's attitude toward those deeply depraved?

27. What is acceptable worship?

28. What place has tradition in Christian thinking?

29. What can we learn about the church from the Old Testament?

30. Indicate how David and Hezekiah shepherded God's people the Jesus way.

31. Why are kings Jehoshaphat and Hezekiah given so much attention in Chronicles?

32. How are Scriptural rules to be applied in church meetings? How does 2 Chronicles 30 throw light on cases where rules are broken?

33. In what ways did the people of Hezekiah's day express the unity displayed in Acts 4:32?

34. Are we devoting ourselves wholeheartedly to the service of God?

35. How should we consider the sufferings that come to Christians?

36. What is the difference between a test and a temptation?

37. What does Manasseh's life teach us?

38. What are the benefits and disadvantages of a nation state in which the church is closely associated?

39. How does the New Testament use the Passover festival?

40. When did the Babylonian exile begin and end?

41. In what way was the Babylonian exile a picture of the final punishment?

42. Distinguish between punishment and discipline.

43. Consider the place of Cyrus in the purposes of God.

Bibliography

Commentaries

Ackroyd, P. R. *I & II Chronicles, Ezra, Nehemiah* Torch Bible Commentaries (London: SCM, 1973).

Braun, R. L. *1 Chronicles* Word Bible Commentary 14 (Waco: Word Books, 1986).

Bolen, T. *The Date of the Davidic Covenant* (JETS 65, 2022).

Dillard, R. B. *2 Chronicles* Word Bible Commentary 15 (Waco: Word, 1987).

Japhet, S. *I & II Chronicles* The Old Testament Library (London: SCM, 1993).

Johnstone, W. *1 and 2 Chronicles*, vol. 1: *1 Chronicles 1–2 Chronicles 9: Israel's Place Among the Nations*; vol. 2: *2 Chronicles 10–36: Guilt and Atonement* JSOT Suppl. Series 160 (Sheffield: Sheffield Academic Press, 1993).

Knoppers, G. N. *1 Chronicles 1–9 A New Translation with Introduction and Commentary* Anchor Bible 12A (New York: Doubleday, 2004).

1 Chronicles 10–29 A New Translation with Introduction and Commentary Anchor Bible 12B (New York: Doubleday, 2004).

Merrill, E. H. *Kingdom of Priests* (Grand Rapids: Baker, 1987).

Murphy, J. G. *The Books of Chronicles* Hand-Books for Bible Classes (Edinburgh: T & T Clark, undated).

Myers, Jacob M. *I Chronicles: Introduction, Translation and Notes* Anchor Bible 12 (New York: Doubleday, 1965).

II Chronicles: Translation and Notes Anchor Bible 13 (New York: Doubleday, 1965).

Payne, J. Barton. '1, 2 Chronicles' pp. 301-562 in *The Expositor's Bible Commentary* editor F. E. Gaebelein vol. 4 (Grand Rapids: Zondervan Publishing House, 1988).

Pratt, Richard L. *1 and 2 Chronicles,* A Mentor Commentary (Fearn, Ross-shire: Christian Focus Publications, 1998).

Rudoph, W. *Chronikbücher* Handbuch zum Alten Testament (Tübingen: Mohr, 1955).

Selman, M. J. *1 and 2 Chronicles,* 2 vols. Tyndale Old Testament Commentaries (Leicester: Inter-Varsity Press, 1994).

Wilcock, M. *The Message of Chronicles,* The Bible Speaks Today (Leicester: Inter-Varsity Press, 1987).

'1 and 2 Chronicles' in 21st Century edition of *The New Bible Commentary* eds. Carson, France, Motyer, Wenham (Leicester: Inter-Varsity Press, 1994), pp. 388-419.

Willi, T. *Die Chronik als Auslegung* (Göttingen: Vandenhoeck & Ruprecht, 1972).

Williamson, H. G. M. *1 and 2 Chronicles,* The New Century Bible Commentary (London: Marshall Morgan & Scott, 1982).

Supplementary works

Ackroyd, Peter R. 'The Chronicler as Exegete,' *JSOT* 2 (1977), pp. 2-32.

The Chronicler in his Age, JSOT Sppl. Series 101 (Sheffield: Sheffield Academic Press, 1991).

'The Temple Vessels: A Continuity Theme', *Supplements to Vetus Testamentum* 23 (1972), pp. 166-181, and reprinted in *Studies in the Religious Tradition of the Old Testament* (London: SCM Press, 1987) chapter 4.

Braun, R. L. 'Solomonic Apologetic in Chronicles', *JBL* 92, 1973, pp. 503-16.

'Solomon, the Chosen Temple Builder: The Significance of 1 Chronicles 22, 28, 29 for the Theology of Chronicles', *JBL* 95, 1976, pp. 581-90.

'A Reconsideration of the Chronicler's Attitude toward the North', *JBL* 96, 1977, pp. 59-62.

Butler, T. C. 'A Forgotten Passage from a Forgotten Era (1 Chr xvi. 8-36), VT 28 (1878) pp. 142-50.

Dillard, R. B. 'Reward and Punishment in Chronicles: the Theology of Immediate Retribution' *WTJ* 46 (1984), pp. 164-72.

Evans, Paul. 'Divine Intermediaries in 1 Chronicles 21– An Overlooked Aspect of the Chronicler's Theology,' *Biblica* 85.4 (2004), pp. 545-58.

Eveson, P. H. 'Prayer Forms in the Writings of the Chronicler,' unpublished M.Th. dissertation (University of London, 1979).

Graham, M. P., McKenzie, S. L. and Knoppers, G. N. (eds.), *The Chronicler as Theologian. Essays in Honour of Ralph W. Klein*, JSOT (London: T & T Clark, 2003).

McKenzie S. L. and Suppl. Series 371 (London: T & T Clark International, 2003).

Japhet, S. 'The Supposed Common Authorship of Chronicles and Ezra–Nehemiah Investigated Anew,' *VT* 18, 1968, pp. 332-372.

The Ideology of the Book of Chronicles and Its Place in Biblical Thought (Frankfurt am Main: Peter Lang, 1997 revised edition).

Johnson, M. D. *The Purpose of the Biblical Genealogies: With Special Reference to the Setting of the Genealogies of Jesus.* 2nd edition (Cambridge: Cambridge University Press, 1988).

Kelly, Brian E. *Retribution and Eschatology in Chronicles* JSOT Suppl. Series 211 (Sheffield: Sheffield Academic Press, 1996).

Mason, Rex. *Preaching the Tradition. Homily and hermeneutics after the exile* (Cambridge: Cambridge University Press, 1990).

Meyers, J. M. 'The Kerygma of the Chronicler,' *Interpretation* 20 (1966), pp. 257-73.

Murray, D. F. 'Retribution and Revival: Theological Theory, Religious Praxis, and the Future in Chronicles,' *JSOT* 88 (2000), pp. 77-99.

Plöger, O. 'Reden und Gebete im deuteronomistischen und chronistischen Geschichtswerk' in *Festschrift für Günther Dehn* ed. W. Schneemelcher (Neukirchen: Kreis Moers, 1957) pp. 35-49.

Theokratie und Eschatologie 1959 translated by S. Rudman as *Theology and Eschatology* (Oxford: Blackwell, 1968).

von Rad, G. 'The Levitical Sermon in I and II Chronicles' in *The Problem of the Hexateuch and other Essays* (Edinburgh: 1966), pp. 267-80.

Riley, William. *King and Cultus in Chronicles. Worship and the Reinterpretation of History* JSOT Suppl. Series 160 (Sheffield: Sheffield Academic Press, 1993).

Wenham, J. 'Large Numbers in the Old Testament,' *Tyndale Bulletin* 18 (1967), pp. 19-53.

Williamson, H. G. M. 'The Accession of Solomon,' *VT* 26 (1976), pp. 351-61.

Israel in the Books of Chronicles (Cambridge: Cambridge University Press, 1977).

'Eschatology in Chronicles' *Tyndale Bulletin* 28 (1977), pp. 115-154.

Zvi, Ehud Ben. *History, Literature and Theology in the Book of Chronicles* (London: Equinox Publishing, 2006).

Subject Index

Scripture Index